FOUNDATIONS
OF AMERICAN
CONSTITUTIONALISM

FOUNDATIONS
OF AMERICAN
CONSTITUTIONALISM

David A. J. Richards

New York Oxford
OXFORD UNIVERSITY PRESS
1989

Oxford University Press

Oxford New York Toronto
Delhi Bombay Calcutta Madras Karachi
Petaling Jaya Singapore Hong Kong Tokyo
Nairobi Dar es Salaam Cape Town
Melbourne Auckland

and associated companies in
Berlin Ibadan

Published by Oxford University Press, Inc.,
200 Madison Avenue, New York, NY 10016

Oxford is a registered trademark of Oxford University Press

Library of Congress Cataloging-in-Publication Data

Richards, David A. J.
Foundations of American constitutionalism / David A.J. Richards.
p. cm.
Includes bibliographical references and index.
ISBN 0-19-505939-5
1. United States—Constitutional law—Interpretation and
construction. 2. United States—Constitutional history. I. Title.
KF4550.R475 1989   89-3025
342.73'02—dc19   CIP

9 8 7 6 5 4 3 2 1
Printed in the United States of America
on acid-free paper

In Loving Memory of My Father,
Armand J. Richards,
1910–1981,
"He was a verray, parfait gentil knyght"

Preface

This book takes up and further investigates the general approach to American constitutional law and interpretation implicit in my earlier work, *Toleration and the Constitution.*[1] The aims of *Toleration and the Constitution* were first, to sketch a new methodology of constitutional interpretation that gives appropriate weight to text, history, interpretive conventions, and political theory, and second, to demonstrate the fruitfulness of that methodology by developing in some detail a unified interpretive account of the American constitutional law of religious liberty, free speech, and constitutional privacy. Further research and reflection have led me to believe that the explanatory and critical power of this approach can only be fully developed and stated if its methodology could be shown to bear fruit in a more general interpretive account of the project of American constitutionalism as an original blend of interpretive history and political philosophy. Constitutional interpretation today is best understood within the framework of that project, which it best explicates when it carries forward the project in the same spirit as its remarkable founders. In that sense, this book finds common ground with the politically conservative impulse that takes the interpretation of the founders' intent as a key issue in understanding constitutional interpretation in general, but it goes on to argue that the best interpretation of that impulse cannot be aligned with the conventionally understood agenda of some political conservatives. Indeed, some such conservatives are, so I will argue, radical ideologues who mock anything that founders' intent could reasonably be taken to mean.

Foundations of American Constitutionalism offers an interpretive theory of the founders' project and argues that this project is the key to the understanding of the constitutional interpretation of their enduring legacy, the U.S. Constitution, as amended. It gives central play to the arguments of history, political science, and political philosophy that they self-consciously used and often transformed in their great work of constitutional design. The political philosophy of the founders was, I argue, clearly Lockean; however, their constructivist enterprise of constitutional design was framed by their own political experiences as colonists, revolutionaries, and framers of and leaders

[1] New York: Oxford Univ. Press, 1986.

under the state constitutions and federal Articles of Confederation, and the sense they made of these experiences in light of the critical insights and constructive alternatives offered by the interpretive history and political science of Machiavelli, Harrington, Montesquieu, and Hume. The political theory of the U.S. Constitution is best understood in light of the humanist methods of reflection and argument that the founders brought to their task, including the ways they understood their place in the history of republican thought and practice and justified themselves to one another and to the nation at large in its great democratic deliberation over their work. Those methods of argument do not inevitably lead to all details of the constitutional design, about which leading founders often fundamentally disagreed. However, they do constitute a substantive political theory calling, in general, for constitutionally guaranteed independent centers of political authority and accountability, and we best interpret the design on which the founders did agree and its later amendments when we see this design as reflecting such methods of argument.

This political theory may now be so powerful for Americans that we can deny that our institutions reflect, in contrast to European politics, any political theory at all.[2] However, that familiar American denial of political theory makes us uncritical about the essential values of our only unifying public philosophy—democratic constitutionalism—and debases standards of public debate about essential issues of constitutional interpretation in ways unworthy of the responsibilities of free people under the rule of law.[3]

We have historically seen such debased standards of argument articulated in terms of the overarching commitment of democracy to majoritarianism, against which the Constitution is tested and often found wanting. Arguing from the Progressive Left against socially regressive decisions of the Supreme Court of the United States, J. Allen Smith[4] set the stage for the debunking of the founders by historians like Beard,[5] Parrington,[6] and Hofstadter[7] by invoking majority rule, which the Constitution obviously frustrates. Smith thus condemned the Constitution because it flouted majoritarianism, but he nowhere defended the idea that democracy was identical with unqualified majority rule (a position from which he later retreated[8]); moreover, he misunderstood, as did Beard, Parrington, and Hofstadter, the distinctive commitment

[2] See, e.g., Daniel J. Boorstin, *The Genius of American Politics* (Chicago: Univ. of Chicago Press, 1953).

[3] Cf. Louis Hartz, *The Liberal Tradition in America* (New York: Harcourt, Brace & World, 1955), for example, pp. 20–21, 248–55, 285; Thomas L. Pangle, *The Spirit of Modern Republicanism* (Chicago: Univ. of Chicago Press, 1988).

[4] J. Allen Smith, *The Spirit of American Government*, Cushing Strout, ed. (Cambridge, Mass.: Belknap Press of Harvard Univ. Press, 1965) (originally published, 1907).

[5] Charles A. Beard, *An Economic Interpretation of the Constitution of the United States* (New York: Free Press, 1913). For a classic critique, see Forrest McDonald, *We the People: The Economic Origins of the Constitution* (Chicago: Univ. of Chicago Press, 1958).

[6] Vernon Louis Parrington, *Main Currents in American Thought*, vol. 1 (Norman: Univ. of Oklahoma Press, 1987), pp. 267–356.

[7] Richard Hofstadter, *The American Political Tradition* (New York: Vintage, 1973), pp. 3–21.

[8] See Smith, *Spirit of American Government*, pp. vii–viii.

to democratic equality that motivated the founders.[9] In effect, serious debate over the political theory of the Constitution took place without the participation of essential parties to the debate, who, until relatively recently,[10] conceded serious study of the philosophical assumptions of the founders to elitist and aristocratic political theories.[11] The consequence was a failure to assist in the development and articulation of the powerful internal arguments of interpretive mistake based on interpretive history available to critics of the regressive decisions of the Supreme Court.[12]

More recently, majoritarian arguments sponsor attacks from the Right or Center on decisions of the Supreme Court. From the Right,[13] the Constitution is construed narrowly to express the specific historical understanding of the majorities in the generation that approved it, and to leave all else to contemporary majority rule. Or, from the plausible Center,[14] the more specific texts of the Constitution are construed to reflect the requisite majorities of early generations, but more general texts are assessed in light of a political theory of democracy as fair representation, and discredited if demonstrably inconsistent with that political theory. However, these theories leave unexplained why democratic majorities of earlier generations—often grotesquely nonrepresentative by contemporary standards (excluding women and blacks)—should bind later generations at all, and often reflect a moral skepticism about human rights clearly inconsistent with the understanding of the founders.

Failure to engage the essential arguments of political theory assumed by the founders fails to take them seriously at the level of thought and aspiration that they understood themselves, and uncritically blinds us to our interpretive responsibilities today. We thus badly interpret not only them, but ourselves as well. We can do better, and the argument of this book shows how.

[9] For a useful corrective, see, e.g., Martin Diamond, "The Federalist," in Leo Strauss and Joseph Cropsey, ed., *History of Political Philosophy* (Chicago: Rand McNally, 1963), pp. 573–93; also, Hartz, *Liberal Tradition in America;* Pangle, *Spirit of Modern Republicanism.*

[10] See Rogers M. Smith, *Liberalism and American Constitutional Law* (Cambridge, Mass.: Harvard Univ. Press, 1985); Richards, *Toleration and the Constitution.* There was, of course, good work available in which a more egalitarian perspective was implicit, but the interpretive issues of egalitarian political philosophy were not given the salient role they deserve. The most notable example of this genre was Andrew C. McLaughlin, *The Foundations of American Constitutionalism* (New York: New York Univ. Press, 1932). See also David G. Smith, *The Convention and the Constitution* (New York: St. Martin's Press, 1965).

[11] For a notable exemplar of this genre, see Paul Eidelberg, *The Philosophy of the American Constitution* (New York: The Free Press, 1968).

[12] Lawyers were left, sometimes persuasively, to develop such arguments on their own. For a notable example, see Felix Frankfurter, *The Commerce Clause under Marshall, Taney, and Waite* (Chicago: Quadrangle, 1964).

[13] Edwin Meese, III, "Construing the Constitution," 19 *U.C. Davis L. Rev.* 22 (1985); Robert H. Bork, *Tradition and Morality in Constitutional Law* (Washington, D.C.: American Enterprises Institute, 1984); idem, "Neutral Principles and Some First Amendment Problems," 47 *Ind. L.J.* 9 (1971). For a rather different approach arguing from the right, see Richard A. Epstein, *Takings* (Cambridge, Mass.: Harvard Univ. Press, 1985).

[14] John Hart Ely, *Democracy and Distrust: A Theory of Judicial Review* (Cambridge, Mass.: Harvard Univ. Press, 1980).

We need a new start, and the argument in Chapter 1 starts at trying to understand the familiar American appeal to founders' intent. Because that appeal cannot be plausibly understood in any of the several ways urged by various contemporary theorists, a new approach is called for. That approach must take seriously the founders' extensive interpretive and critical uses of history to articulate both the normative and empirical methodologies and working assumptions they brought to their great work of constitutional constructivism (Chapter 2). That work brilliantly applied these methodologies and assumptions in service of a Lockean theory of political legitimacy and a Harringtonian conception of founding an immortal commonwealth; each of the three structures of American constitutionalism (federalism, separation of powers, and judicial review) reflects the impact of these arguments (Chapter 3). The founders' approach to political legitimacy shaped, in turn, a new conception of legal argument and justification (arguments of principle) that the founders adapted from their common-law arguments as British lawyers interpreting the British constitution in the prerevolutionary controversies. These new forms of constitutional argument explain constitutional interpretation over time; such interpretation (e.g., of the federal system) requires that abstract connotations be ascribed to the constitutional text (Chapter 4). These methods of interpretation enable us freshly to address central interpretive puzzles of American constitutional law: the scope of enumerated rights like religious liberty and free speech (Chapter 5), the justifiability of unenumerated rights like constitutional privacy (Chapter 6), and equal protection as an interpretive and critical response to defects in the 1787 Constitution (Chapter 7). The U.S. Constitution was, I argue, a brilliant expression of European humanist interpretive and critical thought, combining interpretive history (including the comparative political science of Machiavelli, Harrington, Montesquieu, and Hume), the Lockean political theory of legitimate government, and a common-law model for interpretive practice over time that reasonably justifies the Constitution to each generation on terms of respect for rights and the pursuit of the common good. If the founders thus transcended the now-conventional dichotomies among history, political philosophy, and law, then interpreting their project today requires that we do no less. The consequence of failure to educate Americans into the humanist tradition the founders assumed has been constitutionally decadent interpretive argument of the kind put in political play in the United States in the debates over the 1987 Bork nomination to the Supreme Court. The educational responsibility for this problem must be placed squarely on the shoulders of the American institutions most capable of addressing it: American universities and law schools (Chapter 8).

A new understanding of American constitutional interpretation, like that urged here, must be judged by its overall explanatory and critical power in comparison with critical approaches. My argument urges an interpretive methodology that brings history and political philosophy into a fruitful working relationship as constructive components in the overall interpretive approach. The argument offered is not therefore a historian's argument nor is it an argument in abstract political theory, but an interpretive argument in which a certain kind of interdisciplinary relationship between good arguments of history and political philosophy plays a central role. Neither history nor philosophy is abused by this process, but rather each is shown to play an important role in a larger interpretive project with its own independent standards of intellectual and moral integrity. Presumably, not all questions of interest to historians or philosophers will be of interest to this interpretive project, and even the questions that are of interest must be framed by the distinctive standards of value appropriate to this interpretive project; however, some such questions are relevant, and my concern here is to make clear how and why this is so as a distinctive truth of American constitutional interpretation today. My argument introduces this interpretive procedure as the founders' most enduring contribution to American constitutionalism; indeed, our interpretive interest in the founders is, so I argue, motivated by understanding the ways in which they used and developed these arguments in terms of which they both approached their great work and conceived their enduring heritage to posterity. The cumulative force of the book's argument is that we make the best interpretive sense not only of them but also of the tradition that followed them in light of this way of thinking about the interpretive responsibilities of good constitutional argument.

Such an argument must be long, complex, and detailed to do justice to its large subject, constitutional interpretation. It must take an imaginative journey of the spirit through the complex web of empirical methodologies and normative assumptions implicit in the founders' great work, displaying perspicuously not only the context of thought and action assumed by them but also their remarkable intellectual, moral, and political originality. The founders of the U.S. Constitution both used and transformed the best political theory and science of their age, and their work was thus the product of one of the most remarkable political achievements of the western humanist tradition of democratic and emancipatory public reason. We can be equal to their achievement and their ambitions only if we take seriously the life of the mind that sustained them and come to understand in such terms our own role in their project. Otherwise, our lack of critical standards leaves us prey to a stupefying complacency supinely content with the intellectual and moral vacancies of bicentennial self-congratulations and the shallow and specious abuse of the idea of founders' intent. We need, now as much as ever, the bracing critical challenge of seeing truly what the founders' achievement was and measuring ourselves accordingly. Confronting truth in this way can sustain a humane wisdom able to understand sentiently the terrifying enormity of what our nescience stands a chance of losing, a critically informed public understanding of the most precious constitutional legacy bequeathed to any people. A journey of the spirit into the foundations of American constitutionalism poses the critical issues of responsible thought and action. Such a long journey will be worthwhile if, at the end, we better understand the American constitutional tradition and our interpretive responsibilities to that tradition as free people under the rule of law. What journey could be more worth taking?

New York D. A. J. R.
December 1988

Acknowledgments

This book was written during a midsabbatical leave taken from New York University School of Law during the spring term of 1988. That leave and the summer researches that anticipated it were made possible by research grants from the New York University School of Law Filomen D'Agostino and Max E. Greenberg Faculty Research Fund.

My thinking about the issues of this book profited from conversations over several years, often in classes or seminars taught together with my colleague, Lawrence G. Sager, whose reflections on majoritarianism and constitutionalism shaped my understanding of central defects in current approaches to constitutional law and helped clarify my thinking about the range of constructive alternatives that might meet our need fundamentally to rethink the issues. I have also learned much from conversations in courses and seminars taught with my colleagues, Ronald Dworkin and Thomas Nagel, and from conversations over the years with my distinguished colleagues in legal history, John Phillip Reid and William Nelson. Ronald Dworkin, Thomas Nagel, William Nelson, John Reid, and Lawrence Sager generously read and wisely counseled me about arguments in this book, and I learned also from comments of Paul Shupack, professor of law at the Cardozo School of Law. My secretary, Patricia Rinaldi-Johnson, ably and patiently assisted me in gathering research materials used in writing this book.

Conversations with Donald Levy, professor of philosophy at Brooklyn College, illuminated and nurtured all my work on this book, and he also generously read and wisely criticized the manuscript. I am grateful as well for the support and encouragement of my sister and friend, Diane Rita Richards, and my mother, Josephine Cona Richards.

Contents

FOUNDATIONS
OF AMERICAN
CONSTITUTIONALISM

It may be a reflection on human nature, that such devices should be necessary to controul the abuses of government. But what is government itself but the greatest of all reflections on human nature?

JAMES MADISON, *The Federalist*, no. 51

There was not any government which he knew to subsist, or which he had ever known of, that would bear a comparison with the new Constitution . . . : legislators have at length condescended to speak the language of philosophy; and if we adopt it, we shall demonstrate to the sneering world, who deride liberty because they have lost it, that the principles of our government are as free as the spirits of our people.

FISHER AMES, in J. Elliot, ed., vol. 2, *Debates in the Several State Conventions on the Adoption of the Federal Constitution* (1836), p. 155 (Massachusetts Convention)

1

Introduction

The American Constitution is the longest lasting written constitution in the world. Americans are famously self-conscious of this fact, which gives to our legal and wider political discourse its distinctive sense of history. Today Americans very actively debate, for example, how we should understand the intent of the founders who wrote and ratified the Constitution in 1787–88, the Bill of Rights in 1789–91, and the Fourteenth Amendment and its due process and equal protection clauses in 1866–68. A remarkable feature of the American constitutional tradition is that not only did the founders aspire to this kind of long-term durability but generations of Americans have also regarded it as common sense. It is, of course, nothing of the kind.

No less a figure than Thomas Jefferson (who did not attend the constitutional convention) had suggested an alternative approach, namely, that each generation should revolt against the old political order and establish a new one by its own best lights.[1] Jefferson did not object in principle to a written constitution. On the contrary, like other prominent figures (e.g., John Adams[2]) of the revolutionary era, he regarded the construction of written republican constitutions at the state and national levels as the central intellectual and political responsibility of the American Revolution. That revolution was fought over the oppressions made possible by the unwritten British Constitution and its lack of appropriate institutional constraints on what Americans regarded as both the unconstitutional and unjust powers asserted by British parliamentary supremacy over the American colonies.[3] Jefferson thus wrote in 1776 no less than three drafts for the Virginia state constitution,[4] and made

---

[1] See, e.g., Adrienne Koch, *Jefferson and Madison: The Great Collaboration* (New York: Knopf, 1950), pp. 62–96.

[2] See, e.g., John Adams, *Thoughts on Government,* in Charles Francis Adams, ed., *The Works of John Adams,* vol. 4 (Boston: Little, Brown, 1851), p. 193.

[3] On the constitutional arguments, see, e.g., John Phillip Reid, *Constitutional History of the American Revolution: The Authority of Rights* (Madison: Univ. of Wisconsin Press, 1986); idem, *Constitutional History of the American Revolution: The Authority to Tax* (Madison: Univ. of Wisconsin Press, 1987).

[4] See Julian P. Boyd, ed., *The Papers of Thomas Jefferson, 1760–1776,* vol. 1 (Princeton, N.J.: Princeton Univ. Press, 1950), pp. 329–65.

yet another proposal in 1783,[5] motivated by the failure of the 1776 Virginia constitution adequately to learn the abusive lessons of British-style legislative supremacy: "[a]n *elective despotism* was not the government we fought for."[6] But Jefferson did object to the idea that any generation's conception of the best form of written constitution should be authoritative for later generations; his 1783 draft constitution thus allowed a relatively easy amendment procedure,[7] and his famous 1789 letter to Madison argued for an abstract moral right of constitutional revolution every nineteen years.[8] Madison, one of the greatest of the founders, disagreed with his good friend and collaborator Jefferson on precisely these points in both *The Federalist* no. 49 and his private correspondence[9] (more fully discussed in later chapters). Madison's view of the intergenerational authority of the written constitution was the view of the founders; indeed it sets the framework of aspiration against which they tested and assessed their work.[10] It is a tribute to their success that it is now the common sense of almost all sides to the continuing American controversies over constitutional interpretation.

There is, of course, a rather gaping logical chasm between what the founders of the Constitution may have intended (namely, that the Constitution should endure over many generations of their posterity), and what role, if any, their intentions should play in current interpretive debates over the meaning of constitutional guarantees. The great architects of the British common-law tradi-

---

[5] See Julian P. Boyd, ed., *The Papers of Thomas Jefferson, 1781–1784*, vol. 6 (Princeton, N.J.: Princeton Univ. Press, 1952), pp. 294–308.

[6] Thomas Jefferson, *Notes on the State of Virginia*, William Peden, ed. (New York: W.W. Norton, 1982), p. 120.

[7] Any two of the three branches of government could, by a two-thirds vote, call a constitutional convention. See ibid., p. 304. Madison criticizes this feature of Jefferson's constitutional thought in *The Federalist*, no. 49, and he made more extended criticisms of Jefferson's 1783 draft constitution in a 1788 letter to Kentucky friends who solicited his constitutional advice. See Robert A. Rutland et al., *The Papers of James Madison, 1788–1789*, vol. 11 (Charlottesville: Univ. Press of Virginia, 1977), pp. 281–95.

[8] Julian P. Boyd, ed., *The Papers of Thomas Jefferson, 1789*, vol. 15 (Princeton, N.J.: Princeton Univ. Press, 1958), pp. 392–97.

[9] For Madison's response to Jefferson's proposal of a constitution only lasting for each nineteen-year generation, see Charles F. Hobson et al., *The Papers of James Madison, 1790–1791*, vol. 13 (Charlottesville: Univ. Press of Virginia, 1981), pp. 18–26; for Madison's response to Jefferson's 1783 draft Virginia constitution, see Rutland et al., *Papers of James Madison, 1788–1789*, pp. 281–95.

[10] Arguments over the Constitution, both for and against, were standardly framed in terms of whether some textual provision or some failure to make some textual provision could meet the critical test for a written constitution accepted by all parties to the debate, namely, that a written constitution should afford an enduring framework of just government for future generations of posterity. To take just two of numerous available examples on both sides of the debate, *The Federalist* standardly appeals to posterity in making its arguments for ratification of the Constitution. See Jacob E. Cooke, ed., *The Federalist* (Middletown, Conn.: Wesleyan Univ. Press, 1961), pp. 89, 145, 210–11, 213, 276–77. And one of the leading antifederalist tracts, *Letters from the Federal Farmer*, powerfully articulates the argument for a bill of rights by reference to the effects of this lacuna on future generations. See Herbert J. Storing, *The Complete Anti-Federalist*, vol. 2 (Chicago: Univ. of Chicago Press, 1981), pp. 324–25.

tion (e.g., Lords Coke and Mansfield) may have intended their work to last forever, but the interpretation of that tradition today cannot reasonably be understood as, centrally, a search for their intents. Indeed, whatever weight the idea of authorial intent may properly have in the interpretation of what a speaker says or a writer writes does not naturally transfer to the interpretation of culture in general or a legal tradition in particular. A complex modern legal culture—whether in the case of the British unwritten or the American written constitution—embodies highly abstract and densely structured collective understandings about the legitimate use of the modern state's monopoly of coercive power. Those collective understandings are the work of many generations of shared historical experience, and their interpretation cannot standardly be understood on the model of the speaker's or writer's meaning.[11]

Although there is no logical requirement that founders' intent play a central role in constitutional interpretation, such a practice has become indigenously American, and one criterion for the acceptability of a theory of the proper interpretation of the U. S. Constitution is that it give weight and sense to this American practice. We require a theory of constitutional interpretation that can do justice to the intergenerational authority of the written constitution and, by extension, give a proper sense to how or why such interpretation pays homage to the founders' intent. In order to set the stage for my own proposal, I examine in this chapter three current proposals for such a theory: the appeal to historical exemplars, the appeal to moral reality, and the appeal to conventions. None of these proposals can, in my view, do justice to constitutional interpretation, because they do not ask sufficiently critical questions about the nature of interpretation in general and constitutional interpretation in particular.

The Appeal to Historical Exemplars

The appeal to historical exemplars, advocated by legal scholars (Raoul Berger[12]), officials of the Reagan administration (former Attorney General Edwin Meese III[13]), and federal judges (Hugo Black[14] and Robert Bork[15]) combines history and constitutional interpretation in the following way. History shows that those who drafted and approved the language of some constitutional text clearly contemplated that the language would apply to x and would

---

[11] See, in general, Ronald Dworkin, *Law's Empire* (Cambridge, Mass.: Harvard Univ. Press, 1986); David Richards, *Toleration and the Constitution* (New York: Oxford Univ. Press, 1986), pp. 20–45.

[12] Raoul Berger, *Government by Judiciary* (Cambridge, Mass.: Harvard Univ. Press, 1977); idem, *Death Penalties* (Cambridge, Mass.: Harvard Univ. Press, 1982).

[13] Edwin Meese III, "Construing the Constitution," 19 *U.C. Davis L. Rev.* 22 (1985).

[14] See the dissent of Justice Black in *Katz* v. *United States,* 389 U.S. 347 (1967).

[15] Robert H. Bork, *Tradition and Morality in Constitutional Law* (Washington, D.C.: American Enterprise Institute, 1984); idem, "Neutral Principles and Some First Amendment Problems," 47 *Ind. L.J.* 9 (1971).

not apply to *y*. Therefore, the failure to apply the language to *x* or its application to *y* is a wrong and abusive interpretation of the meaning of the constitutional text. The starkest and most uncompromising formulation of the view (Berger's)[16] argues that we can thus properly apply the prohibition on cruel and unusual punishment in the Eighth Amendment to torture but not to the death penalty; we can apply the requirement of equal protection in the Fourteenth Amendment to racial discrimination by states in persons' access to the criminal and civil law but not to racial segregation or antimiscegenation laws or blatant gender discrimination. The mediating premise of this account is the founders' intent, because the meaning of constitutional text is based on this intent, which is construed on the model of denotative historical exemplars.

The strict constructionist model of constitutional interpretation derives its appeal from a simplistic philosophical picture of what legal interpretation must be, namely, reading legal texts on a naive model of speaker's meaning: a legal text, including a written constitution, is construed as an utterance of its authors regarding certain things in the world to which the language applies and does not apply. But even speaker's meaning may be interpretively construed at different levels of abstraction. For example, a dean at a meeting of a law faculty may call for hiring excellent new faculty and construe that standard of value as applying to certain candidates A and B, but not to C and D, but the faculty members attending may understand and agree with the standard and not concur in its application; indeed, they may understand the dean's mandate better than he or she does. If anything, the interpretation of legal texts is more disengaged from the subjective applications of the authors of the text (founders, legislators, or whomever). Often the best understanding of legal interpretation is that the purposes of the authors of an authoritative legal text are best assigned a sense in light of the interpretive practices and the governing political theory of the society.

For example, it is a familiar principle of statutory interpretation in the United States to ascribe to the often conflicting and sometimes incoherent data of legislative language, context, and history the purposes of a hypothetically reasonable legislator.[17] Courts ascribe such hypothetical rationality to the legislative process because fundamental constitutional principles of due process and equal protection require that both courts and legislatures rationally pursue constitutionally reasonable purposes of the public interest and respect for basic rights of the person. In order to be consistent with their constitutional duty to apply all law in light of the supremacy of the Constitu-

---

[16] Other advocates of the position argue, not altogether coherently, that some judicial decisions, notably the desegregation decisions, should be excepted from the argument. See, e.g., Meese, "Construing the Constitution," p. 27. My focus here is on the form of the argument advocated with ferocious consistency by Raoul Berger.

[17] See Henry Hart and Albert Sachs, *The Legal Process* (Cambridge, Mass.: Harvard Law School, 1958), pp. 1414–15; see also Reed Dickerson, *The Interpretation and Application of Statutes* (Boston: Little, Brown, 1975), ch. 12; Michael S. Moore, "The Semantics of Judging," 54 *So. Calif. L. Rev.* 151, 246–70 (1981). Cf. J. Willard Hurst, *Dealing with Statutes* (New York: Columbia Univ. Press, 1982), pp. 31–65.

tion, Courts must frame their interpretive task of statutory construction accordingly. One should not construe these familiar features of legal interpretation as wholly disengaging the interpretive process from any contact with legislators' intentions. Rather, the intentions of legislators are shaped, illuminated, and often best understood in light of such interpretive conventions, which are in turn embedded in larger moral and political ideals of constitutionally legitimate government.

The available interpretive range in understanding constitutional texts is surely broader than strict constructionism supposes it to be. For example, an alternative model of the interpretation of the Constitution might focus not on the things to which the clauses would have been applied when they were originally drafted and approved, but to the more abstract intentions of those clauses.[18] The interpretive consequence of this alternative reading of such constitutional texts is that the founders' denotative examplars, interpretively decisive on the strict constructionist model, would not enjoy this pivotal role. More abstract intentions may be construed to apply differently in various periods depending on changing factual circumstances (what counts as commerce among the states, or a violation of the Fourth Amendment's protection of privacy in light of new technologies of electronic surveillance) and normative perspectives (cruel and unusual punishment, equal protection, constitutional privacy). The founders, no less than my hypothetical law dean, would not be the ultimate authority on the best interpretation of their mandates—either for their own generation or later generations.

The strict constructionist model of constitutional interpretation suppresses both the question of such a range of interpretive choices and the ways of adjudicating among them. We need now to address the latter metainterpretive issue, that is, which style of interpretation is the better reading of the intergenerational authority of the U. S. Constitution? All sides to this debate would presumably agree that the preferable selection among available interpretive positions is that view that makes the best sense of the context and aspirations of the founders and of the text on which they agreed. It would be more controversial whether and to what extent later judicial practice should be given weight in this assessment, because some strict constructionists take the constitutionally fundamentalist stance that the text of the Constitution is prior to any later interpretive practice, which often may be rejected by appeal to the text itself. It would be still more controversial whether and in what way political theory should play any role in this assessment. However, all these parameters of assessment converge on one result, namely, that many of the relevant constitutional clauses are best construed as expressing abstract intentions.

The text of the Constitution clearly does not require that we ascribe to the founders an intent to bind their generation or later generations by their own conception of how the language should be applied. The range of application of pertinent text even in 1787 or 1791 or 1868 was often enormously controversial

---

[18] See Ronald Dworkin, *A Matter of Principle* (Cambridge, Mass.: Harvard Univ. Press, 1985), pp. 33–71 (distinguishing concrete and abstract intentions).

even among the founders, and the generality of the language chosen may have glossed over such disagreements in application. It is not reasonable to ascribe to the founders an intent to bind others to their denotative exemplars when the language studiously and for good reason refuses to do so, and when available conventions of the judicial role at the time included the common-law model of case-by-case elaboration of general concepts and abstract principles—and indeed when, as H. Jefferson Powell has made clear,[19] the founders would have rejected the appeal to denotative exemplars as a sound model of legal interpretation in general and constitutional interpretation in particular.

The case for the strict constructionist model is no less unreasonable if we try to make sense of the founders' aspiration for the intergenerational authority of the Constitution. Binding interpretation to historical referents ascribes the unreasonable intent to apply abstract language acontextually to the design, ignoring changes in relevant considerations of fact and value that would lead reasonable interpreters to apply the text differently in various historical circumstances. The ascription of that intent mocks the founders' self-conscious choice of more abstract language—in the words of an important document used in their drafting of the final constitution—"to insert essential principles only; lest the operations of government should be clogged by rendering those provisions permanent and unalterable, which ought to be accomodated [sic] to times and events."[20] The founders were well aware of cultural evolution and social change,[21] and indeed anticipated massive changes in American economic and political life under the Constitution they framed.[22] They drew up a constitutional charter so that its interpretation would be contextually sensitive to the impact of such changes on the reasonable elaboration of constitutional structures and principles enduring over time precisely because later generations would find them reasonable. Only the ascription of abstract intentions to the text coheres with such enduring value in the constitutional design.

Some substantive clauses of the Constitution (in particular, the general normative clauses) derive their force and meaning from a larger political and

---

[19] H. Jefferson Powell, "The Original Understanding of Original Intent," 98 *Harv. L. Rev.* 885 (1985).

[20] Max Ferrand, ed., *The Records of the Federal Convention of 1787*, vol. 4 (New Haven, Conn.: Yale Univ. Press, 1966), p. 37. This document was in the handwriting of Edmund Randolph with emendations by John Rutledge, and "is fundamental in the development of the final draft of the Constitution" (idem).

[21] Leading social and economic theorists of the Scottish Enlightenment had developed a four-stage theory of cultural evolution, culminating in commercial society. Importance primary sources include Adam Ferguson, *An Essay on the History of Civil Society* (London: T. Caddel, 1773); James Millar, *The Origins of the Distinction of the Ranks*, reprinted in William C. Lehmann, *John Millar of Glasgow 1735–1801* (Cambridge: Cambridge Univ. Press, 1960); Adam Smith, *The Wealth of Nations* (New York: Modern Library, 1937). For important secondary literature on these and other sources, see Ronald L. Meek, *Social Science and the Ignoble Savage* (Cambridge: Cambridge Univ. Press, 1976); Peter Stein, *Legal Evolution: The Story of an Idea* (Cambridge: Cambridge Univ. Press, 1980).

[22] James Madison prominently used this perspective at the constitutional convention. See Farrand, ed., *Records of Federal Convention*, vol. 1, pp. 422–23, 431, 585–86; vol. 2, pp. 124, 203–4, 236, 268–69.

moral culture that perceived the human rights guaranteed by these clauses as grounded in enduring inviolable principles of justice, thus affording a constitutionally guaranteed benchmark of respect for inalienable human rights that was the very test for legitimate government.[23] The interpretation of these clauses, as abstract principles contextually sensitive to reasonably relevant changes in factual and normative circumstances, is alone consistent with this background moral understanding of constitutional legitimacy.[24]

It may be somewhat more controversial, for reasons already advanced, whether an interpretive approach should be preferred solely because it better explains the judicial elaboration of constitutional doctrine over time. But it is surely a good reason for preferring an approach—clearly superior on grounds of context and text—that makes better sense, as the ascription of abstract intentions clearly does, of how traditions of interpretation (including judicial review) have construed constitutional language over time. It is unreasonably question-begging to appeal to data like the founders' denotative exemplars as the reason for dismissing the interpretive weight of traditions of judicial review over time when the whole force of the appeal to denotative exemplars rests on an unreasonable theory of the founders' intent. Perhaps long-standing patterns of judicial review should sometimes be criticized and delegitimated on the grounds of an appeal to a better interpretation of the Constitution itself, which the judicial tradition has in some way gotten deeply wrong. But such arguments are only as valid as is their independent cogency as interpretations of the text; the strict constructionist model offers no such weighty reasons and thus cannot wholly ignore the interpretive traditions, including those of judicial review, that customarily use the abstract-intention approach to constitutional interpretation in ways that often illuminate and properly elaborate the founders' project of enduring political principle.[25]

It is still more controversial whether and in what way political theory should figure in the adjudication among variant interpretive approaches. But any interpretive approach that rests on an unexamined conception of political legitimacy that will not bear examination must discredit itself. In fact, strict constructionism rests on an undefended and questionable positivistic interpretation of popular sovereignty as the foundation of political legitimacy. According to this view, the people—the fount of constitutional legitimacy—imposed constitutional limits on the state in terms of the founders' sense of the application of constitutional language at the time it was drafted and approved,[26] and

---

[23] See, in general, Bernard Bailyn, *The Ideological Origins of the American Revolution* (Cambridge, Mass.: Belknap Press of Harvard Univ. Press, 1967); Gordon S. Wood, *The Creation of the American Republic, 1776–1787* (New York: W.W. Norton, 1969); Morton White, *The Philosophy of the American Revolution* (New York: Oxford Univ. Press, 1978); idem, *Philosophy, The Federalist, and the Constitution* (New York: Oxford Univ. Press, 1987).

[24] The explication of this background moral understanding will preoccupy later chapters of this book.

[25] Cf. Paul Brest, "The Misconceived Quest for the Original Understanding," 60 *B.U. L. Rev.* 204 (1980).

[26] See Berger, *Death Penalties*, p. 66.

any later interpretive deviation, no matter how long-standing and entrenched (e.g., in judicial tradition), is illegitimate. But the argument cannot withstand critical examination either at the level of its jurisprudence or the political theory that motivates its jurisprudence.

As jurisprudence, the argument assumes legal positivism (law is construed as given by the norms accepted by the final authority on law in the legal system). However, a classical difficulty with positivism is that it has problems in explaining legally authoritative constitutional limits on the sovereign as the final authority on law in the legal system.[27] In particular, how, in a constitutional order like the United States, should we understand the sovereign? If understood as the historical persons who approved the original Constitution, why then, as a matter of democratic legitimacy, should they bind a later generation long removed in time who never participated in the original decision? If understood in the context of the current generation, how do we know who they are or what they approve when, as a matter of fact, they may not understand the nature of constitutional arguments and institutions, and when the very authority of those arguments and institutions rests on the constraints it imposes on a factionalized populism unmindful of constitutional principles? Contemporary positivists acknowledge that the traditional sovereign of classical positivism gives a strained and often distorted reading of the facts of modern democratic constitutionalism, and they correspondingly abandon the futile search for or invention of a fictionalized sovereign.[28] Such forms of positivism identify valid law by reference to critical attitudes reflected in contemporary conventions of judicial interpretation, identification, and application, not with the founders or some other sovereign.[29] This view has the consequence that strict constructionism rejects. That is to say, in conflicts between judicial review and the founders' intent—understood as denotative exemplars—it is judicial review, not denotative exemplars, that should govern.

The positivistic jurisprudence of strict constructionism is motivated by a political theory of democratic legitimacy, namely, popular sovereignty. But, popular sovereignty is as essentially contestable an interpretive concept as democracy itself,[30] and we need to do political theory in order to sort out various interpretations of the concept and to decide which among them is better or worse. Strict constructionism opts for the founders' denotative exemplars because it interprets popular sovereignty as the majorities who ratified the work of the constitutional convention in a process that was, by the standards of the age, remarkably democratic. One cannot underestimate the im-

---

[27] See H.L.A. Hart, *The Concept of Law* (Oxford: Clarendon Press, 1961), pp. 49–76; idem, *Essays on Bentham* (Oxford: Clarendon Press, 1982), pp. 220–68. Cf. Joseph Raz, *Practical Reason and Norms* (London: Hutchinson, 1975).

[28] See Hart, *Concept of Law;* Raz, *Practical Reason and Norms;* idem, *The Concept of a Legal System* (Oxford: Clarendon Press, 1970); idem, *The Authority of Law* (Oxford: Clarendon Press, 1979); Neil MacCormick, *Legal Reasoning and Legal Theory* (Oxford: Clarendon Press, 1978).

[29] See sources in previous note. See also Hart, *Essays on Bentham,* pp. 243–68.

[30] See W.B. Gallie, "Essentially Contested Concepts", in *Philosophy and the Historical Understanding,* 2d ed. (New York: Schocken Books, 1968), ch. 8.

portance of the ratification process in the new conception of constitutional legitimacy that Americans pioneered, which is explored further in later chapters. But there are powerful reasons in democratic political theory for resisting the interpretation that strict constructionism places on these facts.

We need to be quite clear about what strict constructionism requires, namely, that a contemporary generation should be bound to the *denotative exemplars* of a generation long dead. But, as we have already seen, there are insuperable interpretive difficulties in making sense of the Constitution in this way, and it follows that ratification—whatever its meaning—cannot bear this meaning. Ratification, on the strict constructionist model, is essentially an act of personal will about very concrete issues, but the continuing democratic legitimacy of the Constitution is for us precisely that it is an act of judgment with authority that derives from the way it addresses permanent issues of ensuring equal justice and the public interest against the corruption of power, including democratic power, by politics. Indeed, our interpretive interest in the founders (see Chapter 4) is motivated by our interest in the kinds of arguments they used at this level of thought and deliberation about justice in politics. It follows that strict constructionism can give no adequate answer to a fundamental question of constitutional legitimacy: why should a contemporary generation be bound to the will of a generation long dead? It offers highly concrete and often controversial putative facts of legal history about the will of past generations, but does not enter into the public judgments of enduring political principle that interpretively explain how those facts made interpretive sense in the circumstances of 1787, 1791, or 1868—let alone how those judgments could make or be supposed to make (as the founders clearly intended) continuing *interpretive* sense in contemporary circumstances.[31] Why should recondite facts of legal history of this sort be the measure of an acceptable public understanding of principles of constitutional law today? Constitutional interpretation cannot make sense, as a matter of democratic political theory, of the founders' intent in the way strict constructionism requires.

Interpretive history plays a central role in constitutional interpretation in the United States, and the reasons for this will be explained in succeeding chapters. But strict constructionism (unearthing the founders' denotations) is an unsound theory of the place of history in constitutional interpretation because it raises the wrong questions and thus obfuscates the interpretation of the historical meaning of the American constitutional system.[32] It is bad interpretive history because it fails to take seriously the founders' own uses of history and of abstract judgments of political theory and science in their great work of political constructivism. The overreactive consequence to the abusive historiography of strict constructionism is the radical rejection of history as a tool of legal interpretation. The appeal to moral reality and the appeal to conventionalism are two rejections that are considered in the following paragraphs.

---

[31] These interpretive difficulties in Berger's use of legal history are more fully explored in Richards, *Toleration and the Constitution,* pp. 41–45.

[32] See the source cited in the previous note.

The Appeal to Moral Reality

Once the appeal to historical denotative exemplars is rejected as a sound approach to the elaboration of constitutional law, one natural move made by some recent theorists has been either to eschew what they call interpretive theories of law for noninterpretive appeals to moral reality (Michael Perry[33]), or to argue that constitutional interpretation itself is just the appeal to the best moral theory indicated by the constitutional text generally. Constitutional text, history, and tradition, this school argues, should be understood in light of this moral theory and, if necessary, revised and even excised in service of the best moral theory (Michael Moore,[34] John Hart Ely[35]). Whether given the noninterpretive or interpretive ways of approaching the problem, the basic line is one of ignoring history for an appeal to the best immediate moral results. So understood, the approach is a kind of neolegal realism in that we are not bound by any past history or conventions, but must—in the attempt to do justice—simply make the world the best place it can be. Unlike the old legal realism, this new approach does not construe making the world the best place in utilitarian terms, but in antiutilitarian terms—if, in the view of the relevant theorist or policymaker, an antiutilitarian theory of justice is the better theory of justice and the better reflection of moral reality.

The choice posed by these theories of American constitutional interpretation is false because it is between history or convention and critical morality. It is false in both directions. The exclusive appeal to critical morality may ignore the more cogent political theory implicit in the text, history, or conventions of American public law. For example, theories as crude as that of Learned Hand[36] or as sophisticated as that of John Hart Ely[37] appeal to a critical political theory (namely, utilitarianism) and excise the larger or smaller portions of text, history, and convention that, in their respective views, are inconsistent with this political theory. But they fail to take seriously the cogency of antiutilitarian, rights-based arguments in political theory,[38] and the ways in which a closer attention to the text, history, and conventions of American public law clarify the permanent value of such a theory in general. In the other direction, critical morality is often a central interpretive tool in understanding the place of text, history, and convention in the interpretation of the American constitutional tradition.

[33] Michael J. Perry, *The Constitution, the Courts, and Human Rights* (New Haven, Conn.: Yale Univ. Press, 1982).

[34] Michael S. Moore, "A Natural Law Theory of Interpretation," 58 *So. Calif. L. Rev.* 279 (1985).

[35] John Hart Ely, *Democracy and Distrust: A Theory of Judicial Review* (Cambridge, Mass.: Harvard Univ. Press, 1980).

[36] Learned Hand, *The Bill of Rights* (New York: Antheneum, 1968).

[37] For fuller critical discussion of Ely's theory along these lines, see Richards, *Toleration and the Constitution*, pp. 14–19.

[38] See, in general, John Rawls, *A Theory of Justice* (Cambridge, Mass.: Harvard Univ. Press, 1971).

In *Toleration and the Constitution,* I made this latter point in the context of clarifying the central place of John Locke's political theory in understanding the text, history, and interpretive conventions surrounding the religion clauses of the First Amendment.[39] John Locke's political theory has undergone and is still undergoing a sharp reassessment by critical historians. Locke appears to be a much more radical political thinker than both the British Whig tradition and their revisionist critics supposed him to be,[40] and the deeper critical understanding of his political theory brings out not only his obvious importance at the time of the American Revolution but also the long-standing role of his views of religious tolerance in shaping American culture and the remarkable American commitment to religious freedom in central constitutional traditions.[41] The interpretive importance of these arguments of critical historiography for American constitutional interpretation of the First Amendment is, however, best articulated in the terms of a contemporary critical political theory (that of John Rawls, for example) that argues for the priority of civil liberties on the model of religious toleration.[42] A good political theory of this sort appears not only to illuminate the deep structure of Locke's political theory, as political theory, but also interpretively to clarify the historical record, texts, and traditions saliently shaped by this political theory. No great political theory, including Locke's, is the last word on its own best interpretation, and critical advances in political theory may enable us better to understand and interpret the permanent truths implicit in the theory and to distinguish these from its lapsing untruths. Such an advance in political theory clarifies in the same way the best interpretation of the constitutional traditions shaped by the theory. It helps us articulate, for example, the abstract background rights to which the constitutional tradition shaped by the theory appeals,[43] and thus advances interpretive understanding of the best enduring arguments of constitutional principle today, at the same time and precisely because it also advances interpretive understanding of text, history, and conventions.

This argument regarding Locke particularly and political theory generally is, if anything, of more general and fundamental importance in understanding the American constitutional tradition than it was previously assumed to be by this author. The objective of this book is thus to give justification for this

---

[39] See Richards, *Toleration and the Constitution,* Chapters 4 and 5.

[40] See, e.g., Richard Ashcraft, *Revolutionary Politics and Locke's Two Treatises of Government* (Princeton, N.J.: Princeton Univ. Press, 1986); idem, *Locke's Two Treatises of Government* (London: Allen & Unwin, 1987); James Tully, *A Discourse of Property* (Cambridge: Cambridge Univ. Press, 1980).

[41] See, e.g., John Dunn, "The Politics of Locke in England and America in the Eighteenth Century," in *Political Obligation in the Historical Context* (Cambridge: Cambridge Univ. Press, 1980), pp. 53–77. The libertarian religious foundations of Locke's political theory are a central point of idem, *The Political Thought of John Locke* (Cambridge: Cambridge Univ. Press, 1969).

[42] Rawls, *Theory of Justice,* pp. 195–257.

[43] For a development of the idea of abstract background rights in legal interpretation in general, see Ronald Dworkin, *Taking Rights Seriously* (Cambridge, Mass.: Harvard Univ. Press, 1977), pp. 81–130.

broad claim for the role of political theory in constitutional interpretation, because constitutional interpretation belies the sterile dichotomies of history on convention and political theory. Moral and political theory, in conjunction with interpretive history, plays a central role in American constitutional interpretation and understanding of legal tradition.

The Appeal to Conventions

It is natural to resist this vision of the interpretive nature of law by questioning its necessity. The intellectual duties involved (interpretive history and political philosophy) are simply more demanding or more controversial than the task requires. American legal education—with its traditions of separation from the larger intellectual dialogue of the universities—makes this resistance the natural common sense of many academic lawyers, who are poised uneasily between the university and the practicing bar. The most appealing theory for such resistance is the positivistic insistence that law is neutrally given to us by legal authority independent of any requisite need for interpretive history, let alone political philosophy. Once strict constructionism's version of historical positivism (meaning is given by the founders' denotative exemplars) is rejected because of its indefensible theory of interpretation, the natural alternative within the positivistic paradigm is an appeal to ongoing conventions. That approach, as advocated by Schauer[44] and Monaghan,[45] captures the common sense of constitutional law as a living tradition, which is not deadly bound to a distorting mythology of the founders' intent, and gives a straightforward account of easy constitutional cases (namely, those cases at the core of existing conventions). The account, however, does not advance understanding of the interpretive process, and gives a false view of central issues in constitutional interpretation.

The appeal of positivistic conventionalism is that it eases the otherwise burdensome intellectual responsibilities of constitutional interpretation. That is to say, we need merely the lawyerly explication of the conventions of constitutional law as revealed through interpretation aand application. Our understanding of this interpretive process of explication is not advanced by dividing it into predictable regularities in judgment (governed by convention) and less predictable regularities (not thus governed), because all such judgments reveal interpretation and thus require explanation, and positivistic conventionalism offers none.

Indeed, it is a recurring experience in the interpretive practices of American constitutional law that current legal conventions, in the sense identified by positivistic conventionalism, do not correctly explicate the meaning of the

---

[44] Frederick Schauer, "An Essay on Constitutional Language," 29 *U.C.L.A. L. Rev.* 797 (1982); idem, "Easy Cases," 58 *So. Calif. L. Rev.* 399 (1985).
[45] Henry Monaghan, "Our Perfect Constitution," 56 *N.Y.U. L. Rev.* 353 (1981).

Constitution. Rather, such conventions are themselves interpretively wrong because they fail to reflect the best interpretive history of the principles of government implicit in the relevant text and its historical context, and the political theory that best justifies these principles. On such internal interpretive grounds, the Supreme Court may correctly confess mistake and overrule a long line of precedents that rest on this mistake.

My point is not limited to the internal interpretive criticism of some current widely held judicial consensus on an interpretive issue, because such criticism may—consistent with positivistic conventionalism—be explained by appeal to some larger positivistic convention held by other legal authorities (e.g., Congress or the president). There may be an unambiguous standing convention, in which the Supreme Court, Congress, the president, and the nation at large all concur, and yet such a convention may be interpretively wrong. As an example, the long-held national acceptance of executive usurpation of the war powers arguably was and is interpretively wrong with regard to text, to the 1787 historical understanding, to authoritative constructions thereof, and to the political theory of separation of powers that justifies the role of the Congress in declaring war.[46] Objections like these are not only quite meaningful, but sometimes true. Any theory of constitutional meaning, like positivistic conventionalism, that makes these objections meaningless or false fails to capture the sense of some of our most vitally important interpretive practices as a free people under the rule of law.

The interpretation of constitutional law cannot be identified with the positivistic conventions of the living constitution, because they leave no logical space for some of our most essential interpretive practices. To understand such practices of lawyerly explication, we must engage in interpretive history and political philosophy. The theory of positivistic conventionalism of the American law school is inadequate to the practice of American constitutional law.

The very appeal to easy cases, on which positivistic conventionalism builds its case, is often interpretively illusory, as examples of internal interpretive criticism clearly show. Many of these cases, once regarded as easy, came to be regarded as difficult, which shows that the conventionalist dichotomy between easy cases (at the core of the convention) and hard cases (at the periphery) is itself question-begging, and subject to shifts that turn on the kinds of deeper interpretive inquiries that conventionalism itself cannot explain.

[46] For historical understanding, see Max Farrand, ed., *Records of the Federal Convention*, vol. 2, pp. 318–19. For supportive political theory, see Madison, writing as Helvidius, in Thomas A. Mason et al., eds., *The Papers of James Madison, 1793–1795* (Charlottesville: Univ. Press of Virginia, 1985), pp. 64–74, 80–87, 95–103, 106–110, 113–120; answering Hamilton, writing as Pacificus, in Harold C. Syrett et al., eds., *The Papers of Alexander Hamilton, 1793–1794* (New York: Columbia Univ. Press, 1969), pp. 33–43, 55–63, 65–69, 82–86, 90–95, 100–106, 130–135. For judicial construction, see *Prize Cases*, 67 U.S. (2 Black) 635 (1863). See generally Louis Henkin, *Foreign Affairs and the Constitution* (New York: W.W. Norton, 1972), Chapters 2–4.

A Constructive Alternative?

The kinds of mistakes just identified and discussed in a range of current theories of constitutional interpretation suggest that constitutional law must be more self-critical about the nature of interpretation in general and constitutional interpretation in particular. The mistakes made by these theories standardly depend on failures to be sufficiently critical about complexities in the very idea of interpretation (for example, different levels of abstraction at which meaning may be assessed), including the range of competing interpretive conceptions that are in fact available and the reasons of interpretive history and political theory for preferring one such conception over others. Such theories often seek a kind of talismanic algorithm of certainty in making interpretive judgments (e.g., historic denotative exemplars, or utilitarian aggregation, or positivistic conventionalism), a simplistic decision procedure free of the demands of interpretive history and political philosophy. But such certainty is illusory if it rests on recondite facts of legal history that make no continuing interpretive sense today, or on an unexamined utilitarianism that makes no sense of the protection of inalienable rights at the core of the American constitutional tradition, or on conventions that make no sense of interpretive practices central to our constitutional community. The problem with these theories is that they oversimplify the practice of constitutional interpretation in the United States, and thus fail to meet minimal standards of explanatory (let alone critical) adequacy.

We need to return to the point at which we started, namely, the interpretation of the founders' intent as an indigenously American feature of our interpretive practices as a constitutional community. None of the approaches examined here takes this idea sufficiently seriously. One of them (strict constructionism) fails to explain how and why the idea has or should have interpretive appeal today, and the other two simply change the subject. But our interpretive choices are not between a history that makes no interpretive sense of our values and practices today and a political theory or conventionalism that makes no sense of history; it is a fault in contemporary constitutional theory that it has thus narrowed and cramped our perspective of the constitution to the terms of such polarized alternatives. We need to discover a constructive alternative that transcends such sterile dichotomies.

We have, remarkably, such an example at hand: the construction of the U. S. Constitution with its remarkable blend of interpretive history and political theory. Americans take interpretive instruction from their founders, in a way no other nation does, because they reasonably understand their interpretive responsibilities today within the terms of critical discourse set by the founders and their ambitions for an enduring project of democratic constitutionalism. That project did not isolate history from practice, or political theory from history. Its enduring achievement was a method of argument, of collective democratic deliberation about permanent problems of justice in politics, and ways of solving them that transcended such dichotomies. Americans, as a people, are particularly moved to attend to the written legacy of the founders because their method and context of argument (for reasons that are later developed in Chapter 4) is a reasonable way of understanding and giving effect to American institutional structures and arguments that secure legitimate government in the United States today. It may, therefore, be the test of our interpretive responsibilities today that we rediscover these methods of argument, and there is no better way to do so than to interpret the intent of the founders themselves by the lights they brought to their task. To start with, we need to take seriously the multiple layers of interpretive history the founders brought to their task and the critical uses to which they put such history in their understanding of their great project of constitutional construction.

2

The Founders' Interpretive Uses of History

Historical argument may come into play in legal argument in a number of ways that are analogous to various historiographic conceptions of method and purpose[1]: cyclical conceptions of recurrent growth and decay (Polybius or Machiavelli on constitutional processes[2]), religious and eventually secular theories of a providential order of progressive meaning in history (the Whig theory of history[3]), mythical conceptions of an idealized past against which present religious or political corruption is critically assessed (the primitive Saxon constitution[4]), and critical historiography based on rigorous standards of authentication of records against which hypotheses of the explanation of human action in history are critically assessed (competing explanatory theories of the decline of powerful political-legal orders[5]). Such uses of history in law cannot always be profitably sharply distinguished; the historically minded American revolutionaries often combined several such approaches in offering an analysis of the corruption of the British constitution and stating the grounds in both law and justice for revolution from it.[6] Furthermore, early

[1] For studies of such different approaches to history, see J.H. Plumb, *The Death of the Past* (Boston: Houghton Mifflin, 1971); Herbert Butterfield, *The Origins of History* (New York: Basic Books, 1981); R.G. Collingwood, *The Idea of History* (Oxford: Clarendon Press, 1946).

[2] See, e.g., Bruce James Smith, *Politics and Remembrance* (Princeton, N.J.: Princeton Univ. Press, 1985), pp. 26–101.

[3] See Herbert Butterfield, *The Whig Theory of History* (New York: W.W. Norton, 1965).

[4] See J.G.A. Pocock, *The Ancient Constitution and the Feudal Law* (Cambridge: Cambridge Univ. Press, 1957); idem, *Politics, Language and Time* (New York: Atheneum, 1973).

[5] See, e.g., Edward Gibbon, *The Decline and Fall of the Roman Empire,* 3 vols. (New York: Modern Library); Paul Kennedy, *The Rise and Fall of the Great Powers* (New York: Random House, 1987).

[6] Relevant primary sources include John Dickinson, *Letters of a Farmer in Pennsylvania* (1768), reprinted in Paul Leicester Ford, ed., *The Writings of John Dickinson,* vol. 1 (Philadelphia: Historical Society of Pennsylvania, 1895), pp. 279–406; James Wilson, *Considerations on the Nature and Extent of the Legislative Authority of the British Parliament* (1774), reprinted in Robert Green McCloskey, ed., *The Works of James Wilson,* vol. 2 (Cambridge, Mass.: Belknap Press of Harvard Univ. Press, 1967), pp. 721–46; Thomas Jefferson, *A Summary View of the Rights of British America* (1774), in Julian P. Boyd, ed., *The Papers of Thomas Jefferson, 1760–1776,* (Princeton, N.J.: Princeton Univ. Press, 1950), vol. 1, pp. 121–37; John Adams, *Novanglus*

American constitutional thought—fired by the revolution—framed its thinking about constitutional construction at the state and federal levels in similar terms.[7]

It is a remarkable feature of the American constitutional tradition that Americans regarded both their revolution and their formation of these constitutions as raising the same tests of both moral legitimacy and political intelligence and will[8]; indeed, the moral test of the revolution was, for leaders like John Adams and Thomas Jefferson, the quality of the constitutionalism it would yield.[9] Americans evinced the power for them of this imaginative truth when, after the political success of the revolution and in the circumstances of some prosperity, they experienced a sense of collective crisis in the 1780s in part because the utopian expectations of the American Revolution were discredited by apparent failures of constitutional design at the state and federal levels.[10] The problem was not only the anomalous unicameralism of the Pennsylvania constitution,[11] or the insufficient observance of the separation of powers in the constitution of Virginia,[12] or even the admired procedure of ratification and Harringtonian structures of John Adams's Massachusetts constitution—which had not avoided Shays' Rebellion.[13] The problem was

---

(1774), reprinted in Charles Francis Adams, ed., *The Works of John Adams* (Boston: Little, Brown, 1851), vol. 4, pp. 11–177. For useful commentary, see H. Trevor Colbourn, *The Lamp of Experience* (Chapel Hill: Univ. of North Carolina Press, 1965).

[7] Pertinent arguments at the state level include, for example, Carter Braxton, *A Native of This Colony*, in Charles S. Hyneman and Donald S. Lutz, eds. *American Political Writing during the Founding Era, 1760–1805* (Indianapolis, Ind.: Liberty Press, 1983), pp. 328–39 (appealing to the British constitution as a model); *Demophilus*, in idem, pp. 340–67 (appealing to the ancient saxon constitution as a model); *Four Letters on Interesting Subjects*, in idem, pp. 368–89 (need for new departure from historical practice in Pennsylvania and Britain); John Adams, *Thoughts on Government*, in C.F. Adams, ed., *Works of John Adams*, vol. 4, pp. 193–209 (consulting the best republican writers to suggest a model constitution for states).

[8] For the contrasting approaches on this issue of the American and French revolutionaries, see Hannah Arendt, *On Revolution* (Harmondsworth, Middlesex, England: Penguin, 1977), pp. 55–7, 61, 67–8, 75, 91.

[9] In this spirit, John Adams writes his very influential *Thoughts on Government* (1776); takes a central role in drafting the admired Massachusetts state constitution of 1780, reprinted in C. F. Adams, ed., *Works of John Adams*, vol. 4, pp. 219–67; and writes one of the most important apologia for American constitutionalism, *A Defence of the Constitutions of Government of the United States of America*, in idem, vol. 4, pp. 278–588; vol. 5, pp. 3–496; vol. 6, pp. 3–220. Thomas Jefferson writes no less than three draft constitutions for Virginia in 1776 and proposes yet another in 1783; see Boyd, ed., *Papers of Thomas Jefferson, 1760–1776*, vol. 1, pp. 329–65; idem, *Papers of Thomas Jefferson, 1781–1784*, vol. 6, pp. 294–308.

[10] See Gordon Wood, *The Creation of the American Republic, 1776–1787* (New York: W. W. Norton, 1969), pp. 394–95, 415.

[11] See ibid., pp. 438–46, 449–50. For a useful general consideration of the early state constitutions, see Willi Paul Adams, *The First American Constitutions*, Rita and Robert Kimber, trans. (Chapel Hill: Univ. of North Carolina Press, 1980).

[12] See Thomas Jefferson, *Notes on the State of Virginia*, William Peden, ed. (New York: W.W. Norton, 1954), pp. 118–29.

[13] The 1780 Massachusetts constitution was adopted only after the 1778 constitution had been rejected. For an important criticism of the latter, see Theophilus Parsons, *The Essex Result*, in Hyneman and Lutz, *American Political Writing during Founding Era*, vol. 1, pp. 480–522. Unlike

also a crisis of republican legitimacy, because the state and the federal constitutions were not cumulatively adequate responses—either procedurally or substantively—to the challenge and opportunity of constitutional construction in the fortunate circumstances of the United States. In this sense, the constitutional convention culminated a national deliberation on constitutionalism, in which both the state constitutions and Articles of Confederation were equally the objects of critical assessment and reconstruction.[14] That sense of challenge and opportunity fired the founders to initiate with the American people a great collective democratic deliberation on constitutionalism; they brought to their deliberation more extensive and critical uses of history than they had previously used.

The constitutional "experiment" (as the founders referred to it[15]) was designed, discussed, and ratified with a remarkably developed and articulate critical self-consciousness of its place in a complex fabric of thought and practice about legitimate government in western culture. The Constitution, followed shortly by the Bill of Rights, was thus the product of self-conscious reflection on, among other things:

> Past republican experiments (e.g., Greece, Rome, the Florentine and Venetian republics, the Cromwellian commonwealth) and the republican political theory and science of their emergence, stability, and decline (e.g., Polybius, Machiavelli, Guicciardini, Giannotti, Sarpi, Harrington, Locke, Sidney)[16]

---

other state constitutions (drafted and approved by state legislatures), the 1780 constitution was drafted by a specially elected constitutional convention and ratified by the people in an election called for this purpose. The legislature was bicameral with a house of representatives representing the people and a senate of forty proportioned to districts in accord with the amount of public taxes paid by inhabitants. A governor was separately elected by the people with a power of veto over legislation, except those repassed by two-thirds of each house of the legislature. Consistent with Harrington, there was a rising scale of property and residence requirements for representatives, senators, and the governor. See Wood, *Creation of the American Republic,* pp. 434–35. An independently elected executive with a veto power was a constitutional innovation of John Adams, who preferred an absolute not a suspensive veto. See R.R. Palmer, *The Age of the Democratic Revolution,* vol. 1 (Princeton, N.J.: Priceton Univ. Press, 1959), p. 225. On Harrington, see J.G.A. Pocock, ed., *The Political Works of James Harrington* (Cambridge: Cambridge Univ. Press, 1977); for useful commentary, see Zera S. Fink, *The Classical Republicans* (Evanston, Ill.: Northwestern Univ. Press, 1945), pp. 52–89. On Shays' Rebellion, see Forrest McDonald, *E Pluribus Unum* (Indianapolis, Ind.: Liberty Press, 1979), pp. 249–56.

[14] See Wood, *Creation of the American Republic,* pp. 465–67, 474–75, 564; Jack N. Rakove, *The Beginnings of National Politics: An Interpretive History of the Continental Congress* (Baltimore, Md.: Johns Hopkins Univ. Press, 1979), pp. 389–96.

[15] For example, at the Virginia ratification convention, Madison observes: "I can see no danger in submitting to practice an experiment which seems to be founded on the best theoretic principles": Jonathan Elliot, ed., *Debates in the Several State Conventions on the Adoption of the Federal Constitution,* vol. 3 (Philadelphia: Lippincott, 1836) (hereafter referred to as Elliot, ed., *Debates*); and at the South Carolina convention, Charles Pinckney admits, "our Constitution was in some measure an experiment," and "that he considered it the fairest experiment ever made in favor of human nature," idem, vol. 4, p. 262.

[16] See Douglass Adair, *Fame and the Founding Fathers* (New York: W.W. Norton, 1974), pp. 107–23; Fink, *Classical Republicans;* J.G.A. Pocock, *The Machiavellian Moment* (Princeton,

Various ancient and modern federal systems and their comparative success and failure[17]

Both explanatory and normative theories of federalism, separation of powers, a mixed or balanced constitution, and the British constitution (e.g., Aristotle, Hume, Blackstone, Montesquieu)[18]

Traditions (including British common law) of respect for basic rights of the person and the classic arguments calling for the protection of such rights as conscience and free speech (e.g., Locke, Milton)[19]

The founders used such interpretive history to make critical sense of American political experience in which they were often active participants[20] (i.e., colonial self-government, the struggles with Britain centering on concepts of political representation, the republican experiments in the states after the revolution, and the abortive federalism of the Articles of Confederation).[21] Such arguments framed the ways in which Americans thought about the complex mixture of both material and ideological interests (encompassing both commercial prosperity and respect for rights of the person) that were at stake in their constitutional experiments, including the range of alternative ways of coordinating pursuit of these interests in a durable republican constitutional framework (as we shall see at length later).

The founders intensively subjected the American political experience to the test of history because they had come to see their own republican experience in the light of a comparative political science, which was methodologically committed in the same way that Machiavelli had framed the proper study

---

N.J.: Princeton Univ. Press, 1975); William Bouwsma, *Venice and the Defense of Republican Liberty* (Berkeley: Univ. of California Press, 1968).

[17] See, e.g., James Madison's *Notes on Ancient and Modern Confederacies*, in Robert A. Rutland et al., eds., *The Papers of James Madison, 1786–1787* vol. 9 (Chicago: Univ. of Chicago Press, 1975), pp. 3–24; idem, *Additional Memorandums on Ancient and Modern Confederacies*, in Robert A. Rutland et al., eds., *The Papers of James Madison, 1787–1788* vol. 10 (Chicago: Univ., of Chicago Press, 1977), pp. 273–83. See also *The Federalist* no. 9 (Hamilton), no. 18–20 (Madison).

[18] See Adair, *Fame and the Founding Fathers*, pp. 75–123; Wood, *Creation of the American Republic;* Bernard Bailyn, *The Ideological Origins of the American Revolution* (Cambridge, Mass.: Harvard Univ. Press, 1967); Pocock, *Machiavellian Moment*, pp. 333–552.

[19] See, e.g., Locke's *Letters on Toleration,* in *The Works of John Locke*, vol. 6 (London: Thomas Davison, 1823); John Milton, *Areopagitica,* in J. Max Patrick, ed., *The Prose of John Milton* (Garden City, N.Y.: Anchor, 1967), pp. 247–334.

[20] Of the fifty-five who attended the convention, three had been in the Stamp Act Congress, seven in the First Continental Congress, eight had signed the Declaration of Independence, thirty had done some military service and fifteen were hardened veterans, forty-two had served at some time or another in the Congress of the United States, all but two or three had served as public officials of colony or state, and perhaps twenty had helped write constitutions of their states and six worked as codifiers of state laws. See Clinton Rossiter, *1787: The Grand Convention* (New York: W.W. Norton, 1966), pp. 145–46.

[21] See, in general, Wood, *Creation of the American Republic.* For useful studies focusing on representation alone, see J.R. Pole, *Political Representation in England and the Origins of the American Republic* (London: Macmillan, 1966); Jack P. Greene, *Peripheries and Center: Constitutional Development in the Extended Polities of the British Empire and the United States 1607–1788* (Athens: Univ. of Georgia Press, 1986).

of the Florentine republican experience: "In all cities and in all peoples there are the same desires and the same passions as there always were,"[22] therefore the study of these passions in the past (e.g., the Roman republic) can clarify today how "the same effects are produced."[23] Americans knew and admired the European thinkers who had powerfully applied Machiavelli's methodological procedures to the more recent study of politics (e.g., Montesquieu and Hume), and they learned much from them, as we shall shortly see. However, they believed as well that the American political experience and circumstances made possible a range of political imagination and experimentation beyond any European thought and practice could offer. Shortly before the constitutional convention, John Adams, one of the most important constitutional thinkers of the age,[24] made this point to a European and American audience in the first volume of his great apologia of American constitutionalism, *A Defence of the Constitutions of Government of the United States of America:*

> The United States of America have exhibited, perhaps, the first example of governments erected on the simple principles of nature; and if men are now sufficiently enlightened to disabuse themselves of artifice, imposture, hypocrisy, and superstition, they will consider this even as an era in their history. . . . It will never be pretended that any persons employed in that service had interviews with the gods, or were in any degree under the inspiration of Heaven, more than those at work upon ships or houses, or laboring in mer-

---

[22] Niccolò Machiavelli, *Discourses,* Bernard Crick, ed., Leslie J. Walker, trans. (Harmondsworth, Middlesex, England: Penguin, 1970), p. 207.

[23] Ibid., p. 517.

[24] See, e.g., R.R. Palmer, *Age of Democratic Revolution,* vol. 1, pp. 221–28, 267–76. Madison, for example, writes Jefferson on June 6, 1787 from the constitutional convention noting the impact of the publication of the first volume of Adams' *A Defence* on American thinking. Madison's comments are biting: "Men of learning find nothing new in it. Men of taste many things to criticize," but he concludes the book to be "a powerful engine in forming the public opinion" both because of its author's stature and because "the book has merit," Rutland et al., eds., *Papers of James Madison, 1787–1788,* pp. 29–30. Madison's criticisms appear to center on fear that the book would be used "to revive the predilections of this Country for the British Constitution," idem, p. 29. On the unjustified failure of historians to take Adams seriously as a major force in shaping American constitutionalism, see Ralph Lerner, *The Thinking Revolutionary* (Ithaca, N.Y.: Cornell Univ. Press, 1987), pp. 18–29. One historian, for example, has denied that *A Defence* had any impact on the Constitution; see Merrill D. Peterson, *Adams and Jefferson: A Revolutionary Dialogue* (Oxford: Oxford Univ. Press, 1976), p. 43. Another conceded the major importance of *Thoughts on Government* to early American constitutional thought, but denied the relevance of *A Defence;* see Wood, *Creation of the American Republic,* pp. 203, 580–87. To note just one powerful example of Adams' influence on the constitutional thought of the convention, the Constitution adopts from Massachusetts the idea of an independently elected executive with a suspensive veto, which was a constitutional innovation of Adams (though Adams preferred an absolute veto), defended at excruciating length in *A Defence.* See R.R. Palmer, *Age of Democratic Revolution,* vol. 1, p. 225; Adams, *A Defence,* pp. 358–59. *The Federalist* acknowledges the adoption of the Massachusetts approach; see Jacob E. Cooke, ed., *The Federalist,* (Middletown, Conn.: Wesleyan Univ. Press, 1961), pp. 464, 499. Hamilton's appeal for support of the idea to "the adepts ablest in political science," (idem, p. 445) would have been understood to refer to Adams.

chandise or agriculture; it will forever be acknowledged that these governments were contrived merely by the use of reason and the senses, as Copley painted Chatham; . . . as Dwight, Barlow, Trumbull, and Humphries composed their verse, and Belknap and Ramsay history; as Godfrey invented his quadrant, and Rittenhouse his planetarium; as Bolyston practised inoculation, and Franklin electricity; as Paine exposed the mistakes of Raynal, and Jefferson those of Buffon. . . . Neither the people, nor their conventions, committees, or subcommittees, considered legislation in any other light than as ordinary arts and sciences, only more important.[25]

Adams laid American claim to a new era in the history of European political theory and practice, and leading founders powerfully justified their accomplishment to the nation at large in precisely such terms. James Wilson thus spoke to the Pennsylvania ratification convention:

Government, indeed, taken as a science may yet be considered in its infancy; and with all its various modifications, it has hitherto been the result of force, fraud, or accident. For, after the lapse of six thousand years since the Creation of the world, America now presents the first instance of a people assembled to weigh deliberately and calmly, and to decide leisurely and peaceably, upon the form of government by which they will bind themselves and their posterity.[26]

And Hamilton thus opened *The Federalist:*

It seems to have been reserved to the people of this country, by their conduct and example, to decide the important question, whether societies of men are really capable or not, of establishing good government from reflection and choice, or whether they are forever destined to depend, for their political constitutions, on accident and force.[27]

This sense of enlarged political intelligence and opportunity can only be understood against the background of the ways Americans critically interpreted a European political history marred, in Adams' forthright terms, by "artifice, imposture, hypocrisy, and superstition." The founders' uses of this history contain admixtures of all the four approaches to history already noted, but their predominant strain was a form of critical historiography in the service of an interpretive history of republican thought and practice, which the founders regarded themselves as both continuing and radically transforming in a new way. We can come to no reasonable understanding of the founders' project if we do not explicate these methodologies and their main critical results: particularly the emancipation of religious and political intelligence,

[25] Adams, *A Defence,* pp. 292–93.

[26] Merrill Jensen, ed., *Documentary History of the Ratification of the Constitution,* vol. 2 (Madison: State Historical Society of Wisconsin, 1976) (hereafter referred to as Jensen, *Documentary History*), p. 342.

[27] Cooke, ed., *The Federalist,* p. 3.

the political psychology of faction, classical republicanism as a negative exemplar, the political psychology of fame, stages of history and commercial republics, and the British constitution as a negative or positive exemplar. This chapter examines each of these points as the basic building blocks that set the stage for the examination in later chapters of the founders' aspiration to an enduring written constitution (Chapter 3) and the kind of constitutional interpretation that best does justice to that project (Chapter 4). In each case, as we shall see, Americans took seriously the best political science available, but they often transformed it into their own independent assessment of how best to meet the challenge before them.

The Emancipation of Religious and Political Intelligence

The founders brought to their great work certain distinctive assumptions about the emancipation of religious and political intelligence that were made possible by fortunate American circumstances. The point is not merely that the founders understood themselves to be participants in the best Enlightenment thought of Scotland, England, France, and others and defined their work as an elaboration and extension of such thought,[28] sometimes submitting their work to wider European critical debate.[29] Rather, such Enlightenment thought was readily absorbed and distinctively used by Americans because they interpreted it as advancing more long-standing trends in American life—in particular, a democratizing emancipation of religious and political intelligence, an intelligence thus uniquely capable of seizing the great opportunity posed to Americans by Wilson and Hamilton. Leading American lawyers and constitutionalists, like John Adams, saw no inconsistency between their work as students of British common law and their mastery of Enlightenment history, political science, and philosophy; the best legal and constitutional argument depended on such procedures in order to understand its distinctive values and principles. Enlightenment in law, history, religion, and philosophy was one process.

John Adams had made precisely this prophetic point in his important 1765

---

[28] See, generally, Wood, *Creation of the American Republic;* Bailyn, *Ideological Origins of American Revolution;* Forrest McDonald, *Novus Ordo Seclorum* (Lawrence: Univ. Press of Kansas, 1985); Morton White, *The Philosophy of the American Revolution* (New York: Oxford Univ. Press, 1978); idem, *Philosophy, The Federalist, and the Constitution* (New York: Oxford Univ. Press, 1987); Henry Steele Commager, *The Empire of Reason* (Garden City, N.Y.: Anchor, 1977), pp. 176–235; Henry May, *The Enlightenment in America* (New York: Oxford Univ. Press, 1976), pp. 88–101, 153–76, 197–251.

[29] Americans profited, for example, from the support and critical advice of the British philosopher Richard Price. See, e.g., Richard Price, *Two Tracts on Civil Liberty, the War with America, the Debts and Finances of the Kingdom* (New York: Da Capo Press, 1972); idem, *Observations on the Importance of the American Revolution and the Mean of Making It a Benefit to the World* (New Haven, Conn.: Meigs, Bowen & Dana, 1785). For a good general treatment, including discussion of Turgot's critical letter to Price and John Adams' monumental response, *A Defence,* see Palmer, *Age of Democratic Revolution,* vol. 1, pp. 239–82.

essay, *A Dissertation on the Canon and Feudal Law.*[30] Adams wrote from the perspective of the Puritan tradition of deep learning and its commitment to rights of human nature "antecedent to all earthly government."[31] Only such learning (including study of the "philosophers of Greece and Rome"[32] and "the ancient seats of liberty, the republics of Greece and Rome"[33]) enabled the Puritans and their posterity to analyze critically the ways in which people in general had been deprived of any fair respect for their basic rights by the unjust tyrannies over the human mind wrought by Constantine's establishment of Catholic Christianity as the religion of the Roman Empire and "the two greatest systems of tyranny that have sprung from this original, . . . the canon and the feudal law."[34] The oppressive force of these twin tyrannies ("encroaching, grasping, restless, and ungovernable"[35]) legitimated unnatural hierarchies of both religious and political power over people "by reducing their minds to a state of sordid ignorance and staring timidity."[36] Puritan learning cultivated critical standards of intellectually and morally independent inquiry not held hostage to these tyrannies, and such inquiry was increasingly available to all: "we are all of us lawyers, divines, politicians, and philosophers."[37] A public culture—fostered by such learning—had thus made possible rediscovery not only of "the constitution of human nature and that religious liberty with which Jesus has made them free"[38] but also "a right, an indisputable, unalienable, indefeasible, divine right to that most dreaded and envied kind of knowledge, I mean, of the characters and conduct of their rulers."[39] Adams thus identified the "great struggle that peopled America" not with "religion alone, as is commonly supposed" but "a love of universal liberty,"[40] and interpreted a main aim of the Puritans to be "a government of the state more agreeable to the dignity of human nature, than any they had seen in Europe, and to transmit such a government down to their posterity, with the means of securing and preserving it forever."[41] Fidelity to "the great compact"[42] required the exercise of the great rights it guarantees, including morally independent historical research into the "principles of government"[43] and the testing of state power against their demands, including, if necessary, assertion of the right to revolt.[44]

---

[30] C.F. Adams, ed., *Works of John Adams,* vol. 3, pp. 448–64.
[31] Ibid., p. 449; cf. p. 463, idem.
[32] Ibid., p. 452.
[33] Ibid., p. 454.
[34] Ibid., p. 449.
[35] Ibid.
[36] Ibid., p. 450.
[37] Ibid., p. 456.
[38] Ibid., p. 454.
[39] Ibid., p. 456.
[40] Ibid., p. 451.
[41] Ibid., p. 453.
[42] Ibid., p. 459.
[43] Ibid., p. 462.
[44] See ibid., pp. 456–57.

Adams's essay was an advocate's paean to the New England mind.[45] Its praise of New England's respect for religious liberty was certainly over-stated[46]; Adams himself, like his fellow commonwealthsmen of Massachusetts, proved unable to make as radical a break with traditional views of church–state relations as much less Puritan Virginia had on the question of religious liberty under the leadership of Jefferson and Madison.[47] However, Adams's argument gives a perspicuous representation of generic features not only of the American revolutionary mind but its evolving constitutional mind as well. For Americans, both revolutionary and constitutional argument depended on the cultivation of a morally independent critical reflection on the history of religion and politics not held hostage to the religious and political tyrannies that this history often embodied, and that reflection was made possible by and also facilitated respect for the inalienable rights of human beings. In contrast to the more doctrinaire approach of French revolutionary and constitutional thought,[48] Americans linked critical history and respect for rights. In this, they showed themselves to be very much the thoughtful posterity of John Locke.[49]

[45] See, in general, Perry Miller, *The New England Mind: The Seventeenth Century* (Cambridge, Mass.: Belknap Press of Harvard Univ. Press, 1939); idem, *The New England Mind: From Colony to Province* (Cambridge, Mass.: Belknap Press of Harvard Univ. Press, 1953).

[46] On Puritan intolerance, see Perry Miller, *Orthodoxy in Massachusetts 1630–1650* (Cambridge, Mass.: Harvard Univ. Press, 1933).

[47] Article III of the Declaration of Rights of the Massachusetts constitution of 1780, in both Adams' draft and the finished constitution, declared religion to be the foundation of morality and of the state, authorized the legislature to "enjoin" people to go to church, and required the use of public funds to maintain the churches, which allow any "subject" to have his or her own contribution paid to the denomination of choice. See Palmer, *Age of Democratic Revolution*, vol. 1, p. 227. In contrast, Jefferson's Bill for Establishing Religious Freedom, adopted in Virginia in 1786, not only guaranteed the free exercise of religion but forbade any state aid to religion. See Julian P. Boyd, ed., *The Papers of Thomas Jefferson, 1777–1779,* vol. 2 (Princeton, N.J.: Princeton Univ. Press, 1950), pp. 545–53. For Madison's important *Memorial and Remonstrance against Religious Assessments,* written in support of adoption of Jefferson's Bill, see Robert A. Rutland et al., eds., *The Papers of James Madison, 1784–1786,* vol. 8 (Chicago: Univ. of Chicago Press, 1973), pp. 295–306.

[48] For illuminating comparisons of the American and French traditions along these lines, see, in general, Arendt, *On Revolution.* See also, Palmer, *Age of Democratic Revolution,* vols. 1 and 2.

[49] The Lockean foundations of American thought during this period cannot be underestimated. For example, the important American theologian and philosopher, Jonathan Edwards, had conceived his religious and ethical views very much within the framework of Locke's philosophy. For a good study of this point, see Perry Miller, *Jonathan Edwards* (New York: William Sloan Associates, 1949). For a useful general study, see Thomas L. Pangle, *The Spirit of Modern Republicanism: The Moral Vision of the American Founders and the Philosophy of Locke* (Chicago: Univ. of Chicago Press, 1988). Pangle gives insufficient attention and weight, in my judgment, to the focal importance to Americans of Locke's argument for toleration and rather overstates the case for Locke's artful subversion of traditional religious values. Locke's arguments are, in fact, remarkably straightforward and clear, but he was certainly as radical a thinker in both religion and politics as Pangle supposes him to be. He would, of course, have identified his radicalism with the proper form of Protestant Christianity, and there seems to be no reason whatsoever to question Locke's evident and profound Christian religiosity and the integrity of his argument that much traditional religion and politics had to be questioned and reformed on such grounds.

Americans did not, any more than Locke, base arguments of human rights or of morality in general on history,[50] because they were quite prepared, as Locke taught them they must be,[51] to test historical political practice against objective standards of political legitimacy (including respect for rights and pursuit of the public good), and to base the right to revolution on the failures of such practice to meet these standards.[52] However, Locke had taught them as well that a critical analysis of history could often clarify the ways in which corrupt abuses of power had subverted the very intellectual, moral, and political foundations of recognizing, let alone implementing, the inalienable rights of human nature. Such analysis could afford invaluable historical instruction in the need for political and constitutional principles protecting against such corruption.

Locke's argument for a principle of religious toleration illustrated this generic pattern of argument.[53] Indeed, the argument for religious toleration was taken by Americans, as Adams's essay clearly shows, to be a kind of model for political argument in general. Locke's critical attack on the theory and practice of religious persecution was not just on an abstract structure of argument that was demonstrably wrong, but on the pivotal historical role of this argument in the corruption of both religion and politics.[54]

Locke, like Bayle,[55] thus examined the argument offered by Augustine of Hippo to justify religious persecution of heresy,[56] and criticized Augustine's conception that there can be a politically just criterion for an erring conscience, a diabolically willful failure to accept evident religious truths. Fundamentally, Augustine's argument turned on the conviction of the truth of certain religious beliefs; everyone, however, had such a conviction of the truth of their religious beliefs. Accordingly, the argument would justify universal persecution by everyone of everyone else, which neither a just God nor the law of

---

[50] Indeed, Locke is notable among his generation precisely for his failure to make use in his political theory of legitimacy of any appeal to the history of the ancient constitution. See, e.g., Pocock, *Ancient Constitution and Feudal Law*, pp. 46, 187–8, 235–8, 348, 354–61.

[51] See John Locke, *The Second Treatise of Government*, in *John Locke, Two Treatises of Government*, Peter Laslett, ed. (Cambridge: Cambridge Univ. Press, 1960), pp. 424–46. For useful commentary, see Richard Ashcraft, *Locke's Two Treatises of Government* (London: Allen & Unwin, 1987); Ruth W. Grant, *John Locke's Liberalism* (Chicago: Univ. of Chicago Press, 1987).

[52] See *The Declaration of Independence*, in Jensen, ed., *Documentary History*, vol. 1, pp. 73–76. For useful commentary on the natural law and rights background of the Declaration and Constitution, see Carl L. Becker, *The Declaration of Independence* (New York: Vintage, 1958); White, *Philosophy of American Revolution;* Edward S. Corwin, *The "Higher Law" Background of American Constitutional Law* (Ithaca, N.Y.: Cornell Univ. Press, 1955).

[53] See John Locke, *Letters Concerning Toleration*, in *Works of John Locke*, vol. 6.

[54] For a fuller analysis, see David Richards, *Toleration and the Constitution* (New York: Oxford Univ. Press, 1986), pp. 89–98.

[55] See Pierre Bayle, *Philosophique Commentaire sur ces paroles de Jesus Christ "Contrain-les d'entree,"* in *Oeuvres Diverses de Mr. Pierre Bayle*, vol. 2 (A la Haye: Chez P. Husson et al., 1727) (hereafter referred to as *Philosophique Commentaire*), pp. 357–560. For a useful recent general study, see John Kilcullen, *Sincerity and Truth: Essays on Arnauld, Bayle, and Toleration* (Oxford: Clarendon Press, 1988).

[56] For fuller discussion, see Richards, *Toleration and Constitution*, pp. 86–88.

nature could have intended. In effect, one theological system, among others equally reasonable, was made the measure of enforceable truths.[57]

The crux of Locke's argument was the biased sectarian conception of enforceable rational truth that Augustine assumed, a corruptive judgment that failed to respect the just freedom of persons to exercise their inalienable right to conscience. The putatively irrational heretic was supposed to be unfree and marred by a disordered will. However, that judgment about the absence of freedom was itself corruptively biased and degraded our right to reasonable freedom of conscience, because conscience was made subject to the judgments of others. In order to ensure respect for the right to conscience of all on fair terms, a political principle of toleration was in order that deprived the state of the power to make and enforce such sectarian judgments over conscience.

The moral nerve of the argument for the right to conscience was that persons are independent originators of reasonable claims on one another as ethical beings, and that the demands of ethics and of an ethical God could only be both known and practically effective in our lives when persons' right to conscience was appropriately respected. Otherwise, the demands of ethics would be confused with public opinion or popular taste or a tradition based on "artifice, imposture, hypocrisy, and superstition."[58] This association of religious conscience with ethical imperatives was, of course, pervasively characteristic of the Judaeo-Christian tradition and its conception of an ethical and personal God acting through history.[59] Locke and Bayle were religious Christians in this tradition; they regarded themselves as returning Christianity to its ethical foundations (e.g., reminding Christians of the toleration of the early patristic period[60])—"that religious liberty," as Adams termed it, "with which Jesus made them free."[61] Disagreements in speculative theology—which had grounded Augustinian persecutions for heresy—were for them patent betray-

---

[57] This was hardly a decisive refutation of Augustine's argument. John Kilcullen's perceptive comment on Bayle's argument for toleration observes: "As a refutation of the Augustinian theories which in the seventeenth century gave religious intolerance its motive, or gave other motives a religious guise, Bayle's book does not really succeed. To the followers of St Augustine some of Bayle's premises would have seemed false or arbitrary, including some which today may seem trivial and self-evident. The Augustinians were not refuted: they died out without successfully training later generations" (Kilcullen, *Truth and Sincerity,* p. 2).

[58] John Adams, *A Defence,* p. 292.

[59] For the distinctive force of this conception in the Old Testament's narrative style and sharp repudiation of different conceptions of divinity in surrounding cultures, see Herbert Schneidau, *Sacred Discontent: The Bible and Western Tradition* (Baton Rouge: Louisiana State Univ. Press, 1976); Dan Jacobson, *The Story of Stories* (New York: Harper & Row, 1982); Robert Alter, *The Art of Biblical Narrative* (New York: Basic Books, 1981). On the personality of the western conception of the divine and its broader cultural significance for western ethics, politics, and science, see Denis de Rougemont, *Man's Western Quest,* Montgomery Belgion, trans. (Westport, Conn.: Greenwood, 1973); on the impersonality of India's concept of the divine, see Arthur Danto, *Mysticism and Morality* (New York: Harper, 1973), pp. 40–41.

[60] See, e.g., Bayle, *Philosophique Commentaire,* pp. 387–88.

[61] John Adams, *A Dissertation on the Canon and Feudal Law,* in C.F. Adams, ed., *Works of John Adams,* vol. 3, p. 454.

als of essential Christianity, because they prevented people from regulating their lives by the simple and elevated ethical imperatives of Christian charity.

The most acute criticism from Locke and Bayle of Augustinian persecution was of the particular significance of its corruption of ethics in the broader corruption of religion and politics, and the motivation of their arguments for the inalienable right to conscience was a new interpretation of what ethics was, one that made possible the emancipation of religion and ethics from their historical corruptions. Locke thus linked a free conscience to the autonomous exercise of the moral competence of each and every person as a democratic equal to reason in ways accessible to all reasonable beings about the nature and content of the ethical obligations imposed on persons by an ethical God,[62] and thought of these obligations as centering on a core of minimal ethical standards reflected in the Gospels.[63] Furthermore, ethics, for Bayle (as for Kant), was only a vital force in life when one independently acknowledges its principles and imposes them on one's life.[64] The very point of respect for conscience, for Locke and Bayle, was to ensure that each and every person was guaranteed the moral independence to determine the nature and content of ethical obligations and that state enforcement of sectarian religious beliefs did not taint this inalienable moral freedom with speculative theological disagreements that had corrupted the central place of this democratic conception of ethics in what both regarded as true religion. On this conception, religion did not embed us in ontological and political hierarchies of being that were characteristic of many of the world's cultural traditions,[65] but it made possible, indeed emancipated, a respect for persons that was expressive of their rational freedom. The right to conscience had a focal role in a just polity because it made possible the intellectual and moral foundations for reasonable self-government.

It was decisively important in the distinctive formation of American constitutionalism that Americans regarded religious beliefs, properly understood, as vehicles of moral and political emancipation in this Lockean way.[66] Locke and his American posterity thus faced frontally the central puzzle for religious Christians and democrats: how is it that a religion like Christianity (a religion for Locke of democratic equality and civility) had long been associated in the West with the legitimation of antidemocratic institutions like hereditary monarchy? Lockean Americans thus confronted the tension in traditional Christianity between a conception of radical freedom from existing roles, and the

---

[62] See, in general, John Colman, *John Locke's Moral Philosophy* (Edinburgh: Edinburgh Univ. Press, 1983).

[63] See John Locke, *The Reasonableness of Christianity,* in I.T. Ramsey, ed. (Stanford, Calif.: Stanford Univ. Press, 1958).

[64] Bayle, *Philosophique Commentaire,* pp. 367–72, 422–33.

[65] Van Leeuwen notes peculiarly western antiontocratic concerns. See, in general, Arend Th. van Leeuwen, *Christianity in World History,* H.H. Hoskins, trans. (New York: Charles Scribner's Sons, 1964).

[66] See, in general, Alan Heimert, *Religion and the American Mind: From the Great Awakening to the Revolution* (Cambridge, Mass.: Harvard Univ. Press, 1966).

coercive claims (e.g., heresy prosecutions) of the Christian political community over the minds and hearts of people.[67] This critical question was particularly poignant for Locke and the Lockean revolutionary and constitutionalist
Americans a century later because they believed, as Adams's essay makes
clear, that a properly understood Protestant Christianity supplied the ethics of
personal self-government that made possible the theory and practice of democratic self-government. How could Christianity have for millennia thus betrayed its essential emancipatory purposes, degrading a just human freedom
into the acceptance of morally arbitrary hierarchies of religious and political
privilege and power?

The American constitutional tradition chose to answer this question in a
way that repudiated the alternative Erastian conception of civil religion familiar to the founders in the classical republican tradition as elaborated by Machiavelli[68] and Rousseau.[69] The challenge to all republican theorists after the
ancient world was to understand whether and how republican political practice could exist in a nonpagan world—in particular, in the world of commitment to the Judaeo-Christian religious synthesis. After all, the great historical
examples of republican rule—Athens, Sparta, Rome, Carthage, and the
like—were all pre-Christian or pagan societies, and the reawakening of interest in republican theory and practice in the Renaissance naturally posed the
question of whether and how republicanism could be squared with Christian
commitments.

The classical republican answer by Machiavelli, Rousseau, and Marx[70] was
the Erastian conception of civil religion, which was an established church
regulated by state power to appropriately emancipatory ends. On this analysis, the great defect in the relationship of church and state since Constantine
was the independence of the church from state control, and its consequent
capacity to corrupt republican aims and values by theocratically defined ends.
This view was naturally, though not inevitably, linked to the kind of Voltairean
anticlericalism familiar to Europeans from republican Venice and Florence
and the associated classical republican tradition revived by Machiavelli.[71] On
this view, Judaeo-Christian values, whatever their truth value, were intrinsically dangerous, and must be confined and tamed to the ends of secular
authority by the assertion of supreme secular authority over religious life on
the model of Roman or Spartan civil religion. Even the political science of

---

[67] For an illuminating recent study of this tension from the perspective of issues of gender, see
Elaine Pagels, *Adam, Eve, and the Serpent* (New York: Random House, 1988).

[68] See Machiavelli, *Discourses*, pp. 139–52.

[69] See Jean Jacques Rousseau, *The Social Contract and Discourses*, G.D.H. Cole, trans. (New
York: Dutton, 1950), pp. 129–41.

[70] See Karl Marx, *On the Jewish Question*, in *Karl Marx: Early Writings*, T.B. Bottomore,
trans. (London: C.A. Watts, 1963).

[71] See Bouwsma, *Venice and the Defense of Republican Liberty*, pp. 1–51, 417–638. For a good
general study of Machiavelli's subversive attitude to Christian thought and practice, see Mark
Hulliung, *Citizen Machiavelli* (Princeton, N.J.: Princeton Univ. Press, 1983).

Montesquieu and Hume—though not endorsing classically republican civil religion—supported Erastian established churches.[72]

Americans like Jefferson and Madison gravitated to a quite different constitutional conception that culminated in the religion clauses of the First Amendment,[73] because they took a different view of how Judaeo-Christian belief and republican values interconnected, namely, the familiar American union of equally intense personal religiosity *and* republicanism. On this view, stated by Locke, the essential moral message of Christian belief—namely, the democratic liberty and equality of all persons—was supportive of republican values of equal liberty under law, but had been corrupted from its proper supportive role by Constantine's wholly heretical and blasphemous establishment of Christianity as the church of the Roman Empire. The problem was not that Constantine had opted for the wrong form of established church—one subordinating secular to religious authority—but that, as Americans like Jefferson and Madison came increasingly to see,[74] he had wedded religious to secular authority *at all*. A more radical separation of religious and political authority was required in order to preserve the integrity of each, in particular, to preserve the moral independence of conscience against which the legitimate claims of state power could then be assessed.

Americans, following Locke, thus gave prominence to the right to conscience because such historical reflection led them to believe that only the protection of conscience from sectarian corruption enabled people to emancipate themselves from the "artifice, imposture, hypocrisy, and superstition"[75] that prevented persons from knowing and giving weight to the natural rights of human nature in both religion and politics. Locke took as the central problem of politics the ways in which distortions of self-interest prevented persons from fairly adjudicating controversies over such rights, and argued that the legitimacy of state power depended (in a way we must examine in the next chapter) on securing greater impartiality in the enforcement of such rights.[76] The specific argument for toleration was that a legitimate state could have no power to enforce sectarian conscience because such power was corruptively biased in ways that cannot impartially enforce the right to conscience. Locke's removal of the issue from the scope of legitimate power rested on a penetrating analysis of the subversion of rationality itself by the self-deceiving excesses of a mind so impassioned by sectarian zeal[77] and dead-

[72] For commentary on Montesquieu's Erastian conception of religion, see Thomas L. Pangle, *Montesquieu's Philosophy of Liberalism* (Chicago: Univ. of Chicago Press, 1973), pp. 249–59. On Hume, see David Miller, *Philosophy and Ideology in Hume's Political Thought* (Oxford: Clarendon Press, 1981), pp. 117–18.

[73] See, in general, Richards, *Toleration and the Constitution,* Chapters 4 and 5.

[74] Americans elaborate this principle beyond Locke, whose arguments focus on free exercise, not antiestablishment. For discussion of the ways Americans adapted and elaborated Locke's arguments, see ibid., pp. 88–116.

[75] John Adams, *A Defence,* p. 292.

[76] See, in general, Grant, *John Locke's Liberalism.*

[77] See, e.g., John Locke, *On the Conduct of the Human Understanding,* in *Works of John Locke,* vol. 3, pp. 212, 216, 235, 267–68. On the importance of getting clear about Locke's

ened by oppressive custom[78] that it was incapable of any impartial or fair-minded assessment of dissenting, let alone heretical, views.[79] Toleration was thus required as a prophylaxis against an irrationalism that made impossible the satisfaction of minimal demands for the reasonable justification of the power of the state.[80]

This pattern of argument was of quite general application, because the same kind of critical historical analysis was necessary to come to terms with the ways in which corrupt religious and political power had made people incapable of knowing and implementing the natural rights of human nature due them in politics. John Adams's *Dissertation on the Canon and Feudal Law* illustrates not only how well revolutionary Americans had absorbed and used this pattern of argument for purposes of understanding their rights against an oppressive government, but also how imaginatively they were prepared to extend it to the more general discussion of what Adams calls "the grounds and principles of government."[81] Americans would shortly need to develop such arguments further in order to grapple with their political experiences in the revolution and under the early state and federal constitutions, and to articulate constructive alternatives more consistent with both respect for rights and pursuit of the public interest. They naturally turned again to the critical use of interpretive history in the service of advancing their aims of religious and political emancipation, but now at a more penetrating level of analysis of the enduring pathologies of political psychology.

Political Psychology: The Theory of Faction

The study of political psychology had been a preoccupation of the American revolutionary mind, which adapted to American circumstances the theory of the corruptibility of unaccountable power that absorbed from the Whig opposition literature in Britain the claims of constitutional abuse with which Americans passionately identified.[82] Americans had learned, for example, from Trenchard and Gordon's *Cato's Letters*[83] a political psychology that explained

---

distinctive thought about a flawed human nature, see W.W. Spellman, *John Locke and the Problem of Depravity* (Oxford: Clarendon Press, 1988).

[78] See Locke, *Conduct of Human Understanding*, pp. 208, 230, 231–32, 268, 276–77.

[79] See Ibid., pp. 266–69, 271, 276–77.

[80] I am indebted here to the discussion of Ruth W. Grant, *John Locke's Liberalism*, pp. 180–92. For a different interpretation of Locke's argument, centering on the irrationality of coercion to secure any belief at all, see Jeremy Waldron, "Locke: Toleration and the Rationality of Persecution," in Susan Mendus, ed., *Justifying Toleration* (Cambridge: Cambridge Univ. Press, 1988), pp. 61–86.

[81] John Adams, *A Defence*, p. 462.

[82] The best general study remains Bailyn, *Ideological Origins of American Revolution*. See also Caroline Robbins, *The Eighteenth-Century Commonwealthman* (Cambridge, Mass.: Harvard Univ. Press, 1959); Bernard Bailyn, *The Origins of American Politics* (New York: Vintage, 1967).

[83] John Trenchard and Thomas Gordon, *Cato's Letters: Essays on Liberty, Civil and Religious,*

unconstitutional abuses in terms of the distortions of judgment by passion and the resulting dominance of oppressive "factions"[84] that were unconcerned with the public interest; furthermore, they came to think of constitutional reform, following Trenchard and Gordon, as a study in how such blinding political passions might be regulated[85] by frequent elections or rotation in office[86] or, following Burgh's *Political Disquisitions*,[87] by a more representative legislature. The Whig opposition literature heavily depended on the further elaboration of methods of analysis learned from Machiavelli's study of classical republicanism[88] and applied to British circumstances by, among others, Algernon Sidney[89] and James Harrington.[90] The Whig oppositionists thus argued as Cato,[91] or Brutus,[92] or Junius,[93] and others in ways, of course, that Americans were to imitate.[94]

However, Americans confronted new circumstances when they were compelled critically to reflect on the defects in the early state and federal constitutions, and they had to rethink the terms of analysis they had absorbed from the Whig opposition literature. Those terms of analysis had been congenial to Americans because they made critical sense of the political psychology of threatened oppression they had come to fear from a government not properly accountable to them.[95] However, the experience of political oppression under the early state and federal constitutions could not be explained in such simplistic terms. The state legislatures were certainly much more fairly representative than the British House of Commons, and there was no hereditary element anywhere in the American constitutions, state or federal. Yet many Ameri-

---

and Other Important Subjects, 4 vols. (printed in 2 vols.: vols. I and II in vol. 1; vols. III and IV in vol. 2) (New York: Da Capo Press, 1971) (copy of 6th ed., published in London, 1755).

[84] See, for example, Trenchard and Gordon, *Cato's Letters,* vol. I, pp. 83, 104, 108, 114, 121, 130, 139, 178; vol. II, pp. 11, 48, 66, 130, 131, 301; vol. III, p. 118; vol. IV, pp. 248, 284. A faction is defined as "the gratifying of private Passion by publick Means" (idem, vol. II, p. 48).

[85] See ibid., vol. II, pp. 43–56.

[86] See ibid., vol. IV, pp. 81–86.

[87] James Burgh, *Political Disquisitions: An Enquiry into Public Errors, Defects, and Abuses* (New York: Da Capo Press, 1971), 3 vols. (first edition, published in London, 1774–1775).

[88] See, for example, Trenchard and Gordon, *Cato's Letters,* vol. I, pp. 108–9, 154, 180–1, 247, 249; vol. II, pp. 265–66; vol. III, p. 118.

[89] See Algernon Sidney, *Discourses Concerning Government* (New York: Arno Press, 1979), pp. 104–5, 112–14, 117–19.

[90] See, for example, James Harrington, *The Commonwealth of Oceana,* in Pocock, ed., *Political Works of James Harrington,* pp. 166, 178, 203, 234, 261, 310, 311. For very illuminating commentary on Machiavelli, Sidney, Harrington, and others, see Fink, *Classical Republicans.* See also Robbins, *Eighteenth-Century Commonwealthman.*

[91] See, in general, Trenchard and Gordon, *Cato's Letters.*

[92] See ibid., vol. I, pp. 163–77, 227–36.

[93] See, in general, George Woodfall, ed., *The Letters of Junius* (London: George Routledge & Sons, n.d.).

[94] See McDonald, *Novus Ordo Seclorum,* pp. 67–68.

[95] On these American fears and their ideological background, see, in general, Bailyn, *Ideological Origins of American Revolution.*

cans of the revolutionary generation had concluded, like Jefferson, that "an *electoral despotism* was not the government we fought for."[96] The problem appeared to be more fundamental, and Americans like James Madison were accordingly stimulated to reinterpret Whig political psychology in ways illuminated by the general political science offered by Montesquieu and Hume, a political science (as we shall see in the next section) that enabled Americans—in contrast to much Whig opposition thought—to conceive of the range of constructive alternatives not in imitation of classical republicanism but in sharp rejection of it.

One of Montesquieu's more striking points of analytical politics was his elaboration of the Machiavellian observation of the incommensurability of political virtue and vice with moral virtue and vice.[97] Machiavelli wrote from the perspective of those "constituting and legislating for a commonwealth,"[98] and argued that, for this purpose, "it must needs be taken for granted that all men are wicked and that they will always give vent to the malignity that is in their minds when opportunity offers."[99] The argument was not that moral virtue and vice did not exist and were not important, but that the task of what Montesquieu later called the "legislator"[100] required attention to the sorts of motives that characterize political life. A better constitution and better laws could only be framed in light of a realistic assessment of such motives, for example, a mixed constitution might be framed on the assumption that only a balance of power among disparate factions (motivated to oppress other factions) could realistically secure equal liberty for all.[101] Montesquieu's "legislator"—when designing political constitutions—took, following Machiavelli, a view of *political* psychology that Judith Shklar has recently called "thoroughly misanthropic."[102] In effect, the political virtues requisite for the proper functioning of a good constitution were distinguished from any conception of moral or religious virtue.[103] As Shklar observes, "The English, said Montesquieu, have an excellent constitution, and are solid citizens, but are perfectly awful people."[104]

David Hume's analytical political psychology developed Montesquieu's point even more trenchantly when he endorsed the

---

[96] Jefferson, *Notes on the State of Virginia*, p. 120.

[97] See, e.g., Baron de Montesquieu, *The Spirit of the Laws*, Thomas Nugent, trans. (New York: Hafner, 1949), vol. 1, p. 297.

[98] Machiavelli, *Discourses*, p. 111.

[99] Ibid., pp. 111–12.

[100] Montesquieu, *Spirit of the Laws*, vol. 2, p. 156.

[101] For useful commentary on Machiavelli's originality in making this argument, see Quentin Skinner, *Machiavelli* (New York: Hill and Wang, 1981), pp. 65–67.

[102] Judith Shklar, *Ordinary Vices* (Cambridge, Mass.: Belknap Press of Harvard Univ. Press, 1984), p. 197.

[103] See, for example, Montesquieu's criticism of Bayle for confusing religious and political virtue, in *Spirit of the Laws*, vol. 2, pp. 31–32; and his criticism of the Christian ideal of speculation (a religious virtue) as a political vice (idem, vol. 2, p. 19).

[104] Shklar, *Ordinary Vices*, p. 33.

maxim, that, in contriving any system of government, and fixing the several checks and controls of the constitution, every man ought to be supposed a *knave,* and to have no other end, in all his actions, than private interest.[105]

Hume, like Montesquieu, did not suppose that all human conduct was motivated by private interests; indeed, he defended a general moral and political philosophy based on capacities of human nature for sympathetic benevolence that was motivated by identification with the interests of all other persons.[106] Hume squared the maxim of his political science with his moral and political philosophy of sympathetic benevolence by noting how "somewhat strange" it is that the "maxim should be true in *politics* which is false in *fact*"[107]; furthermore, he explained the limited truth of the maxim in politics by facts of group psychology that are central to political life, namely, the dynamics of group identification and psychology such that

> men are generally more honest in their private than in their public capacity, and will go greater lengths to serve a party, than when their own private interest is alone concerned. Honour is a great check upon mankind: but where a considerable body of men act together, this check is in a great measure removed, since a man is sure to be approved of by his own party, for what promotes the common interest; and he soon learns to despise the clamours of adversaries.[108]

Elsewhere, Hume analyzed further these facts of political psychology as "factions"[109] of two different kinds: personal (*i.e.,* familial or clan-based) and real (subdivided into those from interest, from principle, and from affection).

The theory of political man of Montesquieu and Hume addressed the nature of political life, and supplied the more penetrating perspective on their experience that Americans needed to understand the critical defects in their state and federal constitutions.[110] The evolving political thought of James

---

[105] David Hume, "Of the Independency of Parliament," in *Essays Moral, Political, Literary* (Oxford: Oxford Univ. Press, 1963), p. 40.

[106] Hume's most penetrating statement of the view is *A Treatise of Human Nature,* in L.A. Selby-Bigge, ed. (Oxford: Clarendon Press, 1964), book III. See also David Hume, *An Enquiry Concerning the Principles of Morals,* in *Enquiries,* L.A. Selby-Bigge, ed. (Oxford: Clarendon Press, 1963).

[107] Hume, "Of the Independency of Parliament," p. 42.

[108] Ibid., pp. 42–43.

[109] See Hume, "Of Parties in General," in *Essays Moral, Political, and Literary,* p. 55.

[110] Montesquieu is cited by all sides to the debates over the Constitution at every stage, and his views are discussed by Madison, for example, in *The Federalist* at no. 47. See, in general, Paul Merrill Spurlin, *Montesquieu in America 1760–1801* (New York: Octagon, 1969). Hume is cited by Hamilton at the concluding essay of *The Federalist,* p. 594 (Jacob E. Cooke, ed.), and his maxims of political psychology, earlier noted in the text, are quoted by Hamilton in his 1775 essay, *The Farmer Refuted,* in Harold C. Syrett and Jacob E. Cooke, eds., *The Papers of Alexander Hamilton, 1768–1778,* vol. 1 (New York: Columbia Univ. Press, 1961), pp. 94–95. Madison's use of Hume is inferential, but the inference is well justified by Douglass Adair in his classic study of the matter; see Adair, *Fame and the Founding Fathers,* pp. 93–106. On the reasons why a good

Madison—in a memorandum prepared for his use at the constitutional convention, speeches at the convention, correspondence with Jefferson after the convention, and finally the argument in *The Federalist* no. 10—exemplified how this perspective framed the American project of drafting, debating, criticizing, and ratifying the Constitution.

In his important memorandum, "Vices of the Political System of the United States,"[111] Madison analyzed defects not only in the Articles of Confederation but also in the state constitutions; in particular, Madison took alarm not only at the bad policies pursued by state laws but also at their unjust failure to respect rights. Moreover, such laws brought "into question the fundamental principle of republican Government, that the majority who rule in such Governments, are the safest Guardians both of public Good and of private rights."[112] The difficulty was not only in the representative bodies, but, more fundamentally, also in the political psychology of the people themselves. The mistake of American republicanism heretofore was that it had—consistent with much Whig opposition thought—focused on the political corruptibility of government officials, not on the corruptibility of the people themselves. However, the facts of political psychology applied to all political actors, as Madison had come to see. Republican government was distinguished by the power it gave the people to be political actors, but it could claim no legitimate exemption from the laws of political psychology; the political power of the people was as subject to these laws as the power of a hereditary monarch or aristocracy. American constitutionalism must—consistent with its commitment to the uses of emancipated religious and political intelligence in service of the rights of human nature—take account of these facts, and frame its task accordingly.

Madison characterized the facts of political psychology pertinent to the American situation in Humean terms:

> All civilized societies are divided into different interests and factions, as they happen to be creditors or debtors—Rich or poor—husbandmen, merchants or manufacturers—members of different religious sects—followers of different political leaders—inhabitants of different districts—owners of different kinds of property &c &c.[113]

By definition, such factions pursued their own private interests at the expense of the interests and rights of others, and the commitment of republican government to majority rule would allow majority factions untrammeled power to achieve their ends at the expense of the public interest and the rights of minorities.

Madison considered three motives as possible limits on the oppressive power of such majority factions: interest, character, and religion. However,

---

republican like Madison might have wanted not explicitly to acknowledge dependence on Hume, see Theodore Draper, "Hume and Madison," *Encounter*, vol. 58 (Feb. 1982), p. 34.
[111] Rutland et al., eds., *Papers of James Madison, 1786–1787*, pp. 345–58.
[112] Ibid., p. 354.
[113] Ibid., p. 355.

the political psychology of faction was such—especially under the circumstances of republican government—that none of them was constitutionally adequate. The ugly Humean truth about faction was that a person's critically independent judgment—as a person of conscience—about their long-term interests and about justice to others would be distorted by their group identifications. Madison echoed Hume's earlier-quoted way of putting the point:

> However strong this motive [respect for character] may be in individuals, it is considered as very insufficient to restrain them from injustice. In a multitude its efficacy is diminished in proportion to the number which is to share the praise or the blame.[114]

Indeed, Madison underscored the special ferocity of this type of factionalized injustice under republics: the sense of justice in a republican community reflects public opinion, but public opinion "is the opinion of the majority" so that "the standard [of critical public opinion] is fixed by those whose conduct is to be measured by it."[115] Furthermore, religion—so far from being a constraint on majority factions—was often its worst expression:

> The conduct of every popular assembly acting on oath, the strongest of religious Ties, proves that individuals join without remorse in acts, against which their consciences would revolt if proposed to them under the like sanction, separately in their closets.[116]

Madison reproduced and elaborated this argument in his addresses to the constitutional convention on June 6[117] and June 26, 1787[118] and in his letter of October 24, 1787 to Jefferson that both explained and criticized the work of the convention.[119] At the convention, Madison argued that it was not enough that new powers be given to the federal government; it must provide

> more effectually for the security of private rights, and the steady dispensation of Justice. Interferences with these were evils which had more perhaps than any thing else, produced this convention.[120]

The oppressive force of faction was well supported by history and by contemporary examples in America, one example of which Madison acidly brought to stage center: "We have seen the mere distinction of colour made in the most enlightened period of time, a ground of the most oppressive dominion

---

[114] Ibid.

[115] Ibid.

[116] Ibid., p. 356.

[117] Max Farrand, ed., *The Records of the Federal Convention*, vol. 1 (New Haven, Conn.: Yale Univ. Press, 1966), pp. 134–36, 138–39.

[118] Ibid., pp. 421–23.

[119] See Rutland et al., eds., *Papers of James Madison, 1787–1788*, pp. 206–219.

[120] Farrand, *Records of Federal Convention*, vol. 1, p. 134 (speech of June 6, 1787).

ever exercised by man over man."[121] A central task of the Constitution was to take seriously the corruptive force of many such factions and "to protect [the people] agst. the transient impressions into which they themselves might be led."[122] Madison later wrote to Jefferson in no uncertain terms about the felt need to address the problem of the oppressions by majority factions of minority rights at the state level:

> The injustice of them has been so frequent and so flagrant as to alarm the most stedfast [sic] friends of Republicanism. I am persuaded I do not err in saying that the evils issuing from these sources contributed more to that uneasiness which produced the Convention, and prepared the public mind for a general reform, than those which accrued to our national character and interest from the inadequacy of the Confederation to its immediate objects.[123]

Indeed, Madison's main criticism of the Constitution was conceptualized in such terms: it had not gone far enough in affording strong institutional constraints on such majority factions.[124]

In *The Federalist* no. 10, Madison defended the Constitution to the nation at large on the basis of the constraints it imposed on "the violence of faction."[125] Madison defined a faction as follows:

> By a faction I understand a number of citizens, whether amounting to a majority or minority of the whole, who are united and actuated by some common impulse of passion, or of interest, adverse to the rights of other citizens, or to the permanent and aggregate interests of the community.[126]

In his memorandum prepared for the convention, Madison had earlier pointed to the especially malign force of faction under republican government, namely, its erosion of citizens' capacity for critical moral independence by a public opinion that is often the self-serving opinion of majority factions. The argument of *The Federalist* no. 10 generalized this theme.

Republicans valued liberty above all. We know that liberty for Madison[127] crucially included the inalienable right to conscience that made possible religious and political emancipation (see previous section), including the exercise of public judgment in drafting and ratifying a constitution. However, such

---

[121] Ibid., p. 135.

[122] Ibid., p. 421 (Madison's later speech of June 26, 1787).

[123] Rutland et al., ed., *Papers of James Madison, 1787–1788*, p. 212.

[124] Madison had unsuccessfully defended at the convention and defends to Jefferson the need for a congressional negative on the laws of the states. See Rutland et al., ed., *Papers of James Madison, 1787–1788*, p. 209–14.

[125] *The Federalist*, p. 56.

[126] Ibid., p. 57.

[127] For the primacy of the right of conscience in Madison's thought about rights, see his 1785 *Memorial and Remonstrance against Religious Assessments*, Rutland et al., ed., *Papers of James Madison, 1784–1786* pp. 295–306, and his 1792 essay, "Property," in Robert A. Rutland et al., eds., *The Papers of James Madison, 1791–1793*, vol. 14 (Charlottesville: Univ. Press of Virginia, 1983), pp. 266–68.

liberty "is to faction, what air is to fire, an aliment without which it instantly expires."[128] The argument of *The Federalist* no. 10 has often been interpreted in light of the special emphasis it gives "the most common and durable source of factions, . . . the various and unequal distribution of property."[129] Its pivotal argument, however, turns on why the uncompromisable republican value placed on liberty of judgment is inconsistent with the kind of uniformity of judgment and action that would preclude faction:

> As long as the reason of man continues fallible, and he is at liberty to exercise it, different opinions will be formed. As long as the connection subsists between his reason and his self-love, his opinions and passions will have a reciprocal influence on each other; and the former will be objects to which the latter will attach themselves.[130]

In effect, sectarian disagreements (whether religious, economic, or political) will be unleashed by the republican commitment to protection of the liberty of judgment in exercising our faculties ("the first object of government"[131]), and the disagreements thus unleashed will, under majority rule, lead to sectarian oppression. The argument amplified Madison's earlier theme about the self-subverting character of the untrammeled majoritarianism Americans had associated with republican rule: the subversion of the moral independence of free people by a factionalized public opinion was generalized to the subversion of republican liberties by the factions that those liberties necessarily unleashed. Some constructive alternatives had to be defined that might transcend the horns of this republican dilemma.

Classical Republicanism as a Negative Exemplar

American thinking about such alternatives was remarkably stimulated by an interpretation of the history of both confederacies and republican government (including their own political experience) in light of the political psychology of faction. The history of confederacies, for example, was studied and debated in depth, and the failures of such confederacies were analyzed as a consequence of the uninhibited scope they gave to state factions that pursued parochical interests at the expense of the rights of other states, their citizens, and the national interest.[132] The unhappy American experience under the Articles of

---

[128] *The Federalist*, p. 58.

[129] Ibid., p. 59. See, e.g., Charles A. Beard, *An Economic Interpretation of the Constitution of the United States* (New York: Free Press, 1941), pp. 14–15, 153–54. For cogent criticism of Beard's interpretation, see White, *Philosophy, The Federalist, and the Constitution*, pp. 74–81.

[130] *The Federalist*, p. 58.

[131] Ibid.

[132] See, e.g., Madison's memoranda prepared for the constitutional convention, "Notes on Ancient and Modern Confederacies," in Rutland et al., ed., *Papers of James Madison, 1786–1787,* pp. 324; "Vices of the Political System" pp. 345–58. For the constitutional convention, see, e.g., Farrand, ed., *Records of Federal Convention* vol. 1, pp. 143 (Wilson), 285–86 (Hamilton), 317, 320

Confederation had repeated these lessons of history, and the founders—in light of that history—perceived both the need and opportunity to construct a constitutional alternative that would better address the corruptive political psychology of state factionalism. The study of history in this case led Madison to see clearly the imaginative poverty of available historical examples, and to be open to an experimental adaptation of a Harringtonian utopian model[133] that might deal with these problems in ways that also grappled with the republican dilemma (see Chapter 3).

Americans also brought to bear the political psychology of faction on the critical study of the history of republican government itself, a study antici-pated by Harrington[134] and persuasively elaborated for Americans by Montes-quieu and Hume.[135] That study enabled Americans to redefine the project of republican government by way of negative contrast to the factionalized poli-tics of classical republicanism,[136] that is, the classical democratic models of antiquity and the Renaissance with their Aristotelian[137] and Machiavellian[138] focus on the actively engaged and participating citizen-soldier.

Political activity on the classical model was the central activity of civilized social life, preoccupying—as the slave and sexist society of ancient Athens permitted—the entire space of a well-lived life with the absorbing tasks of

---

(Madison), 343 (Wilson), 448 (Madison). For ratification debates, see, e.g., Elliot, *Debates*, pp. 128–32 (Madison in Virginia debates). For *The Federalist*, see nos. 18–20 (Madison).

[133] Madison almost certainly studied at this point Hume's utopian essay, "Idea of a Perfect Commonwealth," in *Essays Moral, Political, and Literary*, pp. 499–515 (elaborating on Harring-ton's *Oceana*). See Adair, *Fame and the Founding Fathers*, pp. 93–106.

[134] Harrington, inspired by Machiavelli's political science of ancient republics, made his own study of such republics and consequently urged that republican government must take seriously the political psychology of faction, especially religious sectarianism (see *Commonwealth of Oceana*, in Pocock, ed., *Political Works of James Harrington*, p. 204), and design constitutional structures accordingly to minimize the oppressive tendencies of faction in republican politics. As he put the point: " 'Give us good men and they make us good laws' is the maxim of a dema-gogue. . . . But 'give us good orders, and they will make us good men' is the maxim of a legislator and the most infallible in the politics" (idem, p. 205). Harrington's model endorses, however, many elements of Machiavelli's republicanism of civic participation, including a central focus on the citizen-soldier, in a way that Montesquieu and Hume did not.

[135] Both Montesquieu and Hume use their political psychology in the critical assessment of different political regimes, arguing that institutional structures should be so arranged so that the facts of political psychology work out in the way that is most consistent with independently specified aims of justice and the public good. For this reason, both thinkers are skeptical of the classical republican ideal of the small city-state motivated by the virtue of Machiavellian civic moralism as a model for contemporary states. On Montesquieu, see Pangle, *Montesquieu's Philosophy of Liberalism*, pp. 48–106. On Hume, see James Moore, "Hume's Political Science and the Classical Republican Tradition," 10 *Can. J. Pol. Sci.*, pp. 809–39 (1977); Miller, *Philoso-phy and Ideology in Hume's Political Thought*, pp. 121, 150–1.

[136] See, e.g., *The Federalist*, pp. 61–65 (Madison). For extended comparisons, see John Ad-ams, *A Defence*, vol. 4 (pp. 273–588), vol. 5 (pp. 3–496), and vol. 6 (pp. 3–220).

[137] See, e.g., Aristotle, *The Politics of Aristotle*, Ernest Barker, trans. (New York: Oxford Univ. Press, 1962), pp. 92–110.

[138] See, e.g., Machiavelli, *Discourses*, pp. 265–90.

democratic participation.[139] Correlatively, Athens proudly touted its regime of free speech as an aspect of the more ultimate evaluative aim of democratic participation.[140] This conception of free speech had no place for the idea of a legitimately private sphere immune from politics, a point bluntly made by Pericles: "We do not say that a man who takes no interest in politics is a man who minds his own business; we say that he has no business here at all."[141] Family life, for example, was contemptuously remitted to the morally inferior class of women, whose labor had moral weight only insofar as it released men for public life[142]; work was often for slaves, thus releasing citizens for civic life in the agora.[143] Furthermore, the political system, which was committed to free speech only as an aspect of political participation, failed to understand a Socratic individualism rooted in a moral conception external to and often critical of politics, including the conception of free speech that served this distinctive moral conception.[144] Indeed, the Athenian state ruthlessly persecuted uses of free speech that were expressive of an individualistic moral conception—uses interpreted, by the Athenian democracy, to be impious and heretical and thus worthy of death.[145]

The classical conception specified a richly elaborated theory and practice of democratically controlled collective political life.[146] However, that conception exhaustively identified the moral aims of democracy with voting and participation, and their constitutive role in the flowering of human excellences like civic generosity, military courage, heroism, and patriotism, that is, the perfectionist virtues of Aristotelian ethics.[147]

Theories of normative ethics are standardly distinguished into teleological and deontological types.[148] Teleological theories define right action in terms of the tendency of an action to result in the greatest net aggregate of goods over evils; in contrast, deontological theories are those that do not define right

---

[139] See, e.g., Paul A. Rahe, "The Primacy of Politics in Ancient Greece," 89 *Amer. Hist. Rev.* 265 (1984); M.I. Finley, *Politics in the Ancient World* (Cambridge: Cambridge Univ. Press, 1983); idem, *Democracy Ancient and Modern,* rev. ed. (New Brunswick, N.J.: Rutgers Univ. Press, 1985).

[140] See Pericles' Funeral Oration, in Thucydides, *History of the Peloponnesian War,* Rex Warner, trans. (Harmondsworth, Middlesex, England: Penguin, 1954), p. 147.

[141] Thucydides, ibid.

[142] See Aristotle, *Politics,* pp. 8–38.

[143] See, e.g., ibid., pp. 9–17. For pertinent comparisons of ancient and modern conceptions of work, see Hannah Arendt, *The Human Condition* (Garden City, N.Y.: Doubleday, 1959).

[144] For statement of such a conception, see Richards, *Toleration and the Constitution,* Chapters 6 and 7.

[145] Socrates makes precisely this predictive point about his own fate at the hands of his fellow Athenians in Plato, *Gorgias,* Terence Irwin, trans. (Oxford: Clarendon Press, 1979), pp. 101–2. For a recent political study of the trial that rather misses the underlying conflicts of philosophical principle, see I.F. Stone, *The Trial of Socrates* (Boston: Little, Brown, 1988).

[146] See, e.g., Finley, *Democracy Ancient and Modern.*

[147] See, in general, Aristotle, *Nicomachean Ethics,* Martin Ostwald, trans. (New York: Bobbs-Merrill, 1962).

[148] See, e.g., John Rawls, *A Theory of Justice* (Cambridge, Mass.: Harvard Univ. Press, 1971), pp. 22–27, 30.

action in such teleological terms. Perfectionist moral theory is a teleological theory that defines the relevant goods and corresponding evils in terms of the greatest exercise and display of developed capacities of talent, creativity, and general excellence, including artistic and intellectual performance and military courage and prowess. Aristotle's perfectionism, like Nietzsche's,[149] assumed that such competencies were quite unequally distributed, and thus justified, as a matter of principle, both slavery and the subjection of women[150] as ways of better realizing perfectionist ends, for example, releasing artists or patriotic men from forms of work that frustrated their capacity to realize more fully the only goods of ultimate moral worth, namely, superior achievement of talent, creativity, military courage, genius, and comparable excellences.[151]

Aristotelian perfectionism was thus fundamentally elitist, because it construed slavery and the subjection of women as wholly natural; indeed it morally required ways to preserve the proper role of the talented elite. The theory and practice of classical republicanism assumed such perfectionist aims and supposed the extraordinary demands of classical republican participation to be instrumental in the full flowering of human excellence. In particular, the moral theory of classical republicanism emphasized perfectionist heroism in the service of the ultimate unit of value, the polis, which defined the indispensable context for the fostering and display of the elitist human excellences. Democratic participation was valued intrinsically as the matrix for the exercise and display of the perfectionist virtues.

Americans defined the distinctive aims of their own constitutional republicanism by a process of critical historical reflection on the history of the theory and practice of these classical republics. This criticism discredited classical republicanism as a model for American constitutional thought in a way that explains the sharp objection Americans took to the European thinkers, like Rousseau and others, for whom such models had a powerful continuing appeal.[152] More affirmatively, such reflection clarified for Americans every level

---

[149] For fuller discussion, see David A.J. Richards, *A Theory of Reasons for Action* (Oxford: Clarendon Press, 1971), pp. 116–17.

[150] For fuller discussion and relevant citations, see ibid., p. 117.

[151] Contemporary forms of perfectionist moral theory are not, of course, inevitably wedded to such conclusions. See, e.g., Vinit Haksar, *Equality, Liberty, and Perfectionism* (Oxford: Clarendon Press, 1979); Joseph Raz, *The Morality of Freedom* (Oxford: Clarendon Press, 1986). An alternative kind of teleological theory, utilitarianism, identifies goods and evils in terms of pleasures and pains that are, in principle, more equally distributed among all sentient creatures than the excellencies of Aristotelian perfectionism. See, e.g., Henry Sidgwick, *The Methods of Ethics*, 7th ed. (London: Macmillan. 1963).

[152] John Adams is illustrative. He had cited Rousseau with approval in his 1765 essay, *Dissertation on the Canon and Feudal Law*, pp. 454–55, and he even described his work on the Massachusetts state constitution of 1780 as "Locke, Sidney and Rousseau and De Mably reduced to practice," in idem, vol. 4, p. 216; he also cited Rousseau's works approvingly for their empirical views about particular societies (the dominant power of the nobles in Poland) and about the general evil in civilized men in *A Defence*, idem, vol. 4, pp. 367, 409. However, he later repudiated Rousseau's political theory as resting, like that of Turgot and Condorcet, on a perfectionism untested by the kind of experience to which American constitutionalists appealed in framing their constitutions. See, in general, Zoltan Haraszti, *John Adams and the Prophets of Progress* (Cam-

of their distinctive constitutional project, namely, its fundamental political principles and aims, requisite constitutional structures, and the kinds of motivational demands on the citizenry appropriate to its stability.

Madison opined, in *The Federalist* no. 51, "justice is the end of government,"[153] and construed the need for constitutional government as affording constraints on factions that are, by the definition of *The Federalist,* no. 10, "adverse to the rights of other citizens, or to the permanent and aggregate interests of the community."[154] Americans like Madison thus thought of constitutional governments as to be assessed and tested in light of independent values of respect for equal rights and pursuit of the public good. The test of legitimate government was the degree to which its constitutional structures respected equal rights and gave equal weight to all human interests. Fundamental American political principles were thus egalitarian. Faction was construed as an evil in republican politics because its political psychology corrupted equality: members of the faction regarded outsiders as less politically worthy, perhaps as unworthy or even evil (religious sectarianism) or, as Madison's example of the evil of slavery attests,[155] as subhuman. Furthermore, majority factions, under simple majority rule, violated the rights of outsiders and ignored their interests. That was, for Americans, the republican dilemma: republican majority rule flouted the principles at the foundation of republican legitimacy.

The basic American normative test of constitutional legitimacy was foundationally egalitarian (see Chapter 3),[156] and thus the elitist Aristotelian moral perfectionism of classical republicanism was unacceptable. Certainly, even by the best lights of 1787, Americans were unwilling to implement fully their

---

bridge, Mass.: Harvard Univ. Press, 1952). Adams, of course, was stimulated to write his monumental *A Defence* by Turgot's criticism of American constitutions. See *A Defence,* pp. 278–302. On the rejection of Rousseau's political theory by Americans, see Paul Merrill Spurlin, *Rousseau in America 1760–1809* (University, Alabama: Univ. of Alabama Press, 1969), pp. 57–70. Webster, for example, rejected the views of *The Social Contract* as "chimerical" and "Experience does not warrant them," idem, p. 61. For Madison's criticism of "theoretic politicians," see *The Federalist,* p. 61. In the debates over ratification of the Constitution, Rousseau is cited, and then quite rarely, by anti-Federalists; see e.g., Herbert J. Storing, *The Complete Anti-Federalist,* vol. 4 (Chicago: Univ. of Chicago Press, 1981), pp. 251–52.

[153] *The Federalist,* p. 352.

[154] *The Federalist,* p. 57. In *A Defence* (p. 318), Adams reversed this order but was to similar effect: "the end of government is the greatest happiness of the greatest number, saving at the same time the stipulated rights of all."

[155] See Farrand, ed. *Records of Federal Convention,* vol. 1, p. 135 (Madison's speech of June 6, 1787).

[156] Hamilton, for example, defended a lifetime elective monarchy and senate at the constitutional convention on the model of the British constitution. See ibid., pp. 282–93. However, his argument for such institutions was, following Hume, that history showed that such institutions were more likely to secure an impartial conception of the public interests of all alike, that is "the happiness of our Country" (idem, p. 284). There is no suggestion here or elsewhere that Hamilton justified his views on perfectionist grounds, but rather as alternative ways of securing the egalitarian conception of justice and the public good he shared with the other founders. See, for a good study of Hamilton's distinctive views, Gerald Stourzh, *Alexander Hamilton and the Idea of Republican Government* (Stanford Calif.: Stanford Univ. Press, 1970).

political principles, but they often tragically knew, by such lights, when they were compromising principle (e.g., the Constitution's legitimation of slavery). Madison's characterization of slavery at the convention as "the most oppressive dominion ever exercised by man over man"[157] illustrates the point. Americans like Madison, Jefferson,[158] and many others[159] knew that slavery was the republican abomination it was precisely because they accepted a political and moral theory of equality that was inconsistent with the Aristotelian perfectionism that, in the participational democracy of ancient Athens, *required* slavery.

American constitutional thinkers, as diverse as Thomas Jefferson and John Adams, experienced no comparable moral or cognitive tension between their beliefs in equality and their advocacy of a natural aristocracy of republican leaders.[160] However, that was not because they assumed, *sub silentio,* Aristotelian moral perfectionism, but because they quite rightly thought that the belief that government must respect equal rights and give equal weight to all legitimate human interests required a constitutional government that would realistically mobilize and direct the best available talent for leadership of the nation in ways that would better secure such equal rights and the public interest (see, for further elaboration of this theme, the discussion of the theory of fame later in this chapter). Such talent was not valued intrinsically in the way that perfectionism requires, but as instrumental to the ends of republican equality. The perfectionist interpretation of American constitutionalism standardly rests on such a confusion of levels of justification,[161] a mistake the founders did not make. As we shall see (Chapter 3), the founders thought of the legitimacy of the Constitution as resting on an egalitarian conception of respect for equal rights and pursuit of the common interests of all, and their instrumental arguments of constitutional design (including mobilizing a natural aristocracy)

[157] Farrand, *Records of Federal Convention,* vol. 1, p. 135.

[158] See, e.g., Jefferson, *Notes on the State of Virginia,* pp. 162–63.

[159] See, in general, Herbert J. Storing, "Slavery and the Moral Foundations of the American Republic," in Robert H. Horwitz, ed., *The Moral Foundations of the American Republic,* 3rd ed. (Charlottesville: Univ. Press of Virginia, 1986), pp. 313–32; but cf. Paul Finkelman, "Slavery and the Constitutional Convention," in Richard Beeman et al., *Beyond Confederation* (Chapel Hill: Univ. of North Carolina Press, 1987), pp. 188–225.

[160] See, e.g., Merrill D. Peterson, *Adams and Jefferson: A Revolutionary Dialogue* (Oxford: Oxford Univ. Press, 1978), pp. 111–15. Adams and Jefferson agree on the importance of a natural aristocracy, but disagree over what should count as "natural" for this purpose. Harrington had used the idea of a "natural aristocracy" as a prominent feature of his political theory of republicanism; see, e.g., Harrington, *Commonwealth of Oceana* (pp. 173, 259), and *The Art of Lawgiving* (p. 677), both in Pocock, ed., *Political Works of James Harrington.*

[161] See, e.g., Paul Eidelberg, *The Philosophy of the American Constitution* (New York: Free Press, 1968), which systematically misinterprets the founders' arguments in this way. In effect, for Eidelberg, any argument for a branch of government less directly accountable to the people is construed as an aristocratic argument grounded in perfectionist principles, for example, arguments for the Senate as opposed to the House (idem, pp. 147, 157, 165, 259–60) and, of course, arguments for the judiciary (idem, pp. 242, 247–48). In each case, the relevant arguments are, in fact, for constitutional structures that will better secure respect for equal rights and the pursuit of the public interest in ways the give equal weight to all human interests (free of the distortions of faction).

are justified at that deeper level. We may certainly question the validity of one or another of these arguments, and should certainly question blatant failures of republican justification like the legitimation of slavery; however, such questions are raised within the framework of egalitarian justification assumed by the founders, not outside it. Indeed, the uneasy republican conscience of the founders about some of these questions (slavery) makes my point.

Reflection on classical republicanism especially clarified for Americans their distinctive principles of equal respect for inalienable human rights. The concept of human rights was foreign to classical political thought,[162] and Americans—in view of their profound beliefs in the importance of such rights in the emancipation of both religion and politics—naturally distinguished their own project from the classical republican tradition based on an Aristotelian perfectionism that was devoid of the idea of human rights. No constitutional thinker more sharply saw the difference nor more acutely articulated its constitutional significance than James Madison.

Americans, as we have seen, regarded their revolutionary and constitutional project as both an expression and a defense of the inalienable rights of human nature (the bases of reasonable self-government) that had been denied by a tyrannical religious and political tradition. They set themselves such a high standard of critical historical and political argument in order to ensure that they met this challenge wisely by standards of independent critical moral and political intelligence that were not subject to these corrupt traditions. The founders' study of history led them to believe that the propensity to such sectarian tyrannies was a permanent fact of political psychology (the theory of faction), and no political order could be exempt from its force, including the one they were framing. They thus conceived the enduring value of the Constitution as its procedural and substantive protections of such spheres of reasonable self-government from the continuing tyrannies of entrenched power that they anticipated. In effect, they could not concede to the power of the state under the Constitution an authority over the very intellectual and moral sources of political emancipation that gave life to their entire project. By defining spheres of private life that were immune from the factionalized oppressions of majority rule, the American conception of inalienable human rights expressed this vision. The rights to conscience and free speech were prominent among such rights (notably so in the political thought of Madison[163]), because they preserved a critical moral distance between the factionalized power of the state and the capacity for critical moral independence

---

[162] For pertinent discussion, see David Richards, "Rights and Autonomy," 92 *Ethics* 3 (1981), pp. 7–9. The discussion of the differences between the ancient and modern world in this respect was a prominent theme of Benjamin Constant. See, in general, Stephen Holmes, *Benjamin Constant and the Making of Modern Liberalism* (New Haven, Conn.: Yale Univ. Press, 1984).

[163] See, e.g., on religious liberty, Madison's *Memorial and Remonstrance against Religious Assessments,* in Rutland et al., eds., *Papers of James Madison, 1784–1786* pp. 295–306; on free speech, see *Madison's Report on the Virginia Resolutions,* Elliot, ed., vol. 4, pp. 546–80. For fuller discussion of the rights of religious liberty and free speech, see Richards, *Toleration and the Constitution,* Chapters 4–7.

of the citizen, including criticism of and challenge to abuses of the authority of the state.

Because founders like Madison conceived of legitimate political power in this way, they took sharp critical objection to the conception of classical republicanism that political life per se was comprehensive of the value in living and that other forms of life had value, if at all, only by reference to politics. To the contrary, American respect for rights gave a constitutional significance and value to private spheres of life and enterprise, including, as we shall see, a productive life in agriculture or business. Political power had to be tested against the reasonable judgment of free people as to whether the state respected rights and pursued the public good, and voting and participational rights were to be defined, weighted, and structured in whatever ways that secured that the state indeed respected rights and pursued the public good. American republican political theory certainly accorded voting rights an important place in the idea of basic rights of the person, but their definition and scope was importantly to be judged against the background of how they respected the rights of the person overall and used political power for the public good. Property qualifications for voting might, for example, be thought to be required for independent voters who checked arbitrary power and preserved rights, as they were by many Americans in 1787.[164]

Madison took particularly forceful objection on such grounds to the structures of mass democratic participation that were characteristic, for example, of the ancient Athenian democracy. Any such political structure must, for Madison, be tested against its tendency to secure respect for rights and the public good, but such mass assemblies were loci of oppressive majority factions:

> A common passion or interest will, in almost every case, be felt by a majority of the whole; a communication and concert results from the form of Government itself; and there is nothing to check the inducements to sacrifice the weaker party, or an obnoxious individual. Hence it is, that such Democracies have ever been spectacles of turbulence and contention; have ever been

---

[164] See, e.g., Willi Paul Adams, *First American Constitutions,* pp. 164, 196–217, 293–307; and, in general, Pole, *Political Representation.* Madison himself recommended property qualifications for voters for the senate in his critical discussion of Jefferson's 1783 draft constitution for Virginia as a model for the Kentucky state constitution; see Robert A. Rutland et al., *The Papers of James Madison 1788–1789* vol. 11 (Charlottesville: Univ. Press of Virginia, 1977), pp. 287–88. Of course, from its beginnings, American democratic constitutionalism has distributed the franchise more broadly than comparable democracies (e.g., than Great Britain). This was attributable, at least in part, to the broader diffusion of property in the United States than Britain; see, e.g., Pole, *Political Representation,* pp. 205–6). The progressive elaboration of constitutional principles (including the fourteenth, fifteenth, nineteenth, and twenty-sixth amendments) has expanded the scope of the democratic franchise still more broadly and equitably, for example, the reapportionment of voting power in accord with one person/one vote; see *Baker* v. *Carr,* 369 U.S. 186 (1962); *Reynolds* v. *Sims,* 377 U.S. 533 (1964). It is, of course, consistent with the American conception of voting rights that, as the maldistribution of voting rights is perceived to frustrate effective respect for equal rights under law and pursuit of the public good, the scope and distribution of such voting rights should in these ways be more fully and fairly extended in service of these goals.

found incompatible with personal security, or the rights of property; and have in general been as short in their lives, as they have been violent in their deaths. Theoretic politicians, who have patronized this species of Government, have erroneously supposed, that by reducing mankind to a perfect equality in their political rights, they would, at the same time, be perfectly equalized and assimilated in their possessions, their opinions, and their passions.[165]

Such a political structure might treat people equally if, as Madison remarked in his October 24, 1787 letter to Jefferson, they were a "homogeneous mass of Citizens"[166] so that the oppression of one would oppress all equally. However, the modern republican dilemma, as we saw earlier, was for Madison posed by a respect for rights that, in American circumstances, precluded such homogeneity. It was one of Madison's more brilliant insights to see the absence of such homogeneity not as a republican vice, but as an opportune circumstance for an alternative constitutional structure that would use American heterogeneity to secure better the ends of republican government (see Chapter 3).

Madison identified such mass assemblies with an unreasoned and unreasonable mob rule that had made republicanism so discredited a form of constitutional government:

In all very numerous assemblies, of whatever characters composed, passion never fails to wrest the sceptre from reason. Had every Athenian citizen been a Socrates; every Athenian assembly would still have been a mob.[167]

Madison tested constitutional designs by whether its political structure sustained arguments of public reason that respected rights and secured the public good. Such mass assemblies were parts of unacceptable constitutional designs because they were dominated by the political psychology of faction that would undermine even a Socratic conscience.

Classical republicanism was a kind of Madisonian exemplar of republican corruption. He presented representation as a constitutional principle because it would better secure bringing public reason to democratic politics.[168] With characteristic precision, however, Madison denied that the representative principle was completely unknown to classical democratic polities, a claim made by other founders.[169] Rather,

the true distinction between these and the American Governments lies *in the total exclusion of the people in their collective capacity* from any share in the

---

[165] *The Federalist*, pp. 61–62.

[166] Rutland et al., eds., *Papers of James Madison, 1787–1788*, p. 212.

[167] *The Federalist*, p. 374.

[168] See ibid., no. 10.

[169] Notably, by James Wilson in his opening address to the Pennsylvania ratifying convention: "One fact, however, is certain, that the ancients had no idea of representation, that essential to every system of wise, good, and efficient government," Jensen, ed., *Documentary History*, vol. 2, p. 343.

latter, and not in the *total exclusion of representatives of the people,* from the administration of the former. The distinction however thus qualified must be admitted to leave a most advantageous superiority in favor of the United States.[170]

Madison's indictment of classical republicanism must carry over to its reigning political psychology, perfectionist civic virtue. From Madison's perspective, for example, the perfectionist public morality of ancient Sparta—so admired by Rousseau[171]—expressed yet another form of faction, a thought John Adams stated with characteristic bluntness:

> Separated from the rest of mankind, they lived together, destitute of all business, pleasure, and amusement, but war and politics, pride and ambition; . . . as if fighting and intriguing, and not life and happiness, were the end of man and society; as if the love of one's country and of glory were amiable passions, when not limited by justice and general benevolence. . . . Human nature perished under this frigid system of national and family pride.[172]

Aristotelian perfectionism—as the reigning political psychology of the ancient republics—was, from the founders' perspective, the key to their political vice: such a conception of civic virtue expressed and reinforced a parochial and insular ideology of vapid patriotism and empty glory that blinded the people to their just claims that government respect rights and equally pursue the happiness of all.[173]

For both Madison and Adams, the motivating public morality of American republicanism was an ethics of equal respect, in which public power was limited and directed in ways designed both to respect inalienable equal rights of persons and to pursue the public good. That egalitarian ethics—crucially made possible (on Locke's view, discussed earlier) by respect for each person's equal liberty of conscience—could be met by and reasonably justified to our common human nature,[174] and could, therefore, only impose burdens of civil duty that could be reasonably borne by all persons and justified to them as reasonable demands. The perfectionist elitism of classical republicanism imposed self-sacrificing ideals of heroic excellence well beyond what could thus be reasonably demanded of all persons, indeed it was often blatantly inconsistent with the reasonable demands of what Madison and Adams would

---

[170] *The Federalist,* p. 428.

[171] See, e.g., Jean Jacques Rousseau, *Considerations on the Government of Poland,* in F.M. Watkins, trans., ed., *Rousseau: Political Writings* (Edinburgh: Nelson, 1953), pp. 162–67.

[172] John Adams, *A Defence,* p. 554.

[173] Cf. John P. Diggins, *The Lost Soul of American Politics* (New York: Basic Books, 1984), pp. 69–99.

[174] Cf. T.M. Scanlon, "Contractualism and Utilitarianism," in Amartya Sen and Bernard Williams, eds., *Utilitarianism and Beyond* (Cambridge: Cambridge Univ. Press, 1982), pp. 103–28.

call "human nature."[175] In effect, the enforcement at large of such controversial perfectionist ideals by the state would impose a factionalized moral view that obfuscates the legitimating responsibility of the state to respect inalienable human rights and to pursue the public good. For example, the civic virtue of the ancients *legitimated* not only slavery and the subjection of women (e.g., in contrast to the founders' clear unease with the harsh political realities that perpetuated slavery in the new republic[176]), but also a rampant imperialism of military adventure and glory.[177] The civic virtues of classical republicanism were—as both Montesquieu[178] and Hume[179] had taught the founders—often masks for political manipulation and tyranny, an elitist ideology that blinded people to the moral demands of equality.

Americans needed to discover a political psychology more consistent with their egalitarian principles. The stability of a constitutional order founded on such principles could not make motivational demands on all citizens that ordinary human nature could not bear, and the elitist and heroic demands of Aristotelian perfectionism could not, even if not ideologically distorted, satisfy this egalitarian requirement.[180] Americans understandably sought a more minimal and less demanding political psychology to provide the operative premises within which a stable constitutional structure could operate. A quite antiheroic political psychology about faction—in addition to its sober political realism—had this appeal for the founders, as did another assumption of political psychology, the theory of fame.

Political Psychology: The Theory of Fame

It is a misunderstanding of the American constitutional project to suppose that the founders' use of the theory of faction or their skepticism about Aristotelian civic virtue committed them to a general theory of psychological and ethical egoism of the sort associated with the political theory of Thomas

[175] Madison writes, "What is government itself but the greatest of all reflections on human nature?" (*The Federalist,* p. 349). Adams writes of Sparta: "Human nature perished under this frigid system of national and family pride" in C.F. Adams, ed., *Works of John Adams,* vol. 4, p. 554.

[176] See, e.g., Storing, "Slavery and the Moral Foundations of the American Republic"; but cf. Finkelman, "Slavery and the Constitutional Convention."

[177] See Finley, *Politics in the Ancient World,* p. 17; idem, *Democracy Ancient and Modern,* p. 87. Machiavelli had, if anything, idealized these features of classical republicanism in his attempt to revive republican ideals in the Renaissance. See, in general, Hulliung, *Citizen Machiavelli.* The American rejection of classical republicanism is, *pari passu,* a rejection of this aspect of Machiavelli's republicanism in favor of an alternative conception.

[178] See, e.g., Montesquieu, *Spirit of the Laws,* pp. 34–39. For pertinent commentary, see Pangle, *Montesquieu's Philosophy of Liberalism,* pp. 48–106; Shklar, *Ordinary Vices,* pp. 33, 196–97, 233.

[179] See, e.g., Moore, "Hume's Political Science and the Classical Republican Tradition"; Miller, *Philosophy and Ideology in Hume's Political Thought,* pp. 121, 150–1.

[180] See, in general, Martin Diamond, "Ethics and Politics: The American Way," in Robert H. Horwitz, ed. *Moral Foundations of the American Republic,* pp. 75–108.

Hobbes[181] or the social theory of Mandeville[182]; American constitutionalism does not rest on Hobbesian foundations.[183] Neither Madison nor Adams, for example, denied that a sense of justice existed or that people often conscientiously acted on it, or that such a sense of justice must play an important role in both the people and leadership under constitutional republicanism. To the contrary, Madison argued in *The Federalist:* "republican government presupposes the existence of these qualities in a higher degree than any other,"[184] and construed its constitutional tasks "to obtain for rulers, men who possess most wisdom to discern, and most virtue to pursue the common good of the society; and . . . to take the most effectual precautions for keeping them virtuous."[185] Furthermore, he defended the Constitution near the end of the Virginia ratifying convention—against anti-Federalist arguments for additional checks against human depravity—as follows:

> Nor do I . . . expect the most exalted integrity the sublime virtue [of the people]. But I go on this great republican principle, that the people will have virtue and intelligence to select men of virtue and wisdom. Is there no virtue among us? If there be not, we are in a wretched situation. No theoretical checks, no form of government can render us secure. To suppose that any form of government will secure liberty or happiness without any virtue in the people, is a chimerical idea.[186]

These remarks were not disingenuous; they described in part the kind of astonishing devotion to public service that was typical of both Madison and Adams in their own lives as political leaders,[187] and the quality of leadership they might reasonably have anticipated under the American constitutions.

Neither Madison nor Adams was a moral skeptic, and each had views about objective values of inalienable rights and the common good in terms of

[181] See, in general, Thomas Hobbes, *Leviathan,* Michael Oakeshott, ed. (Oxford: Basil Blackwell, 1960). It may also be an injustice to attribute such a view to Hobbes. There is some question whether Hobbes himself actually believed in psychological and ethical egoism as facts of human nature as opposed to truths of political science about the nature of political life under conditions of radical intellectual and religious heterogeneity in the English Civil War. His actual ethical views may have endorsed aristocratic values far more demanding than the mean picture of *Leviathan.* See Keith Thomas, "The Social Origins of Hobbes's Political Thought," in K.C. Brown, ed., *Hobbes Studies* (Oxford: Basil Blackwell, 1965), pp. 185–236. My appreciation for this point is to John Rawls.

[182] See Mandeville, *The Fable of the Bees,* Phillip Harth, ed. (Harmondsworth, Middlesex, England: Penguin, 1970). For useful commentary, see M.M. Goldsmith, *Private Vices Public Benefits: Bernard Mandeville's Social and Political Thought* (Cambridge: Cambridge Univ. Press, 1985).

[183] For examples of this mistaken view, see Frank M. Coleman, *Hobbes and America* (Toronto: Univ. of Toronto Press, 1977); George Mace, *Locke, Hobbes, and the Federalist Papers: An Essay on the Genesis of the American Political Heritage* (Carbondale and Edwardsville: Southern Illinois Univ. Press, 1979).

[184] *The Federalist,* p. 378.

[185] Ibid., p. 384.

[186] Elliot, *Debates,* pp. 536–37.

[187] See Rakove, *Beginnings of National Politics,* p. 225.

which polities, including the design of constitutions, should be assessed.[188] However, they believed—consistent with both their own experience as politicians and their arduous studies of the history of political life—that important truths of *political* psychology must be taken seriously at the stage of constitutional design of an enduring framework for a *political* life in which those objective values were to be respected; furthermore, they learned much, in this connection, from the introspective psychology of human nature of the age, a psychology of the unstable personal and social passions that often distorted our calmer and more impartial reason.[189] At the constitutional convention, Madison had responded to Gouverneur Morris's evident distrust of politicians in some regions and trust of those in other regions in a way that shows the force of these assumptions:

> To reconcile the gentln. [sic] with himself it must be imagined that he determined the human character by the point of the compass. The truth was that all men having power ought to be distrusted to a certain degree.[190]

The importance of these psychological assumptions to American constitutional thinking cannot be appreciated in isolation from their use in the protection of certain values.

American constitutional thought, as we saw in our earlier discussion of Adams's 1765 *Dissertation on the Canon and Feudal Law,* was a generalization to political life of critical arguments of interpretive history in service of the emancipation of moral and religious intelligence, for example, Locke's argument for religious toleration. That argument combined a normative claim (the inalienable right to conscience) and a historical explanation of how that claim had been obfuscated by a corrupt tradition (a sectarian conception of religious truth), and used the historical explanation in the construction of a political principle that protected the normative claim. The argument depended on a critical use of the interpretive history of religious persecution, in particular, the underlying psychology of intolerance that appealed to a sectarian conception of religious truth to condemn all disagreement with that truth as irrational to the point of madness. The range of reasonable discourse about religion was thus stunted, and our natural right to a free conscience (engaging in such

---

[188] For Madison, see *The Federalist* nos. 10 and 51; for Adams, "the end of government is the greatest happiness of the greatest number, saving at the same time the stipulated rights of all," John Adams, *A Defence,* p. 318.

[189] Important primary sources, familiar to American thought, include Francis Hutcheson, *An Essay on the Nature and Conduct of the Passions and Affections,* Paul McReynolds, ed. (Gainesville, Fl.: Scholars' Facsimiles & Reprints, 1969); and Adam Smith, *The Theory of the Moral Sentiments* (Indianapolis, Ind.: Liberty Classics, 1976). For one of the most enduring philosophical achievements in this genre, see Hume, *Treatise of Human Nature.* For useful general commentary on the psychological literature of the age and its influence on the American constitutionalists, see Arthur O. Lovejoy, *Reflections on Human Nature* (Baltimore, Md.: Johns Hopkins Press, 1961), which was a much needed corrective to Carl L. Becker, *The Heavenly City of the Eighteenth-Century Philosophers* (New Haven, Conn.: Yale Univ. Press, 1932).

[190] Farrand, *Records of Federal Convention,* vol. 1, p. 584.

discourse) abridged. The political principle of toleration forbade any such abridgement that was grounded in a sectarian conception of religious truth, and thus protected the right to conscience.

This kind of argument had such generative force for Americans like Adams and Madison because it showed how a historically informed understanding of the self-protecting political power of a dominant religion expressed itself in a religious psychology of intolerance. Taking that psychology seriously reflected no skepticism about religion or ethics, but was, for Locke and Bayle, the way to emancipate our religion and ethics from a tradition corrupted by power and privilege.

When leading American constitutional thinkers like Madison and Adams addressed themselves to the political psychology that was appropriate to the task of a constitutional framer, it was thus quite natural that they should gravitate to the theory of faction. That theory naturally generalized the argument for religious toleration to politics in a way that generally made coherent sense not only of indigenous preoccupations of American religion but also of American experience under the British and under the early state and federal constitutions. Such use of the theory of faction—as a general account of *political* psychology—no more rested on skepticism about justice and the common good than the narrower theory of religious factions—assumed by the argument for toleration—rested on skepticism about religion and ethics. To the contrary, both the broader and narrower theories of faction rested on reliable generalizations about the nature of *political* power and how such power, unless circumscribed, threatened rights and the common good. In particular, the theory of faction did not deny that people had moral consciences and often pursued justice and the public good in light of their own independent judgment; rather, it took seriously—as a constitutional order centrally committed to the right of conscience must—the dynamics of a political psychology most likely to corrupt, as Madison acutely observed,[191] even the Socratic conscience. If such a theory of political psychology was skeptical, it was not skeptical about rights or the public good but of the way political power—motivated by sectarian commitments to a person, group interests, or idea (Madison's Humean theory of faction)—prevented persons from fairly giving weight to the rights and interests of those outside one's sectarian circle.

These purposes of the political psychology of the theory of faction were complemented, in American constitutional thought, by the theory of fame, namely, that aspirations for political power were often motivated by a competitive emulativeness for admiration and reputation from both the present generation and later generations. If Madison (following Hume) was America's deepest theorist of faction, John Adams (following Adam Smith) was its most probing theorist of the political psychology of fame.[192]

---

[191] *The Federalist*, p. 374.

[192] Adams gave his most extended philosophical explication of this theory in his *Discourses on Davila*, in C.F. Adams, ed., *Works of John Adams*, vol. 6, pp. 232–81. *Discourses* quotes passages from Smith's *Theory of the Moral Sentiments* in support of his views. See *Discourses on*

The theory of fame may be regarded as the American response to the political psychology of civic virtue in classical republicanism. American constitutionalists certainly believed, as we have seen, that people often acted from a sense of justice and the common good, and they designed the Constitution with the expectation that these motives would have an important place in the political psychology of constitutionalism. However, they rejected the Aristotelian conception of civic virtue with its heroic requirements of civic participation, its identification of all values with the political sphere, and its rejection of rights and private life. Nonetheless, Madison and Adams were personally obsessed by public service and accepted the need for a leadership capable of such public service well beyond that expected or demanded of citizens at large. The theory of fame dealt with the place of these motives in constitutional politics, addressing, in part, the motivations of the founders themselves.[193]

The theory of fame, like that of faction, arose from a critical use of interpretive history in what Adams called "the science of government," "the knowledge of the means of actively conducting, controlling, and regulating the emulation and ambition of the citizens."[194] As we saw earlier, both Adams and Jefferson accepted the idea of a natural aristocracy of persons who were especially talented for public service, and Adams molded the theory of fame to the distinctive ways American constitutionalists thought about the political psychology of such leaders (Adams' powerful interpretation of the political psychology underlying the American constitutions must be distinguished from his more controversial interpretation of the constitutions themselves[195]). The critical focus of the theory of fame was the political psychology of men aspiring to power, in particular, enlightened natural aristocrats aspiring to leadership positions. The very drive for such power was, Adams argued, a passion for emulative distinction, and such passion distorted knowledge:

> Does not the increase of knowledge in any man increase his emulation; and the diffusion of knowledge among men multiply rivalries? . . . On the contrary, the more knowledge is diffused, the more the passions are extended, and the more furious they grow. Had Cicero less vanity, or Caesar less ambi-

---

Davila, pp. 258–62; see, in general, Smith, *Theory of Moral Sentiments.* See also John A. Schutz and Douglass Adair, *The Spur of Fame* (San Marino, Calif.: Huntington Library, 1980). For useful commentary on the role of the theory of fame pervasively in the thought of the founders, see, in general, Adair, *Fame and the Founding Fathers.* On the powerful role of the idea in the political thought and life of Alexander Hamilton, in particular, see Stourzh, *Alexander Hamilton and the Idea of Republican Government.*

[193] See, in general, Adair, *Fame and the Founding Fathers.*

[194] John Adams, *Discourses on Davila,* p. 248.

[195] Adams meant to be describing a political psychology that he took to pervade the distinctive approach of the American constitutions, exemplified, for example, by the Constitution's bicameralism and strong separation of powers, including an independent executive with a suspensive veto. Americans, including Madison, often disagreed with Adams' highly idiosyncratic and often intemperately overstated tendency to interpret these institutions on the model of the British class-balanced unwritten constitution. See, e.g., Lance Banning, *The Jeffersonian Persuasion: Evolution of a Party Ideology* (Ithaca, N.Y.: Cornell Univ. Press, 1978), pp. 94–100, 155–60.

tion, for their vast erudition? . . . There is no connection in the mind between science and passion, by which the former can extinguish or diminish the latter. It, on the contrary, sometimes increases them, by giving them exercise.[196]

If the theory of faction debunked majority rule in light of the ugly facts of group psychology, the theory of fame debunked the virtue of natural aristocrats in light of the distorting motives of pandering for popular emulative distinction. The contrast to the role of Aristotelian civic virtue in classical republicanism could not be sharper. Adams trenchantly distinguished the American political psychology of fame and its correlative constitutional structures (independent and mutually checking centers of power) from French dependence on virtue and their "whimsical and fastastical projects"[197] (e.g., Turgot's centralization of political power in a unicameral legislature[198]). Adams insisted, as Madison had in his theory of faction and his earlier-cited riposte to Gouverneur Morris at the constitutional convention, that republican constitutionalism could not reasonably exempt itself from the facts of political psychology.

> Amidst all their exultations, Americans and Frenchmen should remember that the perfectibility of man is only human and terrestrial perfectibility. Cold will still freeze, and fire will never cease to burn; disease and vice will continue to disorder, and death to terrify mankind. Emulation next to self-preservation will forever be the great spring of human actions, and the balance of a well-ordered government will alone be able to prevent that emulation from degenerating into dangerous ambition, irregular rivalries, destructive factions, wasting seditions, and bloody, civil wars.[199]

The theory of fame, like that of faction, did not rest on any general Hobbesian skepticism about objective values of justice and the common good. It rested, rather, on the kind of sober historical inquiry into the nature of power in American constitutional thought and the pained and probing introspective psychology of puritan inwardness that Americans like Adams were capable of bringing to the analysis of their own obsessions, including their drive to be founders of the American constitutions (Adams of the Massachusetts constitution, Madison of the federal constitution).[200] Such inquiries were attempts to find our common human nature as political beings, the facts of political psychology that constitutional framers had to take seriously if they were to secure enduring *political* principles, that is, principles intended to be respected in political life per se. The American constitutions assumed no dispensation from

---

[196] John Adams, *Discourses on Davila*, p. 275.

[197] Ibid., p. 276.

[198] See John Adams, *A Defence*, pp. 278–81.

[199] John Adams, *Discourses on Davila*, p. 279.

[200] For an illuminating commentary on Adams and the larger intellectual milieu of the age on which he and other American constitutional thinkers draw, see Lovejoy, *Reflections on Human Nature*.

the laws of political psychology, but instead they rested precisely on psychological assumptions that one could reasonably expect all citizens to be capable of sustaining. Both the theory of faction and that of fame expressed this anti-heroic, antiperfectionist, egalitarian political psychology.[201] So, too, did the founders' picture of America's future as a commercial republic.

Stages of History and Commercial Republics

Both Madison and Adams formulated their respective theories of faction and fame against a contextual background of assumptions about America's present and future place in the commercial stage of history that they understood to be, following Scottish social theory, civilized. Adams claimed that the scope of emulative competition, as a motive in politics, had markedly increased with "the progress of science, arts, and letters,"[202] rendering more necessary "the checks of emulation and the balances of rivalry in the orders of society and constitution of government."[203] Madison characterized the pervasive growth of disparate factions of "a landed interest, a manufacturing interest, a mercantile interest, a monied interest, with many lesser interests" in American life as a matter "of necessity in civilized nations."[204] The historical basis of their economic and social thinking was made quite explicit by Madison in his October 24, 1787 letter to Jefferson, which explained why, in American circumstances, the assumptions of classical republicanism that the interest of the majority could not conflict with the interest of the minority "assume or suppose a case which is altogether fictitious":

> We know however that no Society ever did or can consist of so homogeneous a mass of Citizens. In the savage State indeed, an approach is made towards it; but in that State little or no Government is necessary. In all civilized Societies, distinctions are various and unavoidable. A distinction of property results from that very protection which a free Government gives to unequal faculties of acquiring it. There will be rich and poor; creditors and debtors; a landed interest, a monied interest, a mercantile interest, a manufacturing interest. These classes may again be subdivided according to the different productions of different situations & soils, & according to different branches of commerce, and of manufactures. In addition to these natural distinctions, artificial ones will be founded, on accidental differences in political, religious or other opinions, or an attachment to the persons of leading individuals. However erroneous or ridiculous these grounds of dissention and faction, may appear to the enlightened Statesmen, or the benevolent philosopher, the bulk of mankind who are neither Statesmen nor Philosophers, will continue to view them in a different light. It remains then to be enquired whether a

---

[201] See, in general, Diamond, "Ethics and Politics: The American Way."
[202] John Adams, *Discourses on Davila,* p. 275.
[203] Ibid., p. 276.
[204] *The Federalist,* p. 59.

majority having any common interest, or feeling any common passion, will find sufficient motives to restrain them from oppressing the minority.[205]

Madison thus formulated the republican dilemma against the background of a stage of history, which, in effect, imposed the dilemma on republican thought because unqualified majority rule—in view of that background—violated the essential purposes of republican government, those of respecting rights and pursuing the public good.

American constitutional thinkers were, again, very much the posterity of John Locke in bringing to normative and analytical politics an interpretation of how underlying historical developments shaped the need for constitutional institutions, for example, Locke's idea that the separation of powers and the balance of powers were requirements of legitimate government only at a later stage in the historical development of societies (after the invention of money).[206] Locke's historical method had been based in part on inferences drawn from anthropological data, namely, the books on the Indians of North America that he had studied.[207] That kind of use of comparative data had, for Americans, been powerfully elaborated and enriched by Montesquieu's comparative political science (including studies of the ancient and modern world).[208] However, the development of the approach into a diachronic, stadial history of social, economic, and political change was the achievement of the thinkers of the Scottish Enlightenment whose methods and results, as we have already seen (e.g., Hume and Smith), were much on the mind of America's leading constitutional thinkers.

Adam Smith was—in lectures unpublished in his lifetime[209]—the pioneering intelligence among the Scots of a theory of four stages of history, namely, hunting, pasturage, agriculture, and commerce[210]; furthermore, Americans, including Madison, were clearly familiar with these views in, among others, the published works of Adam Ferguson and John Millar.[211] Ferguson, for

---

[205] Rutland et al., eds., *Papers of James Madison 1787–1788*, vol. 10, pp. 212–13.

[206] See Locke, *Second Treatise of Government*, pp. 356–61. For pertinent commentary, see Grant, *John Locke's Liberalism*, pp. 87–88, 160.

[207] See Ashcraft, *Locke's Two Treatises of Government*, p. 145.

[208] See, in general, Montesquieu, *Spirit of the Laws*. Other important works of Montesquieu also rested on a use of the comparative method, sometimes brilliantly and elliptically imaginative, at other times historical. For each approach, respectively, see Montesquieu, *The Persian Letters*, J. Robert Loy, trans. (New York: Meridian, 1961); idem, *Considerations on the Causes of the Greatness of the Romans and Their Decline*, David Lowenthal, trans. (Ithaca, N.Y.: Cornell Univ. Press, 1968).

[209] For Smith's unpublished lecture notes, see Adam Smith, *Lectures on Jurisprudence*, R.L. Meek et al., eds. (Indianapolis, Ind.: Liberty Classics, 1982). Smith incorporates aspects of the theory in *The Wealth of Nations*. See, e.g., Adam Smith, *The Wealth of Nations* (New York: Random House, 1937), pp. 356–96.

[210] For useful commentary, see Ronald L. Meek, *Social Science and the Ignoble Savage* (Cambridge: Cambridge Univ. Press, 1976); Peter Stein, *Legal Evolution: The Story of an Idea* (Cambridge: Cambridge Univ. Press, 1980).

[211] See Adam Ferguson, *An Essay on the History of Civil Society* (London: T. Caddel, 1773); John Millar, *The Origin of the Distinction of Ranks*, reprinted in William C. Lehmann, *John*

example, had observed that "to the ancient Greek, or the Roman, the individual was nothing, and the public every thing,"[212] an attitude expressed by disdain for commerce[213] and by total devotion to classical republican civic virtue[214] and to war as the main business of public life[215]; in contrast to such "rude" societies,[216] "civilized" or "polished"[217] societies were marked by commerce and the division of labor[218] and the inequalities that arose from differential rewards for different talents and occupations.[219] Millar—in an argument prophetic of *The Federalist* no. 10—gave a rights-based interpretation to this social and economic transition:

> A nation of savages, who feel the want of almost every thing requisite for the support of life, must have their attention directed to a small number of objects, to the acquisition of food and clothes, or the procuring shelter from the inclemencies of the weather; and their ideas and feelings, in conformity to their situation, must, of course, be narrow and contracted. . . . According as men have been successful in . . . improvements, and find less difficulty in the attainment of bare necessaries, their prospects are gradually enlarged, their appetites and desires are more and more awakened and called forth in pursuit of the several conveniencies of life; and the various branches of manufacture, together with commerce, its inseparable attendant, and with science and literature, the natural offspring of ease and affluence, are introduced, and brought to maturity. By such gradual advances in rendering their situation more comfortable, the most important alterations are produced in the state and condition of a people: their numbers are increased; the connections of society are extended; and men, being less oppressed with their own wants, are more at liberty to cultivate the feelings of humanity: property, the great source of distinction among individuals, is established; and the various rights of mankind, arising from their multiplied connections, are recognised and protected: the laws of a country are thereby rendered numerous; and a more complex form of government becomes necessary, for distributing justice, and for preventing the disorders which proceed from the jarring interests and passions of a large and opulent community.[220]

Millar of Glasgow 1735–1801 (Cambridge: Cambridge Univ. Press, 1960), pp. 173–322. These two works appear in Madison's 1783 "Report on Books for Congress"; see William H. Hutchinson and William M.E. Rachal, *The Papers of James Madison 1783*, vol. 6, at p. 86 (numbered as 156 and 157). Madison owned his own copy of Ferguson's *Essay on History*, p. 86, and Millar's *Origin of Distinction of Ranks*, p. 154.

[212] Ferguson, *Essay on History*, p. 92.

[213] Ibid., p. 154.

[214] Ibid., pp. 264–70, 326–33.

[215] Ibid., pp. 246–47.

[216] Ibid., p. 154.

[217] Ibid., p. 335.

[218] Ibid., pp. 301–7.

[219] Ibid., pp. 308–14.

[220] Lehmann, *John Millar of Glasgow*, p. 176.

In effect, the transition from the "rude" societies of military glory to the "polished" society of commerce[221] was the transition from the conditions of necessity (including slavery[222]) to freedom,[223] a freedom that Millar, like Madison, identified with the exercise of our "wonderful powers and faculties" that have led "to the noblest discoveries in art or science, and to the most exalted refinement of taste and manners."[224] Rousseau's picture of primitivist liberty was thus, for Millar (like Madison[225]), based on a dangerous political mythology about the facts of primitive social, economic, and political life.[226]

Smith, Ferguson, and Millar gave a stadial historical explanation to the civilizing role of commerce in history that had earlier been identified and discussed by Montesquieu and Hume. In contrast to the malign insularity, thirst for glory, and military conquest of the participatory classical republics, both Montesquieu and Hume emphasized the role of commercial life and exchange in creating incentives for peaceful and broader ties for reciprocal cooperation among diverse peoples. For Montesquieu, such commerce was nothing short of world revolutionary[227]; for Hume, commerce had been an essential cause of the growth of the capacity for public liberty in civilized societies.[228] The Scottish social and economic theorists built on the political science of Montesquieu and Hume, introducing explanatory mechanisms for the complementary development of economic and political institutions. Adam Smith, citing Hume, summarized one important causal mechanism uniting commerce and political liberty:

> Commerce and manufactures gradually introduced order and good government, and with them, the liberty and security of individuals, among the inhabitants of the country, who had before lived almost in a continual state of war with their neighbours, and of servile dependency upon their superiors.[229]

These perspectives defined the context within which American constitutional thinkers, like Madison, made arguments like those in *The Federalist* no. 10, and debated in the constitutional convention the importance of a reasonable anticipation of future changes in the American economy in designing a

---

[221] Ibid., pp. 284–87.

[222] Ibid., pp. 315–16.

[223] Ibid., pp. 290, 294–95, 315–16.

[224] Ibid., p. 198.

[225] See *The Federalist*, p. 61, referring to "theoretic politicians."

[226] Ibid., pp. 294–95.

[227] See Montesquieu, *Spirit of the Laws*, vol. 2, pp. 316–73. For useful commentary, see Pangle, *Montesquieu's Philosophy of Liberalism*, pp. 200–48.

[228] See, e.g., Hume, *Essays Moral, Political, and Literary*, the essays "Of Civil Liberty," pp. 89–97; idem, "Of the Rise and Progress of the Arts and Sciences," pp. 112–38; idem, "Of Commerce," pp. 259–74; idem, "Of Refinement in the Arts," pp. 275–88; "Of the Populousnessness of Ancient Nations," pp. 381–451. For useful commentary, see Duncan Forbes, *Hume's Philosophical Politics* (Cambridge: Cambridge Univ. Press, 1975), pp. 296–98.

[229] Smith, *Wealth of Nations*, p. 385.

constitution intended to endure.[230] Madison, as opposed to Beard,[231] was no more an economic determinist than were Montesquieu, Hume, Smith, Ferguson, and Millar. Diverse economic interests (including different amounts and kinds of property)—"the most common and durable source of factions"[232]— were central to the best American constitutional thought because its exponents brought to the task of constitutional construction an interpretation of diachronic political history that was absorbed from the Scottish Enlightenment, a history that placed America at a historical stage that was opportune for a new and enduring experiment in the understanding of republican liberties. That history was not reductive, because it assumed objective moral and political values worth protecting (e.g., respect for basic rights of the person) and argued that those values could only be protected if one also appropriately attended to the background institutions (e.g., a fairly and sensibly regulated commercial economy) that made war and servile dependencies unnecessary as the motor of political life and supplied the prosperity, economic independence, and diversity within which a high political value could reasonably be placed on the constitutional protection of independent judgment in the exercise of one's faculties ("the first object of Government"[233]) by guarantees of basic rights of the person.

It is important to the understanding of the founders' project to clarify what these contextual assumptions do and do not mean about the role of equality in the American constitutional tradition. Madison, for example, put his argument in a way that apparently endorsed inequality. Regarding the protection of our faculties, he inferred "protection of different and unequal faculties of acquiring property"[234] and thus "different degrees and kinds of property."[235] He condemned political factions to achieve the ends of religious sects equally with those "for an equal division of property, or for any other improper or wicked project."[236] At the constitutional convention, he put the apparent point even more bluntly:

> No agrarian attempts have yet been made in this Country, but symptoms of a leveling spirit, as we have understood, have sufficiently appeared in a certain quarter to give notice of the future danger. How is this danger to be guarded agst. on republican principles?[237]

[230] See, e.g., Farrand, *Records of Federal Convention,* vol. 1 pp. 422–23; vol. 2, pp. 123–24.
[231] See Beard, *Economic Interpretation of the Constitution of the United States,* pp. 14–15, 153–54.
[232] *The Federalist,* p. 59.
[233] Ibid., p. 58.
[234] Ibid.
[235] Ibid.
[236] Ibid., p. 65. For comparable kinds of objections made at the constitutional convention, see Farrand, ed., *Records of Federal Convention,* vol. 1, pp. 26–27, 51, 58 (Randolph); idem, p. 48 (Gerry, objecting to "the danger of the levilling [sic] spirit").
[237] Farrand, ed., *Records of Federal Convention,* vol. 1, pp. 422–23.

Harrington had proposed constitutionally imposed limitations on the amount of real property people could hold (the agrarian of *Oceana*[238]) in the interest of maintaining republican principles of equality, and Madison's attack on the agrarian in the name of "republican principles" suggests a normative belief in economic inequality and a conviction that the U.S. Constitution, in contrast to Harrington's, would inhibit attempts to disturb it.

However, we know that Madison was to found with Jefferson (during the Washington administrations) the Republicans (a party that was the spiritual heir to the Country party of Bolingbroke in Britain),[239] which had an ideological program that defended, sometimes on constitutional grounds, an egalitarian, agrarian vision of American farmers against the kinds of corruptive inequalities they associated with Hamilton's program (while secretary of the treasury) for a commercial, manufacturing country fueled by public credit, British investment, and a sound system of public finance.[240] Furthermore, Jefferson had urged in Virginia in 1776 an allocation of fifty acres of public land to all persons who were without that amount, which certainly suggests Harrington's worries about the impact of unequal landholdings on republican politics.[241] Indeed, in clear support for a redistributive role for the state in maintaining a more egalitarian distribution of resources, Madison wrote in 1792 that

> the great objection should be to combat the evil [of faction] by withholding *unnecessary* opportunities from a few, to increase the inequality of property, by an immoderate, and especially an unmerited, accumulation of riches. . . . By the silent operation of laws, which, without violating the rights of property, reduce extreme wealth towards a state of mediocrity, and raise extreme indigence towards a state of comfort.[242]

Such redistributive policies would presumably include inheritance and taxation laws.[243] Had Madison changed his mind? We can only understand and properly interpret views of the sort he expressed as a framer and later if we construe all these statements in a spirit that ascribes a reasonable sense to them all consistent with the contextual background they assumed.

---

[238] The agrarian of *Oceana* sought to limit acquisitiveness and control redistribution by enforcing divisibility of inheritance so that, with certain deviations not worth elaboration here, no one could hold land with a value greater than £ 2,000. For the details, see Harrington, *The Commonwealth of Oceana*, in Pocock, *Political Works of James Harrington*, pp. 231, 237; see also, p. 62.

[239] See, in general, Isaac Kramnick, *Bolingbroke and His Circle: The Politics of Nostalgia in the Age of Walpole* (Cambridge, Mass.: Harvard Univ. Press, 1968).

[240] See, in general, Banning, *Jeffersonian Persuasion*.

[241] See Merrill D. Peterson, *Thomas Jefferson and the New Nation* (Oxford: Oxford Univ. Press, 1970), p. 106.

[242] James Madison, "Parties," in Rutland et al., eds., *The Papers of James Madison, 1791–1793* vol. 14 (Charlottesville: Univ. Press of Virginia, 1983), p. 197. See also Madison's 1821 note added to his record of his convention speech on rights of suffrage (Farrand, *Records of Federal Convention*, vol. 3, pp. 450–55).

[243] See Pangle, *Spirit of Modern Republicanism*, pp. 97, 298–99.

Harrington wrote for a precapitalist economy and he defended, following Machiavelli, acquiring colonies by military conquest in which citizens may hold land.[244] Suppose Madison believed, as Harrington probably did, that all persons have an abstract right to equal resources in choosing how to live their lives.[245] It would not follow, in view of Madison's quite different conception of the relationship of economic and political institutions, that Harrington's agrarian would serve equality in American circumstances; indeed, it might frustrate it in ways that could explain the founders' spirited rejection of it.[246]

Madison's conception of a commercial republic depended on a capitalist conception of commerce, not military conquest, as the driving force for social life, and he sometimes used the term "property" to refer to what we would call resources, which could not be measured by land alone ("property" including, for example, a wide range of rights of the person, among which "[c]onscience, . . . the most sacred of all property, . . . being a natural and unalienable right"[247] was prominent). Suppose that Madison assumed that such resources in American circumstances were presently distributed equally[248]; he certainly had argued along such lines at the convention: "as the Govts. the laws, and the manners of all were nearly the same, and the intercourse between different parts perfectly free, population, industry, arts, and the value of labour, would constantly tend to equalize themselves."[249] Suppose also that Madison believed, as Locke did,[250] that a diverse commercial life among the people (laying the bases of liberal freedoms) could not be secured without some unequal rewards that would stimulate, unleash, and even emancipate the exercise of native faculties to perform for the public good,[251] and the failure to secure such rewards would discourage economic growth in ways that appreciably worsen both the level and distribution of resources and thus worsen equality

[244] See Harrington *Commonwealth of Oceana*, pp. 159–60, 180, 238–39, 273–74.

[245] On this conception of equality, see Ronald Dworkin, "What is Equality? Part 2: Equality of Resources," 10 *Phil. & Pub. Aff.* 283 (1981).

[246] For some earlier endorsements of the idea of an agrarian, see Wood, *Creation of the American Republic*, p. 64; for an abortive such proposal in a early draft of the 1776 Pennsylvania state constitution, see idem, p. 89.

[247] See Madison's essay "Property," in Rutland et al., eds., *Papers of James Madison 1791–1793* vol. 14, p. 267.

[248] Charles Pinckney had made precisely this claim at the constitutional convention in defense of his argument that models taken from the ancient and modern world, which depended on less egalitarian circumstances, should not be regarded as models for the United States. See Farrand, ed., *Records of Federal Convention*, vol. 1, pp. 397–404. Madison, in response, did not disagree, but urged that Pinckney had underestimated the range of different factions that characterized American social, economic, and political life, and certainly underestimated the likelihood that certain justifiable inequalities (*i.e.*, those, perhaps, consistent with equality of resources) would later arise in American circumstances giving rise to factions that could gain sufficient political power to achieve unjust ends. Indeed, these latter observations led to Madison's remark about his fears of "agrarian attempts." See idem, pp. 422–23.

[249] Ibid., vol. 1, p. 585.

[250] See, for pertinent commentary, Pangle, *Spirit of Modern Republicanism*, pp. 168–69, 308 (n. 6).

[251] See, in general, Joyce Appleby, *Capitalism and a New Social Order: The Republican Vision of the 1790s* (New York: New York Univ. Press, 1984).

itself. From this perspective, an absolute constraint on the amount of land one could acquire (an agrarian) would undesirably compromise such incentives, and would therefore be both unjust and against the public good and condemned on such grounds (as it was by the founders). In contrast, the Republicans' objection to Federalist policies might be based on a view of the best interpretation of equal resources, one more likely to preserve the fair bases of a diverse and economically independent people against a recurrence of the mercantile dependencies of British oppression. Jefferson's proposal for the distribution of public lands would enhance both equality and the broadly distributed bases for incentives for the exercise of faculties that better perform for the public good[252]; furthermore, Madison's advocacy of the redistributive aims of equitably designed inheritance and taxation laws would be justified as ways of securing equality without unreasonably compromising incentives.

Americans might reasonably disagree about what economic policies would thus serve equality. Some might believe that broadly distributed agricultural landholding was fundamental to republican equality and resist economic policies that supported commerce and manufacturing at the expense of agriculture; others might believe that equality of resources would be generally enhanced by a balanced program of support of agriculture, commerce, and manufacturing that would, cumulatively, support and encourage one another. Jefferson, Madison, and Hamilton in the 1790s took different views of which policies pursued the public good and of whether certain federal policies were or were not therefore constitutional.[253] Indeed, views on these questions might change over time; for example, Madison, in light of painful political experience, came in a later period to question and reject some of his earlier views on these questions.[254] However, Americans on all sides of these debates were not disowning equality as a central republican value; rather, they were giving it different interpretations in ways reasonably sensitive to background assumptions about economics, politics, and the domestic and international policies most likely to secure their common values. The founders had greater consensus about the effects of an agrarian under American circumstances. They did not therefore abandon republican equality; instead, they implemented it. We certainly cannot reasonably ascribe to them a consensus of principle about the constitutional sanctity of economic inequalities,[255] al-

---

[252] See, in general, Appleby, *Capitalism and New Order.*

[253] See, in general, Banning, *Jeffersonian Persuasion.*

[254] Ibid., pp. 290–302.

[255] For an attempt to read the Constitution along these antiredistributive lines, see Richard A. Epstein, *Takings: Private Property and the Power of Eminent Domain* (Cambridge, Mass.: Harvard Univ. Press, 1985). Epstein's argument invokes Locke but makes no attempt to engage Locke's complex views nor attend to the ways in which the founders, in light of Scottish economic and social thought, interpreted and elaborated Lockean ideas. For attempts to come to terms with Locke's economic and other views in a more sensible way, see Pangle, *Spirit of Modern Republicanism;* James Tully, *A Discourse on Property: John Locke and His Adversaries* (Cambridge: Cambridge Univ. Press, 1980).

though we should not overlook either their republican myopia on the related issues of poverty and slavery.[256]

The founders framed their constitutional thought around the idea of America as a commercial republic in part because they had been persuaded by Montesquieu and the Scottish theorists that emerging institutions of commercial exchange were important conditions for the kinds of political values they believed were the enduring values of republicanism, and they therefore had a responsibility to secure constitutional institutions that would sustain and direct the historical development of such commerce in the right way. However, they also came to see a diverse and thriving commercial life as a natural and appealing answer to their search for a system of political motivations for the citizenry at large that would support the stability of republican institutions and also be consistent with their egalitarian political principles.[257]

Military glory and conquest had been fundamental constituents of much of classical republicanism; indeed, Machiavelli's revival of this republicanism, if anything, idealized Roman imperialism.[258] In contrast, the republican founders of America had come to see the participatory politics (see earlier discussion of the theory of faction) and religion of the classical republics (see earlier discussion of civil religion) as suspect because devotion to the polis had rested on heroic, elitist, and perfectionist demands; they rejected this political conception as hostile to everything they had painfully achieved in both politics and religion, namely, the emancipation of reasonable capacities of self-government and respect for the spheres of private rights that protected such capacities from manipulative sectarian tyrannies that had denied such rights and thus stunted human nature. Civic republicanism was yet another such tyranny, because it made demands that reasonable human nature could not bear and often degraded as subhuman (slavery) or less than fully human (women) much of the human race as tools for pursuit of its vapid and immoral ideals of conquest and subjugation. Americans needed an antiheroic, antielitist, antiperfectionist basis for life in a political community of persons capable of regarding one another as equal and free and according respect to the values of both private and public life.

Life in commerce was usually neither heroic, nor elitist, nor perfectionist. Such a way of life required only minimal reciprocal fairness in responsibilities and benefits; there were in this case none of the extraordinary demands of character or genius suitable to the special callings of saints and heroes. The very emphasis of commerce on common human interests gave no weight to controversially sectarian perfectionist ideals.[259]

---

[256] See, e.g., Edmund S. Morgan, *American Slavery American Freedom: The Ordeal of Colonial Virginia* (New York: W.W. Norton, 1975), pp. 322, 324–25, 381–87.

[257] See, in general, Lerner, *Thinking Revolutionary*, pp. 195–221.

[258] See, in general, Hulliung, *Citizen Machiavelli*.

[259] For discussion of many of these points, see Albert O. Hirschman, *The Passions and the Interests: Political Arguments for Capitalism before Its Triumph* (Princeton, N.J.: Princeton Univ. Press, 1977).

It was therefore a deeply egalitarian impulse that led Americans, including anti-Federalists,[260] to agree that the national government must be accorded a power over the regulation of commerce. The states under the Articles of Confederation had factionalized the regulation of commerce and thus failed to secure a fair and effective framework for commercial exchange among the states and with foreign nations.[261] Securing such a framework would guarantee that commercial life would support republican institutions.[262] The pervasive force of commerce in American social life would thus, when appropriately regulated by the national government, reinforce the commitment of citizens to republican institutions not because such institutions imposed heroic, elitist, perfectionist demands, but because allegiance was a fair and reciprocal return for the ways such institutions both respected persons' rights not to be subject to such demands (leaving normative space for the values of private life), and advanced the human interests of all alike.

Commerce was, for the founders, a civilizing influence because it provided an arena in which the capacities and interests that all persons shared could be engaged and offered a peaceful intercourse among diverse peoples and regions. Commercial factions were thus much on Madison's mind because they were expressions of republican liberty, which commercial life sustained, and yet they threatened its civilizing universalism. The Articles of Confederation were thus irredeemably flawed, in the minds of Madison and others, because they had structured the regulation of commerce (as a power of the states) in a way that made commerce the unjust vehicle of balkanizing state factionalism and oppression; commerce was not regulated as the republican agent of peaceful intercourse among equals for mutual advantage, but it was and would be the basis of trade wars and worse.[263] The challenge of the republican dilemma was how and whether republican institutions could preserve the civilizing functions of commerce without subversion by its intrinsic propensity to faction. Americans were familiar with only one example of a nation on the American scale that had preserved the civilizing tasks of commerce, namely, Great Britain; yet, the British constitution was not republican in the American sense. One of the founders' central interpretive tasks was to decide whether the American project of a commercial republic was to follow or reject the British example.

---

[260] See, e.g., Storing, ed., *Complete Anti-Federalist*, vol. 2, p. 164 (*Letters of Centinel*); idem, p. 239 (*Letters from The Federal Farmer*). At the constitutional convention, the alternative plan to the Virginia proposal added a power over commerce to the powers of the national government; see Farrand, ed., *Records of Federal Convention*, vol. 1, p. 243.

[261] See, e.g., *The Federalist*, pp. 39–41, 65–73.

[262] Hamilton appealed to this principle in his June 18, 1787 address to the constitutional convention; see Farrand, ed., *Records of Federal Convention*, vol. 1, p. 284. It, of course, pervades the general argument of *The Federalist*.

[263] See, e.g., *The Federalist*, pp. 39–41, 65–73.

The British Constitution: Negative or Positive Exemplar?

Americans had fought a revolution over the constitutional interpretation of the British constitution.[264] Two of the most prominent intellectual leaders of that revolution (Jefferson and Adams) were major figures in the unfolding dialogue of American constitutionalism at the state and federal levels; three others (James Wilson, John Dickinson, and Alexander Hamilton) attended the constitutional convention at which one of them (Wilson[265]) was a dominant force; the same three (Wilson, Dickinson, and Hamilton) played major roles in the public discussions leading to ratification.[266] The important contributions they had all earlier made to the American case regarding the unconstitutionality of the British Parliament's legislation for the colonies were learned, often brilliant interpretive achievements,[267] which identified this generation of Americans as among the best British lawyers of the age. As such accomplished lawyers, they took even greater pride than other Americans in the British constitution, and they experienced a poignant despair when Britons proved unable to fulfill their vision of these constitutional ideals. It was not merely that events proved the British constitution to be somewhat different modality of constitutionalism than they had thought it to be; that might have been bearable. Rather, "the truth is, the English have no fixed Constitution."[268]

The ideology of the American Revolution rested on that interpretive judgment,[269] and the generation of American lawyers who had made the judgment—with all the intellectual and moral powers they could muster— could not be satisfied in their consciences until they had justified that inter-

---

[264] See Bailyn, *Ideological Origins of the American Revolution;* John Phillip Reid, *Constitutional History of the American Revolution: The Authority of Rights* (Madison: Univ. of Wisconsin Press, 1986); idem, *Constitutional History of the American Revolution: The Authority to Tax,* (Madison: Univ. of Wisconsin Press, 1987); idem, *In Defiance of the Law* (Chapel Hill: Univ. of North Carolina Press, 1981).

[265] See, in general, Charles Page Smith, *James Wilson; Founding Father 1742–1798* (Chapel Hill: Univ. of North Carolina Press, 1956).

[266] See, e.g., James Wilson, "Speech in the State House Yard," in Jensen, ed., *Documentary History,* vol. 2, pp. 167–72, and Wilson's opening address to the Pennsylvania ratifying convention, idem, pp. 339–63. See John Dickinson, *Letters of Fabius,* in Paul Leicester Ford, ed., *Pamphlets on the Constitution of the United States Published during Discussion by the People 1787–1788* (Brooklyn, N.Y., 1888), pp. 165–216. For Alexander Hamilton, see *The Federalist.*

[267] The primary sources are Dickinson, *Letters of a Farmer in Pennsylvania* (1768); Wilson, *Considerations on the British Parliament* (1774); Jefferson, *Summary View of Rights* (1774); John Adams, *Novanglus* (1774). (See footnote 6 above.) Alexander Hamilton, *A Full Vindication of the Measures of the Congress, &c,* in Harold C. Syrett and Jacob E. Cooke, *The Papers of Alexander Hamilton 1768–1778,* vol. 1 (New York: Columbia Univ. Press, 1961), pp. 45–77; Hamilton, *The Farmer Refuted, &c,* idem., pp. 80–165.

[268] *Four Letters on Interesting Subjects,* in Hyneman and Lutz, *American Political Writing during Founding Era* vol. 1, p. 384. For illuminating commentary about evolving American thought about the nature of constitutionalism, see Bailyn, *Ideological Origins of the American Revolution,* pp. 67–68, 175–98.

[269] See, in general, Bailyn, *Ideological Origins of the American Revolution* and *Origins of American Politics.* See also Reid, *Constitutional History of the American Revolution: The Authority of Rights,;* idem, *Constitutional History of the American Revolution: The Authority to Tax.*

pretive judgment by explaining what a constitution was and how it should be designed to secure its essential purposes. The work of these and other Americans in the design of state and federal constitutions was thus as much an interpretive as a constructive act, in which they continued what they as lawyers had undertaken, in their interpretations of the British constitution, namely, making the best sense of a valued and valuable practice within the genre they understood to be constitutional government. Because they had concluded that the British constitution was not truly of that genre, they had to turn to the history of government itself (including that of Britain) to explain to themselves and to the world what that genre was, why a revolution had to be fought over a failure to take the genre seriously as a matter of interpretive principle, and how its interpretive principles should be understood.

The U.S. Constitution was, of course, a creative act of statesmanship, but its authority for the Americans who framed, discussed, and ultimately ratified it was the interpretive judgment about constitutionalism that sustained it. We cannot therefore do justice to its authority for them or its continuing authority for us unless we come to terms with that judgment and understand our own place in its interpretation. That judgment, however, was very much formed in the process of the continuing reflection among Americans about the place of the British constitution in the interpretive history of constitutionalism.

Some Americans, including some founders (e.g., Edmund Randolph of Virginia[270] and Alexander Hamilton of New York[271]), had—in light of their political experience under the early state and federal constitutions[272]—come to reexamine the revolutionary generation's judgment, which they (Hamilton) had helped shape, about the British constitution. No one, of course, would have questioned that the British had unconstitutionally and unjustly oppressed their American colonies, and that the revolution was therefore justified. However, the failure of the British to extend their own constitutional principles to their colonies was not sufficient justification to discredit the

---

[270] At the constitutional convention, Randolph observed of the British constitution: "He did not mean however to throw censure on that Excellent fabric. If we were in a situation to copy it he did not know that he should be opposed to it; but the fixt genius of the people of America required a different form of Government" (Farrand, ed., *Records of Federal Convention*, vol. 1, p. 66).

[271] At the constitutional convention, Hamilton admitted that "This view of the subject almost led him to despair that a Republican Govt. could be established over so great an extent. He was sensible at the same time that it would be unwise to propose one of any other form. In his private opinion he had no scruple in declaring, supported as he was by the opinions of so many of the wise & good, that the British Govt. was the best in the world: and that he doubted much whether any thing short of it would do in America" (Farrand, *Records of Federal Convention* vol. 1, p. 288).

[272] See, especially, Hamilton's bitter 1784 *Letters from Phocion,* in Harold C. Syrett and Jacob E. Cooke, *The Papers of Alexander Hamilton 1782–1786,* vol. 3 (New York: Columbia Univ. Press, 1962), pp. 483–97, 530–58, in which Hamilton attacked the New York legislature for passing anti-Tory laws that were, in his view, blatantly unconstitutional. He argued, among other things, that such legislative oppression of constitutional rights discredited the cause of the American Revolution, for it showed the world that republican constitutionalism was "an *ignis fatuus*" and "we shall have betrayed the cause of human nature" (idem, p. 557).

British constitution per se, which was now intemperately praised by a former revolutionary leader like Adams as "the most stupendous fabric of human invention."[273] The passionate Adams overstated and misstated the nature of his admiration of the British constitution,[274] but Hamilton had meant what he said at the constitutional convention when he despaired "that a Republican Govt. could be established over so great an extent" pointing, for an instructive alternative model in such circumstances, to the British example.[275] From this perspective, republican government was, as Montesquieu appeared to conclude,[276] essentially the government of small, often economically backward, militaristic city-states. However, the American government contemplated an enormous territory, a potentially huge population, and a thriving commercial life, and the British constitution—with its mixture of hereditary and republican elements—was the historically validated model for such governance. As it was finally framed and ratified, the U.S. Constitution was, at best, a *faute de mieux,* or the best that could consensually be achieved consistent with an unfortunate American republicanism that rejected, in principle, the legitimacy of any form of the hereditary principle.

However, other prominent founders (e.g., notably among them James Wilson of Pennsylvania and James Madison of Virginia) argued both at the constitutional convention[277] and in the ratification debates[278] that the American Constitution afforded a unique opportunity to defend republican principles on a new basis. Their defense clearly profited from the interpretive arguments that the revolutionary generation (including Wilson himself) had made on the basis of the British constitution. Both Wilson and Madison gave central play, for example, to arguments of fair representation in the design of a national government that was to have power over taxation and commerce[279]; importantly, these were debates that Americans had rehearsed earlier as interpretive arguments for the unconstitutionality of such powers

[273] John Adams, *A Defence,* p. 358; cf. idem, p. 296.

[274] Adams' doctrine was that an upper house and an independent executive would prevent aristocratic domination, and it was these abstract features of the British constitution that he admired (whether or not British public life corresponded to the model). He was neither a monarchist nor an aristocrat, and thought it was best for the senate and executive to be popularly elected. See Palmer *Age of the Democratic Revolution* vol. 1, p. 275.

[275] Farrand, *Records of Federal Convention,* vol. 1, p. 288.

[276] See Montesquieu, *Spirit of the Laws,* vol. 1, pp. 8–13, 19–108. For pertinent commentary, see Pangle, *Montesquieu's Philosophy of Liberalism,* pp. 48–106.

[277] See, e.g., pp. 134–36 (Madison), 218–19 (Madison), 260–61 (Wilson), in Farrand, *Records of Federal Convention,* vol. 1.

[278] See, e.g., pp. 167–72 (Wilson), 339–63 (Wilson), in Jensen, *Documentary History,* vol. 2; pp. 128–32 (Madison), 399–400 (Madison), in Elliott, *Debates,* vol. 3. See also *The Federalist,* nos. 10–37, 47–51 (Madison).

[279] For Wilson, see, e.g., Jensen *Documentary History,* pp. 342–44. For Madison, see *The Federalist,* no. 10. At the constitutional convention, both Wilson and Madison took violent objection, as a matter of basic political principle, to equal state representation in the Senate because it violated what they took to be principles of fair representation. See, e.g., Farrand, *Records of Federal Convention,* vol. 1, pp. 51 (Madison), 179–80, 605–6 (Wilson); vol. 2, pp. 8–10 (Madison), 10–11 (Wilson).

of the British Parliament over its American colonies.[280] This time the debates were over how polities should be represented in a parliament with lawmaking power over them, which had been part of the colonial debates with Britain at least since Benjamin Franklin's abortive Albany Plan of 1754[281]; they now resolved them in light of principles of fair representation that were the key to solving the republican dilemma itself (see Chapter 3). The debates over framing and ratifying the Constitution thus elaborated many of the substantive interpretive arguments made earlier as claims of unconstitutionality under the British constitution, including claims not only about representation,[282] but also about standing armies,[283] juries,[284] judicial independence,[285] plural office holding and the separation of powers,[286] the establishment of religion,[287] and the like. However, the American debt to these earlier debates cuts deeper than the discrete issues of substance into a radical rethinking of the very foundations of constitutional legitimacy and the methods of argument that were appropriate to the purposes of constitutional government. That led Americans to reinterpret radically the history of the British constitution in light of these conceptions and to rediscover a constitutionalism that had been lost since Harrington, which was the written constitution of "an immortal commonwealth."[288]

It is fundamental to the understanding of the evolving American constitutionalism, which was crystallized by the American Revolution, that the interpretive arguments of the American revolutionaries about the British constitution were framed by an interpretive conviction about the nature of constitutionalism. That conviction (as much British as American) was articulated by Jefferson, among others:

> Not only the principles of common sense, but the common feelings of human nature must be surrendered up, before his majesty's subjects here can be persuaded to beleive [sic] that they hold their political existence at the will of a British parliament.[289]

That common sense, Wilson argued, rested on basic maxims of legitimacy:

---

[280] See, in general, Pole, *Political Representation;* Greene, *Peripheries and Center.*

[281] See Henry Steele Commager, ed., *Documents of American History* 9th ed. (Englewood Cliffs, N.J.: Prentice-Hall, 1973), pp. 43–45; for a related proposal, see Galloway's Plan of Union, idem, pp. 81–82. For commentary on the Albany Plan, see Greene, *Peripheries and Center,* pp. 154, 157–158, 168.

[282] Bailyn, *Ideological Origins of the American Revolution,* pp. 163–64.

[283] See ibid., pp. 61–63, 112–16.

[284] Ibid., p. 74.

[285] Ibid., p. 105ff.

[286] See, e.g., Bernard Bailyn, *The Ordeal of Thomas Hutchinson* (Cambridge, Mass.: Belknap Press of Harvard Univ. Press, 1974), pp. 52–54, 112–13, 117–18, 183–84.

[287] See Bailyn, *Ideological Origins of the American Revolution,* pp. 246–72.

[288] See Harrington, *Commonwealth of Oceana,* pp. 209, 321–31.

[289] Jefferson, *Summary View of the Rights of British America,* p. 126.

All men are, by nature, equal and free: no one has a right to any authority over another without his consent: all lawful government is founded on the consent of those who are subject to it. . . . This rule is founded on the law of nature: it must control every political maxim: it must regulate the legislature itself.[290]

Adams accused the British of obfuscating such common sense by "clouds and vapors . . . raised . . . by the artifices of temporal and spiritual tyrants."[291] Dickinson concluded that the interpretive issue was one of basic constitutional principle: without constraints on the power of parliament, Americans lacked "constitutional security" as free people with rights.

"For WHO ARE A FREE PEOPLE? Not *those,* over whom government is reasonably and equitably exercised, but *those,* who live under a government so *constitutionally checked* and *controuled* [sic] that proper provision is made against its being otherwise exercised.[292]

Law, for Americans, was a historical study of the principles to which the American people had thus consented over time,[293] and the common law, the repository of such consent, was equated with human rights.[294] American lawyers accordingly tested the claims of the British Parliament against such principles, found that it violated them, and concluded that it was therefore acting unconstitutionally.

Americans' claims would have made sense to the seventeenth-century common-law mind of Lord Coke, who had declared:

We are but of yesterday (and therefore had the need of the wisdom of those that were before us), and had been ignorant (if we had not received light and knowledge from our forefathers) and our days upon the earth are but as a shadow in respect of the old ancient days and times past, wherein the laws have been by the wisdom of the most excellent men, in many successions of ages, by long and continual experience (the trial of light and truth) in his head the wisdom of all the men in the world, in any one age ever have effected or attained unto.[295]

However, British constitutional thought had evolved by the late eighteenth century into Blackstone's positivist picture of parliament as "the place where the absolute despotic power, which must in all governments reside some-

---

[290] Wilson, *Considerations on the British Parliament,* p. 723.

[291] John Adams, *Novanglus,* p. 124.

[292] Dickinson, *Letters of a Farmer in Pennsylvania,* p. 356.

[293] See H. Colbourn, *Lamp of Experience,* pp. 20, 25, 84, 125.

[294] See ibid., pp. 25, 77. James Wilson was to elaborate this view, as a criticism of Blackstone's theory of law, in his *Lectures on Law.* See McCloskey, ed., *Works of James Wilson* vol. 1, pp. 98–125.

[295] Quoted in J.G. A. Pocock, *The Ancient and the Feudal Law: A Study of English Historical Thought in the Seventeenth Century* (Cambridge: Cambridge Univ. Press, 1987), p. 35. For commentary on Coke's conception, see idem, pp. 30–55.

where, is entrusted by the constitution of these kingdoms."[296] Parliament, which had once been conceived by Coke as the high court for controversies over the constitutional principles that bound it and all Britons, had now become a sovereign legislative body that was itself the source of such principles and thus not accountable to them.[297] In effect, the American and British interpretive disagreement was so intractable because it was over two different, irreconcilable pictures of what the British constitution was.[298]

Americans themselves sometimes confused matters by combining elements of both constitutions. The constitutional debates within Massachusetts are illustrative. James Otis, for example, combined arguments about the unconstitutionality of parliamentary power, the power of executive courts to declare such statutes void[299] (citing Vattel[300]), and the ultimate power of parliament to decide such issues[301] (a power that Vattel had not endorsed[302]). Furthermore, Thomas Hutchinson, defending the British position, acknowledged the arguments of natural rights that are central to the American constitutional case and yet made parliament the sole judge of such rights.[303] Executive courts could not have the power to judge whether the government has exceeded its power because no constitution was a fixed, immutable blueprint for living, but was instead a growing, malleable arrangement that flexibly accommodated personal and group grievances over time. For Hutchinson, the power of parliamentary supremacy was the proper vehicle for this kind of historically evolving unwritten constitution.[304]

When Governor Hutchinson decided in 1773 that he would prove to the Massachusetts legislature the supremacy of parliament over it, he failed to take into consideration the nature of evolving American constitutional thought, which was no longer satisfied with Otis's confused amalgam of Coke's common-law principles and absolute parliamentary supremacy over the interpretation of those principles. Citing Vattel, the answer of the House—which John Adams helped prepare—appealed to a fixed constitution to which the legislature was

---

[296] William Blackstone, *Commentaries on the Laws of England*, vol. 1 (Chicago: Univ. of Chicago Press, 1979), p. 156.

[297] For pertinent commentary, see Bernard Bailyn, ed., *Pamphlets of the American Revolution 1750–1776* (Cambridge, Mass.: The Belknap Press of Harvard Univ. Press, 1965), pp. 409–17.

[298] See Reid, *In Defiance of Law*, pp. 32–49. For a useful recent general study on the quite different evolutions of the idea of popular sovereignty in Britain and the United States, see Edmund S. Morgan, *Inventing the People: The Rise of Popular Sovereignty in England and America* (New York: W.W. Norton, 1988).

[299] See James Otis, *The Rights of the British Colonies Asserted and Proved* (1764), in Bailyn, ed., *Pamphlets of American Revolution*, pp. 476–77.

[300] See ibid., p. 477.

[301] See ibid., pp. 447, 448, 454–55.

[302] In fact, Vattel had, with much greater clarity than Otis, argued that the constitution was prior to the legislature and could be changed only by the people not the legislature. See M. De Vattel, *The Law of Nations or Principles of the Law of Nature* (Dublin, Ireland: Luke White, 1792), pp. 30–32.

[303] See Bailyn, *Ordeal of Thomas Hutchinson*, pp. 52–54, 112–13, 117–18, 183–84.

[304] See ibid., pp. 102–3.

accountable,[305] and defined that constitution in terms of the deliberative consent of the people.[306]

Hutchinson's defense of parliamentary supremacy rested on a style and vision of constitutional argument quite similar to that cultivated by the political science of both Montesquieu and Hume. In *The Spirit of the Laws,* Montesquieu, for example, developed a comparative science of political institutions that was designed both to identify the cultural, demographic, and climatic conditions congenial to particular institutions and to recommend those institutions that would, given such appropriate circumstances, best advance the normative ends that political life should pursue. For Montesquieu, the end of politics was and should be "political liberty," "a tranquillity of mind arising from the opinion each person has of his safety."[307] Montesquieu had blamed the fall of the Roman republic not on individuals but "on man—a being whose greed for power keeps increasing the more he has it, and who desires all only because he already possesses much,"[308] and in *The Persian Letters* he conceived the corruptions of untrammeled political power on the model of Roxanne's indictment of Uzbek's erotic tyranny:

> How could you have thought that I was naive enough to imagine that I was put in the world only to adore your whims? That while you pampered yourself with everything, you should have the right to mortify all my desires? No! I might have lived in servitude, but I have always been free. I have rewritten your laws after the laws of nature, and my spirit has ever sustained itself in independence.[309]

Montesquieu offered an empirical and normative method of constitutional argument likely to assist legislators[310] in preserving spheres of personal security against temptations to such abusive and intrusive tyrannies over the emotions, minds, and lives of persons who are morally free "after the laws of nature." He recommended the British constitution in this spirit because the British government used both a balanced constitution of classes (i.e., commons, lords, and monarchy) and a separation of functional powers (i.e., legislative, executive, and judicial) as institutional devices that limited and interconnected political powers in ways that secured a just public liberty and the common good in a large commercial society.[311] Montesquieu entertained no illusions that the British constitution was itself the product of political science; his account would be quite consistent with the view that its structure was the consequence both of

---

[305] See John Phillip Reid, *Briefs of the American Revolution* (New York: New York Univ. Press, 1981), pp. 69, 141. On John Adams' role, see idem, pp. 45–53.

[306] See ibid., pp. 140–41.

[307] Montesquieu, *Spirit of the Laws,* vol. 1, p. 151.

[308] Montesquieu, *Considerations on the Causes of the Greatness of the Romans and Their Decline,* pp. 106–7.

[309] Montesquieu, *Persian Letters,* p. 279.

[310] See, e.g., Montesquieu, *Spirit of the Laws,* vol. 2, pp. 156–70.

[311] See ibid., vol. 1, pp. 151–62.

Charles I's "Answer to the Nineteen Propositions[312] and of the historical accident that subsequent British constitutional theory and practice organized itself around its argument.[313] If anything, Montesquieu discredited the ambition to found constitutions in light of reflective political intelligence; he acidly criticized Harrington's political science of constitutional constructivism: "Of him, indeed, it may be said that for want of knowing the nature of real liberty he busied himself in pursuit of an imaginary one; and that he built a Chalcedon, though he had a Byzantium before his eyes."[314] Harrington had, as it were, constructed an ill-conceived utopia for a hypothetical founder (namely, Oliver Cromwell[315]) when he had all about him the basic constitutional structures that, in the light of Montesquieu's political science, were shown to preserve "real" as opposed to Harrington's "imaginary" liberty. Montesquieu thus recommended a style of constitutional argument that identified the real normative values that comparative political science showed to be best realized in certain historically evolving political structures. Such argument would have its natural audience in the hereditary aristocracies capable of asserting their power in service of Montesquieu's constitutional structures and aims (e.g., reviving those ancient French aristocratic institutions that might act as a constraint on the tyrannical power of the French monarchy).

Hume's conception of constitutional argument rested on a similar use of comparative political science and critical historiography to develop in Britain a new kind of philosophical politics, a moderate impartiality in political judgments of "new power and subtlety, reinforced by experimental philosophy used as political hygiene."[316] Like Montesquieu, Hume thought of governments as the product of long-standing practices and understandings that secured the benefits of cooperative social and economic life and not as the product of reflective choice[317]; furthermore, he advocated uses of reflective political theory, science, and history that sometimes clarified the wisdom of such practices. For example, he had argued—against Whig oppositionist thought—that certain conventional practices (e.g., use by the monarch of appointments to secure parliamentary support) served valid constitutional purposes.[318] Such critical arguments could also be used in the assessment of

---

[312] See Corinne Comstock Weston, *English Constitutional Theory and the House of Lords 1556–1832* (London: Routledge & Kegan Paul, 1965), pp. 5, 24–43. Part of the Answer is reprinted at idem, pp. 263–65.

[313] See, in general, ibid.

[314] Montesquieu, *Spirit of the Laws*, vol. 1, p. 162.

[315] Harrington's euphemism for Cromwell as his "sole legislator" was "Olphaus Megaletor," in *Commonwealth of Oceana*, p. 183. *Oceana* was also dedicated to Cromwell.

[316] Forbes, *Hume's Philosophical Politics*, p. 219.

[317] See, e.g., Hume, *Treatise of Human Nature*, p. 490; idem, "Of the Original Contract," in *Essays Moral, Political, and Literary*, p. 452.

[318] See Hume, "Of the Independency of Parliament," in *Essays Moral, Political, and Literary*, p. 40. Hamilton cited this argument at the constitutional convention; see Farrand, *Records of Federal Convention*, vol. 1, p. 381. On the impact of this and other Humean arguments on Hamilton's political thinking about the relationship of the executive and the legislature, see in general, Stourzh, *Alexander Hamilton and Republican Government*.

better and worse governments and policies,[319] and Hume was even willing to·
argue, in ways that would galvanize Americans' attention, that Harrington's
utopian political science might in favorable circumstances be useful in con-
structing constitutional arrangements.[320] However, the general framework of
Hume's thought was comprehensively utilitarian political and moral philosophy in which publicly understood and reliable conventions (the artificial malleable virtues of justice) played a central role.[321] In this spirit, Hume tended to
construct more nearly impartially critical standards for constitutional arguments; these standards accorded with his enlightened utilitarian political philosophy about the proper direction of the historically evolving pattern of
malleable conventions of existing British institutions. Hume, both as a political philosopher and as a historian, articulated critical standards of thought less
ideologically dependent on the existing patterns of factionalized political argument then current in British politics. In his *The History of England,*[322] Hume
self-consciously sought to develop new standards of impartiality in general
political argument by steering a path of studied critical independence of ideologically polar views that he rejected, for example, the Whig view of Charles
I's malignity,[323] and the Jacobite views of James II's virtue and the vice of the
Glorious Revolution.[324] Hume defended critical historiography because it lib-
erated political discussion from the "despicable"[325] distortions of Whig political history and theory. He included among those distortions that Lockean
theory of political legitimacy that sought to hold the state accountable to the
reserved rights of free people.[326] Hume, like Montesquieu, was a constitutionalist, because he sought to identify the constraints on power that would protect what he took to be the central value in politics, the security of property
and person under law.[327] However, he conceived of constitutional argument as
essentially a balanced assessment of historically evolving conventions in service of utilitarian aggregation (i.e., the net aggregate of pleasure over pain of

---

[319] See Hume, "That Politics May Be Reduced to a Science," in *Essays Moral, Political, and
Literary,* p. 13.

[320] Hume, "Idea of a Perfect Commonwealth," in *Essays Moral, Political, and Literary,* p. 499.
For commentary, see Miller, *Philosophy and Ideology in Hume's Political Thought,* pp. 158–59;
Forbes, *Hume's Philosophical Politics,* pp. 182–83. For Madison's attention to Hume's argument,
see Adair, *Fame and the Founding Fathers,* pp. 93–106.

[321] See Hume, *Treatise of Human Nature,* Book III. For general commentary, see J.L. Mackie,
Hume's Moral Theory (London: Routledge & Kegan Paul, 1980); Jonathan Harrison, *Hume's
Theory of Justice* (Oxford: Clarendon Press, 1981). For particular commentary on the artificial
virtues, see Frederick G. Whelan, *Order and Artifice in Hume's Political Philosophy* (Princeton,
N.J.: Princeton Univ. Press, 1985).

[322] See David Hume, *The History of England* 6 vols. (Indianapolis, Ind.: Liberty Classics,
1983).

[323] For Hume's sympathetic view of Charles I, see ibid., vol. 5, pp. 210–11, 236, 355.

[324] For Hume's critical view of James II and favorable view of the Glorious Revolution, see
ibid., vol. 6, pp. 520–31.

[325] Ibid., p. 533.

[326] See ibid.; also, Hume, "Of the Original Contract," in *Essays Moral, Political, and Literary,*
p. 452.

[327] See, e.g., Forbes, *Hume's Philosophical Politics,* pp. 165–67.

all sentient beings)—a structure of argument self-consciously hostile to antiutilitarian arguments of Lockean natural rights that often expressed, for Hume, the politics of faction. The mentality required by the evolving British constitution of parliamentary sovereignty found Hume's new politics of impartiality naturally congenial.[328]

Hutchinson's constitutional argument in defense of the British constitution of parliamentary sovereignty was in this vein. He found the sovereignty of parliament appealing because such authority gave discretionary play to historically evolving institutions that were open to "successive alterations of the British constitution that, historically, have been made to accommodate personal or group grievances"—not "immutable blueprints of government inscribed on parchment at a particular point in time" but "living, growing, malleable arrangements of things."[329] Indeed, the British constitution was the perfection of this mode of constitutional argument, as both Montesquieu and Hume clearly saw.

When Americans, however, were confronted with these arguments for parliamentary sovereignty in their interpretive debates over the British constitution, they rejected them as both unconstitutional and unjust. In their view, these arguments were transparently unconstitutional because they understood the historically evolving principles of the British constitution to say that parliament lacked the extent of legislative power it had claimed over the colonies. These arguments were unjust because they denied the basic rights of Americans as free people to fair political representation.[330] Americans rapidly came to see British insistence on the principle of parliamentary sovereignty not as a constitutional or moral argument at all, but as a bare assertion of factionalized self-aggrandizing power masquerading as an elevated impartiality in the balanced assessment of evolving historical practice for the greater good of all. American "common sense"[331] concluded that the British did not take seriously the arguments that the Americans had made, often at great and learned length, about violations of their constitutional and moral rights; furthermore, they interpreted the British appeal to parliamentary sovereignty as an insult to everything Americans took constitutional argument to be. Constitutional prin-

---

[328] Hume, in fact, came to desire American independence, but not for the reasons urged by the revolutionaries and their British radical supporters, but because the empire put too great a burden on British politics. See J.G.A. Pocock, *Virtue, Commerce, and History* (Cambridge: Cambridge Univ. Press, 1985), pp. 125–41.

[329] Bailyn, *Ordeal of Thomas Hutchinson*, p. 103.

[330] See, e.g., Dickinson, *Letters of a Farmer in Pennsylvania* (1768); Wilson, *Considerations on the British Parliament* (1774), reprinted in McCloskey, ed., *The Works of James Wilson*, vol. 2, pp. 721–46; Jefferson, *A Summary View of the Rights of British America* (1774); John Adams, *Novanglus* (1774). (See footnote 6 above.) Hamilton, *Full Vindication of the Measures of the Congress, &c;* idem, *The Farmer Refuted, &c.* (See footnote 267 above.)

[331] This mode of argument had become so conventional among Americans by 1776 that Thomas Paine could literally call his important pamphlet advocating arguments for revolution against Great Britain by the name of common sense. See Thomas Paine, *Common Sense*, Isaac Kramnick, ed. (Harmondsworth, Middlesex, England: Penguin, 1979). For commentary, see Eric Foner, *Tom Paine and Revolutionary America* (New York: Oxford Univ. Press, 1976).

ciples were, for Americans, the test of power; however, for the British, power had become self-legitimating or sovereign. If the Britons thought that the arguments they had offered to their colonies were constitutional in nature, Americans had to conclude that the British Constitution of 1776 was not the constitution they had always supposed it to be; indeed, from their perspective, it was "no fixed Constitution"[332] at all.

Americans soon learned from their early experiments with state and federal constitutions that the principle of parliamentary sovereignty that they had rejected as a principle of the British constitution was no better as a principle of their domestic constitutions; as Jefferson acidly put the point in his criticism of the Virginia constitution of 1776: "An elective despotism was not the government we fought for."[333] These constitutions had typically been passed as ordinary legislation by state legislatures, and accorded most governing and appointment authority to the legislature.[334] However, when the councils of censors of Vermont and Pennsylvania met to review the constitutional compliance of the legislatures, they reported a sorry record[335]; furthermore, Americans throughout the nation were confronted by comparable records of unjust and unconstitutional laws enacted by the most fairly representative legislatures in human history.[336] American constitutional thought could no longer rationalize its rejection of parliamentary sovereignty in the revolutionary controversies as a rejection of unfairly representative legislative sovereignty; the constitutional problem cut deeper into the very foundations of what Americans required of constitutional argument.

American constitutional thought had to reexamine its historical premises, and it turned, as we have already seen, to the extensive uses of interpretive history we have examined in this chapter. In particular, Americans had to reexamine their interpretive debates over the British constitution, and to ask yet again what was the gravamen of their interpretive controversies over that constitution. Americans had believed in a valued and valuable form of constitutional government of which, like Montesquieu and Hume, they regarded Britain's government as the central interpretive exemplar offered by history. They had been rudely disabused of that interpretive conviction by the events of the American Revolution, and they had to ask, now more critically than ever, what was the strand of the British constitutional tradition they had so admired and that they had so wrongly supposed to be still extant in the Great Britain of 1776. Americans had to turn again to reexamine their history as former Britons and their own constitutional history under the early state and federal constitutions, reviewing both in light of the interpretive historical arguments that had been at the heart of their best constitutional arguments over the British constitution.

---

[332] *Four Letters on Interesting Subjects* (see footnote 7 above), p. 384.
[333] Jefferson, *Notes on the State of Virginia*, p. 120.
[334] See, for good general discussions, Wood, *Creation of American Republic*, pp. 127–255; Willi Paul Adams, *First American Constitutions*.
[335] Wood, *Creation of American Republic*, pp. 407–8.
[336] Ibid., p. 404.

That analysis led Americans both to form a new conception of constitutional legitimacy and to use it in the framing, discussion, and ratification of a new kind of written constitution (Chapter 3); that conception, in turn, led them to deepen their understanding of the kind of interpretive common-law legal arguments they had used as British constitutional lawyers and that would be required of American lawyers and citizens under the 1787 Constitution (Chapter 4). Their normative and constitutional innovation was, as one would expect in a people so conscious of history, conceived as a historical rediscovery of a strand of British constitutionalism that had been neglected since Harrington.[337] Near the conclusion of the Virginia ratifying convention, Zachariah Johnson made reference to their historical rediscovery:

> The historical facts to which I allude happened in a situation similar to our own. When the Parliament of England beheaded King Charles I, conquered their enemies, obtained liberty, and established a republic, one would think that they would have had sufficient wisdom and policy to preserve that freedom and independence which they had with such difficulty acquired. What was the consequence? That they would not bend to the sanction of laws or legal authority. For the want of an efficient and judicious system of republican government, confusion and anarchy took place. . . . This is like our situation in some degree. It will completely resemble it, should we lose our liberty as they did. It warns and cautions us to shun their fate, by avoiding the causes which produced it.[338]

The founders certainly knew that Montesquieu and Hume had questioned the very idea of deliberative design of constitutional government, and they were familiar as well with the Scottish social theory of constitutions as nondeliberative, spontaneous social evolutions.[339] However, their reflection on both British and American constitutionalism led them to believe that the normative demands they made of constitutions had to be expressed in a new, historically self-conscious, deliberative way. America needed both normative guarantees and founders.

John Dickinson—himself a founder—made both pertinent points in his justification of the Constitution to the nation at large. The normative foundation of the Constitution was its "*organization* of the contributed rights in society,"[340] but its continuing authority over the American people must be displayed as a historical appeal to its founders:

---

[337] See, in general, Francis D. Wormuth, *The Origins of Modern Constitutionalism* (New York: Harper & Row, 1949).

[338] Elliot, ed., *Debates,* vol. 3, pp. 648–49.

[339] See, e.g., Ferguson, *Essay on History of Civil Society,* pp. 205–8, 225; Millar, *Origin of Distinction of the Ranks,* pp. 177–78. For pertinent commentary, see Ronald Hamowy, *The Scottish Enlightenment and the Theory of Spontaneous Order* (Carbondale: Southern Illinois Univ. Press, 1987).

[340] Dickinson, *Letters By Fabius,* p. 181.

In a contest between citizens or citizens, or states and states, the standard of laws may be displayed, explained and strengthened by the well-remembered sentiments and examples of our forefathers, which will give it a sanctity far superior to that of their eagles so venerated by the former masters of the world. This circumstance . . . may secure the blessings of freedom to succeeding ages.[341]

[341] Ibid., p. 188–89.

3

Political Legitimacy and Constitutional Founding

The founders brought three levels of analysis to the American project of constitutionalism and its uses of interpretive history (discussed at length in the previous chapter): they transformed the Lockean political theory of legitimacy into a new conception of constitutional deliberation and justification, they realized the Harringtonian dream of "an immortal commonwealth"[1] by recovering the idea of founders, and they analyzed the essential constitutional structures requisite to their political theory and constitutional aims (i.e., federalism, the separation of powers, and judicial independence and review).

Political Legitimacy and Constitutional Justification

Americans had confronted basic issues of political legitimacy in their constitutional interpretation of the British constitution, their arguments for revolution, and their deliberations over their experiments in constitutional construction at the state and federal levels. The American position in all these areas rested on a remarkably consistent and nearly universal attitude to the legitimacy of political power, namely, John Locke's contractualist political theory of reserved rights of the person against which the legitimacy of political power was tested. As British constitutional lawyers, the Americans refused to make sharp positivistic distinctions between constitutional law and political morality, because they took a view of law that construed good legal argument about constitutional principles as a historical inquiry into the pattern of consent they took to be required by Lockean contractualism. James Wilson, for example, argued that, under the principles of the British constitution, "all men are, by nature, equal and free: no one has a right to any authority over another without his consent"[2]

[1] See James Harrington, *The Commonwealth of Oceana,* in J.G.A. Pocock, ed., *The Political Works of James Harrington* (Cambridge: Cambridge Univ. Press, 1977), pp. 209, 321–2.
[2] James Wilson, *Considerations on the Nature and Extent of the Legislative Authority of the British Parliament* (1774), reprinted in Robert Green McCloskey, ed., *The Works of James Wilson,* vol. 2 (Cambridge, Mass.: Belknap Press of Harvard Univ. Press, 1967), p. 723.

(citing Burlamaqui's contractualist theory of sovereignty[3]), and that its constitutional principles were accordingly to be inferred by a historical inquiry into the terms on which the people, construed as "equal and free," can be understood to have consented to obey the power of the state. That study showed, Wilson argued, that

> secure under the protection of their kind, they [the Americans] grew and multiplied, and diffused British freedom and British spirit, wherever they came. Happy in the enjoyment of liberty, and in reaping the fruits of their toils; but still more happy in the joyful prospect of transmitting their liberty and their fortunes to the latest posterity, they inculcated to their children the warmest sentiments of loyalty to their sovereign . . . . Lessons of loyalty to parliament, indeed they never gave. . . .[4]

Americans did not always agree in their historical accounts of the essential features of the British constitution (e.g., Jefferson gave prominence to the Saxon constitution,[5] which Adams regarded as illusory[6]). However, in the constitutional debates with Britain, there was a remarkable convergence in both their historical methodologies in making constitutional arguments and their substantive conclusions.[7] Of course, Americans also believed that Britain's unconstitutional treatment of them could be independently shown to be unjust,[8] and they eventually came to believe that it was sufficiently unjust to justify revolution.[9] However, their constitutional arguments were, as legal arguments, foundationally dependent on a Lockean theory of justice that

---

[3] See *ibid.*, p. 723, note c. For Burlamaqui's statement of his view, see, e.g., J.J. Burlamaqui, *The Principles of Natural and Politic Law,* vol. II Nugent, trans. (Philadelphia: Merriam, 1830), pp. 33–34. For pertinent commentary, see Ray Forrest Harvey, *Jean Jacques Burlamaqui: A Liberal Tradition in American Constitutionalism* (Chapel Hill: Univ. of North Carolina Press, 1937).

[4] Wilson, *Considerations on the British Parliament,* p. 740.

[5] See, e.g., H. Trevor Colbourn, *The Lamp of Experience* (Chapel Hill: Univ. of North Carolina Press, 1965). pp. 169–71.

[6] See ibid., p. 93.

[7] See, for three remarkably convergent such accounts, Wilson, *Considerations on the British Parliament;* Thomas Jefferson, *A Summary View of the Rights of British America* (1774), in Julian P. Boyd, ed., *The Papers of Thomas Jefferson, 1760–1776* (Princeton, N.J.: Princeton Univ. Press, 1950), vol. 1; John Adams, *Novanglus* (1774), reprinted in Charles Francis Adams, ed., *The Works of John Adams* (Boston: Little, Brown, 1857), vol. 4.

[8] Indeed, the Americans combined such arguments with their more legal arguments. Wilson's *Considerations on the British Constitution* contains, for example, both a more abstract moral argument about the legitimate scope of power of a parliament, pp. 722–35, and a more historical argument about the constitutional principles that apply to the American colonies (pp. 735–45). Wilson clearly regarded these arguments as interdependent and convergent, as one would expect in view of his assumption that British constitutionalism, properly understood, embodied a substantive theory of justice.

[9] See *The Declaration of Independence,* in Merrill Jensen, ed., *The Documentary History of the Ratification of the Constitution,* vol. 1 (Madison: State Historical Society of Wisconsin, 1976), pp. 73–75.

they took to be fundamental for the understanding of the British constitution and its proper interpretation. For them, law was an interpretive study of history,[10] but a history guided by normative reflection on what that history revealed about, for example, the common law as an expression of human rights.[11] That interpretive study was understood by them to be an expression of Lockean political theory, and American conviction about that theory had such depth that, when it appeared to the Americans that the British had decisively and irremediably contemptuously disregarded that theory, Americans revolted in order to create constitutional forms that were consistent with it.[12]

Thomas Jefferson justified the American Revolution on the ground that Britain had violated "certain unalienable Rights"[13] in ways that compelled revolution:

> Prudence, indeed, will dictate the Governments long established should not be changed for light and transient causes; and according all experience hath shewn, that mankind are more disposed to suffer, while evils are sufferable, than to right themselves by abolishing the forms to which they are accustomed. But when a long train of abuses and usurpations, pursuing invariably the same Object evinces a design to reduce them under absolute Despotism, it is their right, it is their duty, to throw off such Government, and to provide new Guards for their future security.—Such has been the patient sufferance of these Colonies; and such is now the necessity which constrains them to alter their former Systems of Government. The history of the present King of Great Britain is a history of repeated injuries and usurpations, all having in direct object the establishment of an absolute Tyranny over these States.[14]

[10] See Colbourn, *Lamp of Experience*, pp. 20, 25, 84, 125.

[11] See ibid., pp. 25, 77.

[12] The British not unreasonably took the view that their conception of parliamentary sovereignty was indeed required by Lockean political theory as the necessary protection against the abuses in power by the monarch of the prerogative, and that the parliament must have lawmaking power over the colonies because the only alternative (namely, that the monarchy should have exclusive powers over the colonies, i.e., to veto colonial legislation and to make certain appointments) excessively augmented the prerogative. From this perspective, when Americans like Wilson and Jefferson took the view that indeed only the monarch had any powers over the colonies, they confirmed British Whigs' worst fears. For an illuminating study of these misunderstandings, see John Phillip Reid, *In Defiance of the Law* (Chapel Hill: Univ. of North Carolina Press, 1981). For Wilson's and Jefferson's arguments, see Wilson, *Considerations on the British Parliament;* Jefferson, *Summary View of the Rights of British America.* In fact, however, Blackstone, the leading jurisprudential defender of parliamentary sovereignty, argued that Locke had gone too far in suggesting that the people retained sovereignty. See William Blackstone, *Commentaries on the Laws of England,* vol. 1 (Chicago: Univ. of Chicago Press, 1979), pp. 52, 156–57.

[13] *The Declaration of Independence,* in Jensen, ed., *Documentary History,* vol. 1, p. 73.

[14] Ibid., p. 73.

The ideas were familiarly Lockean[15]; its language also was remarkably like Locke's language in *The Second Treatise of Government*[16]:

> Such *Revolutions happen* not upon every little mismanagement in publick affairs. *Great mistakes* in the the ruling part, many wrong and inconvenient Laws, and all the *slips* of humane frailty will be *born by the People,* without mutiny or murmur. But if a long train of Abuses, Prevarications, and Artifices, all tending the same way, make the design visible to the People, and they cannot but feel, what they lie under, and see, whither they are going; 'tis not to be wonder'd, that they should then rouze [sic] themselves, and endeavour to put the rule into such hands, which may secure to them the ends for which Goverment was at first erected.[17]

The political theory that justified revolution called, on the same grounds, for what Jefferson called "new Guards for their future security"; the theory that called for new constitutions naturally was the framework within which they were discussed and assessed. The debates over the 1787 Constitution, for example, were conducted within a framework of remarkable consensus—by both Federalists and anti-Federalists—about Lockean contractualism. George Washington, president of the constitutional convention, transmitted the Constitution to the consideration of Congress, on behalf of the framers, in words that characterized the task of the convention as guided by difficult contractualist deliberations:

> It is obviously impracticable in the foederal government of these States; to secure all rights of independent sovereignty to each, and yet provide for the interest and safety of all—individuals entering into society, must give up a share of liberty to preserve the rest. The magnitude of the sacrifice must depend as well on situation and circumstance, as on the object to be obtained. It is at all times difficult to draw with precision the line between those rights which must be surrendered, and those which may be reserved; and on

---

[15] See, in general, Carl L. Becker, *The Declaration of Independence* (New York: Vintage, 1958); Morton White, *The Philosophy of the American Revolution* (New York: Oxford Univ. Press, 1978). For a less balanced account focusing too narrowly on the Scottish influences on Jefferson's moral and political thought, see Gary Wills, *Inventing America: Jefferson's Declaration of Independence* (Garden City, N.Y.: Doubleday, 1978). The Declaration of Independence did use "life, liberty, and the pursuit of happiness" as the ends of government in contrast to Locke's "Life, Liberty and Estate," in *The Second Treatise of Government,* in John Locke, *Two Treatises of Government,* Peter Laslett, ed. (Cambridge: Cambridge Univ. Press, 1960), p. 341 (sec. 87), but that usage, adapted by Jefferson from Burlamaqui, was a natural elaboration of Locke's conception of a natural law derived from God's creation of our natures, as free and rational beings made in His image, to pursue our ends. See, for discussion, White, *Philosophy of the American Revolution,* pp. 163, 182, 186, 213–16, 220, 230, 232–36, 269. The pursuit of happiness, thus understood, is the consequence of respect for the inalienable rights of human nature, that is, our creative freedom reasonably to pursue our ends. It is, as White makes clear, not properly understood as a utilitarian idea. See, e.g., idem, pp. 230–39.

[16] For commentary on this point, see White, *Philosophy of American Revolution,* pp. 243–34.

[17] Locke, *Second Treatise of Government,* p. 433 (at sec. 255).

the present occasion this difficulty was encreased by a difference among the several States as to their situation, extent, habits, and particular interest.[18]

Leading Federalist commentators supported the Constitution on contractualist grounds of protecting rights and securing the public good.[19] Furthermore, anti-Federalists—who often violently disagreed with the substance of the Constitution—invariably stated their criticisms in terms of a failure of the Constitution to meet acceptable benchmarks of contractualist legitimacy.[20] For example, the important anti-Federalist essays, *Letters from The Federal Farmer* and *Essays of Brutus,* plausibly indicted the Constitution for its failure to contain a bill of rights that would—consistent with American contractualism—expressly reserve from state power the inalienable rights of the person,[21] that is, those rights that "cannot be surrendered," namely, "the rights of conscience, the right of enjoying and defending life, etc."[22]

We need to understand the Lockean theory of political legitimacy that held such sway over the American revolutionary and constitutional imagination, and the transformation of this political theory by the founders into a new conception of constitutional deliberation, argument, and justification.

Locke's political theory may be usefully understood as a generalization to politics in general of the argument for religious toleration discussed in the previous chapter. That argument—pioneered by Locke and Bayle[23]— depended on the critical analysis of a historical rationale for religious persecution, namely, that the illegitimate political power of a dominant religion had been allowed to impose on society at large a factionalized conception of religious truth that sanctified unnatural hierarchies of power and privilege. Both Locke and Bayle condemned the political uses to which the argument had been put in the history of the West, because it had stunted and stultified the capacities of the human mind and heart to engage the emancipatory and egalitarian moral teaching of historical Christianity. Locke, in contrast to

---

[18] See Jensen, ed., *Documentary History,* vol. 1, p. 305.

[19] See, e.g., Oliver Ellsworth, *The Letters of a Landholder,* in Paul Leicester Ford, ed., *Essays on the Constitution of the United States* (Brooklyn, N.Y.: Historical Printing Club, 1892), pp. 147, 151; John Dickinson, *Letters of Fabius,* in Paul Leicester Ford, ed., *Pamphlets on the Constitution of the United States Published during Discussion by the People 1787–1788* (Brooklyn, N.Y., 1888), pp. 174–80; *The Federalist,* passim, but see, especially, nos. 10, 51.

[20] See, e.g., *Essays of Brutus,* in Herbert J. Storing, ed., *The Complete Anti-Federalist* (Chicago: Univ. of Chicago Press, 1981), vol. 2, pp. 372–73; *An Old Whig,* in idem, vol. 3, pp. 33–37; *Philadelphiensis,* idem, p. 119; *William Penn,* idem., p. 169; *John DeWitt,* idem, vol. 4, p. 21; *A Columbian Patriot,* idem, pp. 272–73; *Essays by Republicus,* idem, vol. 5, pp. 161–62; *The Impartial Examiner,* idem, pp. 175–76; *A Plebeian,* idem, vol. 6, pp. 129–30. For pertinent commentary on the common contractualist assumptions of the Federalist Publius in *The Federalist* and anti-Federalist Brutus in *Essays of Brutus,* see Richard C. Sinopoli, 29 *Polity* 331 (1987).

[21] See Storing, ed., *Complete Anti-Federalist,* vol. 2: *Letters from The Federal Farmer,* pp. 324–5; *Essays of Brutus,* pp. 372–77.

[22] *Essays of Brutus,* p. 373.

[23] For full discussion, see David Richards, *Toleration and the Constitution* (New York: Oxford Univ. Press, 1986), pp. 89–95.

Bayle,[24] generalized the scope of the argument to include the very legitimacy of political power. In effect, for Locke, injustices like religious persecution could not be localized to personal religion or even ethics; they undermined the general conditions for the legitimate exercise of political power by one person over another.[25]

The heart of Locke's political thinking was that the authority the inalienable right to conscience had in religion and in ethics carried over to politics. Parallel corruptions of power to those that had stunted and stultified the religious and moral capacities of persons carried over to people's political capacities. His political theory thus combined a normative component (respect for the inalienable human rights of persons conceived as free, equal, and rational) and a historical component (the structures of illegitimate power that had stunted our capacities to exercise religious, moral, and political freedom consistent with these rights).

The normative component of Locke's political theory (namely, inalienable human rights) rested on the reasonable moral and political inquiry that he believed was made possible and practicable once the political force of the argument for religious persecution was circumscribed by the acceptance of the argument for religious toleration. Such reasonable inquiry must be conducted—Locke had argued in his epistemology[26]—in light of experience, and reasonable inquiry into such experience demonstrably justified a theological ethics in which persons—understood to be made in God's image of rational creative freedom[27]—had inalienable rights, rights they could not surrender (e.g., to conscience and to life).[28] Such rights were inalienable because, as normative claims, they secured to each and every person (understood as free, rational, and equal) the final, ultimate, and uncompromisably nonnegotiable control over the resources of mind and body that is essential to exercising our rational and reasonable powers in living a complete life as independent and morally accountable creative agents.[29] Locke's theory of political legitimacy rested on working out the consequences for politics of the objective moral and political value of such rights for persons, including

---

[24] For fuller discussion, see ibid., p. 90.

[25] When Locke wrote of the conditions that would justify revolution, he thus described the pertinent convictions people would entertain: "they were persuaded in their Consciences, that their Laws, and with them their Estates, Liberties, and Lives are in danger, and perhaps their Religion too," *Second Treatise of Government* pp. 422–23 (sec. 209). On the importance of the issue of religious liberty in Locke's thought about politics and revolution, see Richard Ashcraft, *Revolutionary Politics and Locke's Two Treatises of Government* (Princeton: Princeton Univ. Press, 1986), e.g., pp. 483, 487–88, 494–97, 500. See also, in general, John Dunn, *The Political Thought of John Locke* (Cambridge: Cambridge Univ. Press, 1969).

[26] John Locke, *An Essay Concerning Human Understanding,* 2 vols., Alexander C. Fraser, ed. (New York: Dover, 1959).

[27] See, e.g., James Tully, *A Discourse on Property: John Locke and his Adversaries* (Cambridge: Cambridge Univ. Press, 1980), pp. 3–50.

[28] See, in general, John Colman, *John Locke's Moral Philosophy* (Edinburgh: Edinburgh Univ. Press, 1983).

[29] See, in general, A. John Simmons, "Inalienable Rights and Locke's *Treatises,*" 12 *Phil. & Pub. Aff.* 175 (1983); Tully, *Discourse on Property.*

their right to a politics that allowed them reasonably to know and claim such rights in both their private and public lives.

Post-Lockean moral thought in Britain and North America—to wit, the eighteenth-century philosophy of a moral sense[30]—often questioned the theological argument of Locke[31] not on the ground of its conclusions about inalienable human rights, but rather, that the reasonable argument to such rights was, if anything, more direct, less intellectually circuitous, more available to all persons of common sense.[32] Locke had maintained that ethics was demonstrable, but had not published any such demonstration; rather, in accord with his commitment to theological ethics, he argued that the Gospels sufficed as a practical guide to conduct.[33] The theory of the moral sense—consistent with a Lockean epistemology—filled this gap with a distinctive kind of experience available to everyone's moral sense. Although moral philosophers disagreed among themselves about emotional versus intellectual interpretations of the deliverances of the moral sense (notably, Hutcheson[34] versus Price[35]), they agreed that the moral sense justified inalienable human rights.[36] Indeed, if

[30] See, e.g., Third Earl of Shaftesbury (Anthony Ashley Cooper), *An Inquiry Concerning Virtue or Merit,* in L.A. Selby-Bigge, ed., *British Moralists,* vol. 1 (New York: Dover, 1965), pp. 1–67; Francis Hutcheson, *Illustrations on the Moral Sense,* in Bernard Peach, ed. (Cambridge Mass.: Belknap Press of Harvard Univ. Press, 1971); Hutcheson, *Inquiry Concerning the Original of Our Ideas of Virtue or Moral Good,* in Selby-Bigge, ed., *British Moralists,* vol. 1, pp. 68–177; idem, *A System of Moral Philosophy,* 2 vols., in *Collected Works of Francis Hutcheson,* vols. 5 and 6 (Heildesheim: George Olms Verlagsbuchhandlung, 1969); idem, *A Short Introduction to Moral Philosophy,* in *Collected Works of Francis Hutcheson,* vol. 4; Joseph Butler, *Fifteen Sermons Preached at the Rolls Chapel,* W.R. Matthews, ed. (London: G. Bell & Sons, 1969); Richard Price, *A Review of the Principal Questions in Morals,* D.D. Raphael, ed. (Oxford: Clarendon Press, 1974).

[31] Both Shaftesbury and Hutcheson, who shape the moral sense theory of the age, specifically deny that the concept of ethics depends either on God's will or on divine punishment. See, e.g., Shaftesbury, *Inquiry Concerning Virtue,* pp. 15–16, 23–24, 45–47; Hutcheson, *Inquiry Concerning the Original of our Ideas of Virtue,* pp. 71–72, 79, 85–86, 90–92, 122–23, 125. Because the experience of ethics is defined by an independent moral sense, the very content of such ethics depends on the exercise of this natural sense, in terms of which, in fact, we define our concept of a good and just God, not conversely. For both Shaftesburgy and Hutcheson, the concept of ethics as linked to divine will and punishment degrades the intrinsic appeal and power of both ethical reasoning and motivation, and thus degrades the concept of an ethical god.

[32] See, e.g., Hutcheson, *Short Introduction to Moral Philosophy,* pp. 24–25, 124.

[33] See, in general, Colman, *John Locke's Moral Philosophy.* For Locke's central work of normative ethics, see John Locke, *The Reasonableness of Christianity,* I.T. Ramsey, ed. (Stanford Calif.: Stanford Univ. Press, 1958). Locke's attempt to extract an essential normative ethics from a form of Bible criticism of the Gospels appears to have been immensely influential. See, for a notable example of such influence, Dickinson W. Adams, ed., *Jefferson's Extracts from the Gospels: The Papers of Thomas Jefferson,* Second Series (Princeton, N.J.: Princeton Univ. Press, 1983).

[34] See Hutcheson, *Illustrations on the Moral Sense;* idem, *Inquiry Concerning the Original of Our Ideas of Virtue.*

[35] See Price, *Review of the Principal Questions in Morals.*

[36] See, e.g., Hutcheson, *Short Introduction to Moral Philosophy,* pp. 24–25, 124; Richard Price, *Supplemental Observations on the Nature and Value of Civil Liberty and Free Government,* in Richard Price, *Two Tracts on Civil Liberty, the War with America, the Debts and Finances of the Kingdom* (New York: Da Capo Press, 1972), p. 11. See also Price, *Review of the Principal Questions of Morals,* pp. 178–81, 214.

anything, moral sense theory gave more direct and robust support for an inalienable right like conscience because the failure to respect this right (e.g., by religious persecution on the grounds of political enforcement of a sectarian view of religious truth) was now construed, by Jefferson among others, as a corruption of the moral sense itself.[37] Moral sense theorists, as diverse as Hutcheson and Price, thus both used and elaborated Locke's political theory, indeed (in Britain) in the defense of the program of the radical Whig oppositionists so admired by the Americans.[38]

No one of them more acutely articulated the underlying issue of rights than the British moral philosopher, Richard Price, who was, after Thomas Paine, the most important British defender of the American revolutionary and constitutional achievements.[39] In his *Observations on the Nature of Civil Liberty* (1776), Price articulated the emerging American political theory in the terms that "in every free state every man is his own Legislator,"[40] by which he meant institutional protections of certain basic equal liberties of all persons. He identified these liberties as physical, moral, religious, and civil, and described them thus:

> By PHYSICAL LIBERTY I mean that principle of *Spontaneity,* or *Self-determination,* which constitutes us *Agents;* or which gives us a command over our actions, rendering them properly *ours,* and not effects of the operation of any foreign cause.—MORAL LIBERTY is the power of following, in all circumstances, our sense of right and wrong; or of acting in conformity to our reflecting and moral principles without being controuled [sic] by any contrary principles.—RELIGIOUS LIBERTY signifies the power of exercis-

---

[37] The corruptibility of the moral sense by factual and other misbeliefs was a point made by Kames; see Henry Home Kames, *Essays on the Principles of Morality and Natural Reason,* R. Wellek, ed. (New York: Garland Publishing, 1976), pp. 136–49. And for Bolingbroke, the history of intolerance exemplified such corruption of ethics, including the ethics of the Gospels, by speculative theology; see Lord Bolingbroke, *The Works of Lord Bolingbroke,* vol. 3 (London: Frank Cass, 1967), pp. 373–535. Jefferson was deeply influenced by these views of Kames and Bolingbroke, which he linked to the importance of religious liberty. See Adrienne Koch, *The Philosophy of Thomas Jefferson* (Gloucester, Mass.: Peter Smith, 1957), pp. 9–39. For Jefferson's own linkage of religious persecution with moral and religious corruption, see Thomas Jefferson, *Notes on the State of Virginia,* William Peden, ed. (New York: W.W. Norton, 1982), pp. 159–61; the preface to his Bill for Religious Freedom, in Julian P. Boyd, ed., *The Papers of Thomas Jefferson, 1777–1779,* vol. 2 (Princeton, W.J.: Princeton Univ. Press, 1950), pp. 545–46. In his later life, Jefferson subscribed to Joseph Priestley's views on the corruption of true Christianity. See, in general, D.W. Adams, ed., *Jefferson's Extracts from the Gospels,* pp. 14–30; Jefferson's own attempts at Bible criticism were actuated by the attempt to distinguish the gold from the dross.

[38] See, for pertinent commentary, Caroline Robbins, *The Eighteenth-Century Commonwealthman* (Cambridge, Mass.: Harvard Univ. Press, 1959), pp. 185–96, 335–44.

[39] See Corinne Comstock Weston, *English Constitutional Theory and the House of Lords 1556–1832* (London: Routledge & Kegan Paul, 1965), p. 157.

[40] Richard Price, *Observations on the Nature of Civil Liberty, The Principles of Government, and the Justice and Policy of the War with America,* in *Two Tracts on Civil Liberty,* p. 6. See also idem, *Additional Observations on the Nature and Value of Civil Liberty, and the War with America* (in same volume); and idem, *Observations on the Importance of the American Revolution and the Means of Making It a Benefit to the World* (New Haven, Conn.: Meigs, Bowen & Dana, 1785).

ing, without molestation, that mode of religion which we think best; or of making the decisions of our own consciences respecting religious truth, the rule of our conduct, and not any of the decisions of our fellow-men.—In like manner; CIVIL LIBERTY is the power of a *Civil Society* or *State* to govern itself by its own discretion, or by laws of its own making, without being subject to the impositions of *any* power, in appointing and directing which the collective body of the people have no concern; and over which they have no controul [sic].

It should be observed, that, according to these definitions of the different kinds of liberty, there is one general idea, that runs through them all; I mean, the idea of *Self-direction,* or *Self-government.*[41]

Price clearly did not interpret the idea, "every man . . . his own Legislator," to be exhausted by political liberty, because he expressly "placed *Civil* Liberty last, because I mean to apply to it all I shall say of the other kinds of Liberty,"[42] namely, that the point of civil liberty was precisely to guarantee the spheres of physical, moral, and religious liberty that he calls, equally with civil liberty, "*Self-government,*" echoing Locke's justification of freedom as respect for the general exercise of the "*Reason* . . . he is to govern himself by."[43] Hereafter in this book, my reference to this conception will be as the protection of the spheres of reasonable self-government.

These spheres of physical, moral, and religious liberty were understood by Price—consistent with the Lockean political theory he assumed[44]—as guarantees of moral independence, which were in his terms "not effects of the operation of any foreign cause," "without being controued [sic] by any contrary principles," "not any of the decisions of our fellow-men."[45] The idea is not that people form or should form their identities in a social vacuum, but the political point—at the heart of Locke's argument for religious toleration—that only what Price elsewhere called the state's "perfect neutrality"[46] among sectarian views would enable persons themselves reasonably to exercise their judgment as free and self-governing people. The scope of state power was, for this reason, limited to "the free and undisturbed possession of their good names, properties and lives,"[47] that is, goods that are neutral among sectarian disagreements.[48]

It is fundamental to the Lockean conception of political legitimacy—which Price assumes—both that a state may fail to meet the minimal benchmarks that justify the power of the state and that the question of whether it has done

---

[41] Price, *Observations on the Nature of Civil Liberty,* pp. 3–4.

[42] Ibid., pp. 2–3.

[43] Locke, *Second Treatise of Government,* p. 327 (sec. 63).

[44] See, e.g., Price, *Additional Observations on the Nature and Value of Civil Liberty,* p. 25 (citing Locke against Filmer).

[45] Price, *Observations on the Nature of Civil Liberty,* p. 3.

[46] Price, *Observations on the Importance of the American Revolution,* p. 21; cf. idem, p. 29.

[47] Price, *Additional Observations on the Nature and Value of Civil Liberty,* p. 12.

[48] For a recent restatement of this thought, see John Rawls, "Social Unity and Primary Goods", in Amartya Sen and Bernard Williams, eds., *Utilitarianism and Beyond* (Cambridge: Cambridge Univ. Press, 1982), pp. 159–85.

so must be one of which "I my self can only be Judge in my own Conscience."[49] Locke, of course, understood that the right to revolution could not always be justly and effectively exercised, and he assumed that the politics of revolution would require large numbers of people to concur in their judgments about the intolerable injustice of an existing state.[50] However, his conception of political legitimacy depended on inalienable human rights, rights of each and every person that could be surrendered to no other, and the judgment of whether a state's power met or flouted such rights could no more be surrendered to others than the rights themselves.[51]

Locke thought of this conception of political legitimacy as arising at two distinct stages, which correspond to two distinguishable contractualist metaphors that he employed. First, because any legitimate political community must respect the inalienable rights of each and every person subject to its power, the community of such persons must satisfy a criterion of unanimous reasonable consent that they wish a political community to exist. In a stable existing society, Locke believed such consent must be shown by each person's actual reasonable consent to the present form of governance[52]; if such an existing society should break down, people then must unanimously decide whether they choose to continue as a political society.[53] Second, the organization of such people into a form of government should be decided "by the will and determination of the *majority*."[54] Locke thought of majority rule in this context as the only reasonable alternative to unanimity as a *political* decision-making procedure that would respect equality and yet allow political communities to be formed on reasonable terms. He rejected unanimity because many people, on grounds of "Infirmities of Health, and Avocations of Business," would not attend "the Publick Assembly,"[55] and those who attended would have such "variety of Opinions, and contrariety of Interests"[56] that they would never agree. Because some political communities are, in fact, more consistent with respect for rights than a state of nature and because unanimity would preclude the existence of any political community, our reasonable moral interest in having a political community that respects rights required that the decision-making procedure must be by majority rule. Locke's argument does not, in fact, uniquely require majority rule, and might, in fact, require others (e.g., supermajority voting rules) if they would also be superior to unanimity on the grounds that Locke adduced and lead to the framing of governments that were more consistent with political legitimacy, that is, that respect our inalienable human rights. Locke

---

[49] Locke, *Second Treatise of Government,* p. 300 (sec. 21). See also idem, pp. 398 (sec. 168), 422–23 (sec. 209), 445 (sec. 242).

[50] See, e.g., ibid., pp. 397–98 (sec. 168), pp. 422–23 (sec. 209), pp. 435–36 (sec. 230).

[51] See, e.g., ibid., p. 397 (sec. 168), where Locke expressly argues that the right to revolt is a right of "the Body of the People, or any single Man."

[52] See, e.g., ibid., pp. 349–50 (sec. 96), p. 364 (sec. 117).

[53] For useful discussion of these exegetical points, see Ruth W. Grant, *John Locke's Liberalism* (Chicago: Univ. of Chicago Press, 1987), pp. 110–28.

[54] Locke, *Second Treatise of Government,* p. 349 (sec. 96).

[55] Ibid., p. 350 (sec. 98).

[56] Ibid., pp. 350–1.

clearly thought of majority rule as a faute de mieux addressed to the narrow problem of framing constitutions and not to the substance of how those constitutions should be designed; he clearly did not believe that such majority procedures would necessarily result in governments that used majority rule, because the informed majority at the stage of framing the government might reasonably decide that the government most consistent with respect for rights would circumscribe, if not eliminate, majority rule as a principle of political decision making. Such majority rule at the stage of governmental design must, of course, be exercised reasonably in light of our equal rights, and its resulting government, in the event it violated such rights, would be illegitimate and the justifiable object of the right to revolution.[57]

Locke's political theory thus required political judgment by citizens at three stages: the judgment to join the political society, the judgment (if it was necessary) to frame its constitution, and the judgment to decide whether the constitution was any longer politically legitimate. The capacities requisite to such political empowerment had, in Locke's view, been stunted by the same kinds of sectarian tyrannies he analyzed in his argument for religious toleration. The political power of dominant religious groups had for millennia stultified the reasonable exercise of people's religious and ethical judgment, laying the intellectually and morally corrupt foundations of an unjust edifice of entrenched hierarchy and privilege with a power that depended on the unjust disenfranchisement and disempowerment of others. The brilliance of Locke as a democratic political theorist was his deepening of this insight into a general view of the corruptions of political power and the corresponding need to rethink political legitimacy in ways that would politically constrain such power.

If Locke's theory of religious toleration addressed a history of the abusive uses of political power that undermined the intellectual and moral foundations of the exercise of the inalienable right of conscience, his political theory engaged the more general injustice of the abusive uses of political power to undermine the foundations for the exercise of inalienable rights. If much traditional religious teaching was morally bankrupt because it was supported by illegitimate religious persecution, then the same could be said for traditional teaching in politics. "Learning and Religion shall be found to justify"[58] the worst political tyrannies, "and would have all Men born to, what their mean Souls fitted them for, Slavery."[59] Locke's theory of political legitimacy was thus directed at a new conception of political argument, which would as much prohibit political imposition of sectarian religious as political argument. Political power must be justified in a way that does justice to persons who have inalienable human rights, persons understood to have reasonable powers of thought, deliberation, and action, and to be capable and worthy of governing their lives accordingly.

---

[57] For illuminating commentary on these aspects of Locke's political theory, in particular his argument for majority rule, see Grant, *John Locke's Liberalism*, pp. 110–28.

[58] Locke, *Second Treatise of Government*, p. 345 (sec. 92).

[59] Ibid., p. 444 (sec. 239).

Religious persecution was, for Locke, a kind of paradigm of political illegitimacy because it subverted our very capacities for thinking reasonably about essential issues of a well-lived life by the political imposition of an irrationalism that read all isues of religious truth through the Manichaean lens of fixed sectarian convictions. The argument for toleration ruled out such a use of political power because such power subverted the inalienable right to conscience, undermining the intellectual and moral foundation for reasonable forms of public discussion and deliberation that were not subordinate to fixed sectarian commitments. We have seen that Locke thought of the ultimate questions of political legitimacy (including the right to revolt) as addressed to the conscience of each and every person, and the subversion of the integrity of conscience was thus, for him, an irrationalist attack on political legitimacy itself. Locke's political theory of legitimacy sought to define an alternative conception of free public reason as accessible to all, as free of factionalized sectarian distortion, as justifying political demands to the reasonable capacities of each and every person, whose inalienable rights to exercise those capacities were immune from political compromise or bargaining. To do so, political power must be and be seen to be in the service of a just impartiality rooted in respect for the equality of all persons.

The normative component of Locke's theory required that no legitimate political power could be exercised over our inalienable human rights because those rights were, by definition, subject to the power of no other person. The state could, however, play a normatively justifiable role if it assisted in or promoted equal respect for our rights, including the security of our right to conscience, our right to life, and the like. In fact, in the absence of organized political power, Locke argued that each person or the persons associated with them (e.g., family, clans) had a moral right to enforce such claims, but that our historical experience had been that such enforcement was radically unjust; persons were legislatures, prosecutors, judges, and juries in their own cases, and the distortions of self-interest, bias, and vindictiveness resulted in either inadequate or excessive punishment of the guilty or punishment of the innocent.[60] The state performed a politically legitimate role when its institutions ensured a more just distribution of such punishments and of the rights and goods such punishments protect, because such a distribution better secured our equal rights and interests as persons.

Locke was, for a seventeenth-century British political theorist, remarkable for his lack of interest in historical arguments about the ancient British constitution[61] and for his evident hostility to the reasoning of the common lawyers of his age.[62] His theory of political legitimacy quite clearly rested on a morally

---

[60] See, e.g., ibid., pp. 293–4 (sec. 13).

[61] See, e.g., J.G.A. Pocock, *The Ancient Constitution and the Feudal Law* (Cambridge: Cambridge Univ. Press, 1957), pp. 46, 187–88, 235–88, 348, 354–61.

[62] See, e.g., Locke, *Second Treatise of Government,* p. 293 (sec. 12), where Locke compares the clarity of the natural law to "the Phansies and intricate Contrivances of Men, following contrary and hidden interests put into Words"; cf. idem, pp. 299–300 (sec. 20). See also Locke's Fundamental Constitutions of Carolina, secs. 79 and 80, which provide that all statute laws shall

independent and objective conception of justice (including equal human rights), and political arrangements were subject to criticism on grounds of that conception. However, Locke brought to his political theory an acute sense of the ways in which objective moral values had been historically corrupted (e.g., the psychology of religious persecution), and he used it in defining appropriate political principles (e.g., the theory of religious toleration). Locke's constitutionalism equally rested on historically informed convictions about those structures of political power more likely to secure such ends of moral and political principle and even used (as we saw in the previous chapter) anthropological data to define the relevance of historical change to constitutional structures.[63] He defended institutions calling for fair representation in the legislature, for example, because he construed such a constitutional arrangement as more likely to protect people's rights to property on fair terms[64]; furthermore, his defense of an inchoate doctrine of the separation of powers expressed the judgment that, at least in the later historical stages of a society (after the introduction of money),[65] division of the powers of the legislature and the executive (in which Locke included the judicial power) would tend to secure a more impartially just distribution of punishments.[66] There is no reason to believe that Locke supposed that his own appeal to "experience . . . in Forms of Government"[67] was exhaustive, and—in view of his strong views about the corruption of "Learning and Religion"[68] in the assessment of these matters—he invited a kind of historical and empirical inquiry, which was not subordinate to corrupt sectarian politics, in order better to assess these matters. Later American appeals to the best political science then available are very much in the spirit of Locke's constitutionalism, and it is not surprising that, from the more informed later American perspective, Locke's one exploit in framing a written constitution (namely, The Fundamental Constitutions of Carolina[69]) should appear, as it did to John Adams, "a signal absurdity."[70]

Both the American revolutionary and constitutional minds, as we have seen, framed their enterprises on the basis of Lockean political theory, but the

---

be null after a century, and that no comments on the constitutions shall be permitted, *The Works of John Locke*, vol. 10 (London: Thomas Tegg, 1823), pp. 191–92.

[63] For pertinent commentary, see Richard Ashcraft, *Locke's Two Treatises of Government* (London: Allen & Unwin, 1987), p. 145.

[64] See Locke, *Second Treatise of Government*, pp. 378–81 (secs. 138–42).

[65] See ibid., pp. 356–57 (sec. 107), pp. 359–60 (sec. 110), pp. 360–1 (sec. 111).

[66] See ibid., pp. 382–98 (secs. 143–68). Locke separates government's powers into legislative, executive (in which he includes the judiciary), and federative (foreign policy).

[67] Ibid., p. 356.

[68] Ibid., p. 345 (sec. 92).

[69] See *Works of John Locke*, vol. 10, pp. 175–99.

[70] John Adams, *A Defence of the Constitutions of Government of the United States of America*, in Charles Francis Adams, ed., *The Works of John Adams* (Boston: Little, Brown, 1851), vol. 4, p. 463. For pertinent commentary on Locke's proposals, see Edmund S. Morgan, *Inventing the People: The Rise of Popular Sovereignty in England and America* (New York: W.W. Norton, 1988), p. 129; Maurice Cranson, *John Locke: A Biography* (Oxford: Oxford Univ. Press, 1985), pp. 119–20.

constitutional debates leading to the ratification of the U.S. Constitution transformed American thinking about Lockean political legitimacy into a new conception of constitutional argument. Americans had supposed themselves to be invoking Lockean political principles not only in their revolution but also in their framing of the early state and federal constitutions. The claims on the American colonies made by the parliament in the name of the British constitution were politically illegitimate, and the colonies had validly and successfully invoked their Lockean right to revolt. In Lockean terms, consent to the existing form of government had properly been withdrawn, and Americans were now a political community in the sense of Locke's first unanimous contract, free to decide whether to continue as a political community and to frame a new form of government or to disband. Americans, of course, enthusiastically invoked their Lockean right to frame constitutions and—consistent with his argument—used the most easily available procedures of majority rule to frame their constitutions, namely, either the already existing provincial congresses or committees that exercised political powers (Connecticut,[71] Rhode Island,[72] South Carolina,[73] Virginia,[74] New Jersey[75]) or elections of such bodies to frame constitutions and to exercise ordinary legislative powers (New Hampshire,[76] North Carolina,[77] and Georgia[78]) or elections of bodies mainly to frame constitutions (Delaware,[79] Pennsylvania,[80] Maryland,[81] New York[82]). The members of the continental congress, who were chosen by the state legislatures, drafted the Articles of Confederation, which was approved by the state legislatures.[83]

As we have seen, experience under these constitutions led many Americans to question the very legitimacy of them as forms of government, in particular, the dominant political authority many of them accorded legisla-

---

[71] The general assembly merely confirmed that its republican charter was still in effect, not believing that it was necessary to frame a new constitution. See Willi Paul Adams, *The First American Constitutions,* Rita and Robert Kimber, trans. (Chapel Hill: Univ. of North Carolina Press, 1980), pp. 66–68.

[72] The general assembly merely struck the name of the king and his powers from its republican charter, and did not frame a new constitution. See ibid., pp. 67–68.

[73] See ibid., pp. 70–72 (provisional constitution approved March 26, 1776). A permanent constitution was approved on March 19. 1778 by a general assembly elected to write a constitution and exercise legislative power. See idem.

[74] See ibid., pp. 72–73 (approved June 29, 1776).

[75] See ibid., pp. 73–74.

[76] See ibid., pp. 68–70 (approved on Janauary 5, 1776).

[77] See ibid., pp. 81–82 (adopted on December 18, 1776).

[78] See ibid., pp. 82–83 (approved on February 5, 1777).

[79] See ibid., pp. 74–76 (approved September 21, 1776).

[80] See ibid., pp. 76–80 (approved September 28, 1776).

[81] See ibid., pp. 80–1 (approved November 8, 1776). The congress was also elected to attend to the tasks of the government of a colony at war.

[82] See ibid., pp. 83–86 (approved on April 20, 1777).

[83] See, in general, Merrill Jensen, *The Articles of Confederation* (Madison: Univ. of Wisconsin Press, 1970); Jack N. Rakove, *The Beginnings of National Politics: An Interpretive History of the Continental Congress* (Baltimore, Md.: Johns Hopkins Univ. Press, 1979).

tures, which was a criticism that echoed their own earlier rejection of British constitutional arguments of parliamentary supremacy. Some, like James Wilson,[84] had justified such earlier rejection on the basis of an interpretation of Lockean political legitimacy that they had found in Burmalaqui,[85] namely, that sovereignty "resides originally in the people, and in each individual, with regard to himself"[86] and that the "fundamental laws"[87] that the people impose on the government must be supreme and bodies may reasonably be established to secure that they are.[88] Others, like James Otis and John Adams,[89] had made related criticisms by appealing to Vattel's similar idea,[90] namely, that "legislators derive their power from the constitution, how then can they change it, without destroying the foundation of their authority?"[91] and that resistance may accordingly be justified on the ground of the constitution.[92] Americans found the arguments of Burlamaqui and Vattel so appealing because they were grounded in a Lockean conception of a natural law of human rights,[93] a conception that America's constitutional lawyers, in contrast to Locke, ascribed to the historical tradition they so valued in the British constitution and its common law.

It was a wholly natural step for American constitutional thought to resolve its sense of crisis over the early state and federal constitutions by a new level of deliberation over and ratification of constitutions. The basic idea was forged in the crucible of Massachusetts constitutional politics. Various towns had objected, in principle, to the idea that either the legislature could properly draft or could approve a constitution meant to be supreme over the legislature,[94] and, in the wake of the massive rejection by the towns of the proposed state constitution of 1778, the "first true constitutional convention in Western history, a body of representatives elected for the exclusive purpose of framing a constitution, met in Cambridge on September 1, 1779"[95]; its draft

[84] See James Wilson, *Considerations on the British Parliament (1774)*, p. 723, note c.

[85] See, in general, Burlamaqui, *Principles of Natural and Political Law,* 2 vols.

[86] See ibid., vol. 2, p. 34.

[87] See ibid., p. 46.

[88] See ibid., pp. 46–54.

[89] See James Otis, *Rights of the British Colonies Asserted and Proved,* in Bernard Bailyn, ed., *Pamphlets of the American Revolution 1750–1776* (Cambridge, Mass.: Belknap Press of Harvard Univ. Press, 1965), vol. 1, pp. 477–78, note. Otis, in contrast to other Americans, did not, however, question the ultimate power of parliament over the interpretation of the British constitution, although he did argue that parliament's interpretation of its powers of the colonies was, in fact, wrong. See idem, pp. 409–17. For Adams, see John Phillip Reid, ed., *Briefs of the American Revolution* (New York: New York Univ. Press, 1981), p. 141. On Adams' role in drafting this document, see idem, pp. 119–25.

[90] See M. De Vattel, *The Law of Nations or Principles of the Law of Nature* (Dublin, Ireland: Luke White, 1792)

[91] See ibid., p. 30.

[92] See ibid., pp. 40, 44–47.

[93] See, for pertinent discussion of Burlamaqui's influence on American revolutionary thought in general and Jefferson's thought in particular, White, *Philosophy of the American Revolution.* See also Harvey, *Jean Jacques Burlamaqui.*

[94] See Willi Paul Adams, *First State Constitutions,* pp. 87–90.

[95] Ibid., p. 92.

constitution would go into effect only when independently ratified by the towns. The result, the Massachusetts state constitution of 1780, was the work of John Adams,[96] and was proposed to and ratified by the people of Massachusetts in a way that made possible a new conception of constitutional deliberation and justification.

Americans now could conceive of the task of deliberation over and justification of a constitution as wholly distinct from normal politics, indeed as authoritative over such politics because it rested on firmer foundations of Lockean political legitimacy. Locke had thought of framing a government as a process of reasonable deliberation through majority rule on the structuring of political power in ways more consistent with its legitimate exercise, namely, its respect for inalienable human rights. Americans had learned from bitter experience that this process could not reasonably be interpreted—consistent with the aims of Lockean constitutionalism—as a kind of ordinary majoritarian legislation (Locke had never suggested it could be). Americans now saw that the deeper Lockean point of the constitutionalism over which they had fought a revolution was the quality of the reasonable deliberation it demanded about the proper scope and limits of political power. The people of Massachusetts concluded that legislative supremacy could not do it justice, and that independent thinking—of the caliber displayed in *The Essex Result*'s criticism of the proposed constitution of 1778[97]—must be cultivated, extended, and deepened through new institutional forms that would make the requisite reasonable deliberation possible and practicable.[98]

John Adams later wrote his monumental *A Defence of the Constitutions of Government of the United States of America*[99] to explain to Europeans the quality of deliberation that he believed the American people had now shown could be brought democratically to bear on the issue of framing a constitution. Adams's book is long, turgidly burdened with long extracts from all the writers Adams deemed pertinent, and often carelessly expressed in ways that obscured for Americans his essential argument, namely, that an upper house and independent executive were necessary to prevent aristocratic domination, which would be inconsistent with a Lockean respect for equal rights.[100] However, the approach of the work to the task of constitutional deliberation brilliantly exemplified how Adams and the people of Massachusetts had come

---

[96] See C. F. Adams, ed., *Works of John Adams,* vol. 4, pp. 213–67.

[97] See Theophilus Parsons, *The Essex Result,* in Charles S. Hyneman and Donald S. Lutz, *American Political Writing during the Founding Era 1760–1805* (Indianapolis, Ind.: Liberty Press, 1983), vol. 1, pp. 480–522.

[98] For a useful general study of the different direction of British and American constitutional thought on the issue of sovereignty, see Morgan, *Inventing the People.*

[99] See C. F. Adams, ed., *Works of John Adams,* vols. 4–6.

[100] See R. R. Palmer, *The Age of the Democratic Revolution* (Princeton, N.J.: Princeton Univ. Press, 1959), vol. 1, p. 275. For Adams' reasons for fearing the political power of aristocracies if not balanced by a third branch of government, see, e.g., *A Defence,* pp. 336, 343–45, 354–55, 366, 444–45; on the need for an independent executive to protect people's rights, see idem, p. 585.

to understand its requirements not only institutionally (constitutional convention and ratification by the people) but also substantively.

People gathered their deliberative forces in a constitutional convention and in ratification debates to reflect and decide on a constitutional framework for the exercise of political power that was consistent with human rights. Americans had learned "that neither liberty nor justice can be secured to the individuals of a nation, nor its prosperity promoted, but by a fixed constitution of government, and stated laws, known and obeyed by all."[101] If Americans were concerned only for their own time and place in a still largely unpopulated agricultural society, they could perhaps thrive

> under almost any kind of government, or without any government at all. But it is of great importance to begin well; misarrangements now made, will have great, extensive, and distant consequences; and we are now employed, how little soever we may think of it, in making establishments which will affect the happiness of a hundred millions of inhabitants at a time, in a period not very distant. All nations, under all governments, must have parties; the great secret is to control them.[102]

Constitutional design thus required that people look at political life and forms from a more abstract point of view, garnered perhaps from the kind of comparative political science that Adams (following the example of Montesquieu and Hume) conspicuously displayed in his monumental treatise. Moreover, they must consider the likely pattern of social and economic developments in the society and the impact of political forms on such developments, including on their posterity. If they or their posterity should later suffer from the oppressions of untrammeled political power:

> It will be entirely the fault of the constitution, and of the people who will not now adopt a good one; . . . for what consolation can it be to a man, to think that his whole life, and that of his son and grandson, must be spent in unceasing misery and warfare, for the sake only of a possibility that his great grandson may become a despot![103]

Adams construed Americans' sense of constitutional responsibility to be an exercise of collective democratic deliberation on the corruptive and distributive tendencies of political power such that he regarded ratification of a constitution like that of Massachusetts as the endorsement of a governmental structure that would best control power over many generations of social and economic change consistent with enduring respect for human rights.

The Massachusetts constitution of 1780 exemplified one such pattern of

---

[101] John Adams, *A Defence*, p. 401.
[102] Ibid., pp. 587–88.
[103] Ibid., vol. 5, p. 426.

control of political power.[104] The legislature was bicameral with power balanced between a house of representatives representing the people and a senate of forty with a membership that was proportioned to districts according to the amount of taxes paid by inhabitants. An ascending scale of property holding and residence set the qualifications for the three branches of the legislature: the house, the senate, and the governor. The Governor was the most powerful executive of any state, was separately elected by the people and had a suspensive veto over legislation (subject to override by a two-thirds majority in each house). Judges, most of whom were appointed by the executive, retained their offices indefinitely "during good behaviour."[105] A lengthy bill of rights preceded the constitution, in which the principle of separation of powers was spelled out in detail.

The Massachusetts constitution, though widely admired in the 1780s,[106] was inadequate in controlling Shays' Rebellion,[107] and American constitutional thinkers, notably Madison, had concluded that the quality of deliberation and argument, which had been brought to the constitutional task in Massachusetts, would remain imperfect and incomplete until it had been brought to bear on the general problem of constitutionalism in America, including, of course, the relative powers of state and federal governments.[108] If the legitimacy of the early state constitutions was now in dispute because of the political hegemony of the state legislatures, then such disrepute extended equally to the powers of the state legislatures over the continental congress under the Articles of Confederation; the legislatures elected representatives to the Congress and retained effective discretion over whether to pay requisitions (taxes), and any state could veto a proposed amendment to the Articles (and needed amendments had been thus rejected).[109] When compelled to address the claim that the Constitution's ratification procedure violated the Articles, Madison refused to take it seriously,[110] an impatience rooted in the Lockean theory of political legitimacy that he assumed. Citing the Declaration of Independence,[111] Madison reminded Americans of the "transcendent and precious right of the people to 'abolish or alter their governments as to them shall seem most likely to effect their safety and happiness,' "[112] a remark that suggests issues about the Lockean political illegitimacy of the Articles of

---

[104] For fuller description, see Gordon S. Wood, *The Creation of the American Republic, 1776–1787* (New York: W.W. Norton, 1969), pp. 434–35; and, for a good comparative study of the Massachusetts and other state constitutions, see, in general, Willi Paul Adams, *First State Constitutions*.

[105] Willi Paul Adams, *First State Constitutions,* p. 269 (citing text of Massachusetts constitution of 1780).

[106] See Wood, *Creation of American Republic,* pp. 434–35.

[107] For pertinent commentary, see Forrest McDonald, *E Pluribus Unum* (Indianapolis, Ind.: Liberty Press, 1965), pp. 244–57.

[108] See, e.g., Rakove, *Beginnings of National Politics,* pp. 389–96.

[109] See, in general, Jensen, *Articles of Confederation;* Rakove, *Beginnings of National Politics.*

[110] See *The Federalist,* p. 263.

[111] Ibid., p. 265.

[112] Ibid.

Confederation themselves. If so, Madison's argument was, in effect, that the constitutionalism for which Americans had fought a revolution was not the Articles and that Americans now should be accorded the deliberative opportunity to reject it (precisely because it failed adequately to protect rights and secure the public good) and to achieve a better understanding of their Lockean constitutionalism.[113] That understanding was crucially expressed for Madison, as we shall shortly see, by both the quality of deliberation that the constitutional convention made possible and the kind of deliberative ratification by the people at large (not the state legislatures) that it required.

Americans naturally interpreted this new conception of constitutional deliberation and argument in terms of the Lockean contractualism that some of them (e.g., James Wilson) had earlier used in justifying the sovereignty of the British constitution over parliament. When Wilson—now one of the leading founders—rose at the Pennsylvania ratifying convention to characterize the authority the Constitution would have when ratified, he recalled how Americans, like himself, had rejected in the revolutionary debates Blackstone's doctrine of parliamentary sovereignty, and announced that Americans finally had found practicable institutional forms to express the alternative conception of political legitimacy for which they had fought.

> The supreme, absolute, and uncontrollable authority *remains* with the people. . . . The practical recognition of this truth was reserved for the honor of this country. I recollect no constitution founded on this principle. But we have witnessed the improvement, and enjoy the happiness, of seeing it carried into practice. The great and penetrating mind of Locke seems to be the only one that pointed towards even the theory of this great truth.[114]

The authority of the ratified Constitution was thus identified with a Lockean interpretation of popular sovereignty. The authority of constitutional argument thus understood was supreme over all political bodies and agencies, which explains why Wilson and many others rejected any idea that it would be regarded as a kind of contract between one political body and another (e.g., the British conception of Magna Charta as a contract between the monarchy and the barons).[115] The Constitution was contractualist only in Locke's sense, namely, a contract among the people, not between rulers and ruled.[116] In effect, under the American doctrine of the supremacy of the Constitution, no political body was or could be sovereign, because the Constitution's supremacy rested on the judgments it embodied about political legitimacy, which subordinated all political power to the demands of reasonable justification to persons understood as free and equal bearers of human rights.

---

[113] For other notable references to the revolution in *The Federalist*, see, e.g., ibid., pp. 89, 250, 297, 309, 320.

[114] Jensen, ed., *Documentary History*, p. 472.

[115] See, for Wilson's rejection, ibid., pp. 555–56; see, in general, Wood, *Creation of American Republic*, pp. 541–42, 601–2.

[116] See Wood, *Creation of American Republic*, p. 601.

Americans had finally discovered a new way of thinking about constitutionalism that explained their grievances under the British constitution and their criticisms of the early state and federal constitutions. Constitutional law had to move to a new level of deliberation and justification, and new institutional forms had to be invented that were more adequate to the supremacy of such arguments over ordinary politics. The need for institutional innovation—moved by the demands of abstract political argument and sophisticated comparative political science—led such a historically minded people to look again to history and to reclaim for future generations of Americans the Harringtonian idea of the founders of "an immortal commonwealth."[117]

The Idea of Founders and the Immortal Commonwealth

The self-conscious sense of the founders, as founders, was perhaps their most remarkable use of history, because it represented their choice to identify the American constitutional tradition with Harrington's aspiration to cut Britain free of its corrupt "Gothic model"[118] of balanced classes in the service of a republican aspiration to "an immortal commonwealth"[119] and his use of Machiavelli's political science of Roman republicanism in the service of that aspiration.[120] The idea of founding was fundamental to Roman—in contrast to Greek—political thought,[121] but not as the act of any one person. As Cicero described it:

> [Rome] was founded, not in one generation, but in a long period of several centuries and many ages of men. For, . . . there never has lived a man possessed of so great genius that nothing could escape him, nor could the combined powers of all the men living at one time possibly make all necessary provisions for the future without the aid of actual experience and the test of time.[122]

Machiavelli, in contrast, used his study of Roman republicanism to develop a political science that might profitably be used (e.g., balancing factions in a mixed state[123]) in the sound framing of a republican form of government, and

---

[117] See Harrington, *Commonwealth of Oceana*, pp. 209, 321–22.

[118] See, e.g., James Harrington, *The Prerogative of Popular Government*, in Pocock, *Political Works of James Harrington*, p. 563.

[119] Harrington, *Commonwealth of Oceana*, p. 209.

[120] For an excellent general study, see Zera S. Fink, *The Classical Republicans* (Evanston, Ill.: Northwestern Univ. Press, 1945).

[121] See, for pertinent commentary, Hannah Arendt, *Between Past and Future* (Harmondsworth, Middlesex, England: Penguin, 1968), pp. 98–99, 120–41, 166, 193–94.

[122] Cicero, *De Re Publica*, in *De Re Publica, De Legibus*, Clinton Walker Keyes, Trans. (Cambridge, Mass.: Harvard Univ. Press, 1928), p. 113. See, in general, Neal Wood, *Cicero's Social and Political Thought* (Berkeley: Univ. of California Press, 1988).

[123] For Machiavelli's originality on this point, see Quentin Skinner, *Machiavelli* (New York: Hill and Wang, 1981), pp. 65–67.

he thought of his science as directed to "but one person . . . the prudent organizer of a state whose intention is to govern not in his own interests but in the interests of the fatherland."[124] Founding a state was an act often calling for ruthless genius,[125] a foundation that later generations would "renovate" by returning the state "to their starting points," their "original principles in the case of a republic."[126] Although Machiavelli accepted universal human tendencies to corruption, such tendencies could at least be reasonably retarded by the foundation and renewal of properly designed republics in light of political science.[127]

Harrington adopted both Machiavelli's methodology of political science and his republican ambitions, but he argued, in contrast to Machiavelli's limited hopes to retard corruption, that the proper use of such science could achieve "a commonwealth rightly ordered . . . as immortal, or long-lived, as the world."[128] However, this could be accomplished only if "first, . . . the legislator should be one man, and secondly . . . the government should be made altogether, or at once."[129] Harrington sharply distinguished, as did Adams and later Madison, the normal psychology of people in politics from the normative ends of a republican government. A founder should not trust political virtue because it was often corrupted by faction,[130] or religious virtue because it would "reduce a commonwealth unto a party."[131] A point that was fundamental to the thinking of the American founders was bluntly put by Harrington:

"Give us good men and they will make us good laws" is the maxim of a demagogue. . . . But "give us good orders, and they will make us good men" is the maxim of a legislator and the most infallible in the politics.[132]

The normative end of a commonwealth was "an empire of laws and not of men,"[133] reasonable treatment of all persons as equals under the "law of nature,"[134] and Harrington no more doubted the objective truth of such moral and political values than did Adams or later Madison. The constructivist project of a founder was to take seriously such values, their corruption by normal political psychology, and the need to invent constitutional forms to

---

[124] Niccolò Machiavelli, *The Discourses,* Bernard Crick, ed., Leslie J. Walker, trans. (Harmondsworth, Middlesex, England: Penguin, 1970), p. 132.

[125] See, for commentary on this point, Bruce James Smith, *Politics and Remembrance* (Princeton, N.J.: Princeton Univ. Press, 1985), pp. 26–101; Mark Hulliung, *Citizen Machiavelli* (Princeton, N.J.: Princeton Univ. Press, 1983), pp. 192–3.

[126] Machiavelli, *Discourses* pp. 385–86.

[127] See Fink, *Classical Republicans,* p. 12.

[128] Harrington, *Commonwealth of Oceana,* p. 321.

[129] Ibid., p. 207.

[130] See ibid., pp. 173, 202, 206, 676.

[131] Ibid., p. 204.

[132] Ibid., p. 205.

[133] Ibid., p. 170.

[134] Ibid., p. 171.

channel such political motivations to achieve the ends of egalitarian public reason. In language that anticipated Madison's defense of the separation of powers,[135] Harrington called for a constitutional structure "that there can be in the same no number of men, having the interest, that can have the power, nor any number of men, having the power, that can have the interest, to invade or disturb the government."[136] The Harringtonian approach to constitutional design was exemplified by the analogy of dividing a cake fairly: the way to ensure justice in distribution was not to expect justice in politics, but to structure a political process of choice (you cut the cake first, and I choose my piece second) likely—given normal human motives in politics—to result in equal shares.[137] Harrington's proposals in *Oceana* were unbelievably complex.[138] For present purposes, we must simplify and highlight those features that were significant for later constitutional thought in Britain and America. Writing in a precapitalist society, Harrington used land as the criterion of wealth and of political power, and he imposed an agrarian law that would reduce large landholdings to ensure more nearly equal patterns of land distribution and thus more nearly equal political power[139]; his voting procedures combined elements of both a lottery and voter selection,[140] and political power was subject to regular rotation to ensure broader participation in government through a diverse and nonrecurring political leadership.[141] Under Harrington's proposals, voting by all citizens (in contrast to servants[142]) was structured through successive intermediate representative bodies culminating in a bicameral legislature: a smaller branch of lords or senate (indirectly elected by popular vote) that could only deliberate and propose laws, and a larger house of representatives (directly elected) that could only adopt or refuse. He aimed to ensure the deliberative use of public reason through a refining process of representation[143] by "a natural aristocracy"[144] (in a sense

---

[135] "But the great security against a gradual concentration of the several powers in the same department, consists in giving to those who administer such department, the necessary constitutional means, and personal motives, to resist encroachments of the others" (*The Federalist*, p. 349).

[136] James Harrington, *The Art of Lawgiving*, in Pocock, ed., *Political Works of James Harrington*, p. 658 (italicized in text).

[137] Ibid., p. 172.

[138] See, for a clear and fair exposition of the proposals, Fink, *Classical Republicans*, pp. 52–89.

[139] See Pocock, ed., *Political Works of James Harrington*, pp. 62–63.

[140] Harrington adapted the Venetian ballot that combined such elements; see *Commonwealth of Oceana*, pp. 241–47. On the Venetian republic and its impact on Harrington's thought, see Fink, *Classical Republicans*, pp. 28–89.

[141] See Pocock, ed., *Political Works of James Harrington*, pp. 69–72.

[142] See Harrington, *Commonwealth of Oceana*, pp. 212–13.

[143] Harrington summarized the aims of his constructivist politics in terms of "the soul or faculties of a man . . . refined or made incapable of passion" (*A System of Politics*, in Pocock, ed., *Political Works of James Harrington*, p. 838).

[144] Ibid., p. 173.

similar to the later usage of Adams and Jefferson[145]) accountable to the electorate in ways that would tend to assure equal treatment for all. Politics had to be thus structured because—in terms that prefigure Madison's point about the corruptibility even of Socratic conscience by the politics of "a mob"[146]—Harrington observed that "the body of a people, not led by the reason of the government, is not a people, but a herd."[147]

Harrington insisted that such a design be done by one person, which reflected a distrust of the shallow empiricism of people in general who tended to fall back on immediate historical experience (e.g., of the British constitution of balanced hereditary and other classes).[148] In contrast, Harrington's proposals for an immortal commonwealth rested on an empirically rigorous comparative political science and the use of imaginative political intelligence in the construction of new kinds of political orders in the service of reflective republican values. That kind of judgment would, he assumed, require the possibly ruthless Machiavellian man of genius; *Oceana* was dedicated to Cromwell.

Americans had either read Harrington directly (like Adams[149]) or absorbed his ideas from thinkers in Britain (notably, a whig oppositionist like Francis Hutcheson or a political scientist like Hume[150]) who gave his views prominence. Although they had come to reject some of his views as inappropriate in American circumstances (an agrarian[151]), or unwise (rotation[152]), or inconsistent with American aims and values (notably, Harrington's imperialistic expansionism and perfectionist ideals of military heroism[153]), his ambition

---

[145] Harrington, for example, thinks of this aristocracy as one of merit. See, e.g., Harrington, *Art of Lawgiving*, p. 677.

[146] *The Federalist*, p. 374.

[147] Harrington, *System of Politics*, p. 838.

[148] See ibid., pp. 106, 728–29. 737, 839–40.

[149] In his important 1776 essay on American constitutionalism, *Thoughts on Government*, Adams appealed to Harrington as an authority and indeed used his description of the ends of republican government, "an empire of laws, not of men," as the definition of a republic. See C.F. Adams, ed., *Works of John Adams*, vol. 4, p. 194. In *A Defence*, Adams quoted a long excerpt from Harrington's discussion in *Oceana* of cake division, calling his arguments: "eternal and unanswerable by any man" (C.F. Adams, ed., *Works of John Adams*, vol. 4, p. 410); the quotation is at idem, pp. 410–13. Madison included Toland's edition of Harrington's works in his 1783 Report on Books for Congress; see William T. Hutchinson and William M.E. Rachal, eds., *The Papers of James Madison 1783* (Chicago: Univ. of Chicago Press, 1969) vol. 6, p. 85 (at no. 148).

[150] See, e.g., Francis Hutcheson, *System of Moral Philosophy*, vol. 2, in *Collected Works*, vol. 6, pp. 240–66; idem, *Short Introduction to Moral Philosophy*, in *Collected Works*, vol. 4, p. 299; David Hume, "Idea of a Perfect Commonwealth", in *Essays Moral, Political and Literary* (Oxford: Oxford University Press, 1963), pp. 499–515. For commentary on the Whig oppositionist influence, see Robbins, *Eighteenth-Century Commonwealthman*, pp. 173–74, 190–1.

[151] See, e.g., Max Farrand, ed., *Records of the Federal Convention*, vol. 1 (New Haven, Conn.: Yale Univ. Press, 1966), pp. 422–23 (Madison).

[152] See, e.g., Farrand, ed., *Records of Federal Convention*, vol. 1, p. 376 (Wilson, "agst. fettering elections, and discouraging merit").

[153] Citizenship, for Harrington, involved extensive military service in imperialistic wars in service of a Machiavellian commonwealth of increase. See, for illuminating discussion, Fink, *Classical Republicans*, pp. 79–85. Machiavelli had, of course, powerfully stated the theme of republican imperialism on which Harrington writes a variation. See, in general, Hulliung, *Citizen Machiavelli*.

for an immortal commonwealth struck a responsive chord among American constitutionalists.[154]

American constitutional thinkers, like Harrington, had despaired of the British constitution and its evolving historical conventions; Harrington's acute use of political science in the attempt to emancipate British constitutional thought from its unimaginative historicism must have had a resonance for Americans, who had found British appeals to the historically evolving British constitution of parliamentary supremacy so inexcusably vapid and insulting. Americans needed an alternative way of thinking about constitutionalism, and they naturally identified their situation with the abortive constitutional proposals made during the English Civil War and the interregnum.[155] Harrington's particular proposals appealed to American constitutionalists because his methods and ambitions were so congruent with their sense of their own extraordinary historic opportunity and their responsibility to bring to it the full scope of the emancipated religious, moral, and political intelligence in which they took such natural pride. However, that intelligence could only realize itself if it were not subverted by the corruptive religious, moral, and political traditions that had shackled the natural scope of its reasonable freedom.

This sense of historic opportunity and responsibility led the American founders to bring to their deliberations the interpretive uses of history (discussed in the previous chapter), including the analysis of such history in light of the comparative political science of Machiavelli, Harrington, Montesquieu, Hume, and the contemporary Scottish social theorists. Montesquieu, for example, wrote for a "legislator"[156] who, in felicitous circumstances, could use the normative and empirical insights culled from Montesquieu's idealization of the British constitution to frame such a constitution or a similar such constitution in the appropriately supportive cultural, demographic, and climatic circumstances identified by Montesquieu's political science. A text containing advice of this sort would understandably have enormous power in 1787, because it addressed, clarified, and indeed defined the kind of historic opportunity and task that the founders had before them; the founders, themselves trained in the British constitutional tradition, identified their circumstances as precisely those most favorable to acting on the kind of reflective wisdom that Montesquieu urged on the "legislator." Although Hume defended the British constitution on the ground of long-standing tradition, he had allowed himself the utopian luxury of reflecting on an ideal Harringtonian extended republic, which he offered for a time when "an opportunity might be afforded of reducing the theory to practice, either by a dissolution of some old government, or by the combination of men to form a new one, in some distant part of the

---

[154] On the importance of Harrington for American constitutional thought, see Morgan, *Inventing the People,* pp. 86, 157, 248, 251, 291.

[155] See, in general, Francis D. Wormuth, *The Origins of Modern Constitutionalism* (New York: Harper & Row, 1949); also, Morgan, *Inventing the People,* pp. 55–93.

[156] Baron de Montesquieu, *The Spirit of the Laws* Thomas Nugent, trans. (New York: Hafner, 1949), vol. 2, p. 156.

world."[157] However, the American founders found themselves, miraculously, in precisely such a situation, and Madison, as we shall see, found Hume's advice useful indeed.

The American constitutionalists tested, refined, and elaborated their critical political intelligence in light of such political science because, like Harrington, they had learned to distrust the shallow historicist empiricism of their now-shattered faith in the British constitution; they knew also that the test of their exercise of emancipatory political intelligence would be their capacity for moral independence and reasonable criticism of the traditions that had so stunted and stultified the human mind and heart into acceptance of unnatural hierarchies of power and privilege. Such exercises of critical intelligence included an independent stance from the comparative political science that they had found so illuminating. Americans thus used Montesquieu, sometimes critically, for precisely the Harringtonian purposes he deplored, and they used Hume's often brilliant political science of political impartiality in service of a Lockean theory of political legitimacy that Hume rejected. Furthermore, Americans were certainly absorbed by Harrington's methods and ambitions, but they could not subscribe to the conception of Machiavellian political science as a kind of alternative organon to ultimate religious and moral truth (e.g., laying the foundations of an Erastian civil religion of the state).[158] Americans were absorbed by Harrington for reasons of their own, namely, as a model for the quality of deliberation that was required by their great historic opportunity and responsibility in service of protecting the inalienable human rights that were fundamental to the legitimacy of political power. Consistent with this political theory, they needed a conception of themselves not as Harrington's ruthless man of genius but as participants in a great collective democratic deliberation over a new conception of constitutional argument that would dignify all Americans of their generation in the judgment of history.

Importantly, "the ends" of such constitutional arguments, as Madison put it at the constitutional convention, "were first to protect the people agst. their rulers: secondly to protect [the people] agst. the transient impressions into which they themselves might be led."[159] The authority of such arguments was that their "ends" were those of a "people deliberating in a temperate moment, and with the experience of other nations before them, on the plan of Govt. most likely to secure their happiness."[160] That authority was crucially in play in *The Federalist* no. 49 when Madison defended the founders' conception of a long-enduring written constitution against Jefferson's idea of a written constitution more easily amendable by each generation.[161]

---

[157] David Hume, "Idea of a Perfect Commonwealth," in *Essays Moral, Political, and Literary* (Oxford: Oxford Univ. Press, 1963), p. 500.

[158] See, in general, Leo Strauss, *Thoughts on Machiavelli* (Chicago: Univ. of Chicago Press, 1984); Hulliung, *Citizen Machiavelli*.

[159] Farrand, ed., *Records of Federal Convention*, vol. 1, p. 421.

[160] Ibid.

[161] Madison referred to Jefferson's draft Virginia constitution of 1783, which he had appended to his *Notes on the State of Virginia*. See Jefferson, *Notes on the State of Virginia*, pp. 209–22, in

Madison's argument was an appeal to the extraordinary sort of liberty, opportunity, and reflective capacity that were collectively and democratically brought to the framing and ratification of the U.S. Constitution. The authority of the framers' conception of a written constitution was precisely that it was not the product of routine democratic politics in which competitors for political power brought to all disputes their factionalized perceptions of issues of both principle and policy. Madison thought of the legislative debates of such normal politics as "so many judicial determinations, not indeed concerning the rights of single persons, but concerning the rights of large bodies of citizens,"[162] namely, as a substantive debate about justice in which all parties interpret such claims of justice filtered through their factionalized commitments as either creditors or debtors, farmers or manufacturers, Quakers or Anglicans, and so on. The authority of the Constitution, in contrast, was in the impartiality brought to bear on the construction of constraints on power and the provision of reasonable substantive and procedural arguments limiting the exercise of such routine politics, consistent with a larger Lockean conception of justice, equal rights, and the effective use of collective power to advance the public good. Madison's objection to Jefferson's view of a written constitution was that the sense of a written constitution that was easily changed or modified, eroded the distinctive authority of the framers' intent and undermined its distinctive virtue of constitutional impartiality by the factionalized perceptions of constitutional argument that necessarily arise in normal politics. However, that would unleash yet again Hamilton's "demon of faction,"[163] which it was the very point of the Constitution to tame and civilize. For this reason, the very impartiality of the written constitution must place it beyond any change resembling normal democratic politics. That deeper impartiality expressed a conception of the collective reasonableness of the Constitution itself. Furthermore, Madison argued[164] that amendments must be so designed to approximate the same sort of collective exercise of deliberative reflection on enduring constitutional design.

Madison's argument about the authority of the Constitution was contractualist in Locke's sense; namely, the legitimacy of political power was tested against a political ideal of the acceptability of such power to the free, rational, and equal persons subject to such power.[165] The legitimacy of the Constitution was the way in which it imposed constraints on the power of the state and the power of the people that could be and often were publicly justified to all

---

which Jefferson advocated that—whenever two branches of government should by two thirds vote concur—a constitutional convention of the people shall be called to amend the constitution. See idem, p. 221.

[162] *The Federalist,* p. 59.

[163] Ibid., p. 444.

[164] Ibid., pp. 341–43.

[165] See, in general, Richards, *Toleration and the Constitution.* Cf. John Rawls, *A Theory of Justice* (Cambridge, Mass.: Harvard Univ. Press, 1971); T.M. Scanlon, "Contractualism and Utilitarianism," Amartya Sen and Bernard Williams, eds., *Utilitarianism and Beyond,* pp. 103–28.

persons subject to them as reasonable such limits. It was therefore essential, as founders like Wilson and Madison insisted at the convention,[166] that the Constitution be ratified by one of the most inclusive deliberative processes that any republican government had ever seen; such ratification had normative force because it gave authoritative political expression to the deeper Lockean judgment of reasonable justification.

The authority of an enduring written constitution was, Madison argued, the impartial reasonableness of its written constraints on the power of both the state and the people. However, Madison thought of these constraints as an enduring heritage to posterity, namely, constitutional arguments based on an impartially conceived republican morality enforceable against both the state and the people; furthermore, he and other founders certainly shared Jefferson's bitterly realistic Machiavellian prophecy about the probable direction of America away from its original Lockean aspirations and his view of the responsibilities of American constitutionalists in light of that anticipated declension from republican virtue:

> They should look forward to a time, and that not a distant one, when corruption in this, as in the country from which we derive our origin, will have seized the heads of government, and be spread by them through the body of the people; when they will purchase the voices of the people, and make them pay the price. Human nature is the same on every side of the Atlantic, and will be alike influenced by the same causes. The time to guard against corruption and tyranny, is before they shall have gotten hold on us. It is better to keep the wolf out of the fold, than to trust to drawing his teeth and talons after he shall have entered.[167]

The future integrity of republican morality and the inalienable rights it protected would depend on the quality of constitutional argument that the American people could sustain. Madison had no doubt about the objective truth of that morality, and "a nation of philosophers" might, as Jefferson probably believed, rediscover it in each generation. However, the constitutional responsibility of his generation could not be discharged so cavalierly:

> The reason of man, like man himself is timid and cautious, when left alone; and acquires firmness and confidence, in proportion to the number with which it is associated. When the examples, which fortify opinion, are *antient* as well as *numerous,* they are known to have a double effect. In a nation of philosophers, this consideration ought to be disregarded. A reverence for the laws, would be sufficiently inculcated by the voice of an enlightened reason. But a nation of philosophers is as little to be expected as the philosophical race of kings wished for by Plato.[168]

---

[166] See, e.g., Farrand, ed., *Records of Federal Convention,* vol. 1, pp. 122–23 (Madison), 123 (Wilson), 127 (Wilson); idem, vol. 2, pp. 92 (Madison), 468–69 (Wilson), 469 (Madison), 475–76 (Madison), 477 (Wilson), 561–62 (Wilson).

[167] Jefferson, *Notes on the State of Virginia,* p. 121.

[168] *The Federalist,* p. 340.

Madison (and, as we saw earlier, John Dickinson[169]) in this case anticipated remarkably the normative role that the historical commitment to a written constitution (and its founders) would play in constituting American identity as an enduring republican community over generations. The Constitution had been self-consciously conceived in this way: in the words of the Preamble, to "secure the blessings of liberty to ourselves and our posterity," and all sides to the debates over the constitution—Federalist[170] and anti-Federalist[171]—appealed to the effects on posterity as a crucial test of the legitimacy of the Constitution. Madison's point—against Jefferson—was that the aspiration to such an enduring written constitution could best be achieved by self-consciously using the deeply human sense of history and tradition to maintain in the people at large the capacity for deliberative constitutional argument in service of Lockean political legitimacy. The idea of the founders would play a role in the American constitutional tradition not as a point of reference for ruthless Machiavellian genius but for a quality of public argument and vision among a free people that, as it dignified their generation, may yet dignify ours.

Constitutional Structures

We must now explore how and why the founders, understanding their role in the distinctive way that they did, both constructed and reasonably justified to the nation at large the three distinctive structures of American constitutionalism: federalism, the separation of powers, and judicial review.

Americans had forgotten neither their own history as British colonists, as revolutionaries, or as constitutional framers of and political officials under the early state and federal constitutions, nor the larger history of governments in general and republican government in particular.[172] In Chapter 2, some of the more important critical results of their extensive uses of interpretive history were described, for example, the significance of the emancipation of religious, moral, and political intelligence associated with the argument for religious toleration; the political psychology of faction as a general problem for political life; classical republicanism as a negative exemplar of aims and structures not to be followed; the political psychology of fame and its implications for political leadership; the stage of history and the role of commerce as an agent

[169] See John Dickinson, *Letters of Fabius*, pp. 188–9.

[170] See, e.g., *The Federalist*, pp. 89, 145, 210–11, 213, 276–77; Dickinson, *Letters of Fabius*, pp. 200–1.

[171] See, e.g., Herbert J. Storing, ed., *The Complete Anti-Federalist*, vol. 1, pp. 96, 105, 117, 155, 227, 249, 326, 363–64, 372; idem, vol. 3, pp. 14, 21, 39, 67, 86, 97, 105, 165; idem, vol. 4, pp. 18, 20, 64; idem, vol. 6, pp. 130, 141–42.

[172] For example, three of the framers had been in the Stamp Act Congress; eight had signed the Declaration of Independence; forty-two of the framers had served in the Congress of the United States; all but two or three had served as officials of colony or state; and twenty had helped write the constitutions of their states. See, in general, Clinton Rossiter, *1787: The Grand Convention* (New York: W.W. Norton, 1966), pp. 145–46.

of egalitarian liberal values; and the British constitution as a negative exemplar of constitutional argument.

The constitutional deliberations both at the constitutional convention and in the ratification debates that followed brought to the design of the new federal constitution all of this experience, which was interpreted as the application to human institutions of the experimental philosophy of Bacon, Newton, and Locke.[173] Indeed, the constitution itself was described by its defenders as "in some measure but an experiment," but "the fairest experiment that had been ever made in favor of human nature."[174] The appeal to experience was not, however, understood in a narrow inductive way as if any American republican experiment must not go beyond what history shows can work. If that had been the dominant empirical philosophy of the founders, then the Constitution would *not* have been the result, because none of the relevant historical "experiments" contained anything quite like the Constitution (although some of the state constitutions, notably those of Massachusetts, New York, and Maryland, offered some helpful models to the founders[175]). That, indeed, was the kind of empiricist objection made to the Constitution at the convention: "Where we have no experience there can be no reliance on Reason,"[176] or "experience must be our only guide. Reason may mislead us" (appealing to British political experience).[177] However, proponents of the Constitution like Madison insisted then and later that American experience showed that a more radical republican experiment was needed[178]; indeed the constitutional plan "wd [sic] decide forever the fate of Republic Govt.,"[179] and there was "no danger in submitting to practice an experiment which seems to be founded on the best theoretic principles."[180] Such proponents used the appeal to history as a tool to identify and analyze

---

[173] For example, at the Virginia ratification convention, Wythe opined: "He thought that experience was the best guide, and could alone develop its consequences. Most of the improvements that had been made in the science of government, and other sciences, were the result of experience," Jonathan Elliot, ed., *Debates in the Several State Conventions on the Adoption of the Federal Constitution,* vol. 3 (Philadelphia: Lippincott, 1836) (hereafter referred to as Elliot, ed., *Debates*), p. 587.

[174] Elliot, ed., *Debates,* vol 4, p. 262 (Charles Pinckney at the South Carolina ratifying convention).

[175] Randolph, in his opening address to the constitutional convention, made particular reference to these three states as having constitutional structures that gestured in the right direction, but none of them "provided sufficient checks against the democracy," Farrand, ed., *Records of Federal Convention,* vol. 1, p. 27. The argument of *The Federalist* prominently uses references to the state constitutions, usually to the effect that the proposed federal constitution takes up and uses (sometimes improving) their best features. On the Maryland senate (elected by an electoral college), see, e.g., *The Federalist,* pp. 429–30; on New York's impeachment procedure, see idem, p. 446; on the strong and independent chief executive of Massachusetts, see idem, pp. 464, 499.

[176] Farrand, ed., *Records of Federal Convention,* vol. 1, p. 264.

[177] Ibid., vol. 2, p. 278.

[178] See Elliot, ed., *Debates,* vol. 3, pp. 394, 399–400 (Madison at the Virginia ratifying convention).

[179] Farrand, ed., *Records of Federal Convention,* vol. 1, p. 423.

[180] Elliot, ed., *Debates,* vol. 3, p. 394.

blunders in the theory and practice of republican and federal systems of government, but not as an exhaustive catalogue of constructive republican and federal alternatives; they were prepared, if necessary, to experiment with self-consciously utopian federalist proposals, which were works of imaginative political reason and not of experience (e.g., Hume's neo-Harringtonian utopian commonwealth[181]). Their constructive political imaginations were absorbed in a quite new departure in political thought and value, which they in part pioneered.

Constitutionalism was now to be conceived as addressed to the pathologies of political power in light of the Lockean requirement that political power was only legitimate if, on terms of equal justice, it respected the spheres of reasonable self-government protected by our inalienable human rights and advanced the public interest of all. No form of government (including republicanism) could reasonably exempt itself from the corruptibilities of political power. In particular, republicanism, as Americans had experienced it under the early state and federal constitutions, had not redeemed human nature (as Rousseau may have dreamed it would[182]); it had only given different and, in some respects, more extended opportunities for political power to display its oppressions. American constitutionalists were compelled to rethink fundamentally the question of what they valued in republican government and the structures for the exercise of republican political power that would serve those values. When they had finished their work, neither republicanism nor constitutionalism could ever be thought of in the ways they had once been. To understand the ways in which Americans used and transformed the political theory and science of their age in this process is to appreciate the nature and purposes of the new kind of constitutional argument and justification they innovated in the course of their "political experiments on the capacity of mankind for self-government."[183]

Federalism

American federalism was conceived by Madison as a way of structuring the political power of the federal government to address two central objections to republican government. First, the psychology of faction, from which republican rule was not exempt, had undermined the Lockean legitimacy of majority rule; second, a republican government was impossible in a nation with as large a territory and population as the United States had in 1787 and was likely further to have over time.

Majority rule had, as we have seen, been defended by Locke as the best available *political* decision-making procedure for forming a government that

---

[181] See Hume, "Idea of a Perfect Commonwealth," pp. 499–516. For pertinent commentary regarding Hume's impact on Madison, see pp. 76–106, Douglass Adair, *Fame and the Founding Fathers* (New York: W.W. Norton, 1974).

[182] See Judith Shklar, *Men and Citizens: A Study of Rousseau's Social Theory* (Cambridge: Cambridge Univ. Press, 1985), pp. 65–66.

[183] *The Federalist*, p. 250.

was consistent with respect for rights and pursuit of the public good, because unanimity would preclude agreement on any government and thus on a government that respected rights; however, for ordinary or routine politics, such a decision-making procedure might or might not require majority rule. In *The Federalist* no. 10, Madison argued that the idea that majority rule operating in a direct, nonrepresentative, participatory democracy should be the rule of decision making for ordinary politics wrongly supposed, like classical republicanism and "[t]heoretic politicians"[184] "that by reducing mankind to a perfect equality in their political rights, they would, at the same time, be perfectly equalized and assimilated in their possessions, their opinions, and their passions."[185] In effect, as he put the point in his October 24, 1787 letter to Jefferson: "the interest of the majority would be that of the minority also,"[186] so that majority rule could be depended on—consistent with Lockean political legitimacy—to respect equal rights and give equal weight to all interests in the pursuit of the public good. However, the argument not only was anachronistically based on the homogeneity of society "in the savage State,"[187] but also failed to take seriously the right to liberty of judgment fostered by the religious, moral, and commercial diversities made possible by the circumstances of "civilized Societies"[188] like the United States. The political psychology of faction, which eroded the Lockean legitimacy of majority rule, flourished in such societies because their circumstances made possible and supported the inalienable right to liberty of judgment, a respect for which was at the core of Lockean political legitimacy. Madison posed this as the republican dilemma: majority rule was justified—if at all—by its protection of equal inalienable rights, but respect for such rights gave rise to faction, which subverted the legitimacy of majority rule (majority factions oppressed the rights and ignored the interests of outsiders).

Madison's argument was directed at anonymous "theoretic politicians," but its point may be usefully understood as similar to an argument made earlier by De Lolme, which was explicitly against Rousseau's *Social Contract*—in particular, Rousseau's indictment of British-style representative government. He had argued that "the people of England regards itself as free: but it is grossly mistaken: it is free only during the election of members of parliament. As soon as they are elected, slavery overtakes it, and it is nothing."[189] De Lolme responded that Rousseau, misled by "inconsiderate admiration of the governments of ancient times,"[190] had confused sharing effective political power with liberty.

---

[184] Ibid., p. 61.

[185] Ibid., p. 62.

[186] Robert A. Rutland et al., eds., *Papers of James Madison 1787–1788* (Chicago: Univ. of Chicago Press, 1977), p. 212.

[187] Ibid.

[188] Ibid.

[189] Jean Jacques Rousseau, *The Social Contract*, in *The Social Contract and Discourses*, G.D.H. Cole, trans. (New York: E.P. Dutton, 1950), p. 94.

[190] J.L. De Lolme, *The Constitution of England* (London: G. Wilkie et al., 1807). The first English translation of this work was published in London in 1775, and was much admired by, among others, John Adams. See Palmer, *Age of the Democratic Revolution*, vol. 1, pp. 145–48, 272.

What then is liberty?—Liberty, I would answer, so far as it is possible for it to exist in a society of beings whose interests are almost perpetually opposed to each others', consists in this, that *every man, while he respects the persons of others, and allows them quietly to enjoy the produce of their industry, be certain himself likewise to enjoy the produce of his own industry, and that his person be also secure.*[191]

On this view, "to give one's suffrage is not liberty itself, but only a mean of procuring it, and a mean too which may degenerate to mere form,"[192] as it often did under classical republicanism. Rousseau thus confused politics as a means with its ends, and failed to address the essential questions of modern constitutionalism of how to structure political power in ways that would respect equal rights under law.

Madison was no defender of the British constitution, but he would have agreed with De Lolme about how the essential questions of modern constitutionalism should be posed. Madison was, if anything, an even more severe critic of classical republicanism, because he saw in the large popular assemblies of classical Athens and Rome the worst pathologies of a factionalized subversion of the sovereign authority of conscience itself.[193] In contrast, Madison defined the ends of constitutional government by implicit reference to the Lockean view of the state's legitimacy, namely, its enforcement of a more impartially just protection of equal rights than was possible in the state of nature (where each person or clan would be legislator, prosecutor, judge, jury, and executioner in his own case). Indeed, legislation itself was construed by Madison explicitly on a judicial model of impartiality:

No man is allowed to be a judge in his own cause; because his interest would certainly bias his judgment, and, not improbably, corrupt his integrity. With equal, nay with greater reason, a body of men, are unfit to be both judges and parties, at the same time; yet, what are many of the most important acts of legislation, but so many judicial determinations, not indeed concerning the rights of single persons, but concerning the rights of large bodies of citizens; . . .[194]

Simple majority rule, exercised in large popular assemblies, was judged defective when measured against this conception.

The force of the republican dilemma for Lockean Americans arose from their sense that America was at a distinctive stage of history and their repudiation of the authority of republican models resting on radically different circumstances and values. The same considerations made it necessary for the founders to confront and answer the view of Montesquieu and others that the virtue of

---

[191] Ibid., p. 245.

[192] Ibid., p. 246.

[193] Madison wrote: "passion never fails to wrest the sceptre from reason. Had every Athenian citizen been a Socrates; every Athenian assembly would still have been a mob" (*The Federalist*, p. 374).

[194] Ibid., p. 59.

republics required a small, ideologically homogeneous, often economically backward, and militaristic city-state (e.g., Sparta[195]) that could provide for its safety at best by a loose confederation with other republics.[196] The success of the British constitution in ruling a large territory and population was, from Montesquieu's perspective, precisely that it was not a republic, but a constitution based on commerce and balancing democratic, aristocratic, and monarchical elements.[197] In effect, for Montesquieu, republicanism was an anachronistic form of government for a large commercial state in contemporary circumstances.[198] The advisable solution to the problem facing the American founders would, on this view, be either a loose confederation of republics that were much smaller and less commercial than the states under the Articles of Confederation,[199] or an adaptation of British institutions to the American context, perhaps along the lines of Hamilton's proposal to the constitutional convention: members of a national assembly serving for three years, senators serving for life, an executive serving for life, and powers in the national government to negative state laws and appoint state officials.[200] Of the political theorists of the age, only Hume had taken the contrary view that a properly structured republican government could successfully operate in a large and populous territory,[201] and even he apparently did not maintain the position consistently.[202]

There was no disagreement that more profoundly distinguished the novel constitutional vision of the founders from the older republicanism of the anti-Federalists than their differences over the importance of homogeneity to political order. Leading anti-Federalist advocates argued, for example, that the Constitution failed to take homogeneous class interests sufficiently seriously as a way of balancing power[203] or as the basis for representation,[204] and others insisted that "in a republic, the manners, sentiments, and interests of

---

[195] See, for pertinent commentary, Thomas L. Pangle, *Montesquieu's Philosophy of Liberalism* (Chicago: Univ. of Chicago Press, 1973), pp. 48–106.

[196] See Montesquieu, *Spirit of the Laws*, vol. 1, pp. 126–28.

[197] For pertinent commentary, see Judith N. Shklar, *Montesquieu* (Oxford: Oxford Univ. Press, 1987), pp. 53–54, 106–9.

[198] Cf. ibid., p. 83.

[199] Hamilton cogently made this point about the proper interpretation of Montesquieu against the anti-Federalists in *The Federalist*, pp. 52–54.

[200] For Hamilton's plan, see Farrand, ed., *Records of Federal Convention*, vol. 3, pp. 617–630; for Hamilton's speech in defense of it, see idem, vol. 1, pp. 282–93.

[201] See Hume, "Idea of a Perfect Commonwealth."

[202] See Duncan Forbes, *Hume's Philosophical Politics* (Cambridge: Cambridge Univ. Press, 1975), p. 183.

[203] See *Letters from the Federal Farmer*, pp. 287–88; *Essays by a Farmer, Complete Anti-Federalist*, vol. 5, pp. 43–44, 62; *Address by John Francis Mercer*, idem, p. 104; *Speeches of Patrick Henry in the Virginia Ratifying Convention*, idem, pp. 233–34, 246.

[204] See *Letters from The Federal Farmer*, pp. 230, 265–70. See also *Essays of Brutus*, idem, p. 380; *The Impartial Examiner*, idem, vol. 5, pp. 192–93; *Speech of George Mason in the Virginia Ratifying Convention*, idem, p. 257; *Speeches by Melancton Smith*, in Storing, ed., *Complete Anti-Federalist*, vol. 6, pp. 157–59, 162.

the people should be similar"[205] and that there could be no coherent conception of the public good in a people as heterogeneous as those of the United States. It followed that religious homogeneity should be a basis of republican solidarity,[206] and the Constitution's prohibition of religious qualifications for public office was to be deplored[207]; moreover, states should keep "separate from foreign mixtures"[208] and the Constitution should not permit foreigners to serve in public offices.[209] For the same reasons, anti-Federalist thought repeated interminably the views of Montesquieu and others regarding the need for small territories and populations that were necessary for republicanism, the only circumstances within which the requisite republican homogeneity could be fostered.[210] Furthermore, those few anti-Federalist writers who saw American commerce as supportive of republicanism, defined such commerce essentially in terms of small communities.[211]

Madison, in *The Federalist* no. 10, wrote the central public defense by an American founder of the republican credentials of the federalism proposed by the Constitution against these anti-Federalist arguments. It took on, at once, both challenges to American republicanism: its republican dilemma, and the impossibility of republicanism in America's circumstances. In effect, Madison took what anti-Federalists identified as the Constitution's antirepublican vices—its large territory, heterogeneous populace, and commercial interests— and transformed them into key components of the construction of constitutional structures for the exercise of political power that would respect enduring republican values.

As Douglass Adair has shown,[212] Madison brilliantly synthesized Hume's analytical political psychology and criticism of classical republicanism (see Chapter 2), as well as the form of structural proposal of Hume's neo-Harringtonian utopian essay, "Idea of a Perfect Commonwealth."[213] In that essay, Hume acknowledged that Harrington's "*Oceana* is the only valuable model of

---

[205] See *Essays of Brutus*, p. 369.

[206] See, e.g., *Aristocrotis*, in Storing, ed., *Complete Anti-Federalist*, vol. 3, pp. 205–6.

[207] See, e.g., *Letters of Agrippa*, in Storing, ed., *Complete Anti-Federalist*, vol. 4, p. 114; *Essay by Samuel*, idem, pp. 193, 195–96; *A Friend to the Rights of the People*, idem, p. 242; *Letter by Davis*, idem, pp. 246–48.

[208] See *Letters of Agrippa*, p. 86.

[209] See *A Republican Federalist*, in Storing, ed., *Complete Anti-Federalist*, vol. 4, pp. 184–85.

[210] See, e.g., Luther Martin's *The Genuine Information*, in Storing, ed., *Complete Anti-Federalist*, vol. 2, pp. 48–49; *Letters of Cato*, idem, pp. 110–11; *Letters of Centinel*, idem, p. 141; *Essays of Brutus*, idem, p. 368; *An Old Whig*, idem, vol. 3, p. 32; idem, *The Address and Reasons of the Minority of the Convention of Pennsylvania*, p. 153; *Letters of Agrippa*, idem, vol. 4, p. 76; *Essays by a Farmer*, idem, vol. 5, pp. 31–32; Samuel Chase, *Notes of Speeches Delivered to the Maryland Ratifying Convention*, idem, p. 81; *Speeches of Patrick Henry in the Virginia Ratifying Convention*, idem, p. 233; *Speech of George Mason in the Virginia Ratifying Convention*, idem, p. 256; James Monroe, *Some Observations on the Constitution*, idem, p. 288–89; *Speeches by Melancthon Smith*, idem, vol. 6, pp. 151, 171.

[211] See, e.g., *Letters of Agrippa*, pp. 71, 82, 84, 88, 95.

[212] See Adair, *Fame and the Founding Fathers*, pp. 93–106.

[213] Hume, *Essays Moral, Political, and Literary*, pp. 499–515.

a commonwealth that has yet been offered to the public,"[214] but he rejected the three components of rotation, the agrarian, and the powers of the senate. In particular, Hume objected to the dominant powers of Harrington's senate that provided "not a sufficient security for liberty, or the redress of grievances,"[215] because the representatives of the people could only approve or disapprove legislation that the senate had the sole power to debate and propose. Hume proposed instead the election of local county representatives who would meet in regional bodies to elect county magistrates and representatives to the national senate and who would perform legislative functions under the constitution. The senate would have executive powers and the power to propose legislation for the approval of the regional representative bodies, but a minority of senators might demand that legislation be sent to these bodies; furthermore, county representatives or magistrates might propose legislation to their senator to be submitted in the senate. Hume's proposals also called for an established church[216] and a court of competitors, consisting of senatorial candidates who lost elections but received a sizable number of votes and who would have the powers to initiate proceedings against public officials accused of wrongdoing.[217] Hume supposed that each of the counties would also be a republican government and that the senate or another county could annul its laws.[218] Consistent with his general views on the importance of cultivating standards of philosophical impartiality in political argument, Hume defended these constitutional structures (in particular, the separate regional representative bodies) as ways of securing the representatives of the people more political power than Harrington permitted but in a smaller, more deliberative context (in contrast, "all numerous assemblies, however composed, are mere mob"[219]). In a passage that must have arrested Madison's attention, Hume concluded that

> we shall conclude this subject, with observing the falsehood of the common opinion, that no large state, such as France or Great Britain, could ever be modelled into a commonwealth, but that such a form of government can only take place in a city or small territory. The contrary seems probable . . . . In a large government, which is modelled with masterly skill, there is compass and room enough to refine the democracy, from the lower people who may be admitted into the first elections, or first concoction of the commonwealth, to the higher magistrates who direct all the movements. At the same time, the parts are so distant and remote, that it is very difficult, either by intrigue, prejudice, or passion, to hurry them into any measures against the public interest.[220]

---

[214] Ibid., p. 501.
[215] Ibid.
[216] See ibid., p. 506.
[217] Ibid., p. 505.
[218] See ibid., p. 511.
[219] See ibid., p. 509.
[220] Ibid., pp. 513–15.

Madison imaginatively recast Hume's argument in service of a Lockean theory of political legitimacy that Hume, of course, rejected.[221] Madison took as axiomatic the quite non-Humean idea of inalienable human rights that were, in principle, exempt from the legitimate scope of political power. He rejected, for example, an established church, an idea that Hume had endorsed, because he regarded it as inconsistent with equal respect for the inalienable right to conscience.[222] Indeed, Madison framed the republican dilemma precisely in terms of the reservation of such Lockean rights: "liberty is to faction, what air is to fire,"[223] where liberty is "the reason of man"[224] exercising human faculties and faction "some common impulse of passion, or of interest, adverse to the rights of other citizens, or to the permanent and aggregate interests of the community."[225] The problem was to resolve this dilemma of republican constitutional design, to preserve republican liberties and yet to constrain institutionally the possible exercise of factionalized tendencies of group insularity in ways that secure political action more likely to respect rights of minorities and promote the public good. Madison assumed that some of these republican liberties (e.g., the right to conscience) would be protected by expressed or implied textual reservations of basic rights of the person from state power; he was concerned in *The Federalist* no. 10 about how one of these republican liberties—the right periodically to vote for political leaders—would be so exercised within the institutional structures of the federal system in ways likely to contain the tendencies to faction in the states that had delegitimated the Articles of Confederation. In Madison's thinking, there were two central issues. First, the national government must have supreme authority over the states regarding issues of national concern (e.g., the regulation of commerce, taxation, foreign policy). Second, it must have authority "to secure individuals agst. [sic] encroachments on their rights."[226] In both areas, factions in the states had either compromised the public good of the nation or flagrantly violated rights of the person; American constitutionalism must address both sources of faction if republican government was to be legitimate in the United States.

The key for Madison was the representative structure of the federal system, that is, the representation of citizens in the House of Representatives,

[221] See, e.g., Hume, "Of the Original Contract," in *Essays Moral, Political, and Literary,* pp. 452–73.

[222] See, e.g., *Memorial and Remonstrance against Religious Assessments,* Robert A. Rutland and et al., eds., *The Papers of James Madison 1784–1786,* Chicago, pp. 295–306.

[223] *The Federalist,* p. 58.

[224] Ibid.

[225] Ibid., p. 57.

[226] Rutland et al., eds., *Papers of James Madison 1787–1788,* p. 212. Both these points were emphasized by Madison to Jefferson in his letter of October 24, 1787; idem, pp. 209–214. See also Madison's *Vices of the Political System of the United States,* in Robert A. Rutland et al., and *The Papers of James Madison 1786–1787* (Chicago: University of Chicago Press, 1975), vol. 9, pp. 345–61; his addresses to the Constitutional Convention, Farrand, ed., *Records of Federal Convention,* vol. 1, pp. 134–36, 314–22, 421–23.

and of states in the Senate. The representative principle had two relevant effects on mitigating faction.

The first was the point emphasized by Hume in the just-quoted passage from "Idea of a Perfect Commonwealth," namely, that the very fact of representation would "refine the democracy" (selecting a superior quality of national leadership more focused on respect for rights and steady pursuit of the public good), and the representatives would be sufficiently "distant and remote" from those represented as to make them more capable of exercising a reasonable independence free of "intrigue, prejudice, or passion." The American federal system did not, of course, adopt Hume's specific suggestion of dispersed houses of representatives in each state. It instead used his representative principles in ways that effected his general aims, namely, the selection of a natural political aristocracy (in the sense of Adams and Jefferson) sharply separated from those they represent in order to secure the exercise of politically independent judgment about the protection of rights and pursuit of the public good. Such political independence must be contrasted to the quite limited powers of the single-body Congress under the Articles of Confederation, including short terms, rotation, lack of enforcement authority, and effective veto power of any state over needed amendments. In effect, under the Articles, political power remained largely in the states, in which, from the founders' perspective, parochial and insular factions had thrived.[227] The comparatively greater political independence of the new Congress would enable it to take the more impartial stance over issues of justice and the public good that Lockean legitimacy required.

The second point (the largeness of electoral districts) echoed American debates over the state constitutions, namely, what structures of republican constitutionalism would be more likely to select a natural political aristocracy.[228] Two such solutions play a role in the design of the federal constitution—that is, indirect election of the Senate and large electoral districts—the latter of which Madison thought to be of particular importance.[229] In *The Federalist* no. 10, Madison made the latter point in an original way that was close in spirit to

---

[227] For an excellent recent study, see Rakove, *Beginnings of National Politics*. See also Jensen, *Articles of Confederation*.

[228] For illuminating discussion of American views on the constitutional structures (property qualifications, indirect election, larger electoral districts) likely to secure a natural aristocracy, see Morgan, *Inventing the People*, pp. 249–54.

[229] Madison objected, for example, to Jefferson's proposed revision of the Virginia constitution to achieve a more effective senate in such terms. Jefferson would have grouped the countries of the state into larger districts and then have the voters choose an electoral college for each district to make the final choice of its senators. Madison objected that even if a measure were calculated to satisfy the particular interests of every county or district, it would not necessarily be a good thing for the entire state. Rather, Madison thought the best way to make senators direct themselves to the interest of the state as whole was "by making them the choice of the whole Society, each citizen voting for every Senator," that is, election at large. See Madison's *Observations on Jefferson's Draft of a Constitution for Virginia*, in Julian P. Boyd, ed., *The Papers of Thomas Jefferson, 1781–1784* (Princeton, N.J.: Princeton Univ. Press, 1952), p. 309. For Madison, only size could supply the needed wisdom in representative government.

Harrington's deliberative constitutionalism, namely, that the extensive range of territories and heterogeneous peoples represented in the national government would lead to a kind of deliberation based on identifying and pursuing common grounds among such diverse people.[230] Religious faction would, for example, not easily be expressed through law because the American states were so religiously pluralistic: the Congregationalists of Massachusetts, the Quakers of Pennsylvania, the Anglicans of Virginia, the Catholics of Maryland, and so on. Accordingly, representatives, who must seek common grounds of consensus and agreement to form and legislate national policy, would not be able at the national level to indulge the animosities of one group against another. Rather, the representative principle would tend to shape the direction and content of national politics in ways that would break down factionalized insularity, that is, the tendency of political groups to oppress and degrade outsiders to the group. In short, the representative principle would tend to result in democratic politics that treated persons as equals, irrespective of their religious or other affiliation. Madison defined faction as the tendency of groups not to treat others with respect for their rights or the common good, which meant that the representative principle attacked the nerve of faction, because its politics structured power on the terms of justice and the common good, that is, treating persons as equals. In effect, majority rule, when appropriately structured by the federal system, was made consistent with Lockean political legitimacy, and could be constitutionally justified to the people generally on that basis as a resolution of the republican dilemma.

Madison quite properly defended the republican credentials of the American Constitution by sharply contrasting it to what he called "pure Democracy,"[231] by which he meant classical republicanism. Madison certainly shared the views of Montesquieu and Hume on the evils of small participatory republics, that is, their unmitigated tendency to give maximum expression to the knavery of faction. However, he put his criticism in an original way that was consistent with his Lockean beliefs in reserved rights; namely, such participatory republics were "incompatible with personal security or the rights of property."[232] Indeed, the crushing moral homogeneity of such societies was, from the Lockean perspective of respect for the rights of a morally independent conscience, their vice:

> Theoretic politicians, who have patronized this species of government, have erroneously supposed that by reducing mankind to a perfect equality in their political rights, they would at the same time be perfectly equalized in their possessions, their opinions, and their passions.[233]

For Madison, it was the small and homogeneous nature of such participatory republics that gave expression to such ferocious extremes of factionalized

---

[230] *The Federalist*, pp. 63–64.
[231] Ibid., p. 61.
[232] Ibid.
[233] Ibid., pp. 61–62.

politics, a devouring public sphere with no political breathing space for the moral integrity of private conscience and life. This political pathology, for Lockean liberalism, could not be more erosive of the fundamental aims of constitutionalism, in which political power must be held accountable to the independent ethical judgment of free people about the polity's respect for rights and pursuit of the public good. In effect, the structure of political power in such small, homogeneous societies crushed the very possibility of such independent judgment; such was the political power of the group psychology underlying faction that it subverted the very psychological possibility to maintain the independent moral judgment against which the legitimacy of state power must be tested.[234]

In stunning contrast, the very large territory and heterogeneous population of the American republican experiment—the fatal flaws of the Constitution from the anti-Federalist perspective—could enable America to achieve, through judicious use of the representative principle, what never had been achieved before, namely, an enduring republican government free of crippling propensities to faction that is consistent with justice and the public good. In effect, the proper design of the federal system would use American heterogeneity not as a republican vice to be dreaded and deplored (as the anti-Federalists assumed it to be), but as the most benevolent and fertile of republican virtues. The federal system so structured the exercise of the republican right to vote that political power would tend to originate with the identification and mobilization of national coalitions that transcend the parochial insularities of heterogeneous groups.

The power of Congress to regulate commerce was at the heart of this argument because the diversely heterogeneous commercial relationships, which were already characteristic of American life, were understood by the founders—consistent with Montesquieu and Scottish social and economic thoery—to be useful building blocks in the construction of a polity that respected the values they took to be fundamental to republicanism, namely, liberty and equality. Both the wealth and activity of a diverse commercial life made possible the independent exercise of judgment and faculties fundamental to respect for rights; commercial transactions among heterogeneous peoples also supplied incentives to peaceful and reciprocally advantageous relationships on terms of equality. However, these advantages could only be realized if the commercial factions that were so characteristic of America's stage of economic and social growth could be harnessed in service of such republican values, and Madison's argument for the federal system—if it worked in general—worked, *a fortiori,* for congressional regulation of commerce. The representative principle would so structure the exercise of political power that the diverse commercial factions throughout the nation would need to find a common basis for national policy that would treat them on terms of equality, both respecting equal rights and giving equal weight to their

---

[234] Madison had put the point acidly: "Had every Athenian citizen been a Socrates; every Athenian assembly would still have been a mob" (ibid., p. 374).

interests. In short, commerce, which had been distorted to serve parochial and insular state factions under the Articles of Confederation, would be harnessed to the larger emancipatory and egalitarian purposes of republican government.

It was not accidental, therefore, that Madison's argument in *The Federalist* no. 10 gave as its two central examples of faction religious and political sectarianism and "the various and unequal distribution of property."[235] These bases of heterogeneity were among the most important building blocks for the founders' constructivist project, because they saw the representative structure of the federal system as an appropriate way to heighten the liberating force of respect for rights of both conscience and property.[236] For Madison, the enumerated power of the federal government to regulate interstate and international commerce was coherent with its lack of power over religion. State regulation of secular interests like commerce and no regulation of religion are mutually complementary and reinforcing ways of fostering the civilizing bonds of a community that treated persons as both free and equal.

The point may be generalized. The founders of the U.S. Constitution set themselves against a range of arguments offered by anti-Federalists about the importance of homogeneity to republican government, and indeed defined their distinctive conception of constitutionalism by the contrasting view they took that heterogeneity was to be maximally used and even encouraged to the degree that it might constructively advance republican values. In contrast to the anti-Federalists, the founders thus self-consciously thought of representation and the separation of powers not in terms of the balancing of classes (in the way Montesquieu and Hume thought of the balancing of the British constitution), but the more diverse bases of heterogeneity (including religion, kinds of work and property, regional culture, etc.) that they both saw about them and thought might be usefully encouraged in the future.[237] Furthermore, the founders thus incorporated in the Constitution a prohibition on religious qualifications for public office[238] that, like the later religion clauses of the First Amendment, encouraged religious and moral heterogeneity; they drafted the Constitution in a spirit often self-consciously hospitable to immigrants and future immigrants, whom Madison, for example, undoubtedly saw as yet further constitutionally valuable additions to American heterogeneity[239]; they defined commerce not as an issue of properly local concern, but as a matter of

---

[235] Ibid., p. 59.

[236] On the liberating force of capitalist commercial life in early America, see Joyce Appleby, *Capitalism and a New Social Order: The Republican Vision of the 1790s* (New York: New York Univ. Press, 1984).

[237] Hamilton, for example, took objection to the anti-Federalist idea that classes should be actually represented. See, e.g., *The Federalist*, pp. 219–22.

[238] See U.S. Constitution, Article VI.

[239] At the constitutional convention, Madison was particularly notable for his concern for facilitating immigration. See, e.g., Farrand, ed., *Records of Federal Convention*, vol. 2, pp. 236–37, 268–69.

the highest national interest for Congress (not the states) in regulating a diverse commercial life in ways likely to serve republican morality.

The place of federalism among the other structures of American constitutionalism must be framed by the failure of the constitutional convention to adopt the full scope of the proposal originally made as the Virginia plan.[240] That plan had included an explicit congressional power to negative state laws that were inconsistent with its view of the powers of the state under the constitution, and a council of revision (including "the Executive and a convenient number of the National Judiciary"[241]) with a power to negative acts of Congress (including its negative of state laws) and acts of state legislatures that were inconsistent with the council's view of the constitution. In addition, Virginia proponents of the plan (in particular, Madison) assumed that representation in both bodies of the Congress would be in some proportion to population and/or property in each state.[242] The convention adopted neither the federal negative, nor council of revision, and compromised on the issue of proportional representation (i.e., adopting it for the house of representatives and rejecting it for the senate). Madison offered powerful arguments against each of these rejections at the convention,[243] and, in private correspondence to Jefferson, took the view that one of them (failure to adopt the Humean federal negative) was a fundamental defect.[244] Had the convention not rejected these proposals, it is reasonable to believe that the design of the other important constitutional structures (separation of powers and judicial review) would have either been different or differently understood and elaborated over time. Certainly, these other constitutional structures sometimes filled lacunae left by these rejections. Two latter decisions by the convention may exemplify this point. First, the departure from proportional representation in the senate was balanced by the idea of a powerful and independent executive, which had a suspensive veto power over legislation, was not elected by Congress, and had an electoral constituency based on essentially proportional principles.[245] Second, the rejection of the federal negative and council of revision brought the judiciary to the center of attention as an institution that might perform their functions or equivalent functions in the overall constitutional structure,[246] in particular, Madison's central desideratum of the new

[240] The plan was proposed by Randolph of Virginia; see ibid., vol. 1, pp. 18–23.

[241] Ibid., p. 21.

[242] See, e.g., ibid., vol. 1, p. 151; idem, vol. 2, pp. 8–10.

[243] For Madison on the need for a federal negative, see, e.g., ibid., vol. 1, p. 447; on the need for a council of revision, see idem, vol. 2, pp. 74, 77; on proportional representation, see idem, pp. 8–10.

[244] See Rutland, et al., eds., *Papers of James Madison 1787–1788*, pp. 163–64, 209–14.

[245] The Virginia plan had originally proposed "that a National Executive . . . be chosen by the National Legislature," in Farrand, ed., *Records of Federal Convention*, vol. 1, p. 21.

[246] Indeed, argument over the issue of including the judiciary in a council of revision was essentially framed by such a power's erosion of the separation of powers, that is, "the Judges in exercising the function of expositors might be influenced by the part they had taken, in framing the laws" (ibid., vol. 2, p. 75). In effect, the judiciary should not exercise the quasi-legislative powers of a council of revision in order to preserve the integrity of its role as a court judging the constitutionality of laws when those laws are brought before it in a proper judicial proceeding.

constitutionalism, "to secure individuals agst. [sic] encroachments on their rights."[247]

The readiness of leading founders to characterize the originality of the constitution in terms of its uses of the representative principle[248] must be understood in the sense of representation that they used. John Dickinson's summary of the virtues of the Constitution's basic structures is revealing:

> Our government under the proposed constitution, will be guarded by a repetition of the strongest cautions against excesses. In the senate the sovereignties of the several states will be equally represented; in the house of representatives, the people of the whole union will be equally represented; and, in the president, and the federal independent judges, so much concerned in the execution of the laws, and in the determintion of their constitutionality, the sovereignties of the several states and the people of the union may be considered as conjointly represented.[249]

Representation is here of "a reasonable, not a distracted will,"[250] an appeal to the standard of Lockean political legitimacy, "the judgment of the most enlightened among mankind, confirmed by multiplied experiments"[251] about how "government . . . committed to such a number of great departments" best serves respect for our equal inalienable rights and the use of political power for the public good.

It is representation, so understood, that makes sense of Madison's characterization of legislative power as "so many judicial determinations . . . concerning the rights of large bodies of citizens,"[252] and his argument that the federal system (for the reasons already discussed) would enable Congress to make these judgments in a more acceptable—because more impartially just—way. The political framework of his analysis was, of course, Lockean, because the validity of structuring power through representative institutions was assessed in light of morally independent judgments about how those institutions would be more likely justly to adjudicate claims to equal rights under law. The representative nature of the institutions was not only their deputing political judgments from voters to representatives, but their doing so within constitutional structures that best represent the Lockean ideal of free and rational people living in cooperative social, economic, and political community.

---

[247] Rutland et al., eds., *Papers of James Madison 1787–1788*, p. 212. Madison was himself skeptical that the judiciary would or should bear this constitutional responsibility. See, e.g., Madison's *Observations on Jefferson's Draft of a Constitution for Virginia*, in Robert A. Rutland, et al., eds., *The Papers of James Madison 1788–1789*, vol. 11 (Charlottesville: Univ. Press of Virginia, 1977), at p. 293; Madison's letter to Jefferson of October 17, 1788, objecting to a bill of rights, idem, at pp. 297–300.

[248] James Wilson was, besides Madison, another notable exponent of this view. See, e.g., Jensen, ed., *Documentary History*, pp. 343–44.

[249] Dickinson, *Letters of Fabius*, p. 184.

[250] Ibid.

[251] Ibid., p. 182.

[252] *The Federalist*, p. 59.

Separation of Powers

The American constitutional doctrine of separation of powers was importantly prefigured by Locke's distinctions among legislative, executive, and
federative powers.[253] Locke's formulation of the doctrine did not draw the
American distinctions; the executive power included for him the judicial
power, and the federative power was over foreign policy, which American
constitutionalism considered an executive power. However, the important
point, for American purposes, was not Locke's particular way of formulating
the doctrine (Americans looked for specifics to Montesquieu, not Locke[254]),
but his political and constitutional motivations for drawing a doctrine of this
kind, which answered to the distinctive demands he imposed on the legitimacy
of any political power at all. The Lockean American constitutionalists found
these demands compelling, and their attraction to Montesquieu's more contemporary formulation of the doctrine rested on these demands.

Locke's theory of political legitimacy depended, as we saw earlier, on the
equal and inalienable rights of all persons and the reasonable capacities of
persons to know and implement those rights as self-governing creative and
ethically accountable agents. The question of political legitimacy thus had for
Locke both critical and constructive components. First, no form of political
power could be legitimate if it rested on the systematic deprivation of the
reasonable freedom of the person to know and implement these rights as self-
governing agents; therefore, Locke was accordingly profoundly critical of the
forms of sectarian religious, moral, and political authority that had historically
stunted and stultified these capacities by asserting an illegitimate political
power over conscience and thus politically legitimated arbitrary structures of
power, hierarchy, and privilege. Second, however, a state could serve a politically legitimate function if it were so constitutionally arranged that it not only
respected rights but also more justly enforced those rights than would otherwise be possible. In a state of nature (lacking any such political institutions),
each person would have "*the Executive Power* of the Law of Nature,"[255] that
is, the right to enforce respect for equal rights by other persons. However, the
consequence would be that people would be "Judges in their own Cases," and
"that Self-love will make Men partial to themselves and their Friends."[256] If
each person was thus legislature, executive, judge, jury, and executioner in his
own case or the case of his clan, justice would not be done, and respect for
rights flouted, not secured. Government might have a politically legitimate
role if it secured equal respect for such rights better than a state of nature.

Locke's constitutionalism arose as a way of bridging the gap from illegitimate to legitimate political power. He proposed the political principle of

---

[253] See Locke, *Second Treatise of Government*, pp. 382–84 (secs. 143–48).

[254] For two admirable studies of the history of the idea of separation of powers, see W.B.
Gwyn, *The Meaning of the Separation of Powers* (The Hague: Martinus Nijhoff, 1965); M.J.C.
Vile, *Constitutionalism and the Separation of Powers* (Oxford: Clarendon Press, 1967).

[255] Locke, *Second Treatise of Government*, p. 293 (sec. 13).

[256] Ibid.

toleration as a substantive constitutional constraint on the legitimacy of political power, because it protected against the political enforcement of a sectarian irrationalism that subverted the very possibility of reasonable government respectful of rights. The separation of powers appeared to Locke as a natural constitutional structure for the exercise of political power that would more justly enforce equal rights than a state of nature, and be politically legitimate on that basis. Locke gave particular importance to a constitutional structure that separated legislative and executive powers, because he thought of legislation, as Madison did later, as a kind of collective judgment and definition of the rights in general of all persons, and the executive power as the fair application of these general rights to particular disputes. In effect, all politically legitimate power was understood on a judicial model of impartial judgments about rights either abstractly or in some specific case; the aim of constitutional government was to structure political institutions with the requisite powers and independence to make such judgments and thus fairly respect the equal rights of free people. In contrast, the failure to observe such independent spheres of political responsibility unleashed the corruptibilities of unaccountable and illimitable political power, which Locke equated with "Slavery."[257] Locke's negative exemplar was an absolute monarch, because

> he being suppos'd to have all, both Legislative and Executive Power in himself alone, there is no Judge to be found, no Appeal lies open to any one, who may fairly . . . decide, and from whose decision relief and redress may be expected of any Injury . . . suffered from the Prince or by his Order . . . .[258]

Politically legitimate power must, for Locke, be power subject to morally independent judgment about its respect for rights and pursuit of the public good. His constitutional doctrine, prefiguring the American conception of separation of powers, expressed this normative demand.

The constitutionalism of Montesquieu, like Hume's, did not give central play to rights (alienable or inalienable),[259] and Montesquieu—an advocate (like Hume[260]) of the constitutional uses of hereditary classes—was certainly no republican. However, his constitutionalism rested on a hatred of absolutism and a passionate quest to limit its terrors that Americans shared and from which they learned; moreover, his criticisms and conception of classical republicanism stung Americans, like Madison, to rethink their republican experiment. Mon-

---

[257] Ibid., p. 402 (sec. 174).

[258] Ibid., p. 344 (sec. 91).

[259] See, e.g., Shklar, *Montesquieu*, p. 86 ("Montesquieu never mentioned rights, natural or artificial").

[260] Hume defended the principle of hereditary monarchy, though not the principle of a hereditary aristocracy. See James Moore, "Hume's Political Science and the Classical Republican Tradition," 10 *Can. J. Pol. Sci.* 809 (1977), at p. 819. On Hume's defense of the security of property and person under law as the central values of constitutional government, see Forbes, *Hume's Philosophical Politics*, pp. 165–67.

tesquieu described his ultimate value, "political liberty,"[261] unpretentiously as "a tranquillity of mind arising from the opinion each person has of his safety,"[262] and his motivating concern was about the crippling and debilitating "consequences of intense, systematic, and protracted fear, and those who spread it,"[263] in particular, those with the untrammeled political power thus to blight the human condition. Montesquieu's *The Persian Letters* brilliantly outlined the corruptions of Asiatic despotism on both the despot and those who were tyrannized; his implicit subject of study was the absolutism of Louis XIV,[264] and his analysis remarkably prefigured Arendt's piercing portrait of the ravages of the politics of fear and domination of twentieth-century totalitarianism.[265] Montesquieu intended his constitutional thought to offer alternative political ideas for a large nation-state like France that—consistent with contemporary circumstances—might enable it to respect political liberty. His proposed model for such an alternative was the British constitution.

Montesquieu's idealization of the British constitution was grounded on the way in which the British government used both a balanced constitution of classes (commons, lords, and monarchy) and a separation of functional powers (legislative, executive, and judicial) as institutional devices that limited and interconnected political interests in ways that realized a just public liberty and the common good in a commercial society.[266] Such an allocation of political powers enabled political liberty to flourish among a commercial people throughout the British Empire without the militaristic imperialism of the Roman Empire or the French monarchy.[267] In contrast to Locke, Montesquieu not only isolated the judiciary as a politically independent power, but also regarded its absolute independence as the key to liberty. The judicial power naturally took center stage in a constitutional scheme preoccupied by protecting the value of personal security, because the judiciary possessed the most terrible powers over the lives of individual citizens (e.g., imposition of the death penalty and the infliction of torture). Accordingly, the judicial power must be exercised almost invisibly as an impersonal office free from fearful personal caprice; people should, for example, be judged by their peers and have some option over their judges; juries should be chosen by lot.[268] Montesquieu thought of such powers as "next to nothing,"[269] "the mouth that pronounces the words of the law, mere passive beings, incapable of moderat-

---

[261] Montesquieu, *Spirit of the Laws*, vol. 1, p. 151.

[262] Ibid.

[263] Shklar, *Montesquieu*, p. 41; see also idem, pp. 46, 83–85.

[264] See Montesquieu, *The Persian Letters*, J. Robert Loy, trans. (New York: Meridian, 1961). For commentary, see Shklar, *Montesquieu*, pp. 29–48.

[265] See, e.g., Hannah Arendt, *The Origins of Totalitarianism* (New York: Harcourt Brace Jovanovich, 1973).

[266] See Montesquieu, *Spirit of the Laws*, vol. 1, pp. 151–62. For pertinent commentary, see Shklar, *Montesquieu*, pp. 85–89.

[267] See Shklar, *Montesquieu*, pp. 53–54, 106–9.

[268] For pertinent commentary on these points, see Shklar, *Montesquieu*, pp. 88–89.

[269] Montesquieu, *Spirit of the Laws*, vol. 1, p. 156.

ing either its force or rigor."[270] However, he clearly insisted that it be independent, called it "the masterpiece of legislation to know where to place properly the judiciary power,"[271] and associated its constitutional uses with the revival of the moribund powers of the French hereditary classes in the *parlements* to check the political excesses of monarchical absolutism.[272]

Montesquieu's constitutionalism naturally brigaded hereditary classes and functional powers, but the egalitarian conditions of the social life of Americans, their republican principles, and the historical memory of their constitutional controversies over the oppressions of the British constitution made the British model of a class-balanced constitution unacceptable. Americans may have tolerated a unicameral Congress that combined legislative, executive, and judicial powers when the Congress had little power over individuals[273]; however, once they decided that the new constitution, in contrast to the Articles of Confederation, had to accord to the national government substantial governing powers (including coercion) over the lives of individuals, their Lockean constitutionalism required that these new political powers be structured in terms of constitutionally independent functions that would assure a more just enforcement of rights of individuals both in the abstract and in concrete cases. Montesquieu's constitutional doctrine of the separation of powers naturally appealed to them; however, American republicanism rejected his correlative use of hereditary classes. They had to separate Montesquieu's theory of separation of powers from its association with the class-balanced constitution. American constitutionalists had to innovate alternative constitutional structures to guarantee the requisite spheres of politically independent judgment that their Lockean principles required. Americans, in short, experienced in Montesquieu's endorsement of the British constitution yet another challenge to their innovative quest for both republicanism and constitutionalism, and a corresponding need to think through their long-standing critical objections to the British constitution as a model for Lockean constitutionalism.

John Adams's Massachusetts constitution of 1780 offered the founders a model for an independent executive and bicameral legislature that, on the basis of a critical analysis of the virtues and vices of the British constitution, appealed to both their republican and constitutional aspirations. Montesquieu's interpretation of the British constitution had emphasized the role of the hereditary nobility as a check on the monarch; however, Adams, like De Lolme,[274] believed that the constitutional strength of the British constitution came from a strong executive serving as a needed check against the ambitions

---

[270] Ibid., p. 159.

[271] Ibid., p. 165.

[272] See, for pertinent commentary on these points, Shklar, *Montesquieu*, pp. 4, 79–80, 81–82, 88–89, 113.

[273] On the judicial powers of the continental congress, see, e.g., Richard B. Morris, *The Forging of the Union 1781–1789* (New York: Harper & Row, 1987), pp. 67–68. See, in general, Rakove, *Beginnings of National Politics;* Jensen, *Articles of Confederation.*

[274] See, e.g., De Lolme, *Constitution of England,* pp. 408–11.

of an otherwise dominant aristocracy.[275] Accordingly, Adams had created for Massachusetts the strongest executive among the state constitutions, elected by the people independent of the bicameral legislature and with a suspensive veto (Adams had preferred an absolute veto).[276] Adams's constitutional theory, elaborated at length in his *Defence of the Constitutions of Government,* was that—consistent with the political psychology of fame and a reasonable political science of comparative constitutions—such political independence should be attractive to Lockean constitutionalists as a reasonable way to give the executive the incentives to perform executive functions justly and to resist the ambitions of political leaders in other branches of government that would otherwise corrupt republicanism into aristocracy[277] (on the same grounds, Adams also defended an upper house[278]).

Adams' proposal rested on the kind of critical analysis of the British constitution that one would expect of a leading figure in the prerevolutionary debates over the British constitution, and he took pride in his winnowing of the gold from the dross of British constitutionalism and yet preserving American republican principles: "In America, there are different orders of *offices,* but none of *men.* Out of office, all men are of the same species, and of one blood; there is neither a greater nor a lesser nobility."[279] Adams thus disjoined the separation of powers from the class-balanced constitution, combining republicanism and constitutionalism in answer to Montesquieu. The founders found his institutional innovation in Massachusetts of a strong republican executive and bicameral legislature to be a constitutionally reasonable way of both according political independence to the national executive from the legislative power and better securing the Harringtonian deliberativeness of the legislative power[280]—consistent with both their republicanism and the Lockean motivations of the doctrine of the separation of powers.[281] However, there remained Montesquieu's greatest challenge: "the masterpiece of legislation," and "where to place properly the judiciary power."[282] American consti-

---

[275] On De Lolme and Adams, see R.R. Palmer, *Age of Democratic Revolution,* vol. 1, pp. 145–48.

[276] See Palmer, *Age of Democratic Revolution,* vol. 1, p. 225.

[277] See, e.g., John Adams, *A Defence,* in C.F. Adams, *Works of John Adams,* vol. 4, p. 585; idem, vol. 6, pp. 171–72.

[278] See, e.g., ibid., vol. 6, p. 44.

[279] John Adams, *A Defence,* p. 380.

[280] Adams had suggested bicameralism as early as his 1776 *Thoughts on Government* as a way of securing the kind of deliberative legislative process embodied in Harrington's division of the legislative power between a body that proposes and another that decides. See C.F. Adams, ed., *Works of John Adams,* vol. 4, pp. 193–209; Morgan, *Inventing the People,* p. 248. Indirect election of the Senate was an idea suggested to the founders (as one of the ways of securing a natural aristocracy) by the Maryland state constitution. See *Federalist Papers,* pp. 429–30; Morgan, *Inventing the People,* p. 250.

[281] On the impact of the Massachusetts executive on the thinking of the founders, see *The Federalist,* pp. 327–28, 464, 499. A reference to "the ablest adepts in political science," idem, p. 445, is probably to Adams himself. See also idem, p. 472.

[282] Montesquieu, *Spirit of the Laws,* vol. 1, p. 165.

tutionalists in this case faced a dilemma, posed by an important lapse in Madison's defense of the separation of powers.

When Madison defended the American doctrine of the separation of powers against anti-Federalist criticisms in *The Federalist* no. 47, he argued that the distinctions among powers and personnel in Articles I, II, and III of the U.S. Constitution were as much in line with Montesquieu's theory and ideals as those embodied in Montesquieu's idealized model, the British constitution. Madison characterized the evil that Montesquieu's theory combatted as "tyranny," defined as "the accumulation of all powers, legislative, executive, and judiciary, in the same hands,"[283] in which the same person was legislator, prosecutor, and judge. The background ideal was equal rights before law: "Where the *whole* power of one department is exercised by the same hands which possess the *whole* power of another department, the fundamental principles of a free constitution are subverted."[284] The U.S. Constitution as much embodied this ideal as the British constitution, and thus Montesquieu could not be invoked in criticism of the work of the founders.

Madison was, of course, quite right on the narrow point he chose to address, but he did not discuss Montesquieu's crucial linkage of separation of powers to the class-balanced constitution based on his fear that a classless society would undermine the institutional constraints of the separation of powers through the domination of a single popular faction.[285] Montesquieu would thus naturally have objected to the argument of *The Federalist* no. 10 that, although such a well-designed federal system might limit the expression of certain factions through law, it would provide no defense against superfactions that united persons in many states in a common unreasoning hatred or prejudice against outsiders to their faction. Montesquieu's constitutional fears were not idle. Christians might, for example, enjoy sufficient solidarity not to oppress one another, but quite enough to oppress Jews or atheists; whites might leave one another alone, but there is always racial hatred of blacks, the prejudice Madison himself termed at the constitutional convention as "the mere distinction of colour . . . , a ground of the most oppressive dominion ever exercised by man over man."[286] Montesquieu's constitutionalism—conjoining the separation of powers with balancing hereditary and nonhereditary classes—supposed that only such a linkage would supply a sufficiently strong social basis for a politically independent judiciary that was capable of standing against the ferocity of mass populist factions, the corruptive demon, as Madison saw, of republican rule. Because Madison acknowledged that both the rule of law and various reserved rights of the person were fundamental to the Lockean legitimacy of government, American constitutionalism (in particular, its form of the separation of powers) was inadequate to its ends.

---

[283] *The Federalist*, p. 324.
[284] Ibid., pp. 325–26.
[285] See Pangle, *Montesquieu's Philosophy of Liberalism*, pp. 129–30.
[286] Farrand, ed., *Records of Federal Convention*, vol. 1, p. 135.

Judicial Review

No founder had a more acute sense of this constitutional inadequacy than James Madison, who wrote to Jefferson near the end of the convention: "The *plan should it be adopted* will neither effectually *answer its national object* nor prevent the local *mischiefs* which every where *excite disgusts* agst. [sic] the *state governments.*"[287] Madison's despair, as he explained in his later October 24, 1787 letter to Jefferson, was over the failure of the convention to adopt the Humean federal negative, which he thought indispensable to securing sufficient constitutional power in the national government both to define and to protect its own powers against the states and "to secure individuals agst. [sic] encroachments on their rights" by the states.[288]

The proposed constitutional structures could not for Madison serve these ends, in particular, the protection of rights the violation of which "contributed more to that uneasiness which produced the Convention, and prepared the public mind for a general reform"[289] than any other source. Certainly, Madison understood that the rejection by the convention of both the federal negative and the council of revision left the judiciary available to serve some of these functions, because he had himself observed that "a law violating a constitution established by the people themselves, would be considered by the Judges as null & void."[290] However, at this stage of his political thought,[291] Madison appears to have entertained republican doubts that such final judicial power could extend over congressional legislation,[292] and he certainly believed, as to judicial review of state legislation, it would come too late, frequently not be invoked, and often be disobeyed.[293] None of the founders believed more deeply that American constitutionalism rested on its protection of rights than Madison, and he conceived the construction of the federal system as giving Congress—through exercise of the federal negative—a judi-

[287] Rutland et al., eds., *Papers of James Madison 1787–1788*, pp. 163–94.

[288] Ibid., p. 212.

[289] Ibid.

[290] Farrand, ed., *Records of Federal Convention*, vol. 2, p. 93.

[291] Madison later came to accept this principle. See Editorial Note, *Observations on Jefferson's Draft of a Constitution for Virginia*, in Rutland et al., *Papers of James Madison 1788–1789*, at p. 285.

[292] Madison had written, for example, in 1788 to give his constitutional advice to framers of a state constitution for Kentucky, and had observed (commenting on Jefferson's 1783 draft constitution for Virginia with its proposal for a council of revision):

> It sd. [sic] not be allowed the Judges or the Ex [executive] to pronounce a law thus enacted [i.e., after both houses repass the legislation by supermajorities after a state election called in response to constitutional objection to a law by either the judiciary or the executive], unconstitul. [sic] & invalid.
>
> In the State Constitutions & indeed in the Fedl. [sic] one also, no provision is made for the case of a disagreement in expounding them; and as the Courts are generally the last in making their decision, it results to them by refusing or not refusing to execute a law, to stamp it with its final character. This makes the Judiciary Dept paramount in fact to the Legislature, which was never intended, and can never be proper.

Ibid., p. 293.

[293] See Rutland, et al., eds., *Papers of James Madison 1787–1788*, p. 211.

cial power and role in enforcing these rights over the states. A political body, thus designed, could both protect rights and advance the public good. In contrast, his own experience had been, as he put it to Jefferson in their debate over bills of rights, that, the judiciary notwithstanding, "repeated violations of these parchment barriers have been committed by overbearing majorities in every State."[294] If Jefferson would appeal in response to the judiciary "which if rendered independent, & kept strictly to their own department merits great confidence for their learning & integrity,"[295] then that was a conception of the judicial power that Madison could not yet trust.

It is true that the question whether courts had or should have such a power had arisen in a few state courts,[296] that no less a figure than Alexander Hamilton had defended such a power in both the New York courts and his *Phocion* letters,[297] and that James Iredell (later a justice of the Supreme Court of the United States) had argued in North Carolina that such a power was fundamental to the role of the judiciary under the new American constitution.[298] However, Madison's skepticism rested not only on his distrust of an institution still largely untried, but also on the absence of such an institution in any of the political theory and science of the age. If Americans were to adopt and successfully use such an institution, then it would be their most remarkable institutional reworking and rethinking of the political wisdom of the age.

Put simply, the American doctrine of the separation of powers contained an ingredient not found in either Locke, Montesquieu, or Hume, namely, the supreme power of judicial review on grounds of constitutionality. Locke had not even identified the judiciary as an independent power of government. Montesquieu innovated the identification of the power and gave it a prominent place in his constitutionalism. He moved the American founders by his challenge when he wrote: "it is the masterpiece of legislation to know where to place properly the judiciary power"[299]; however, he thought of the power as "next to nothing,"[300] precisely the passive interpreter of legislative will that the American constitutional rejection of legislative supremacy could not stomach. Furthermore, Hume, in his "Idea of a Perfect Commonwealth," had articulated a number of ways of initiating the impeachment and removal of elected officials—including a court of competitors consisting of all defeated candidates for the senate—to the degree "that politicians in Hume's perfect commonwealth would have little time for any other aspect of public business

---

[294] Ibid., vol. 11, at p. 297.

[295] Charles F. Hobson et al., eds., *The Papers of James Madison 1789–1790,* vol. 12 (Charlottesville: Univ. Press of Virginia, 1979), p. 13.

[296] See Julius Goebel, Jr., *History of the Supreme Court of the United States: Antecedents and Beginnings to 1801,* vol. 1 (New York: Macmillan, 1971), pp. 125–42.

[297] See, e.g., Morris, *Forging of the Union 1781–1789,* pp. 126–28. For Hamilton's *Letters from Phocion,* see Harold C. Syrett and Jacob E. Cooke, eds., *The Papers of Alexander Hamilton 1782–1786* vol. 3 (New York: Columbia Univ. Press, 1962) pp. 483–97, 530–58.

[298] See James Iredell's *To the Public,* in Griffith J. McRee, *Life and Correspondence of James Iredell* (New York: D. Appleton, 1857), pp. 145–49. See also idem, pp. 172–76.

[299] Montesquieu, *Spirit of the Laws,* vol. 1, p. 165.

[300] Ibid., p. 156.

than these indictments and trials of their fellow politicians."[301] However, he did not articulate the idea of judicial review per se.

American constitutionalists were, as we have seen, committed to a Lockean political theory that motivated their institutional innovation of the American doctrine of separation of powers. The constitutional doctrine of separation of powers structured the exercise of politically independent judgment about the issues of equal justice and the public good that are essential to the very legitimacy of political power, and Americans followed Montesquieu's trichotomy (i.e., legislative, executive, and judicial) because it expressed the requisite kind of independence in making more impartial judgments about what the law should be, how it was to be enforced, and how it was to be applied in disputes. However, legitimate political power was, for Americans inspired by Locke, essentially a kind of judicial power, a judgment about our equal inalienable rights, and the reasonable use of power to advance human interests equally; furthermore, their constitutional thought naturally gravitated to a new conception of the judicial power that would constitutionally entrench the supremacy of such judgment, for, as Hamilton put the point in *The Federalist,* "without this, all the reservations of particular rights or privileges would amount to nothing."[302]

Madison had, of course, believed that the representative structure of the federal system would both yield such a quality of natural aristocrat and impose such political incentives to egalitarian consensus that it would suffice to accomplish these ends. However, even Hamilton, after hearing Madison's defense of both these points at the convention, remained skeptical:

> Answer—There is truth in both these principles but they do not conclude so strongly as he supposes—
> —The Assembly when chosen will meet in one room if they are drawn from half the globe—& will be liable to all the passions of popular assemblies . . . .
> Paper money is capable of giving a general impulse. It is easy to conceive a popular sentiment pervading the E states—[303]

Nothing in Madison's constitutionalism could answer Montesquieu's fears of superfactions that might, if anything, flourish in a politically decadent mass democratic culture (one form of the Machiavellian republican corruption the founders anticipated) for whom the mere fact of being in a majority sufficed for virtue and being in a minority sufficed for vice. In short, the representative structure of the federal system—even if Madison's full conception had prevailed—would have been fundamentally incomplete, leaving at hazard precisely the inalienable rights of minorities that *most* require protection.

This issue was sharply posed for the founders when they disjoined Montesquieu's theory of the separation of powers from his class-balanced constitu-

---

[301] James Moore, "Hume's Political Science and the Classical Republican Tradition," 10 *Can. J. Pol. Sci.* 809 (1977), p. 837.
[302] *The Federalist,* p. 524.
[303] Farrand, ed., *Records of Federal Convention,* vol. 1, pp. 146–47.

tion. Montesquieu had thought of an hereditary nobility (of which he was himself a member[304]) as the natural social basis for the kind of judicial independence that his constitutionalism required. American republicanism had rejected this idea, but it needed something like this conception—not merely to apply legislation impartially (as in Montesquieu's judiciary), but to keep the entire constitutional structure accountable to the inalienable human rights that were fundamental to the Lockean legitimacy of any exercise of political power.

The institutional lacuna, which Hamilton sensed in Madison's federalism, was naturally filled by a conception of judicial accountability well beyond Hume's complex scheme of judicial trials for impeachment, namely, the strengthened conception of both constitutionally mandated judicial independence and the role that Hamilton defended in *The Federalist* no. 78 as a kind of counterpoise to Madison's federalism, "an excellent barrier to the encroachments and oppressions of the representative body of the minor party in the community."[305] That institution was a natural expression of American Lockean constitutionalism because it rested on no antirepublican hereditary principle, vindicated the distinctive normative status in American constitutionalism of textually reserved rights, and supplied the kind of institutional independence (a life tenure unique among federal officials) and supremacy that might resist the populist superfactions that the analytical political psychology of the founders gave them every reason realistically to fear. The role of a class-balanced constitution in Montesquieu and Hume—namely, as an independent basis for resistance to political abuses—was thus naturally filled by the weightier American conception of judicial review.

From this perspective, the American constitutional tradition may ironically have remained closer to the spirit of Montesquieu's constitutionalism than the French democratic tradition with its recurrent romance with classical republicanism (Rousseau) and its traditional rejection of American-style judicial review.[306] Montesquieu argued for a hereditary principle as part of the constitutional balance on the instrumental basis that this principle best afforded a kind of intermediating body between monarchical despotism and democratic factions. The U.S. Constitution creatively adapted this argument to American circumstances practically and ideologically incapable of accepting the constitutional principle of hereditary classes—in this case replacing the intermediating role of independent classes with an independent judiciary. This is an argument Montesquieu did not make, but would, unlike Rousseau, have understood.

It is also an argument at least spiritually in line with Hume's philosophical politics, that is, the search for a moderate impartiality of "new power and subtlety, reinforced by experimental philosophy used as political hygiene"[307]

---

[304] See Shklar, *Montesquieu*, pp. 2–4.
[305] *The Federalist*, pp. 522–27.
[306] See, in general, Vile, *Constitutionalism and the Separation of Powers*, pp. 176–211, 239–62.
[307] Forbes, *Hume's Philosophical Politics*, p. 219.

and his corresponding emphasis that legitimate politics ensure judicial independence in dispensing justice.[308] The arguments used in the making of the American Constitution are politically remarkable expressions of this spirit albeit in service of a Lockean theory of political legitimacy that Hume rejected. Hume did not make the argument for judicial review, but instead depended on a complex scheme of competitive impeachments to contain power in his representative republic, a competitive balance likely to ensure some measure of effective political impartiality. However, Hamilton's argument for judicial review was very much in the spirit of Hume's philosophical politics, only in this case in service not of utilitarian impersonality but of Lockean political reasonableness. If Hume's deep understanding of faction in politics led him to cultivate a philosophical approach to politics and the history often used in politics, then he must have hoped that his approach could internally moderate the malign force of faction in politics, through either raising the quality of political debate in Britain or enabling fortunate legislators "in some distant part of the world"[309] to design constitutions better to secure such effective impartiality. The American founders acted very much in this spirit, creating judicial review as the required institutional commitment of a classless constitution to effective guarantees of an independent impartiality over the interpretation of the Constitution itself, by bringing a kind of appeal to principle to bear on often factionalized disputes over the meaning of a written constitution that was intended to endure for ages to come, by a fair-minded reading of constitutional history, and by a voice and vision not factionally interested (see Chapter 4). This is an argument Hume did not make, but would have understood.

The American founders critically used and creatively transformed the arguments of political theory and political science that they brought to their historic task. Judicial review, for example, was an innovation that was responsive to peculiar American political convictions (textual guarantees of reserved rights) and a natural elaboration to such ends of the appeal of Montesquieu and Hume for independently grounded intermediating institutions. The founders thus synthesized a Lockean theory of political legitimacy and the institutional recommendations of Montesquieu and Hume, which was grounded in history, observation, and even utopian imagination. They saw these influences as mutually reinforcing, not as dichotomous alternatives. Above all, they exercised considerable ingenuity and originality in the way they created from disparate and jarring sources the philosophical praxis of American constitutionalism: committed at once to republican self-rule, to reserved inalienable rights of the person, to a commercial life of national common markets regulated by the national government, and to a separation of powers culminating in the Lockean supremacy of judicial impartiality.

---

[308] See James Moore, "Hume's Political Science," p. 838.
[309] David Hume, "Idea of a Perfect Commonwealth," p. 500.

4

Interpreting the Founders over Time

Both the founders' extended uses of past history (Chapter 2) and their sense of their own role in history (Chapter 3) lay the foundation for the inquiry into how to interpret their work over time, to which we must now turn. We need to understand the interpretive commitment to American constitutionalism that both we and the founders share, and, on that basis, to inquire into constitutional interpretation over time (e.g., the interpretation of federalism over time). This chapter will examine both issues and establish an interpretive methodology that will be further elaborated in later chapters.

Interpretation of a Lockean Constitution for Posterity

The founders' project, as we have seen, was to construct structures for the exercise of political power that would give the best interpretation to the constitutionalism for which they had fought a revolution. That interpretive project centered on the authority of a certain kind of written constitution, which achieved in America what had never been attained elsewhere, namely, an enduring republican constitutionalism in a large territory with a heterogeneous and commercial people who were committed to a Lockean theory of political legitimacy. Past political experience was, as Wilson saw, often "the result of force, fraud, or accident"[1]; in contrast, the American opportunity was precisely its freedom, its theoretical clarity and fidelity to fact, and its exercise of collective deliberative choice. At the constitutional convention, Madison framed the issue as "a people deliberating in a temperate moment, and with the experience of other nations before them, on the plan of Govt. most likely to secure their happiness," the "ends" of which "were first to protect the people agst. their rulers: secondly, to protect [the people] agst. the transient impressions into which they themselves might be led."[2]

   The authority of the Constitution, for both the founders and the people,

[1] Merrill Jensen, ed., *The Documentary History of the Ratification of the Constitution*, vol. 2 (Madison: State Historical Society of Wisconsin, 1976), p. 342.
[2] Max Farrand, ed., *Records of the Federal Convention*, vol. 1 (New Haven, Conn.: Yale Univ. Press, 1966), p. 421.

rested on a complex deliberative judgment about the permanent nature of political power, about the inalienable rights of human nature in terms of which the legitimacy of all power must be tested, and about the enduring structures for the exercise of political power that might best harness it to its legitimate ends. That judgment was, of course, made by the American generation of 1787–1788, but its deliberative power and scope, as we have seen, did not extend to themselves alone. The deliberation about constitutionalism that preceded and fired the revolution and then drove their early constitutional experiments ultimately led to a judgment over a Harringtonian interpretation of constitutionalism, and they proclaimed that judgment unequivocally: this constitution would "secure the blessings of liberty to ourselves and our posterity."[3] Certainly, the founders anticipated the need for amendments, but, in fact, amendment has been remarkably infrequent, often itself a clarification of the design (e.g., the Bill of Rights), or a removal of defects that were anticipated by founders themselves.[4] Furthermore, the amendment procedure of the Constitution[5] requires extensive deliberation and approval in order to preserve the founders' sense of a long-enduring constitution that is not easily revised by each generation, a conception, as we saw earlier, that Madison had defended in such terms in *The Federalist* no. 49 against Jefferson's idea of a more easily amendable written constitution.

Madison had argued that the framer's conception of a written constitution had authority precisely because it did not result from the routine democratic politics in which competitors for political power brought to all disputes their factionalized perceptions of principle and policy. Rather, Americans in 1787–1788 had brought to constitutional design the uses of history, political theory, and political science, as well as of political experience under the failed British constitution and their early state and federal constitutional experiments. In particular, they had reached a mature and sober understanding of the corruptibilities of all forms of power (i.e., religious, moral, and political), and the ways in which in human history such power had entrenched arbitrary structures of hierarchy and privilege the acceptance of which rested on stunting the

---

[3] Preamble, U.S. Constitution.

[4] For example, Madison had always preferred a general power in the federal government to negative state laws inconsistent with human rights, and argued, in the debates over the Bill of Rights, for a guarantee of religious liberty and free speech that extended to both the states and the federal government. Madison thus originally proposed to the House of Representatives the following amendment to the 1787 constitution: "No state shall violate the equal rights of conscience, or the freedom of the press, or the trial by jury in criminal cases," Leonard Levy, *Judgments* (Chicago: Quadrangle, 1972), p. 179. Moreover, he knew, as did many founders, that the institution of slavery in southern states obscenely violated the republican principle of equal liberty of person. See, e.g., Farrand, ed., *Records of Federal Convention,* vol. 1, p. 135 ("the most oppressive dominion ever exercised by man over man"); idem, vol. 2, p. 414 (mention of the slave trade "will be more dishonorable to the National character than to say nothing about it in the Constitution"). The founders' sense of basic flaws in the Constitution was later confirmed, and—in the wake of the Civil War—many of them were expressly addressed by the Reconstruction amendments.

[5] See U.S. Constitution, Article V.

capacities of persons to know and to claim the inalienable rights of human nature and the spheres of self-government that such rights protect. American constitutionalism was thus proclaimed by the founders to be an experiment because, on their view of the abuses of political power that largely composed human history to date, experimentation in new structures of political power was required if they were to respond adequately to a challenge that, in Madison's fateful words to the convention, "wd. decide forever the fate of Republican Govt."[6]

Madison had spoken at the convention not only of the protection of the people against their rulers, but also "agst. the transient impressions into which they themselves might be led,"[7] and his argument in *The Federalist* no. 49 amplified this concern to encompass posterity. If later generations of Americans were "a nation of philosophers,"[8] then they might appreciate the deliberative judgment of legitimacy on which the authority of the Constitution rested. However, the founders' achievement for themselves and their posterity could not reasonably be put to such a risk because "a nation of philosophers is as little to be expected as the philosophical race of kings wished for by Plato."[9] The people under American constitutionalism would be as much subject to faction as any other, perhaps more so in view of its protections of liberty: "liberty is to faction, what air is to fire."[10] That constitution could have the continuing authority it deserved only if the deliberative judgment of its founders was accorded the weight of history and tradition: "that veneration, which time bestows on everything, and without which perhaps the wisest and freest governments would not possess the requisite stability."[11]

However, history and tradition must themselves be interpreted by later generations, and their interpretive processes would, as Madison, Dickinson, and others (including anti-Federalists[12]) so clearly saw, be absorbed by study of the founders. We need to understand—consistent with the premises of Lockean political legitimacy that motivated the Constitution—how such interpretation should be understood. Two founders, James Madison and James Wilson, addressed this issue in ways that merit attention here. Madison was concerned with the kind of legitimacy to which an enduring constitution must make claim; Wilson, as a justice of the Supreme Court of the United States, suggested how such claims of legitimacy must shape the interpretive practice of the supreme constitution over time. America's Lockean constitution for posterity must—consistent with the legitimacy of its ratification—be interpreted over time to justify only those exercises of political power that can be

---

[6] Farrand, ed., *Records of Federal Convention*, vol. 1, p. 423.

[7] Ibid., p. 421.

[8] *The Federalist*, p. 340.

[9] Ibid.

[10] Ibid., p. 58.

[11] Ibid., p. 340.

[12] See, e.g., William Symmes, *Speech in Massachusetts Convention*, in Herbert J. Storing, ed., *The Complete Anti-Federalist*, vol. 4 (Chicago: Univ. of Chicago Press, 1981), p. 64; *Letters of Agrippa*, in idem, p. 114.

justified to the people of each generation in the same way that it was justified at its ratification.

Madison had been compelled to address the issue of the amendability of a written constitution during a correspondence with Jefferson that carried to new depths their earlier disagreement. Jefferson, who represented America in France, had become absorbed in discussions among French reformers about whether the ancient debts of the French monarchy should be valid against the new constitutional order then in process of formation,[13] and he took the occasion of a brief illness to write Madison an unusually philosophical letter dated September 6, 1789 about what he took to be the "self evident" principle governing these matters, namely, " *'that the earth belongs in usufruct to the living'*: that the dead have neither powers nor rights over it."[14] Every generation, speaking through a majority, had, according to this view, a natural right to start anew on a clean slate unencumbered by the obligations of a previous generation. On the basis of Jefferson's actuarial calculations of the length of lives of a majority of people at that time aged twenty-one, nineteen years would be "the term beyond which neither the representatives of a nation, nor even the whole nation assembled, can validly extend a debt."[15] Jefferson's preoccupation was the scope of obligation of old national debts, but he generalized the principle memorably thus:

> On similar grounds it may be proved that no society can make a perpetual constitution, or even a perpetual law. The earth belongs always to the living generation . . . . Every constitution then, and every law, naturally expires at the end of 19 years.[16]

Madison responded in a letter of February 4, 1790—predictably in view of *The Federalist* no. 49—and questioned whether, as a practical matter, Jefferson's revisable constitutions would "become too mutable to retain those prejudices in its favor which antiquity inspires, and which are perhaps a salutary aid to the most rational Government in the most enlightened age."[17] He went on to raise two points of political principle. First, a present generation does not write on a morally clean slate, because it may incur obligations to previous generations: "The *improvements* made by the dead form a charge against the living who take the benefit of them."[18] Second, Jefferson's insistence that his principle required the expiration of constitutions and laws would create violent struggles over reviving or revising them, which could only be satisfactorily avoided by assuming tacit consent of each generation to continue obeying

---

[13] See Editorial Note, Julian P. Boyd, ed., *The Papers of Thomas Jefferson 1789,* vol. 15 (Princeton, N.J.: Princeton Univ. Press, 1958), pp. 384–91.

[14] Ibid., p. 392.

[15] Ibid., p. 394.

[16] Ibid., p. 396.

[17] Julian P. Boyd, ed., *The Papers of Thomas Jefferson 1789–1790* (Princeton, N.J.: Princeton Univ. Press, 1961), p. 148.

[18] Ibid.

preexisting constitutions and laws. Madison amplified the importance of this concept:

> May it not be questioned whether it be possible to exclude wholly the idea of tacit consent, without subverting the foundation of civil Society?—on what principle does the voice of the majority bind the minority? It does not result I conceive from the law of nature, but from compact founded on conveniency. A greater proportion might be required by the fundamental constitution of a Society if it were judged eligible. Prior then to the establishment of this principle, *unanimity* was necessary; and strict Theory at all times presupposes the assent of every member to the establishment of the rule itself. If this assent can not be given tacitly, or be not implied where no positive evidence forbids, persons born in Society would not on attaining ripe age be bound by acts of the Majority; and either a *unanimous* repetition of every law would be necessary on the accession of new members, or an express assent must be obtained from these to the rule by which the voice of the Majority is made the voice of the whole.[19]

Madison concluded, somewhat inconsistently, that his "observations are not meant however to impeach either the utility of the [Jefferson's] principle in some particular cases; or the general importance of it in the eye of the philosophical Legislator,"[20] and "that our hemisphere must be still more enlightened before many of the sublime truths which are seen thro' the medium of Philosophy, become visible to the naked eye of the ordinary Politician."[21] However, in fact, his argument—to the extent that it rested on the Lockean conception of political legitimacy that was fundamental to America's new constitutionalism—quite undercut Jefferson's simplistic claim of a recurring nineteen-year natural right of constitutional majoritarianism.

Madison probably sympathized with the spirit of Jefferson's argument because its principle at least interpreted Locke's claim "that *a Child is born a Subject of no Country or Government* . . . ; nor is he bound up, by any Compact of his Ancestors."[22] Locke had made that argument against Filmer's patriarchal historicism, that is, the claim that political legitimacy today had to be traced lineally to the authority of the original father of the human race. Locke, in contrast, argued that no such past figure could have a legitimate political claim on his or her ancestors, because the normative basis of political legitimacy was not history, but respect for the inalienable human rights that protected the spheres of reasonable self-government of free people. For this reason, no past government (including the founders) could, in and of itself,

---

[19] Ibid., p. 149.

[20] Ibid., p. 150.

[21] Ibid.

[22] John Locke, *The Second Treatise of Government,* in John Locke, *Two Treatises of Government,* Peter Laslett, ed. (Cambridge: Cambridge Univ. Press, 1960), p. 365 (sec. 118). See, for useful commentary on Locke's opposition to Filmer's historicism, Richard Ashcraft, *Locke's Two Treatises of Government* (London: Allen & Unwin, 1987), pp. 60–79.

bind a present generation. Madison sympathized with Jefferson's principle as a way of making this Lockean point.

However, Madison could not agree with the doctrinaire way Jefferson had chosen to state this Lockean view because it failed to observe Locke's crucial distinction between two levels of consent. As we saw earlier (Chapter 3), Locke interpreted the requirement that politics must respect inalienable human rights by requiring that all persons who are subject to its power must have reasonably consented in fact to live under a polity; furthermore, from that benchmark of legitimate political community, a majority of such persons had the authority—should the issue properly arise—to decide on that particular form of government most likely in their view to respect equal rights and pursue the public good. If that government should fail to respect rights, then the people have a right to overthrow it; they may then decide (unanimously) whether they should continue as a political community and (by majority rule) on their new form of government. Jefferson conflated the two issues and, in Madison's clear-eyed view, thus undercut the deeper foundations of the entire conception of political legitimacy. That conception rested on respect for inalienable human rights, and Locke gave that point political expression through the requirement of reasonable unanimous consent, which could not, in principle, be given by any reasonable person if it involved abridgment of *any* of their inalienable human rights. Reasonable unanimity was a way of making that deeper point of political legitimacy. However, Jefferson's interpretation of the point spoke of majority rule, to which Madison brilliantly responded that even majority rule—on deeper grounds of Lockean political legitimacy—had legitimate political force only if it was, as it may well not always be, the best *political* decision-making procedure for designing a government to protect inalienable human rights.

Madison's point had particular force in respect to constitutionalism because Jefferson's idea demanded an expiration of constitutions and a majoritarian reframing of them in a completely doctrinaire way that might often result in constitutions less politically legitimate than the one they supplanted. However, Locke's claim had been that revolution was justified when existing constitutions violated inalienable human rights, not that people have some abstract right to the abolition and reframing of their constitutions notwithstanding their justice and wisdom. Locke's drafting of the Fundamental Constitutions of Carolina expresses this view exactly; his stipulation that the Constitutions "shall be and remain the sacred and unalterable form and rule of government of Carolina for ever"[23] presumes that subsequent generations would tacitly consent to the continuing justice and wisdom of the Constitutions and the legal relations (e.g., property rights) under them; if his presumption were correct (i.e., later generations did consent on good normative grounds), the constitutional order would be legitimate and fully binding on

---

[23] See John Locke, *The Fundamental Constitutions of Carolina, The Works of John Locke,* vol. X (London: Thomas Tegg, 1823), CXX at p. 198.

them. Madison found Jefferson's contrary doctrine "dangerous"[24] and not simply because it fundamentally misinterpreted Lockean constitutional legitimacy. It subverted the authority of America's new experiment in Lockean constitutionalism—a political order that more powerfully embodied the ends of Lockean political legitimacy than had any government in human history, and that offered a path-breaking model for how history and tradition might be used constructively to constitute a political community based on a consensus permanently committed to this type of enlightened government. Jefferson's bad Lockean theory was in this instance subverting America's excellent Lockean practice.

Madison's theory of that practice gave posterity the basis for useful appeals to the founders. These appeals did not rely on Filmer's specious reasons of natural patriarchal authority, but relied on reasons of Lockean constitutionalism. This interpretive practice, suitably understood, could constitute a continuing political community with a legitimacy based on its aspiration to satisfy the Lockean requirement of unanimous reasonable consent in each generation in the same way that the original Constitution had for its own generation. We already discussed at some length (Chapter 3) how the American constitutionalists self-consciously recaptured the Machiavellian and Harringtonian idea of the founders, transforming it from ruthless political genius into a historically unique exercise of collective democratic political intelligence of a free people deliberating about the permanent ambitions, structures, and values of Lockean constitutionalism. Ratification of the U.S. Constitution by constitutional conventions elected by the people was, as we saw, fundamental to confirming the Lockean legitimacy of the Constitution. The point was not that everyone in fact consented to ratification (an unrealistic political procedure, as Locke saw), but that the deliberative and democratic character and focus of the ratification process could plausibly be interpreted to have affirmed the distinctive judgment that constitutional structures would contain political power in ways that respected equally the rights and interests of all. Because the Constitution treated people as equals in this way, it could be offered to and accepted by all as, in principle, reasonable and therefore, on Lockean grounds, legitimate. We must now inquire into the implications of such legitimacy for continuing interpretive practice.

At the Pennsylvania ratifying convention, James Wilson also characterized the legitimacy of the new Constitution in Lockean terms: "The great and penetrating mind of Locke seems to be the only one that pointed towards even the theory of this great truth."[25] Wilson had prominently invoked that theory, as we saw earlier (Chapters 2 and 3), in his constitutional arguments about the British constitution in the prerevolutionary period, and he was to give final observance to it in the 1790–1791 *Lectures on Law* that he delivered

[24] Julian P. Boyd, ed., *The Papers of Thomas Jefferson 1789–1790*, vol. 16 (Princeton, N.J.: Princeton Univ. Press, 1961) p. 149.
[25] Jensen, ed., *Documentary History*, p. 472.

as a justice of the Supreme Court of the United States.[26] The latter argument clarifies the kind of interpretive practice that makes the best sense of the founders' thinking about the political legitimacy of the Constitution for both their own and future generations.

Wilson argued that Americans had brought into play a new conception of law that sharply contrasted with Blackstone's positivism. Americans as revolutionaries had rejected Blackstone's theory of British constitutionalism, and they must now decisively reject his position as the theory of both American law in general and constitutional law in particular.[27] Blackstone's positivism rested on a theory of sovereignty, whereby law was defined as the rule prescribed by the requisite sovereign in a particular community. He had defined sovereignty in Great Britain in terms of the legislative sovereignty of parliament,[28] a sovereignty that American prerevolutionary constitutional thought rejected. Wilson argued, as he had in 1774,[29] that Blackstone's supposition of a supreme lawgiving power in government "has never been evinced to be true. Those powers and rights were, I think, collected to be exercised and enjoyed, not to be alienated and lost."[30] All such views had, for Wilson, corruptly sanctified an "implicit deference to authority, . . . the bane of science, . . . the yoke of that intellectual tyranny, by which, in many ages and countries, men have been deprived of the inherent and inalienable right of judging for themselves."[31] However, the simple truth of the matter, available to a democratic common sense emancipated from such tyranny, was that "the dread and redoubtable sovereign, when traced to his ultimate and genuine source" is not parliament or any political body, but "the free and independent man."[32] In contrast to Burke and Blackstone, the point of legitimate government was not to surrender all our rights[33] but to protect them, in order to maintain the ultimate sovereignty of independent conscience over government. Respect for our inalienable human rights, like conscience, enabled us to exercise the reasonable moral capacities available to all persons (the "moral sense"[34]) to know, understand, and implement as free and equal persons the principles of justice ("the law of nature"[35]). The legitimacy of law arose, for Wilson, from the consent of free and equal persons thus understood, a consent "given in the

[26] See James Wilson, *Lectures on Law,* in Robert Green McCloskey, ed., *The Works of James Wilson,* 2 vols. (Cambridge, Mass.: Belknap Press of Harvard Univ. Press, 1967), vol. 1, pp. 69–439; idem, vol. 2, pp. 441–707.

[27] For the core of Wilson's argument against Blackstone, see *Lectures on Law,* vol. 1, pp. 168–96.

[28] See, e.g., William Blackstone, *Commentaries on the Laws of England,* vol. 1 (Chicago: Univ. of Chicago Press, 1979), pp. 91, 156–57.

[29] See James Wilson, *Considerations on the Nature and Extent of the Legislative Authority of the British Parliament* (1774), in McCloskey, ed., *Works of James Wilson,* vol. 2.

[30] Ibid., p. 174.

[31] Ibid., vol. 2, p. 502.

[32] Ibid., p. 81.

[33] See ibid., pp. 585–86, 588–89.

[34] See, e.g., ibid., vol. 1, pp. 124, 142, 225, 378–79.

[35] Ibid., p. 125.

freest and most unbiassed [sic] manner"[36] to the principles that best secure our equal rights and the common interests of all.

Wilson understood such consent broadly:

> This consent may be authenticated in different ways: in its different stages of existence, it may assume different names—approbation—ratification—experience: but in all its different shapes—under all its different appellations, it may easily be resolved into this proposition, simple, natural, and just—All human laws should be founded on the consent of those, who obey them.[37]

However, Wilson clearly thought that consent "given originally" or "given in the form of ratification" was inferior to "what is most satisfactory of all, consent given after long, approved, and uninterrupted experience. This last, I think, is the principle of the common law."[38] Wilson had defined the British constitution in 1774 in terms of a set of principles consensually validated by the history of the common law, and he had held parliament's assertion of powers of taxation over the colonies to be unconstitutional on that basis. What is remarkable is that Wilson, after playing a pivotal role both in insisting (with Madison) on broadly democratic ratification at the convention[39] and in participating in the actual debates over ratification of the Constitution,[40] should still prefer the common law in 1790 as a better model for the kind of consent that conferred Lockean legitimacy on law.

The key to understanding this preference is Wilson's rather idealized picture of the common-law process as a cumulative pattern of deliberative experiments over time:

> a system of experimental law, equally just, equally beautiful, and, important, as Newton's system is, far more important still. This system has stood the test of numerous ages: to every age it has disclosed new beauties and new truths. In improvement, it is yet progressive; and what has been said poetically on another occasion, may be said in the strictest form of asseveration on this,—it acquires strength in its progress. From this system, we derive our dearest birthright and richest inheritance. . . .[41]

The common law, as experiments in the protection of freedom,[42] had thus not only been deliberatively tested over a longer period by larger numbers of people, but its requirements also reasonably adjusted to changing circum-

---

[36] Ibid., p. 102.

[37] Ibid., p. 180.

[38] Ibid.

[39] See, e.g., Farrand, ed., *Records of Federal Convention,* vol. 1, pp. 122–23 (Madison), 123 (Wilson), 127 (Wilson); idem, vol. 2, pp. 92 (Madison), 468–69 (Wilson), 469 (Madison), 475–76 (Madison), 477 (Wilson), 561–62 (Wilson).

[40] See, e.g., Jensen, ed., *Documentary History,* vol. 2, pp. 167–72, 339–63, and passim.

[41] Ibid., vol. 1, p. 183.

[42] See, e.g., ibid., vol. 1, pp. 356–57; see also idem, vol. 2, pp. 560–65.

stances.[43] Finally, custom had continuing force in the protection of liberty that ratification might lack:

> The regions of custom afford a most secure asylum from the operations of absolute, despotick power. To the cautious, circumspect, gradual, and tedious probation, which a law, originating from custom, must undergo, a law darted from compulsion will never submit.[44]

Wilson, like Madison, quite clearly saw that even a ratification as free and deliberative as that of the U.S. Constitution would be of little continuing effect if the interpretation of the Constitution over time did not comparably elaborate its experiment in freedom using this type of common-law basis in ways that could be justified to the community at large with at least as much force as its ratification. He pointed out the continuing need to renew the original principles of the Constitution and thought of both bicameralism[45] and judicial review[46] as constitutional institutions aimed at this end. Presumably, such needed interpretive practices over time must, if the political legitimacy of the Constitution was to be preserved, themselves be politically legitimate in the same way. The natural inference from Wilson's argument would indeed be that they must, if anything, prove their legitimacy in a more complete and pervasive way. Whereas the Constitution was ratified on the basis of contestable judgments about its likelihood to meet better the demands of Lockean political legitimacy in the abstract, its elaboration over time must prove its worth in multitidinous concrete cases stretching over generations, justifying political power to the community subject to that power on terms of equal respect for rights and pursuit of the common interests of all. The political legitimacy of the Constitution would, in effect, have been deliberatively tested over a longer period by larger numbers of people in changing circumstances, and such long-standing and cumulatively successful interpretive practices would exercise a powerful customary constraint over abuses of political power and be further legitimated on that basis.

If Madison suggests that the understanding of constitutional interpretation over time must make sense of a pattern of Lockean unanimous reasonable consent over time, Wilson suggests the further methodological guide that our analysis proceed in two steps: first, giving the best account that can be given of the Lockean legitimacy of the Constitution in 1787–1788, and second, giving an account of how the interpretation of the Constitution over time is at least as politically legitimate as the founders' project. To begin with, then, we must give the best interpretation that can be given to the deliberative ratification of the Constitution by the American generation of 1787–1788. It was, of course, one of the most broadly democratic and deliberative processes in the political

---

[43] Ibid., vol. 1, pp. 354, 360.

[44] Ibid., p. 184.

[45] He justified bicameralism as one institutional way of achieving the aim of renewing original principles. See ibid., pp. 290–2, 414–17, 432–33.

[46] Ibid., pp. 326–31.

history of both the nation and the world to date,[47] and its point was conceived by that generation as political action of a qualitatively different kind from ordinary legislation. Indeed, it was that difference that would—consistent with the Massachusetts example—give American constitutionalism the status of supreme law over all other kinds and forms of ordinary political activity, including legislation. Ratification must have a political force more deeply legitimate than ordinary legislation, and mere numbers (e.g., larger democratic majorities) could not mark the difference.

American constitutionalists innovated a new kind of decision-making procedure both in process and normative object—that required people to think from a new kind of deliberative perspective about the institutions acceptable to people in many different regions of the country, to themselves over the stages of their lives, and to their posterity over time—a deliberative process that showed itself in the kinds of justifications offered to and accepted by Americans (e.g., in *The Federalist*) as the basis for ratification. The ratification process was a natural political expression of the ideal that the constitutional structures to be ratified could sensibly be regarded as having passed the test required by Lockean legitimacy, or at least to have passed a better test of such legitimacy than the ordinary legislative processes in which Americans had rightly lost constitutional faith. The ratification process had authority for Americans not as an expression of will but of judgment, namely, the judgment that the constitutional structures that could gather sufficient support in such a demanding process of ratification had passed a reasonable test of being just. The constitutional structures of federalism, separation of powers, and judicial review had, in effect, so divided, channeled, and constrained political power that Lockean Americans had made and expressed the deliberative judgment that these structures could be reasonably justified to all as securing uses of political power that would respect the equal rights of all and advance the common interests of all alike.

In effect, American constitutionalists created a new kind of political process as a reinterpretation of the moral point of Locke's first stage of unanimous reasonable consent (see earlier discussion in Chapter 3). Locke had regarded that stage as crucial to any kind of legitimate political community, and then regarded majority rule as the only available political procedure that could frame a government consistent with it. However, Locke's argument was problematic at both the normative and constitutional stages. Locke's normative theory of unanimous consent was subject to the kind of decisive objection Hume had made,[48] namely, that a weak requirement of actual consent (i.e., a

---

[47] On the comparative broadness of American suffrage during this period, see Donald S. Lutz, "The First American Constitutions," in Leonard W. Levy and Dennis J. Mahoney, eds., *The Framing and Ratification of the Constitution* (New York: Macmillan, 1987), at pp. 71, 76–77.

[48] Hume made a cogent objection to the Lockean inference of both the freedom and rationality of consent from mere facts of actual submission to authority:

Can we seriously say, that a poor peasant or artisan has a free choice to leave his country, when he knows no foreign language or manners, and lives, from day to day, by the small wages which he acquires? We may as well assert that a man, by remaining in a

veto by possible exit) could not adequately measure what Locke wanted it to measure: the demands of respect for inalienable rights. Furthermore, the Lockean view confused the deliberation appropriate to framing constitutions with the deliberation appropriate for legislation. Americans certainly had found Locke's view of the second constitution-making stage inadequate to the purposes of the first legitimacy-conferring stage, and therefore quite naturally elided the distinction between the two stages into a conception of framing a constitution much closer to the underlying normative theory of political legitimacy that was fundamental to the first stage.

Americans were sometimes no clearer than Locke about the ambiguity in his first stage between a tacit actual consent of all and a reasonable benchmark of respect for the inalienable human rights of all; Madison himself elided the two ideas in his response to Jefferson. However, American constitutional practice rests on a level beyond Locke in the understanding of how constitutionalism might secure the ends of just government, including respect for the rights of all. The authority of the ratification process for Americans like Madison cannot be sensibly understood on the model of the actual consent of all but only in terms of a more demanding normative conception of justifiability to all that is a distinctive American contribution to constitutionalism. The object of the ratification process was not a judgment of actual unanimous consent, but of constructive reasonable consent: the institutions in question could, in principle, be reasonably justifiable to all persons who were subject to political power because these institutions rested on reasonable deliberations about the permanent nature of political power, about the inalienable rights of human nature in terms of which the legitimacy of all power must be tested, and about the enduring structures for the exercise of political power that might best harness it to its legitimate ends. Ratification thus legitimated the Constitution because it was the best available deliberative, free, and broadly egalitarian *political* decision-making procedure that could fairly be interpreted authoritatively to have made such a judgment of legitimacy,[49] namely, that the Constitution was a reasonably justifiable structure of political power for both the present generation and future generations because it secured respect for the rights and interests of all.

As an initial matter, we should examine two interpretations that have been given to this judgment: first, that the judgment of the 1787–1788 generation of its own force binds future generations, and second, that the judgment of later generations stands on its own without interpretive reference to any other. Neither view can be sustained.

---

vessel, freely consents to the dominion of the master; though he was carried on board while asleep, and must leap into the ocean and perish, the moment he leaves her.

David Hume, "Of the Original Contract," in *Essays Moral, Political, and Literary* (Oxford: Oxford Univ. Press, 1963), p. 462.

[49] On the democratizing importance of the new kind of political journalism that the ratification debates used and elaborated and its historical antecedents, see Albert Furtwangler, *The Authority of Publius* (Ithaca, N.Y.: Cornell Univ. Press, 1984).

The first interpretation flouts, of course, the very premises of Lockean political legitimacy and thus cannot be a reasonable interpretation of a judgment resting on such premises. To suppose that the founders took the view that their judgment could of its own force bind later generations ascribes to them the view of political authority of Filmer's patriarchalism, as if the founders could play the role in American constitutionalism that the first father took in Filmer. However, Americans rejected all such views of natural authority and hierarchy, and understood Locke to have decisively refuted them. Certainly, American constitutionalists, who regarded themselves as defending a better form of Lockean constitutionalism than what they had experienced under Britain's view of its own constitution, would hardly have taken a position in 1787–1788 clearly less Lockean than the one British constitutional thought had taken since the Glorious Revolution of 1688.[50]

Contemporary Americans nonetheless invoke this interpretation when they appeal to the founders' denotative exemplars as the measure of constitutional interpretation (see Chapter 1), because the view measures correct contemporary constitutional interpretation solely by the concrete applications given constitutional language in 1787–1788, although those applications make little or no interpretive sense in contemporary circumstances. It is not only quite clear that this is not the view of constitutional interpretation over time that the founders anticipated,[51] but—in view of their convictions about Lockean political legitimacy—it is also not a view they thought of themselves or anyone having either the authority or right to take. In Chapter 1, this point as a general principle of democratic political theory is raised: how, as a matter of democratic principle, could the ratification of a constitution by a generation long dead bind a contemporary generation? We may now see that this objection of political legitimacy to rule by generations long dead was one to which the founders were themselves profoundly committed. The reasonable republican constitutionalism they had fought a revolution to achieve was not one that could ascribe to anyone the authority of Filmer's patriarch. To ascribe to the founders a claim to such authority fails to take them seriously, demeaning what they valued in their own achievement into a historicist patriarchalism that they regarded as morally and politically corrupt. Yet a view of this sort has recently been espoused at the highest levels of government in the United States in the name of the founders' intent (e.g., as a reason for the nomination

---

[50] Locke's theory of revolution and of framing a new government were used by Whigs to justify the Glorious Revolution. See, in general, Edmund S. Morgan, *Inventing the People: The Rise of Popular Sovereignty in England and America* (New York: W.W. Norton, 1988), pp. 94–121. Locke's own views may, in fact, have been rather more radical than those of the Whig establishment. See, in general, Richard Ashcraft, *Revolutionary Politics and Locke's Two Treatises of Government* (Princeton, N.J.: Princeton Univ. Press, 1986). On the American response to the events of 1688, see David S. Lovejoy, *The Glorious Revolution in America* (Middletown, Conn.: Wesleyan Univ. Press, 1972); Morgan, *Inventing the People*, pp. 122–48.

[51] See H. Jefferson Powell, "The Original Understanding of Original Intent," 98 *Harv. L. Rev.* 885 (1985).

of Robert Bork to the Supreme Court). In fact, the view betrays anything the founders' intent could reasonably be taken to mean (Chapters 7 and 8).

The appeal of this interpretation perhaps rests on a conception of appropriate constraints on the interpretive process; otherwise, *any* view taken by a contemporary generation—without any accountability to history, tradition, or interpretive argument more generally—would suffice,[52] which would distort constitutionalism to the ends of the more powerful political factions in play. It is not a reasonable view of constitutional interpretation, for either the founders' generation or our own, that any interpretive argument will do or that the view of any powerful persons or institutions about correct constitutional interpretation is necessarily correct and not open to independent criticism and correction. A theory of constitutional interpretation must preserve space for such criticism, to which even the most interpretively authoritative institutions (like the judiciary) must be held accountable.

However, the choice is not between patriarchal founders and unchecked contemporary political power with no interpretive obligations to make sense of history and tradition. There is an available and reasonable interpretation of the founders' judgment of the legitimacy of the Constitution for their generation and posterity that does justice to them and that makes sense for us as a constitutional community, namely, a community of principle. The founders thought of their own role in later American interpretive practice in this way, and this practice is now motivated to attend to the founders because their deliberations about the community of principle are a reasonable basis for understanding and framing the interpretive responsibilities of this community today.

Political communities, as the anti-Federalists well understood, had historically been constructed around homogenizing sources like a common identity (e.g., religion, a nation, ethnic group, or region) or collective enterprises of war and conquest of outsiders. However, the founders, as we have seen, had come to believe that these sources of political community had, in both religion and politics, subverted the reasonable capacities of persons in spheres of self-government to come to know, understand, and claim a moral equality that transcended all such differences, "a principle of good will as well as of knowledge," as James Wilson put the point, "capable of abstraction, and of embracing general objects."[53] Accordingly, founders like Madison and Wilson embraced heterogeneity[54] as something to be both used and encouraged as part of a *political* doctrine that would use deeper levels of consensus—transcending group identities and enterprises—in service of the moral abstraction that is

---

[52] Is this just a nightmare of conservatives without reality in terms of contemporary constitutional argument? Certainly not. See, e.g., Michael J. Perry, *The Constitution, the Courts, and Human Rights* (New Haven, Conn.: Yale Univ. Press, 1982).

[53] Wilson, *Lectures on Law,* in McCloskey, ed., *Works of James Wilson,* vol. 1, p. 162.

[54] For example, at the constitutional convention, both Madison and Wilson (himself an immigrant) were particularly notable for their concern for facilitating immigration. See, e.g., Farrand, ed., *Records of Federal Convention,* vol. 2, pp. 236–37 (Madison), 237 (Wilson, speaking of his experience as an immigrant), 268–69 (Madison), 269 (Wilson).

fundamental to a new kind of community, one that is capable of a deepened ethical awareness of the reasonable demands of equality incumbent on all persons.

At one level, this new political conception of republican community was less demanding than the Aristotelian perfectionism of classical republicanism (see Chapter 2); certainly, it accorded to private life a dignity foreign to the devouring demands of heroic public service that were characteristic of the ancient republicanism of Athens, Sparta, and Rome. However, at another level, the new American republican community was much less historically comfortable and certainly less accommodating to the natural facts of group identity, and much more ethically demanding in the constraints it imposed on the political power of such groups, which the founders called "factions." Aristotelian perfectionism thus capitalized on the familiar "natural" groups and enterprises it found at hand (e.g., highly talented heroic men, quite untalented men who "are by nature slaves,"[55] and women as such over whom men are the "naturally ruling elements"[56]), and mobilized them in enterprises that would bring such groups to a kind of peak performance of collective excellence. American constitutionalism arose, in part, from a criticism of classical republicanism because the uses of many "natural" groups by ancient societies seemed to the founders clearly corruptive of the moral equality that they took to be fundamental to political legitimacy, by justifying polities that not only failed to respect equal rights but also obfuscated the basic responsibility of the state to advance equally the common interests of all in the service of vapid ideals of military glory and conquest. The centrality of the theory of faction to American constitutional thought was based on the *political* distrust of the unqualified political power of such groups (in their natural human forms), because the group psychology of faction subverted the capacities of moral independence that are fundamental to an ethical conscience that treated all persons as equals. The political power of such factions had, for the founders, to be structured in ways that would support, not subvert, the maintenance of the desired form of political community, and they used constitutional skepticism about group identity in service of this deeper ethical vision of moral community.[57]

The American constitutional project, thus understood, had at its center both a positive and negative conception of political reasonableness that the founders adapted from a long tradition of critical reflection, which they brilliantly extended and transformed. The positive conception was the justification of all exercises of political power in terms of free public reasons accessible

---

[55] Aristotle, *The Politics of Aristotle,* Ernest Barker, trans. (New York: Oxford Univ. Press, 1962), p. 13.

[56] Ibid., p. 35.

[57] It is this skepticism that leads me to find interpretively strained the analogy between American constitutionalism and civil religion. For a recent statement of the analogy, see Sanford Levinson, *Constitutional Faith* (Princeton, N.J.: Princeton Univ. Press, 1988). For criticism of it, see David A.J. Richards, "Civil Religion and Constitutional Legitimacy," 29 *Wm. & Mary L. Rev.* 177 (1987).

to all persons equally. Locke had, of course, stated such a conception, and subsequent philosophical thought had, if anything, interpreted it in an even more democratic way. Wilson, for one, took egalitarian common sense to be exemplified in epistemology by the commonsense theory of Reid and in ethics by the moral sense theorists.[58] The negative conception was the range of sectarian conceptions of religious and political truths, the political enforcement through law of which not only failed to observe the required standards of free public reason, but had also degraded the capacities for public reason of the people at large.

Reflection on both the positive and negative conception, as we saw earlier (Chapter 2), had a long prehistory not only in American but in European thought. The argument for religious toleration of Locke and Bayle rested on the distinction between these two kinds of reasons (the first, but not the second, of which could be legitimately enforced through law) and on an extended criticism of the damage the Augustinian failure to observe the distinction had inflicted on historical Christianity. The methods of argument of Locke and Bayle used the humanist techniques of textual criticism and exegesis that emerged in the Renaissance and had been cultivated by Erasmus and adapted by the great thinkers of the Protestant Reformation.[59] The use of such humanist techniques reopened the great question of western culture that had been settled since Augustine, namely, how should Judaeo-Christian Europe take account of its pagan heritage, the philosophy, science, art, and politics of Greece and Rome. Augustine, for example, had justified the persecutory political powers of Catholicism as the established church of the Roman Empire, and the criticism by Locke and Bayle of his arguments reopened a decision that had had enormous consequences for both religion and politics in Europe. Locke had, of course, expanded the scope of such criticism to include political legitimacy itself, and other humanists, notably Machiavelli (followed by Harrington, Montesquieu, and Hume), had reopened for western thought the relevance of classical republicanism for thinking about modern politics. Augustine's great synthesis was irretrievably shattered, and the task now was to reconstruct critically the foundations of both religion and politics on a sounder basis.

American constitutional thought—of the sort we have already examined at some length—was at the cutting edge of this process, reflecting on the broad range of historical materials that humanist inquiry had made available, including conflicting moral, religious, and political traditions. The moral, religious,

---

[58] On Reid and the philosophy of common sense, see, e.g., *Lectures on Law*, vol. 1, pp. 212–26; for invocations of self-evident truths on this basis, see idem, pp. 202, 209, 225, 394. For appeals to the moral sense, see, e.g., idem, pp. 124, 142, 225, 378–79. See, in general, Thomas Reid, *Essays on the Active Powers of the Human Mind* (Cambridge: M.I.T. Press, 1969); idem, *Essays on the Intellectual Powers of Man* (Cambridge: M.I.T. Press, 1969).

[59] On the important place of humanist methodologies in Protestant thought, see Margo Todd, *Christian Humanism and the Puritan Social Order* (Cambridge: Cambridge Univ. Press, 1987); William J. Bouwsma, *John Calvin: A Sixteenth Century Portrait* (New York: Oxford Univ. Press, 1988).

and political identity of the West had been shattered by its critical confrontation with such conflicting traditions, in particular, the exposure of the unacceptable ways in which they had been synthesized and the need to rethink the issues fundamentally. The natural move amid such conflict was metainterpretive, in other words, to ask deeper questions about what might constitute a better interpretation of a central cultural text like the Bible and how such interpretation should take account of pagan philosophy.[60] However, metainterpretive inquiries of that sort required, in turn, a reexamination of the foundations of reasonable inquiry, belief, and action (e.g., Locke's epistemology[61]), because the entire humanist process rested on the conviction that the political enforcement of orthodox views of truth in these matters had subverted reason in all these areas. Furthermore, corresponding political principles would be needed to allow reasonable inquiry its proper emancipatory scope by forbidding the enforcement through law of such sectarian conceptions (such as Locke's principle of religious toleration).

American constitutionalism gave profound expression to these methods and concerns. Much of prior religious, moral, and political history was suspect, precisely because it had illegitimately degraded free public reason; the founders thus were compelled to make their own independent reasonable inquiry using a broad range of available political models and methodologies, including Machiavelli's and Harrington's political science of classical republicanism and Montesquieu's and Hume's expansion of such study to the British constitution. Such examples were sifted, discussed, and debunked always in service of the Lockean political theory of legitimacy that the founders took to be fundamental to their task, in particular, the emancipation of free public reason. As Wilson put the point at the constitutional convention, "he could not agrcc that property was the sole or the primary object of Govcrnt. & Society. The cultivation & improvement of the human mind was the most noble object."[62] Furthermore, Madison had written in 1785 of conscience as "in its nature an inalienable right"[63] and was to write in quite Lockean terms[64] in 1792: "Conscience is the most sacred of all property; other property depending in part on positive law, the exercise of that, being a natural and unalien-

[60] See, for further discussion of these points, David Richards, *Toleration and the Constitution* (New York: Oxford Univ. Press, 1986), pp. 25–27, 81, 86–88, 95, 125–28.

[61] See, for further discussion, ibid., pp. 55, 59, 100, 106–8, 112.

[62] Farrand, ed., *Records of Federal Convention*, vol. 1, p. 605. Thomas Pangle makes little interpretive sense of Wilson's claim (deeming it mere rhetoric) because his otherwise illuminating recent study of the founders' Lockean constitutionalism does not give due attention and weight to the importance to Wilson and Madison, following Locke, of the right to conscience in the larger project of republican constitutionalism understood as the emancipation of democratic reason. See Thomas Pangle, *The Spirit of Modern Republicanism: The Moral Vision of the American Founders and the Philosophy of Locke* (Chicago: Univ. of Chicago Press, 1988) pp. 74–76.

[63] See James Madison, *Memorial and Remonstrance Against Religious Assessments*, in Robert A. Rutland et al., *The Papers of James Madison 1784–1786*, vol. 8, p. 299.

[64] Locke had written of property quite broadly as a right to self-possession; for example, "every Man has a *Property* in his own *Person*" (*Second Treatise of Government*, p. 305, sec. 27). Property, for Locke, is a general term for personal rights as such. See, e.g., idem, p. 341 (sec. 87).

able right."[65] Americans thus generalized long-standing humanist concerns to political power, imposing a new form of constitutionalism that required legitimate political power to be reasonably justifiable to the sovereign moral intelligence of each and every person subject to such power on terms that respected their moral equality. The power of factions in politics was accordingly constitutionally structured and abridged to serve this end.

The founders well understood how important to their deliberations had been their critical uses of interpretive history, because they largely defined their project by reference to the threats to democratic reason that they had critically identified and analyzed in that history. They framed their entire enterprise as part of a larger humanist project—uniting historical, moral, and political intelligence—that used tools of critically independent reasonable inquiry to advance the scope of free public reason. However, the point of that enterprise (drawing a distinction between the positive and negative conception of reason) itself arose from historical reflection on political abuses associated with the failure to observe the distinction. Humanist thought had often advanced through shifts in application of the distinction that this type of critical inquiry made possible (e.g., Locke gave the argument for religious toleration a broader application to politics than had Bayle). The founders themselves used history extensively in this way (i.e., interpreting the politics of classical republicanism as faction run riot), and they viewed themselves as having a role in the history of their posterity (as founders) because the process of constitutional argument they had innovated on the basis of such critical history could be reasonably elaborated only in the same way (including critical interpretive history of them as founders).

American constitutionalism would be a legitimate form of government for their posterity because it would structure a political community over time that would have the positive aim of all legitimate power being reasonably justifiable to the persons subject to that power and the negative aim of not permitting political power to be used oppressively to pursue factionalized conceptions of political, moral, or religious truth. The founders would have a pivotal educational role to play in the consciousness of later generations, because these generations could reasonably understand the Constitution as a remarkable achievement in the use of emancipatory critical moral and political intelligence in service of the humanist project of democratic reason, and they could define their own interpretive responsibilities as advancing that project in the same way in their own circumstances. Americans of a later generation would, as Lockean political theory requires, interpret the Constitution's legitimacy (its protection of inalienable rights and pursuit of the public good) in their own terms, that is, in terms of the most reasonable argument regarding these issues in their own circumstances. The founders would not rule as Filmerian patriarchs from the grave, but neither would they be interpretively irrelevant. Americans would find in them what the founders themselves anticipated: a

[65] James Madison, *Property,* for the *National Gazette,* in Rutland et al., *Papers of James Madison 1791–1793* (Charlottesville: University Press of Virginia, 1983) vol. 14, p. 267.

history and tradition of public argument about equal rights and common interests to be used by a later generation in service of the fuller elaboration of public reason according to the best lights of their own generation (e.g., shifting applications of the distinction between the positive and negative conception of reason).

Madison's argument in *The Federalist* no. 49 on this point could not be clearer. Such a tradition of historically continuous arguments of principle would serve as a kind of normative counterweight to the otherwise timorous conscience of republican citizens before current majoritarian sentiment that is hostile to the claims of equality:

> If it be true that all governments rest on opinion, it is no less true that the strength of opinion in each individual, and its practical influence on his conduct, depend much on the number which he supposes to have entertained the same opinion. The reason of man, like man himself is timid and cautious, when left alone; and acquires firmness and confidence, in proportion to the number with which it is associated. When the examples, which fortify opinion, are *antient* as well as *numerous,* they are known to have a double effect.[66]

Americans, born in later generations under an enduring written constitution, must define their political responsibilities not only in terms of their factionalized interests as expressed through shifting majorities of the current generation, but also in terms of a text, political theory, and interpretive practice of a number of earlier generations. The interpretation of the written constitution that defines the basic terms of political community will require citizens to think in terms of the larger aspirations and commitments of the political community over time. The weight of history must be interpreted in terms of a larger perspective on constitutional values (that transcends current factions and fashions) that enables citizens to understand and give effect to the constitutional responsibility of the reasonable justification of political power to all on terms of respect for their equal rights and the pursuit of the common interest.

Such an argument by a founder like Madison suggests that he and other founders had as deep an understanding of the historical fragility and the flickering evanescent beauty of the expression of democratic reason that Americans had achieved in the construction of the Constitution of 1787–1788 as Mozart, his contemporary, had of the poignant impermanence of reason in his art.[67] This recognition led Madison, as a constitutionalist, to take seriously indeed the difficult challenge of sustaining over time the intellectual and moral foundations of the new kind of republican political community to which the founders gave expression. The bonds of cohesion would not be the familiar "natural" groups on which previous political thought depended, but a morality of the equality of all persons. The constitution of such a community

---

[66] *The Federalist*, p. 340.
[67] See Brigid Brophy, *Mozart the Dramatist*, rev. ed. (London: Libris, 1988), pp. 195, 266.

over time would require a new kind of education, politics, literature, and law (including judicial review), and the Constitution was the central expression of its demands. Madison and Wilson had each been educated as a new kind of critically reflective and morally independent republican,[68] and they brought to their work as founders the exercise of such historically novel critical powers of democratic intellect (e.g., their extensive critical uses of interpretive history) that would also be required in succeeding generations to sustain the kind of political community that the founders contemplated. The interpretive demands of the Constitution would be central to that kind of continuing republican education of the generations that would follow, and the appeal to history and tradition would remind posterity of both their heritage and their responsibilities as free people.

In fact, it is a distinctive feature of constitutionalism in the United States that Americans are motivated to attend to the founders interpretively, and my criticism in Chapter 1 of a range of theories of American constitutionalism was made because the theories were unable to explain this central fact. My argument to this point has been that the founders importantly anticipated that they might or would play a central role in later constitutional interpretation, but that fact in itself does not explain why Americans are motivated today to attend to them in the way that they distinctively do. The interpretation of the meaning of constitutions or legal systems cannot, as a general matter, be understood on the model of speaker's meaning (Chapter 1). Moreover, the Lockean theory of political legitimacy denies that the intentions of a previous generation can of their own force have authority over later generations. Madison's argument for the interpretive weight of the founders in later American interpretive practice neither self-validates nor explains the weight that the founders in fact have had in that practice. If Lockean Americans are motivated to attend interpretively to the founders today, then that fact must be understood in terms of a distinctively American interpretive practice.

The American interpretive motivation can, however, be explained in terms of the kinds of political value that Americans look for in constitutional argument, namely, that exercises of political power be reasonably justified on

---

[68] Wilson, a Scottish immigrant, had been educated at St. Andrews in the generalist tradition of Scottish university education with its centrally humanist and philosophical emphasis on independent critical thought about ancient and modern history characteristic of the Scottish Enlightenment. On Scottish university education and its contrasts (including use of the vernacular, critical thought about the ancient world, and more democratizing exchanges between student and teacher) to the more specialist training of British universities in ancient languages, see, in general, George Davie, *The Democratic Intellect* (Edinburgh: Edinburgh at the Univ. Press, 1961); on Wilson, see, in general, Charles Page Smith, *James Wilson: Founding Father 1742–1798* (Chapel Hill: Univ. of North Carolina Press, 1956). And Madison had been educated at Princeton by Witherspoon, an immigrant Scot trained at Edinburgh University who brought to Princeton (as its new president) the same views of the role of education in critical republican thought. See, e.g., John Witherspoon, *Lectures on Moral Philosophy*, Jack Scott, ed. (Newark: Univ. of Delaware Press, 1982). For an admirable general treatment of the role of American colleges in the development of the American generation of republican revolutionaries and constitutionalists, see David W. Robson, *Educating Republicans* (Westport, Conn.: Greenwood Press, 1985).

terms of respect for rights and the pursuit of the public good. The founders' Constitution of 1787–1788 proved to be, for later generations of Americans, a successful experiment. Its success is a constitutive fact of American public life and culture. Americans take pride in living under the longest-lasting written constitution in the world, and they think of constitutional argument in terms of the demands for the justification of state power associated with that constitutive fact of their life as a people. Americans think of these interpretive demands as those of a historically continuous community of principle, and thus take an interpretive attitude to constitutional law motivated by the distinctive values they ascribe to the basic constitutional structures of that community of principle. However, the central discovery of American constitutionalism was that these values could not be defined by the normal processes of factionalized politics, but must instead be understood in terms of a more abstract deliberation about and justification of the uses of political power consistent with respect for equal rights and the pursuit of the public good. As we have seen, it was precisely because the nature and focus of the procedures of public thought, deliberation, and judgment of 1787–1788 were a test of which structures could be reasonably justifiable to all in this way (required by Lockean political legitimacy) that the Constitution was authoritatively the supreme law of the land. Americans today are motivated to find the same kind of value in constitutional argument (as distinct from normal politics), and they therefore interpret constitutional principles as a way of best justifying this historically continuous enterprise in contemporary circumstances (i.e., as constraints on political power that are reasonably justifiable to all).

American constitutional interpretation thus seeks to identify impartial tests for the reasonable acceptability to all today of the abstract constitutional principles of a tradition that imposes on each generation such a requirement for the justification of political power. The kind of reasonable argument and deliberation accorded the Constitution in 1787–1788 absorbs Americans committed to that ongoing interpretive enterprise because it held itself to the most fundamental and impartial test of reasonable justification in our history, and, as such, one kind of reflection (among others[69]) that we reasonably consult when we seek to take up today the requisite point of view of impartiality— irrespective of current political fashions and fads—in addressing interpretive questions of constitutional law in terms of the enduring values in abstract constitutional arguments that make the best sense of a continuous tradition marked by the evolving ambition that political power be reasonably justifiable to all. If there had been later comparable constitutional conventions or events in American history or later amendments had not been so naturally understood as developing themes implicit in the events of 1787–1788 (including correcting lapses of principle in its design), Americans might not have been motivated to attend to the founders interpretively in the way they do. How-

---

[69] Other kinds of such reasonable reflection include reasonable patterns of interpretive practice over time (judicial review) and political philosophy that deepens reasonable understanding of concepts like human rights and the public good.

ever, in fact, the deliberations of 1787–1788 were the most abstract, complete, profound, and seminal reflection by a democratic people on the general problem of constitutional government in American history, perhaps in human history. Accordingly, Americans of later generations, living within the framework of a community of principle sponsored by a Harringtonian written constitution, find it often reasonable to consult the deliberative judgments of 1787–1788 to the extent that they find, as they sometimes surely do (e.g., see the remaining argument of this book), that such abstract judgments, suitably interpreted, show how and why constitutional arguments and structures may be reasonably justified to all in contemporary circumstances as constraints on political power on terms of respect for rights and pursuit of the public good. Consistent with their Lockean constitutionalism, Americans find value in the deliberations of 1787–1788 because it often clarifies the demands of their own interpretive enterprise today.

If we think of these demands as the basic requirements of reasonable justification fundamental to democratic political philosophy, then we can understand the interpretation of the founders as a way that the American community of principle uses interpretive history in service of this philosophy— making accessible and available to all its demands. In contrast to the aristocratic perfectionist ethics of classical republicanism, the democratic political philosophy of American constitutionalism cannot—consistent with its democratic nature—require that all citizens be extraordinarily gifted (e.g., at doing philosophy or political science or writing Harringtonian constitutions for posterity), but it does require that its egalitarian demands be publicly justifiable to all in light of democratic reason. American interpretive practice melds together history and political philosophy in service of this egalitarian ambition, in which the interpretation of a history and tradition common to all is centrally deployed in the constitution of a public culture (including education in all its forms) that sustains a people capable of understanding and giving effect to the demands of a community of principle. The need for constituting such a public culture was, of course, much on Madison's mind at the founding:

> In a nation of philosophers, this consideration ought to be disregarded. A reverence for the laws, would be sufficiently inculcated by the voice of an enlightened reason. But a nation of philosophers is as little to be expected as the philosophical race of kings wished for by Plato. And in every other nation, the most rational government will not find it a superfluous advantage, to have the prejudices of the community on its side.[70]

It is a contingent, unusual (in comparison with other democratic peoples), and certainly pivotally important fact of American constitutional history and law that the founders' project is very much our project: both the making and interpreting of the Constitution are a continuous project in which—consistent with Lockean political theory—each generation seeks a higher-order reason-

---

[70] *The Federalist*, p. 340.

able justification for the exercise of political power (qualitatively different from their roles in normal politics) in a historically continuous community of principle. From the founders' perspective, a reflective process of public deliberation and ratification established the authority of the Constitution by making the deeper point of the reasonableness at large of its constraints on political power. From our own, constitutional interpretation must make sense of an enduring written constitution over time, a process in which, as Madison remarkably argued it would, tradition and history, as constructive elements of the identity of persons and communities, are interpretively harnessed to enable us and each generation more fully to respect on fair terms the civilizing demands of Lockean political legitimacy. For the same reasons, Lockean legitimacy—with its requirement of egalitarian justifiability—must require that the very interpretation of the Constitution over time be similarly justifiable to all persons, which explains why the very legitimacy of much constitutional interpretation is associated with its justifiability on grounds of principle.[71] American controversies over constitutional interpretation thus typically debate whether a decision is unprincipled, or, if not, what its principle might be as a way of making the point that the protection of a basic right of the person has or has not been extended to all on terms of equality.

American debates on interpretation standardly rely on background arguments of substantive justice because relevant provisions of the Constitution (e.g., guarantees of inalienable rights of conscience or speech) give such arguments a central place. Arguments of principle cannot, however, be simply equated with arguments of substantive justice.[72] The legitimacy of constitutional interpretations must be principled because the very legitimacy of the Constitution and its existence over time rests on the public justifiability of state power to all persons as equals; interpretive arguments of principle justify state power in this required way (a right extended to some must be reasonably extended to all within its reasonable scope). However, the most principled and coherent justification may not always be substantively just, because the properly understood constitutional tradition may fall short of justice; prior to the Fourteenth Amendment, for example, federal constitutional protection did not extend to many rights violated by the states. Often, however, the very claim of constitutionally justified injustice will be in interpretive dispute, as it profoundly was in the prolonged academic debate over the "neutral principle"[73] of the Supreme Court decision invalidating racial segregation in public schools, *Brown* v. *Board of Education.*[74]

All sides to the academic debate conceded that the decision was substan-

---

[71] See, generally, Ronald Dworkin, *Taking Rights Seriously* (Cambridge, Mass.: Harvard Univ. Press, 1977); idem, *A Matter of Principle* (Cambridge, Mass.: Harvard Univ. Press, 1985); idem, *Law's Empire* (Cambridge, Mass.: Harvard Univ. Press, 1986).

[72] Dworkin makes this point by distinguishing the value of integrity from substantive values of justice and fairness. See, e.g., Dworkin, *Law's Empire*, pp. 176–275.

[73] See, e.g., Herbert Wechsler, "Toward Neutral Principles of Constitutional Law," 73 *Harv. L. Rev.* 1 (1959).

[74] 347 U.S. 483 (1954).

tively just, but they differed over whether its substantive justice corresponded to a coherently reasonable justification of the relevant constitutional provision, the provision's history, and the other cases interpreting the provision.[75] The consequence of that debate over an issue of interpretive principle was what one would expect and should expect from debates over principle—that is, reasonable discussion among a community of equal persons, leading eventually to agreement that a range of principles justify *Brown*, namely, either that all racial classifications are invalid or only those that are racially invidious.[76] Through the kind of reasoning sponsored by debates over principle, we now understand that *Brown* is based on the constitutional principle of substantive equal justice, although we still debate the relative merits of the alternative principles in other cases in which they dictate different results (e.g., affirmative action,[77] discussed in Chapter 7).

The tension between interpretive arguments of constitutional principle and substantive justice is often fundamental to a sound understanding of the American community of principle over time, and requires—consistent with the founders' project—a critical sense of the achievement of the founders themselves. To be precise, the Constitution of 1787 and the Bill of Rights of 1791—remarkable achievements that they are—contain compromises over and even sacrifices of republican principles of which the founders were themselves all too painfully aware. Madison himself, for example, thought that equal representation of the states in the Senate clearly violated basic republican principles of justice in voting.[78] He also preferred a general power in Congress of a negative over state laws when state laws violated inalienable human rights,[79] and preferred, in the debates over the First Amendment, a guarantee of religious liberty and free speech that extended to both the states and the federal government.[80] Moreover, he knew—as did many founders—that the institution of slavery in southern states obscenely violated the republican principle of equal liberty for all persons.[81] Although some of these constitutional compromises were perhaps not as disastrous as a founder like

---

[75] For a sampling of this commentary, see Wechsler, "Toward Neutral Principles of Constitutional Law"; Louis Pollak, "Racial Discrimination and Judicial Integrity: A Reply to Professor Wechsler," 108 *U. Pa. L. Rev.* 1 (1959); C.L. Black, Jr., "The Lawfulness of the Segregation Decisions," 69 *Yale L.J.* 421 (1960). See also Alexander Bickel, "The Original Understanding and the Segregation Decision," 69 *Yale L.J.* 1 (1955).

[76] See Dworkin, *Law's Empire*, pp. 355–99.

[77] See, e.g., *Regents of the University of California* v. *Bakke*, 438 U.S. 265 (1978).

[78] See, e.g., Farrand, ed., *Records of Federal Convention*, vol. 1, pp. 151–52.

[79] For Madison's clearest defense of this view, see his October 24, 1787 letter to Jefferson, in Rutland, et al., eds., *The Papers of James Madison 1787–1788* (Chicago: Univ. of Chicago Press, 1977), pp. 212–14.

[80] Madison originally proposed to the House of Representatives the following amendment to the 1787 constitution: "No state shall violate the equal rights of conscience, or the freedom of the press, or the trial by jury in criminal cases" (Levy, *Judgments*, p. 179). The proposed amendment was not adopted.

[81] For example, at the constitutional convention, Madison observed that the mention of the slave trade "will be more dishonorable to the National character than to say nothing about it in the Constitution" (Farrand, ed., *Records of Federal Convention*, vol. 2, p. 415).

Madison feared (e.g., equal representation in the Senate), the evil of other sacrifices of principle (like the legitimation of slavery and the absence of a constitutional inhibition on the power of states to deprive persons of basic rights) was great in the later judgment of cumulative historical experience. The founders' sense of basic flaws in the community of principle was later confirmed, and—in the wake of the Civil War—many of them were expressly addressed by the Reconstruction amendments.[82]

The "founders" of the Reconstruction amendments brought to their work the same kind of interpretive sense of history that we saw earlier in the founders of the Constitution of 1787, namely, an attempt to learn from past republican and federal mistakes in institutional design, including lessons learned from the Constitution and Bill of Rights themselves. The "founders" of the Reconstruction amendments were not, however, institutional innovators in the sense of the founding fathers, because their interpretive sense of history accepted, indeed elaborated, many of the substantive and procedural constraints of the Constitution and Bill of Rights. Of course, they addressed central defects in the earlier constitutional design: the Thirteenth Amendment (1865) abolished slavery, the Fourteenth Amendment (1868) extended guarantees of basic rights against state action, and the Fifteenth Amendment (1870) prohibited racial discrimination in voting. However, these changes did not innovate principles as much as elaborate the scope of application of preexisting constitutional principles in ways that were often defended by the constitutional founders themselves. For example, when the Fourteenth Amendment extended guarantees of basic rights against state action, it did not innovate new rights but rather took standing guarantees of the 1791 Bill of Rights and expanded their application from the federal government to the states; one of the great lacunae (as Madison clearly saw) in the Constitution's protection of basic rights was thus filled. Even the innovation of quite new terminology of constitutional protection (notably, the equal protection clause of the Fourteenth Amendment) built, as we shall see in Chapter 7, upon standing constitutional guarantees.[83] In general, the Reconstruction amendments, if anything, expanded the community of principle to encompass a more coherent and certainly less flawed conception of the persons and rights protected by republican equality. These amendments were as much interpretive as innovative, and reflect precisely the kind of critical interpretive arguments of principle that the founders used and anticipated that their posterity would continue to use. The "founders" of these amendments were very much the interpretive posterity of the 1787 founders. Because of them, the founders' community of principle was now, in brief, more principled.

Even the interpretation of the founders' principles, unamended by later constitutional developments, must be construed in light of their aspiration to the continuing legitimacy of the Constitution for succeeding generations. Founders like Madison defended the idea of an enduring written constitution

---

[82] See U.S. Constitution, Amendments XIII–XV.
[83] See Richards, *Toleration and the Constitution*, pp. 296–303.

because it would use the deeply human sense of historical tradition in the service of constituting and elaborating a new kind of republican moral community; history reasonably serves this end only when it is interpreted in the same way the founders defended the legitimacy of the constittuion, namely, as a *historically* continuous enterprise of principle among a community of free, rational, and equal persons (i.e., a community of principle over time).

Constitutional interpretation, thus understood, must ascribe a reasonable sense not only to the work of the founders of the Constitution, the Bill of Rights, or the Reconstruction amendments, but also to constitutional interpretation over time, including examples of gravely mistaken theories of constitutional meaning. The American conception of an enduring written constitution expresses a historically continuous interpretive community of public justification on grounds of principle that incorporates all these moments. Accordingly, the conception must be crucially sensitive to the relevant context bearing on the forms that reasonable public justification must take under different circumstances and during different periods. Only contextual sensitivity enables us to read the Constitution as a continuing community bound to a common thread of principles. The absence of this sensitivity may create powerful paradigms of interpretive mistake, paradigms that fail to understand or articulate enduring strands of principle. Consequently, a community of principle must bring its interpretive sense of history to bear as much on interpretive practice over time as on the text of the Constitution, or the founders' sense of history or the founders themselves.

Of course, James Wilson had anticipated the importance of an interpretive practice such as that he idealized in the common-law process, to the continuing legitimacy of a constitution—like the U.S. Constitution, which was initially ratified by a broadly deliberative and democratic process. Indeed, Wilson thought of such a process as—on grounds of Lockean political legitimacy— superior to ratification; a similar view was suggested by Madison against Jefferson when he invoked the importance of some notion of tacit consent to the continuing legitimacy of any form of government, even the most enlightened. My suggestion has been that we make the best sense of both the ratification of the Constitution and its legitimacy over time when we interpret such conventions of tacit consent as expressing a benchmark of constructive reasonable justification to all against which even the legitimacy of Jefferson's constitutional majoritarianism must be tested, and it may very well be found wanting. American constitutionalism thus expresses a distinctive interpretation of Lockean political legitimacy applied to the aspiration to establish an enduring written constitution and the new kind of political community over time it would constitute, namely, that the interpretive practice in each generation must itself be guided by the aspiration of reasonable justification to all (i.e., justifying power to all persons in terms of equal respect for rights and pursuit of the common interests of all). Wilson had powerfully made this point by urging that the common-law process would be more nearly legitimate than initial ratification, because it would have deliberatively tested its Lockean theory of legitimacy over time. Whatever the truth of Wilson's view of the common-law process, he viewed the American interpretive process under its Lockean constitution as a process that must reasonably justify power to each and every person on terms of respecting rights and advancing the public good. However, constitutional interpretation can play this role only if it offers the most reasonable arguments to the community at large about the scope of constitutional protections against abuses of political power. We must now investigate what this means and should mean.

Abstract Connotations and the Contextuality of Constitutional Interpretation: Federalism as a Case Study

The commitment to an enduring written constitution manifested itself in the self-conscious way the founders linked both their style of drafting the Constitution and the style of interpretation they anticipated, namely, one that is historically sensitive to their aspiration to establish an enduring community of principle.[84] An important document used in their drafting of the final constitution stated, for example:

> In the draught of a fundamental constitution, two things deserve attention:
> 1. To insert essential principles only; lest the operations of government should be clogged by rendering those provisions permanent and unalterable, which ought to be accomodated to times and events; and
> 2. To use simple and precise language, and general propositions, according to the example of the (several) constitutions of the several states. (For the construction of a constitution necessarily differs from that of law).[85]

We need now to examine—consistent with this aspiration—how the Constitution should reasonably be interpreted.

The legitimacy of American constitutionalism rests on its aspiration to subject political power over time to the reasonable egalitarian requirements that it respect inalienable rights and secure the public interest. Constitutional law was framed both to secure that certain rights of the person would remain immune from political bargaining, and that the democratic political process should be structured in ways likely to pursue the common interests of all. We need to ask what kinds of constitutional structures lend themselves more to one of these ends of politically legitimate power as opposed to another. American representative democracy does—as the founders conceived it—make government responsive and sensitive to the interests of the electorate, and elected officials, in exercising power within the constitutional structures of the federal system, give appropriate weight to the common interests of all. However, the proper constitutional scope of the domain of electoral preferences is presumably not the proper measure of the equally important domain of principle that

[84] Cf. Powell, "Original Understanding of Original Intent."

[85] Farrand, ed., *Records of Federal Convention,* vol. 4, pp. 37–38. This document is in the handwriting of Edmund Randolph with emendations by John Rutledge; "the document is fundamental in the development of the final draft of the Constitution," idem, p. 37, n. 6.

is also fundamental—as we have seen—to the very legitimacy of constitutional government. Accordingly, the proper interpretation over time of the constitutional structures of the domain of preference must be rather different from those governing the domain of principle.

It will be useful to begin our interpretive analysis of these matters in an area very much at the center of Madison's constitutionalism but at the periphery of contemporary judicial review, namely, federalism. As we observed earlier, a theory of constitutional interpretation must articulate a critical stance against which the interpretive views of powerful contemporary political factions and institutions may be assessed, including the work of the judiciary. Indeed, a good theory should also clarify why some interpretive issues are properly for the judiciary and others less properly so. The U.S. Constitution strikingly contains a range of politically independent institutions (a bicameral legislature, an independently elected executive with a suspensive veto, a life-tenured judiciary), and is superimposed over independent republican state governments and a range of constitutionally protected private spheres of personal self-government (including liberties of religion, speech, and private life). As we saw earlier (Chapter 3), constitutionally guaranteed spheres of political independence were thought of by the founders as ways of securing impartiality in the exercise of political power consistent with a reasonable respect for rights and the pursuit of the public interest. The interpretation of the Constitution itself obviously would play a central role in this process, and interpretive responsibilities would correspondingly be allocated better to serve the underlying conception of political legitimacy.

Federalism is a useful preliminary interpretive case study because it raises questions regarding both how issues of the public interest should be interpreted and why nonjudicial institutions (e.g., Congress) should sometimes have the primary interpretive role in making those substantive judgments. The first question is one of substantive interpretive content, and the second one is of institutional interpretive competence. Both questions are, of course, interpretive, and the examination of federalism shows that sometimes the best interpretation of the Constitution is, for good reason, that a substantive issue should be decided by a nonjudicial body. Our later interpretive investigations will, in contrast, be more centrally in the area of judicial review based on the protection of basic rights of the person on grounds of principle (Chapters 5–7).

Consistent with the aspiration to an enduring written constitution, a distinctively American style of constitutional interpretation has insisted on framing its interpretive task regarding federalism in terms of what the greatest of the early chief justices of the United States, John Marshall, called "a constitution intended to endure for centuries to come, and, consequently to be adapted to the various *crises* of human affairs."[86] Marshall argued that the founders' aspiration to an enduring constitutional government binding on future generations can be given effect only if we read the often general language of the constitutional text in ways contextually sensitive to changing

---

[86] *McCulloch* v. *Maryland*, 4 Wheat. 316, 415 (1819) (emphasis in original).

circumstances. Marshall made the argument in his classical examination in *McCulloch* v. *Maryland*[87] of the appropriate interpretation of Article I, section 8, the grant of enumerated powers to Congress. *McCulloch* was concerned with whether the ascription of implied grants of power to Congress (to wit, to create a national bank) was a fair interpretation of Article I, section 8. Among the expressly granted powers was that of Congress to regulate interstate and international commerce,[88] a power very much at the heart of Madisonian federalism for a large, heterogeneous, commercial republic. Marshall's argument has naturally framed the interpretation of the commerce clause,[89] and we can usefully focus on this interpretive issue as a case study in the interpretation of federalism more generally.

We may understand Marshall's argument in terms of the commonplace semantic distinction between the denotative and connotative meaning of sentences.[90] Very roughly, the denotative meaning of a sentence identifies the things in the world to which the speaker refers; in contrast, its connotative meaning is not the things referred to but the propositional content of the sentence. When the founders of the Constitution gave Congress the power to regulate commerce, they did so by language with both a denotative and connotative meaning. Denotatively, the framers used the language to refer to both things that could and could not be regulated consistent with the language used; such a 1787 denotative meaning, for example, would clearly give Congress the power to regulate trade among the states, but it could not fairly give Congress the power to regulate purely intrastate farm production, reserved, say, for home use and consumption. Connotatively, we would identify the meaning of the commerce clause as the propositional content of "Commerce . . . among the several States," namely, business that affects more states than one.[91] The denotative and connotative meanings are related in that, because the connotative meaning of "Commerce . . . among the several states" is "business that affects more states than one," the 1787 denotative meaning of the text includes trade among the states (because it is business that affects more states than one), but it would exclude farm production for home use (it does not affect other states). We could, alternatively, state the semantic distinction as not between denotation and connotation, but between more concrete and more abstract connotations. In the one case, the connotation would closely describe circumstances as they were in 1787; in the other, the

---

[87] Ibid., 316 (1819).

[88] See U.S. Constitution, Article I, section 8, clause 3.

[89] Marshall himself examined this issue in *Gibbons* v. *Ogden,* 9 Wheat. 1 (1824) and *Willson* v. *Black Bird Creek Marsh Co.,* 2 Pet. 245 (1829).

[90] Frege formulated the distinction as between reference (the things referred to by "the evening star" and "the morning star") and sense (the proposition that would be used to characterize, for example, the defining properties of "the evening star"—that is, "a star that arises and is seen at evening time"). In fact, modern science tells us that both linguistic expressions have the same referent (namely, the planet Venus), but they have, of course, different senses. On Frege, see Gareth Evans, *The Varieties of Reference* (Oxford: Clarendon Press, 1982), pp. 7–41.

[91] See Robert Stern, "That Commerce which Concerns More States Than One," 47 *Harv. L. Rev.* 1335 (1943).

connotation would describe more abstract features not limited to the circumstances in 1787. In either event (denotation versus connotation, or concrete versus abstract connotations), the interpretive choice would be between a semantics more closely and less closely tied to the historical circumstances of 1787.

Marshall argued in part that we best construe the founders' aspiration to an enduring constitution when we read the test in those ways (connotation as opposed to denotation, or abstract as opposed to concrete connotations) less closely tied to the contingent historical circumstances of 1787. If we read the text denotatively or as signifying a highly concrete connotation, then we could reasonably apply the textual grant only to the things to which the founders in their circumstances would have applied the language. Such an interpretive approach would, however, freeze constitutional interpretation to the circumstances of 1787; that is, it would not be contextually sensitive to relevantly changed circumstances that would reasonably alter the scope of application of Congress's regulatory powers (e.g., the change of the American economy from the agrarian economy of 1787 to the industrial and postindustrial technological civilization of the twentieth century). The denotative meaning, for example, would thus forever forbid the application of the commerce clause to farm production of home-consumed products, because the 1787 denotation could not encompass such economic events. However, this denotative meaning of the clause would conflict with a fair reading of its connotative meaning; in other words, "business affecting more states than one" would in the twentieth century plausibly include even such farm production if appreciable parts of the aggregate of such production now withheld from the market might under changed economic circumstances (rising demand for farm goods) be sold in the market and thus appreciably affect market transactions in a now-integrated national economy. On this reading, congressional power could regulate such home farm production.[92] Marshall's argument was that we should in this case interpretively prefer the connotative (or more abstract connotative) meaning because it was equally consistent with the text and, in contrast to the 1787 denotative (or, more concrete connotative) meaning, would advance and not frustrate the founders' unambiguous aspiration to the long-term durability of the grants of power to Congress.[93] In effect, only the ascription to the commerce clause of an abstract connotation would allow Congress to make a reasonable judgment of how the public interest in this arena should be pursued in contemporary circumstances; in contrast, more concrete connotations would foist on a present generation anachronistic judgments that make no interpretive sense today.

As we have seen (Chapter 3), the federal system was so designed to give power over issues of national concern to a fairly representative Congress in place of the powers of the states over many of these issues under the Articles of Confederation. The Madisonian theory of federalism was directed at the

---

[92] See *Wickard* v. *Filburn,* 317 U.S. 111 (1942).
[93] Cf. *Gibbons* v. *Ogden,* 9 Wheat. 1 (1824).

political evil of faction, in particular, the political power of state factions under the Articles; its remedy was a theory of representation that would accord both sufficient independence and accountability to the Congress in order that its actions would be more free of faction and thus more likely both to respect rights and to pursue the public interest. Congressional regulatory power over interstate and foreign commerce was at the heart of this conception, because the fair and sensible regulation of commercial transactions within the large territory of the United States and abroad would advance the kind and level of peaceful and reciprocally advantageous economic relationships that could sustain the abundance and varied activities that were fundamental to sustaining the political value of the range of equal liberties that republican government protected.

However, Congress could reasonably exercise its constitutional power only if the conception of commerce in the commerce clause reasonably allowed it to judge the contextually relevant changes of national economic circumstances that are central to its mission of securing a national vision of the public interest. Madison had, after all, prominently insisted at the constitutional convention that the economic life of the nation would change and that the Constitution must address such changing economic circumstances[94]; moreover, as we have just seen, the founders expressly drafted the Constitution "to insert essential principles only, lest the operations of government should be clogged by rendering those provisions permanent and unalterable, which ought to be accomodated to times and events."[95] Because the interpretation of congressional powers was so contextually sensitive to relevant social and economic circumstances, we must interpret these grants, including the commerce clause, in a way that will enable Congress to make reasonable judgments about the national interest that are responsive to its interpretation of public purposes under changed circumstances. The abstract connotative interpretation of the commerce clause allows Congress to make these contextually sensitive policy judgments in a way that the denotative or concrete connotative interpretation would not, and should be preferred for that reason. Accordingly, we regard the decisions of the Supreme Court that for a period limited the interpretive power of Congress over these issues[96] as examples of grave interpretive mistake, because they ascribe to the commerce clause and related clauses precisely such an unwarranted denotative or concrete connotative interpretation.[97] Such judicial decisions were wrong because they ascribed to

---

[94] Madison was acutely sensitive to writing a constitution that could anticipate changing economic circumstances, and often was remarkably proleptic about likely changes from an agrarian to more commercial society. See, e.g., Farrand, ed., *Records of Federal Convention*, vol. 1, pp. 422–23, 585–86; idem, vol. 2, pp. 124, 203–4, 236, 268–69.

[95] Ibid., vol. 4, p. 37.

[96] See, e.g., *United States* v. *Darby*, 312 U.S. 100 (1941); *West Coast Hotel Co.* v. *Parrish*, 300 U.S. 379 (1937).

[97] Felix Frankfurter's classic criticism of these decisions is precisely along these lines. See Felix Frankfurter, *The Commerce Clause under Marshall, Taney, and Waite* (Chicago: Quadrangle, 1964).

the Constitution an anachronistic conception of the public interest that could not be reasonably justified in contemporary circumstances, and that thus failed to justify political power for the current generation in the required Lockean way.

The error of these judicial decisions raises the question of institutional interpretive responsibility: does the judiciary have any proper interpretive role over these kinds of questions? The question of appropriate interpretive institutions is obviously shaped by the nature of the issue interpreted. As we saw earlier (Chapter 3), the central issue in the design of the great structures of American constitutionalism was the shaping of political power to make impartial judgments on the issues of Lockean political legitimacy, respect for rights and pursuit of the common interests of all. The bicameral legislature, the executive, and the judiciary were all framed in terms of their impartiality in making the different kinds of judgments that are central to Lockean consti-tutionalism. Moreover, these institutions of the national government were superimposed over both state governments and protected private spheres of self-governing powers over conscience, speech, and personal life, which played important independent roles in maintaining the integrity of interpre-tive argument generally, including criticism of even the most authoritative national institutions.[98] The interpretation of the general constitutional design must allocate interpretive responsibilities among the structures of the national government in ways that take account of both the kind of impartiality each institution enjoys and the kinds of interpretive issues each institution might best judge consistent with the larger demands of Lockean impartiality. The primary interpretive responsibility of Congress over issues of federalism may be understood both in terms of its special competence as an institution and the kinds of interpretive issues that federalism poses.

In this connection, it was common ground among the founders that the grants of power to Congress were intrinsically vague. Indeed, contemplation of "the task of marking the proper line of partition, between the authority of the general, and that of the State Governments"[99] prompted Madison to the most remarkable outburst of political epistemology in all the debates over the Constitution, culminating in a *cri de coeur:*

> Here then are the three sources of vague and incorrect definitions; indistinct-ness of the object, imperfection of the organ of conception, inadequateness of the vehicle of ideas. Any one of these must produce a certain degree of obscurity. The Convention, in delineating the boundary between the Federal and State jurisdictions, must have experienced the full effect of them.[100]

If the very issue would be intractably vague in the mind of the most scrupu-lously impartial observer, then how much worse would it be when viewed

---

[98] On the use of state governments for this purpose, see, in general, *The Federalist,* pp. 179–80, 305, 319–20, 350–1, 359, 376, 404, 582–83.

[99] Ibid., p. 234.

[100] Ibid., p. 236.

from the perspective of "the interfering pretensions of the larger and smaller States"?[101] That, of course, was the situation under the Articles of Confederation, and the Constitution clearly removed the power over the question from the states to the national government. Interpretive responsibility over this kind of issue must devolve on one of the branches of the national government.

Both at the constitutional convention and in the ratification debates, James Wilson had introduced a pertinent distinction to which we should attend. There were, Wilson argued, two kinds of liberty that were the subject of the constitutional contract, namely, civil liberty and federal liberty.[102] Civil liberties included many of the rights guaranteed by state bills of rights and, as such, subject to arguments of principle; however, federal liberty identified the public policy purposes of government granted to the federal government because state regulation of them—though affecting other states—had neither effectively realized their benefits, nor fairly distributed their benefits and burdens. The scope and distribution of such federal liberty were, Wilson argued, a highly discretionary judgment of policy remitted under the Constitution to the judgment of a fairly representative Congress.[103] John Marshall marked a similar distinction when in *Marbury* v. *Madison*[104] he defended the central legitimacy of judicial review as grounded in the defense of principles of liberty and in *McCulloch* v. *Maryland* defended the central role of Congress over the interpretation of the scope of its own powers. On this view, Congress might reasonably be regarded as the high court of the commerce clause.

Experience under the Articles of Confederation had convinced the nation that the states could not responsibly exercise power over the regulation of commerce, because of the dominance of their political processes by parochial and insular factions unconcerned with the larger interests of either justice or the common good. The federal system had been crucially designed to create a national body more nearly capable of addressing these issues; Congress's regulation of business under the commerce clause would accordingly be determined by its reasonable judgment about what kind and scope of regulation would be likely to secure fairly and sensibly a level and quality of economic life that was consistent with both justice and the common good. However, such questions importantly depend on what the political process itself discloses both about the importance of these purposes as against competing ones and about the level of costs people are willing to incur to realize these purposes. Instrumental questions, for example, about more or less efficient ways

---

[101] Ibid., p. 237.

[102] See Farrand, ed., *Records of Federal Convention*, vol. 1, p. 166; Jensen, ed., *Documentary History,* vol. 2, pp. 346–47.

[103] Recent attempts to invoke founders' intent to justify a more substantial role for the judiciary in monitoring Congress in these areas fail to do justice to arguments like Wilson's and others that clearly and for good reason contemplate a central congressional role in these matters. For such attempts, see Raoul Berger, *Federalism: The Founders' Design* (Norman, Oklahoma: Univ. of Oklahoma Press, 1987); Richard A. Epstein, "The Proper Scope of the Commerce Power," 73 *Va. L. Rev.* 1387 (1987).

[104] 5 U.S. (1 Cranch) 137 (1803).

to secure these ends will themselves crucially depend on the weight the political process has given to the ends pursued. There is, in short, no way of even posing these issues outside the political process itself. The essential interpretive issue—the appropriate level of federal regulation—is the basic political issue between Congress and the states, and the federal political process specifies a fair procedure for resolving this interpretive issue, namely, through the politics of the federal system.

Judicial review over such issues would be, as Wilson suggested, otiose, or, as Marshall opined, marginal at best. Marshall argued in *McCulloch* that the judiciary should not abdicate interpretive responsibility entirely, but adopt a highly deferential standard of review under which Congress's interpretive judgment should rarely, if ever, be gainsaid. Such a deferential standard of review, sometimes called the rule of clear mistake,[105] limits the role of judicial review to checking that legislation does not wholly lack a rational basis in the powers conferred by the Constitution; if a congressional statute can be regarded as having some such basis that the Congress might have entertained, then judiciary should not inquire further. The modern judiciary uses this very lenient standard of review in these cases. In effect, Congress's interpretive judgments are rarely[106] disturbed.

It is quite consistent with the rule of clear mistake—as a standard of judicial review—that, although the judiciary will not examine the constitutionality of certain congressional legislation premised on the commerce clause, Congress's interpretive judgment of the scope of its powers under the commerce clause could be wrong in some area.[107] The interpretive judgment that Congress should be the high court of these matters is a judgment of overall institutional interpretive competence, the consequence of which is that the underlying substantive interpretive issues are addressed to a nonjudicial forum, which may make (in its sphere) interpretive mistakes just as the judiciary will (in its sphere). There are, of course, better and worse interpretations of issues of federalism (expressed in the political process through the larger political agendas of American political parties), and those issues are often debated by both political parties and the American people as better and worse interpretations of American federalism.

This interpretive analysis of institutional competence is also quite consistent with a different view of the interpretive questions raised by *state* attempts to regulate interstate commerce. The rule of clear mistake governs

---

[105] For a seminal article defending the rule, see James B. Thayer, "The Origin and Scope of the American Doctrine of Constitutional Law," 7 *Harv. L. Rev.* 129 (1883).

[106] The Supreme Court recently struck down a federal statute grounded on the commerce clause, see *National League of Cities* v. *Usery,* 426 U.S. 833 (1976), but reversed itself nine years later, *Garcia* v. *San Antonio Metropolitan Transit Authority,* 105 S. Ct. 1005 (1985). Strikingly, these five-to-four decisions were not based on the commerce clause, but on the Tenth Amendment. Both the majority and dissent in both cases assumed that the judiciary should use a very deferential standard of review in these cases, which, as a practical matter, conceded to congress a nearly illimitable interpretive authority over purely commerce clause issues.

[107] For a plausible such argument, see Sotirios A. Barber, *On What the Constitution Means* (Baltimore, Md.: The Johns Hopkins Univ. Press, 1984), pp. 91–104.

only within the scope of its application, namely, the interpretive authority of Congress over questions of the scope of exercise of its own powers. However, state regulation of interstate commerce, in areas not occupied by congressional statutes, deserves and receives no corresponding judicial deference.[108] To the contrary, an important motive for the very construction of the federal system was the factionalized ways states had regulated such commerce to the detriment of the legitimate interests of other persons and states. In effect, states were pursuing parochial protectionist interests that unfairly hurt others not themselves fairly represented in the political processes of the state. The theory of the federal system rests on principles of representation because the powers accorded Congress would, because of its representative structure, enable it to make and pursue a fairer and more sensible judgment about these questions. The scope of application of the rule of clear mistake would not, however, extend to cases in which Congress has made no such judgment and in which states have made such judgments on parochial protectionist grounds. If the purpose of the federal system was to produce a deliberative and impartial judgment about the regulation of the economic interests of the nation in ways that secure justice and the public good, then the state political processes are doubly suspect as interpreters of this issue, because they are not politically structured either to make such judgments or to pursue them on fair terms. Accordingly, judicial review properly monitors such state judgments (for both their ends and their means) because they are so suspect for their partiality about the interpretive issues of justice and the public good fundamentally in dispute. Judicial standards of review are more demanding in order to hold such state judgments to standards of impartiality they might otherwise flout.

The received doctrine—a range of interpretive issues not subject to judicial review at all—is the "political question" doctrine. The doctrine is misnamed because it most certainly does not mean that the issues, within the scope of the doctrine, are not interpretive issues to which there are right and wrong answers. Rather, the point is that the interpretive issues of judgment in these cases are more nearly impartially assessed by nonjudicial institutions. The scope of the doctrine is now quite controversial.[109] However, a plausible example of the possible good sense of the doctrine is the interpretive issue of who should decide on the length of time required for ratification by the states of an amendment to the Constitution pursuant to Article V. These amendments are often motivated by hostility to judicial interpretive practice, and it would hardly satisfy Lockean impartiality to make the judiciary the judge of

---

[108] See, e.g., *Raymond Motor Transportation, Inc.* v. *Rice,* 434 U.S. 429 (1978) (state prohibition of trucks longer than 55 feet); *Dean Milk Co.* v. *Madison,* 340 U.S. 349 (1951) (city ordinance prohibiting sales of milk not pasteurized within five miles of city); *Hughes* v. *Oklahoma,* 441 U.S. 322 (1979) (state prohibition of sale of minnows outside state).

[109] See, e.g., Louis Henkin, "Is There a Political Question Doctrine?" 85 *Yale L.J.* 597 (1976); Erwin Chemerinsky, *Interpreting the Constitution* (New York: Praeger, 1987), pp. 97–105.

issues to which it is so much a party. Accordingly, Congress is naturally regarded as the interpretive arbiter of this issue.[110]

Some interpretive issues, on grounds of both the nature of the judicial process and the nature of the issue, constitute the heart of judicial review, namely, arguments of constitutional principle protecting the inalienable rights of the person. Protection of the rights of the person is a requirement of the legitimacy of political power under Lockean constitutionalism, and in the American community of principle these rights must in each generation be reasonably justified to all persons. That process of deliberative reflection and justification requires not only a critical sense of the interpretive history of constitutional principle, but also the rigorous elaboration of those principles in terms of demanding standards of constitutional reasonableness that take seriously and assess reasonably the claim of any and all persons to the full protection of the guarantees of their rights under law. There is no reason to believe that Congress, the executive, the state legislatures, or even the people generally will be fully adequate to these demands of constitutional legitimacy unless there was available an independent judiciary with the primary role fairly and fully to maintain the highest standards of reasonable argument on these issues for the constitutional community at large. The judicial process is in its nature an impartial process of argument over the elaboration of principles that it naturally presses forward to their full natural extent. However, that is, of course, precisely what the very Lockean legitimacy of an interpretive practice of inalienable rights requires. As we saw earlier (Chapter 3), judicial review is the natural culminating point of the architecture of America's experiment in Lockean constitutionalism because it is the most nearly adequate institutional embodiment of its supreme requirement: the impartial and independent judgment of the inviolable rights of the person that must be immune from political bargaining and compromise. In *The Federalist* no. 78, Hamilton made this very point in the most important defense by a founder of the principle of judicial review:

> The complete independence of the courts of justice is peculiarly essential in a limited constitution. By a limited constitution I understand one which contains certain specified exceptions to the legislative authority; such for instance as that it shall pass no bills of attainder, no *ex post facto* laws, and the like. Limitations of this kind can be preserved in practice no other way than through the medium of the courts of justice; whose duty it must be to declare all acts contrary to the manifest tendency of the constitution void. Without this, all the reservations of particular rights or privileges would amount to nothing.[111]

---

[110] The leading case is *Coleman* v. *Miller,* 307 U.S. 433 (1939). For useful commentary on the doctrine, see Fritz Scharpf, "Judicial Review and the Political Question: A Functional Analysis," 75 *Yale L.J.* 517 (1966).

[111] *The Federalist,* p. 524.

It is quite clear that the same preference for abstract over concrete interpretations of the written text applies in this case as in the arena of congressional powers. The Fourth Amendment of the Constitution, for example, protects the "right of the people to be secure in their persons, houses, papers, and effects, against unreasonable searches and seizures." When the founders wrote and ratified that language in 1791, they clearly meant denotatively to forbid certain familiar invasions of the home by arbitrary police power as a way of protecting the connotative proposition of principle of the people's right to a private life shielded from arbitrary state intrusions.[112] If we read the Fourth Amendment only denotatively, as Justice Hugo Black once suggested,[113] then we could not appeal to it to protect invasions of privacy not historically imaginable in 1791, for example, electronic surveillance. This would, of course, introduce the same structural kind of conflict between denotative and connotative meaning that we have just examined in the area of the commerce clause: the 1791 denotative meaning would frustrate the connotative meaning read to protect privacy against the new technological threats that have arisen in contemporary circumstances. However, the denotative interpretation compromises the integrity of the community of principle that is fundamental to the American commitment to an enduring written constitution, because it reads a constitutional text—imposing constraints on state power reasonably justifiable to persons understood as free, rational, and equal—in a way that cannot be so justified, indeed that is crudely insensitive to relevantly changed technological circumstances bearing on the understanding and protection of its underlying principle. Such an unprincipled reading is compelled by neither text nor history, and indeed frustrates the contextually sensitive reasonable community of principle that motivates the very legitimacy of an enduring written constitution. For this reason, our interpretive tradition has preferred in this case as elsewhere the abstract connotative over the denotative or concrete connotative meaning because it more reasonably justifies basic rights on terms of principle; contrary judicial constructions have been decisively rejected as examples of grave interpretive mistake.[114]

Indeed, we should put this point in a more general way. The demands of Lockean legitimacy (namely, the reasonableness of constitutional protections to each and every person subject to law) lead insensibly toward the more abstract readings of constitutional texts. The imperative of reasonable justification to persons as equals constantly presses this interpretive tendency toward abstractness. One can, of course, resist this demand by imposing on the Constitution the external perspective of a radical skepticism about rights that is inconsistent with its text, history, and political theory[115]; such skepticism about rights can easily resist the egalitarian force that arguments of rights

---

[112] See, e.g., Polyvios G. Polyviou, *Search and Seizure* (London: Duckworth, 1982) 1–19 (1982).

[113] See Justice Black's dissent in *Katz* v. *United States,* 389 U.S. 347 (1967).

[114] See *Katz* v. *United States,* 389 U.S. 347 (1967), overruling *Olmstead* v. *United States,* 277 U.S. 438 (1928).

[115] See, e.g., Learned Hand, *The Bill of Rights* (New York: Atheneum, 1968).

must have for those like the founders who took them seriously as protections against the strategic aims of policy or the sentiments of majoritarian taste. However, it cannot be coherent to take the correct view that the protection of rights of the person is central in the American conception of constitutional legitimacy and then to truncate the scope of rights protected by the Constitution in ways that cannot be reasonably justified today on grounds of principle.[116] A claim of constitutionally protected basic rights of the person is, in its nature, an appeal to a right of the person to which all are entitled on equal terms, and the protection of such rights must, as a matter of integrity, always be justified to all in the way that most reasonably takes into account all relevant contextual considerations of both fact and value. This requirement creates, as matter of interpretive legitimacy, a pressure to ascribe to the content of protected rights the level of abstractness often alone consistent with the imperative of reasonable justification to persons as equals.

This pressure takes varied and complex forms in different areas of constitutional interpretation (Chapters 5–7). In all these cases, the ascription of more abstract connotations is often the only way in which a contemporary generation can literally make sense of the authority of the Constitution from 1787–1789 to date, namely, as a historically continuous strand of principles of free speech or privacy or equal protection that made interpretive sense in previous periods and makes interpretive sense today. Indeed, the entire weight of the community of principle, as a counterpoise to contemporary majoritarian nescience (in the terms of *The Federalist* no. 49), is its imperative of disciplined moral and political imagination to articulate constitutional principles in this way, namely, as abstract principles of inalienable rights of which each generation can and must make the best contextual sense in light of democratic reason. In short, the best interpretation of the founders' aspiration to an enduring written constitution is the interpretive ascription of a level of abstractness to textual protections of rights that allows them to serve the ends of the interpretive enterprise of a community of principle. Only such an ascription enables us to read the American constitutional tradition as a strand of enduring principles over time in the way that the founders thought pivotally important to the new kind of republican community they constituted for their posterity. Only this interpretive posture enables us to ascribe a reasonable sense to the founders' remarkable conjoining of historical tradition with the fullest protection of the inalienable rights of the person on terms of principle.

The interpretive coherence of this project requires, when necessary, the use of political philosophy as a mode of critical thinking about how historical principles must be interpreted in contemporary circumstances consistently with the imaginative demands of this community of principle, which must be

---

[116] See, e.g., Gary J. Jacobsohn, *The Supreme Court and the Decline of Constitutional Aspiration* (Totowa, N.J.: Rowman & Littlefield, 1986), who takes this paradoxical position. On the one hand, Jacobsohn insists that the legitimacy of the Constitution can only be understood as a protection of natural rights; on the other, attempts to ascribe abstract intentions to the Constitution are rejected. See idem, pp. 50–53. For a comparable view, see Walter Berns, *Taking the Constitution Seriously* (New York: Simon & Schuster, 1987).

rethought and reconstituted by each generation in light of its background political theory of just government. The community of principle of democratic constitutionalism could not, as Madison put the point, require that all persons be philosophers, but it could require all persons to interpret a historical tradition in a way more likely to make accessible to all the demands of democratic reason. The American melding of interpretive history and political philosophy must thus sometimes call upon political philosophy to make the best interpretive sense to the community at large of these demands. The consequence is that the best interpretation of historical principles is also sometimes a work of transformation by the critical powers of moral and political imagination in the light of emancipatory democratic reason (e.g., the constitutional criticisms of racism and sexism, more fully discussed in Chapter 7). That kind of community functions by making and giving effect to reasonable argument about how in contemporary circumstances historical protections of equal rights of the person should be understood; such arguments sometimes can only be reasonably conducted, as a matter of principled integrity, in terms of larger debates within political philosophy about the better reading of liberty and equality and their appropriate relationship in a comprehensive theory of justice.

The interpretive role of political philosophy in constitutional interpretation has been dismissed on the ground that it introduces too much intractable controversy among academic elites into American constitutional law.[117] That objection supposes there to be some less controversial and more democratic way of addressing issues of constitutional legitimacy, but the alternatives proposed are often more controversial and less democratic.[118] It is part of the genius of American constitutionalism that certain kinds of controversies over both the theory and practice of justice are the organon by which the community comes to a more reasonable understanding of how its arguments of historical principle must be elaborated in contemporary circumstances. Often practice is in advance of theory, but sometimes better arguments of political theory illuminate, deepen, and clarify the interpretive demands that a community of principle must make on free people. Constitutional interpretation imposes interpretive responsibilities, and controversy over the meaning of equality and liberty in just government is an ineliminable component of these responsibilities. The ambition to eliminate from public law such arguments misconceives the place of constitutional argument in the American community of principle. It dismisses as elitist the arguments that sometimes give the most reasonable interpretive justification accessible to all of the meaning of constitutional principles of democratic equality in contemporary circumstances. If it is illegitimately elitist to ask the people at large to think through and guarantee the principled scope of the historical protections of the inalienable rights of democratic freedom that they themselves reasonably cherish as immune

---

[117] See John Hart Ely, *Democracy and Distrust* (Cambridge, Mass.: Harvard Univ. Press, 1980), pp. 43–72.

[118] For further criticisms of Ely along these lines, see Chapters 1 and 7.

from political bargaining, then what sense can we make of the authority of the Constitution itself?

Political philosophy and law sometimes become one because the underlying interpretive issue (the reasonable justification of a constitutionally protected basic right of the person to all persons) turns on a more abstract understanding of equal liberty of conscience (Chapter 5), or of intimate private life (Chapter 6), or of stereotypical degrading prejudices that equal protection condemns as the basis for law (Chapter 7). Such uses of political philosophy are not extraneous to the project of constitutional legitimacy, but they are essential to the kind of moral and political imagination that is required of a community of principle making reasonable claims of legitimacy over time on free people. Such arguments are the public forum of democratic reason through which we come to a more constitutionally legitimate interpretive understanding that moves us beyond the shallow bromides of conventional majoritarian cant into the reasonable discourse of rights of the person to which we are committed as a community of principle, and of free people under the rule of law. The merger of law and political philosophy should, of course, surprise no one who takes the founders seriously at the level of thought and deliberation that they took in their great constructivist work of democratic reason (Chapters 2–4); indeed, the point of their entire project was to constitute institutions that would sustain a people capable of constitutional argument as dependent on the best arguments of democratic reason in their circumstances as the founders had been in their own. The ascription of abstract meanings to the founders' principles is not the betrayal or the trivialization of their project; rather, it is the very condition of making sense of the interpretive weight their project had for them and continues to have for us as a people for whom respect for rights is the condition of politically legitimate power.

Logic would have permitted a different interpretive approach to that which prevailed in America, that is, a preference for denotative over connotative meanings, or more concrete over more abstract connotative meanings. However, the result would almost certainly *not* have been the durable constitution we in fact have had in the United States, which pays the kind of interpretive homage to its founders that is a distinctive feature of American constitutional interpretation (Chapter 1). More frequent amendment would almost certainly have been required; perhaps American constitutional experience would have been more like the changing republican constitutions of France.[119] Our argument makes clear, furthermore, that such an interpretive practice of the founders' Constitution could not have reasonably justified the Constitution to the people at large in the way that its Lockean legitimacy requires. It would have been neither the Constitution that the founders intended nor the document that we have had.

If the advocates of such an interpretive practice would have appealed to

[119] Cf., e.g., Mauro Cappelletti, *Judicial Review in the Contemporary World* 2–6 (Indianapolis, Ind.: Bobbs-Merrill, 1971).

the founders' intent to justify their approach, then they would have been deplorably mistaken (Chapters 1, 7, and 8). Their appeal to the founders would be an abuse of the text, history, and political theory of the founders' Constitution. Indeed, their appeal would not only be interpretively wrong, but it would also express a need that the founders understood as the appetite of a constitutionally corrupt people for fictive Filmerian patriarchs. These are not the posterity of which the founders dreamed, but the victims of the Filmerian nightmare of unreason from which they sought to wake us.

5

Interpreting Enumerated Rights: Religious Liberty And Free Speech

A theory of free speech is, in the American context, a theory of one highly important and visible kind of constitutional interpretation, which is embedded in a larger fabric of related bodies of constitutional interpretation. We relate these interpretive bodies of law in certain well-accepted ways; for example, some free-speech cases are concurrently discussed as cases involving equal protection[1] or religious liberty.[2] However, it is a fairly remarkable indication of the state of constitutional theory that the relations among these interpretive bodies of law are rarely systematically discussed. Indeed, sometimes the very enterprise of general constitutional theory is scouted because it questions the immutable assumptions of such bodies of law considered in hermetically sealed isolation from one another.[3] This chapter challenges that orthodoxy and develops a general approach to the interpretation of constitutionally guaranteed enumerated rights—in particular, the rights of religious liberty and free speech protected by the First Amendment. The interpretive potential of this approach is revealed by the way it takes seriously a thread of historically continuous common principles in different bodies of law, a possibility left unexplored by contemporary constitutional theory. My justification for this approach is with both its interpretive and critical power, because it enables us to understand much of the law of religious liberty and free speech in the modern period, and at the same time advances understanding of some of the central theoretical puzzles of constitutional law, for example, the status of free speech as a critically defensible political value. This chapter begins with the issues of constitutional interpretation, and then turns to the theoretical puzzles.

It is now almost conventional wisdom that the modern doctrine of free speech bears little relation to its history, in particular, to the original understanding of free speech when the First Amendment was drafted and ratified in

---

[1] See, e.g., *Erznoznik* v. *Jacksonville,* 422 U.S. 205 (1975).

[2] See, e.g., *Cantwell* v. *Connecticut,* 310 U.S. 296 (1940).

[3] See Frederick Schauer, "An Essay on Constitutional Language," 29 *U.C.L.A. L. Rev.* 797 (1982).

1791.[4] Accordingly, the theory of free speech typically proceeds in a historical vacuum, or rather its sense of history begins with the World War I Espionage Act and the judicial responses to it.[5] This contracted historical vision naturally confirms the tendencies of the theories of free speech to proceed in isolation from the discussion of larger patterns of interpretive principle. The consequence has been not only historical myopia, but also inadequate contemporary understanding of basic issues of constitutional principle. In fact, the interpretive development of the law of free speech in the modern period is not a historical novelty, and the general theory of constitutional interpretation as proposed earlier has the great virtue of opening one's mind to the larger fabric of historically continuous constitutional principles that the modern law of free speech elaborates in an often remarkably principled way. A better interpretive theory of the founders' intent is, at the same time, a better account of contemporary interpretive practice. This approach clarifies as well all the indeterminate terms that have so undermined the critical force of theories of free speech, in particular, the relation of free speech to the theory of harms and its larger connection to principles of toleration. The discussion begins with general interpretive issues of both history and law, and then turns to the ways in which this approach advances both the interpretive and critical understanding of the modern law of free speech.

Comparison of the Speech and Religion Clauses

Historians of the First Amendment standardly contrast the original highly libertarian understanding of the religion clauses with the extremely circumscribed understanding of the free speech and press clauses. Leonard Levy's work is exemplary of both positions. On the one hand, Levy convincingly argues[6] that the religion clauses of the First Amendment (the free exercise and antiestablishment clauses) wholly deprive the federal government of any power over religion whether by coercion of religious belief or ritual (free exercise), or by endorsement of sectarian religious belief (antiestablishment). This radical understanding was, Levy argues, crystallized by Jefferson in his Virginia Bill for Religious Freedom, defended by Madison in his *Memorial*

---

[4] See, e.g., Leonard W. Levy, *Emergence of a Free Press* (New York: Oxford Univ. Press, 1985); idem, *Legacy of Suppression: Freedom of Speech and Press in Early American History* (Cambridge, Mass.: Belknap Press of Harvard Univ. Press, 1964). But cf. William A. Mayton, "Seditious Libel and the Lost Guarantee of a Freedom of Expression," 84 *Col. L. Rev.* 91 (1984); David A. Anderson, "The Origins of the Press Clause," 30 *U.C.L.A. L. Rev.* 455 (1983).

[5] See, e.g., *Schenck v. United States,* 249 U.S. 47 (1919); *Frohwerk v. United States,* 249 U.S. 204 (1919); *Debs v. United States,* 249 U.S. 211 (1919); *Abrams v. United States,* 250 U.S. 616 (1919).

[6] See Leonard Levy, "No Establishing of Religion: The Original Understanding," in *Judgments* (Chicago: Quadrangle, 1972) pp. 169–224. See also Leonard Levy, *The Establishment Clause* (New York: Macmillan, 1986). For confirmation of Levy's views, see also Thomas J. Curry, *The First Freedoms: Church and State in America to the Passage of the First Amendment* (New York: Oxford Univ. Press, 1986).

and Remonstrance[7] that secured adoption of Jefferson's Bill, and appealed to both generally, and, with respect to the religion clauses, particularly by Madison in his role as the central proponent of the Bill of Rights.[8] Levy argues, however, that the original understanding of the free speech and press clauses cannot reasonably be construed as the comparably libertarian interpretation that there is no federal power over speech.[9] At a minimum, the historical record indicates that the founders contemplated a federal common law of seditious libel; any more libertarian understanding was developed solely in the debates of the late 1790s over the Alien and Sedition Act.[10]

In his later study of the historical record,[11] Levy candidly acknowledges a forceful objection to his earlier views on the original conservative understanding of free speech, namely, James Madison's 1799–1800 *Report on the Virginia Resolutions*[12] (hereafter referred to as *Madison's Report*). Madison defends in the Bill of Rights precisely the proposition that Levy denied was or could reasonably be taken to be the original understanding of free speech—namely, in Madison's own words, "a positive denial to Congress of any power whatever on the subject."[13] If Madison took this view in 1799–1800, then is it not reasonable to construe it as his view in 1791, and, if so, how could there be *better* evidence of a libertarian original understanding? Levy denies the reasonableness of the inference.[14] My focus now is on one aspect of Madison's argument and Levy's interpretation of it, namely, Madison's striking interpretive analogy to the religion clauses.

A leading Federalist argument in defense of the constitutionality of a federal power over seditious libel noted the distinctive language of the religion and speech clauses: under the former, "*respecting* an establishment of religion," or "*prohibiting* [its] free exercise,"[15] in the other "*abridging* the freedom of speech or of the press."[16] Federalists argued that the difference in language justified the interpretive inference that Congress, unlike the religion clauses, could make laws respecting but not abridging speech; that is, Congress could regulate speech through laws like seditious libel laws. Madison precisely denied the inference as follows:

---

[7] See James Madison, *Memorial and Remonstrance against Religious Assessments,* in Robert A. Rutland et al., eds., *The Papers of James Madison 1784–1786,* vol. 8, pp. 295–306.

[8] See David Richards, *Toleration and the Constitution* (New York: Oxford Univ. Press, 1986), pp. 111–121.

[9] See Levy, *Legacy of Suppression.*

[10] See ibid. For pertinent historical background, see John C. Miller, *Crisis in Freedom: The Alien and Sedition Acts* (Boston: Little, Brown, 1951); also, idem, *The Federalist Era 1787–1801* (New York: Harper & Row, 1960).

[11] See Levy, *Emergence of Free Press* (1985).

[12] *Madison's Report on the Virginia Resolutions,* in Jonathan Elliot, ed., *Debates in the Several State Conventions on the Adoption of the Federal Constitution,* vol. 4 (Philadelphia: Lippincott, 1836), pp. 546–80.

[13] Ibid., p. 571.

[14] See, e.g., Levy, *Emergence of Free Press* pp. 315–25.

[15] U.S. Constitution, Amendment I (emphasis added).

[16] Ibid. (emphasis added).

For, if Congress may regulate the freedom of the press, provided they do not abridge it, because it is said only, "they shall not abridge it," and is not said "they shall make no law respecting it," the analogy of reasoning is conclusive, that Congress may *regulate,* and even *abridge,* the free exercise of religion, provided they do not *prohibit* it; because it is said only, "they shall not prohibit it"; and is *not* said, "they shall make no law *respecting,* or no law *abridging* it."[17]

Levy responds that "Madison's argument leaked at its seams,"[18] because "he cleverly proved too much, or nothing at all"[19]; that is, his argument simply shows that the language of the religion clauses could be read to allow what they clearly were meant to forbid, namely, regulations of religion, which does not show that the free speech clauses prohibit any regulation. Although Madison's argument is not conclusive, it is interpretively odd to construe it as disingenuous. He reasonably concludes that the Federalists are imputing "a studied discrimination"[20] to the different language of the two clauses that, if pursued even more studiously, would abuse the meaning of the religion clauses as well. If it abuses one, then it may abuse the meaning of another. Thus, Madison argues about the style of interpretation appropriate to the two clauses of the First Amendment and denies the cogency of the Federalists' linguistic argument.

Madison's alternative interpretive argument is, as one would expect, an argument of both history and principle. Historically, Madison appeals to the language of Virginia's ratification of the Constitution, which called for guarantees of both conscience and speech and to which the First Amendment responded. The Virginia conventions spoke, Madison argues, in terms that linked conscience and speech, namely, "that among other essential rights, the liberty of conscience and freedom of the press cannot be cancelled, abridged, restrained, or modified, by any authority of the United States."[21] Madison observes that

> words could not well express, in a fuller or more forcible manner, the understanding of the Convention, that the liberty of conscience and freedom of the press were *equally* and *completely* exempted from all authority whatever of the United States.[22]

He further notes that, as a matter of principle,

> both of these rights, the liberty of conscience, and of the press, rest equally on the original ground of not being delegated by the Constitution, and conse-

---

[17] *Madison's Report,* p. 577.
[18] Levy, *Emergence of Free Press,* p. 319.
[19] Ibid.
[20] *Madison's Report,* p. 577.
[21] Ibid., p. 576.
[22] Ibid.

quently withheld from the government. Any construction, that would attack this original security for the one, must have the like effect on the other.[23]

Madison's interpretive argument holds that both history and principle support a coextensive level of protection, and that the only textual argument to the contrary rests on "a studied discrimination"[24] that is internally incoherent and therefore not cogent.

Levy's reading of Madison is tendentiously driven by his long-standing commitment to an antilibertarian interpretation of the original understanding of the founders. Levy's argument is very much that of a lawyer; it is almost as if he, like the Federalists, were in legal controversy with Madison. However, there is surely a more natural interpretive approach to Madison's writings, one that is more consistent with the general views of Madison and other founders that the written constitution establishes a continuous community of principle. The founders had a wide range of interpretive views in 1791 about how the First Amendment should be applied; we know, for example, that— whatever Madison's views may have been—James Wilson had argued in the ratification debates over the 1787 Constitution that the scope of the right of free speech[25] would not extend to anyone who "attacks the security or welfare of the government"[26] (i.e., seditious libel laws). However, these divergent views were abstract and still hypothetical, had not been tested by the kinds of arguments of principle over hard cases to which the Constitution would give rise, and certainly could later be reasonably elaborated in diverse ways. Un-questionably, Levy has demonstrated that nothing in the history as of 1791 or in the constitutional text would have determined or required a later libertar-ian application of these clauses. When subsequent debates over application did arise, the founders took different interpretive views. Many of these views were not liberal (e.g., like those of Wilson), but some views, notably Madi-son's, were; there is no reason not to regard his arguments in 1799–1800 as implicit in the original understanding as any other views, as being one among several possible interpretive lines that might later be taken.

Today we discuss the law of free speech against the background of an enormous body of historical and interpretive experience of threats to free speech and how best to guard against them, which appropriately constrains what could reasonably be regarded as a principled argument of law when so much of the law of free speech is properly settled and decidedly liberal. In contrast, the period 1791–1800 was unconstrained by such interpretive experi-ence, a fact underscored by the view of many Americans (like Madison) that

---

[23] Ibid., p. 577.

[24] Ibid.

[25] Wilson, like Madison and other Founders in 1787–1788, believed that free speech and other rights were reserved from federal power without any explicit textual reservation. See, e.g., Madison at the Virginia ratifying convention, Elliot, ed., *Debates,* vol. 3, pp. 620, 626–27; and Hamilton in *The Federalist,* pp. 579–81.

[26] Merrill Jensen, ed., *The Documentary History of the Ratification of the Constitution* (Madison: State Historical Society of Wisconsin, 1976), vol. 2, p. 455.

the British common law of free speech (like its law of religious liberty) could not be necessarily authoritative on the American revolutionary and constitutional commitment to republican legitimacy. Therefore, the issue is not which view better reflects the settled law in 1791, because there was not any law. Rather, the important issue of constitutional principle is whether Madison's views are here, as they often are elsewhere,[27] interpretively powerful as arguments of principle—that is, whether his views are compelling explications of the political theory of republican constitutionalism to which we might appeal in deciding among the wide range of alternative interpretive views otherwise consistent with the text and its history. Certainly, Madison's views were not interpretively frivolous in 1791 or 1799–1800, and are in fact a remarkably useful articulation of reasonably defensible principles of public law today. In short, in this arena, Madison (as a founder) plays precisely the role in contemporary interpretive practice that he anticipated, namely, setting the terms of a reasonable dialogue about the essential interpretive issues for the contemporary American community of principle as it has evolved over time. Americans can reasonably understand the modern law of free speech as a historically continuous elaboration of the arguments of principle central to the Madisonian perspective on free speech.

Madison's argument is not just that the principles of religious liberty and free speech are analogous, but that they rest "equally on the original ground of not being delegated by the Constitution"[28] and are "*equally* and *completely* exempted from all authority whatever of the United States."[29] Why should he, in this way, unify both their justification and their scope of protection? He appears to start from the radical understanding of religious liberty that he shared with Jefferson and that both adapted from Lockean principles of toleration.[30] Republican political theory protects, in this view, the core value of free persons guaranteed equal respect for their right to exercise their reasonable powers regarding ultimate questions of value in living. This value is protected by the inalienable right to conscience, a right that—consistent with the idea that a person's liberty is essential to republican political theory[31]—cannot be surrendered to the state or any person.

On this basis, Locke[32] argues for a principle of toleration that links a free conscience to each and every person's autonomous exercise, as a democratic equal, of his or her moral competence to reason about the nature and content of the ethical obligations imposed on each person by an ethical God. In

---

[27] Consider, for example, Madison's important contributions to the understanding of the federal system *The Federalist* no. 10) and his pivotal role in the understanding of the religion clauses (see e.g., pp. 111–21, Richards, *Toleration and the Constitution*).

[28] *Madison's Report*, p. 577.

[29] Ibid., p. 576.

[30] See Richards, *Toleration and the Constitution*, pp. 89–102, 104–28.

[31] See, e.g., ibid., pp. 98–102.

[32] See John Locke, *A Third Letter for Toleration*, in *The Works of John Locke*, vol. 6 (London: Thomas Tegg, 1823), p. 180.

particular, this principle bars state enforcement of any conception of value in living that selects a sectarian view from among the latitudinarian range of views that reasonable persons might choose. The moral nerve center of Locke's argument for universal toleration is that state enforcement of sectarian views, whether by Protestant or Catholic polities, rests on the illegitimate confusion of the enforcer's beliefs in religious truth with the range of all religious views that might reasonably be believed; in effect, all views, except the sectarian views of the enforcer, are supposed to be unreasonable. Such enforcement cuts the latitudinarian range of reasonable moral freedom to the cramped measure of sectarian belief, and thus degrades the moral powers that both polities believe to be essential to true (Christian) religion and sound ethics.[33] Accordingly, the state must withdraw from making or enforcing such judgments. It must not require that all persons attend one religious service or not attend another. Locke makes the point in terms of legitimately secular and illegitimate religious state purposes: the state may justly pursue the aims of life, liberty, and property that all reasonable persons will need in order to pursue their more ultimate aims (whatever they are), but the state may not enforce the more ultimate sectarian religious aims about which reasonable persons from diverse backgrounds might disagree. Neutrally acceptable state purposes are defined by Locke as being those general aims like "civil interest . . . life, liberty, health, and indolency of body; and the possession of outward things, such as money, lands, houses, furniture, and the like."[34]

Jefferson and Madison apply the Lockean conception of principles of universal toleration beyond Locke's own application of those principles. They not only accord Catholics and atheists the protections of universal toleration,[35] but they also extend its principles to include both the protection of the free exercise of religion and the prohibition of an establishment of religion.[36] In their view, respect for one's inalienable right to his or her conscience requires that the state neither forbid nor require any exercise of religion (free-exercise clause[37]) nor endorse any form of religious teaching (the antiestablishment clause[38]). Just as the free-exercise clause protects the expression of one's current religious beliefs, the antiestablishment clause guarantees that the state will not endorse particular religious teaching in a way that compromises the equal liberty of formation and revision of one's religious beliefs; that is, the state cannot communicate by law the corruptive belief of a religion of true Americans. Lack of a power in the state to abridge religion on the basis of such judgments remits that power to the reasonable judgment of each and every person, who is by that means secured moral independence from state power in the exercise of critical moral powers about basic matters of con-

[33] See Richards, *Toleration and the Constitution*, pp. 89–98.
[34] *Letter Concerning Toleration*, in *Works of John Locke*, vol. 6, p. 10.
[35] See Richards, *Toleration and the Constitution*, pp. 112–14.
[36] See ibid.
[37] See ibid., pp. 140–6.
[38] See ibid., pp. 146–150.

science. The idea is not that the state is always mistaken in making judgments that certain religious views are false or noxious, but that, in principle, judgments of that sort cannot be made by a state committed to equal respect for the right of people to exercise their own reasonable judgments over these matters.[39]

Both the free-exercise and antiestablishment clauses clearly deploy the Lockean distinction between legitimate and illegitimate state purposes. Any infringement of the religious liberty of free exercise can only be justified, for example, by a compelling secular state purpose,[40] and the antiestablishment clause demands that the state not support any form of sectarian religious teaching but pursue only neutrally acceptable state purposes.[41] Consistent with Locke's general argument, the state may incidentally restrict religious free exercise only in the necessary pursuit of a compelling secular state purpose: it might thus, as Locke argued,[42] allow state power to forbid religious rituals involving child sacrifice (i.e., the taking of life, a general good), whereas a state prohibition on animal sacrifices (i.e., preventing the taking of animal life not being a general good in the same way) might be forbidden. In the Virginia Bill for Religious Freedom, Jefferson argues that the line should be divided as follows:

To suffer the civil magistrate to intrude his powers into the field of opinion and to restrain the profession of propagation of principles on supposition of their ill tendency is a dangerous falacy [sic], which at once destroys all religious liberty, because he being of course judge of that tendency will make his opinions the rule of judgment, and approve or condemn the sentiments of others only as they shall square with or differ from his own; that it is time enough for the rightful purposes of civil government for its officers to interfere when principles break out into overt acts against peace and good order; and finally, that truth . . . has nothing to fear from the conflict unless by human interposition disarmed of her natural weapons, free argument and debate. . . .[43]

---

[39] For a recent exploration of the moral foundations of this principle, see Thomas Nagel, "Moral Conflict and Political Legitimacy," 16 *Phil. & Pub. Aff.* 215 (1987).

[40] See, e.g., *Sherbert* v. *Verner,* 374 U.S. 398 (1963); *Thomas* v. *Review Board,* 450 U.S. 707 (1981).

[41] See, e.g., *Lemon* v. *Kurtzman,* 403 U.S. 602 (1971).

[42] Locke naturally appealed to "civil interests" (see pp. 9–10, Locke, *Letter Concerning Toleration*) in defining when the state may and may not restrict or regulate conscience: the state may require that babies be washed if washing is understood to secure health interests, but it may not do so if the aim is not such an interest, for example, in the case of compulsory baptism; the state may not stop a person from killing a calf in a religious ritual if no civil interest would be secured by such a prohibition, but it may forbid the taking of a child's life in such a ritual. See idem, pp. 30–31, 33–34.

[43] Julian P. Boyd, ed., *The Papers of Thomas Jefferson, 1777–1779,* vol. 2 (Princeton, N.J.: Princeton Univ. Press, 1950), p. 546.

He also crisply describes the denial of state power as follows: "it does me no injury for my neighbor to say there are twenty gods, or no god. It neither picks my pocket nor breaks my leg."[44]

Madison shares with Jefferson this principled understanding of the meaning of religious liberty. Madison's advocacy in Virginia of Jefferson's Bill for Religious Freedom, coupled with his own clearly stated dependence on the Virginia understanding as the background for the adoption of the religion clauses of the First Amendment, confirm the place of these principles in the original understanding of the religion clauses.[45] Madison appears, however, to have gone beyond Jefferson in connecting these principles to the principles of free speech.[46]

The argument in *Madison's Report* is a principled elaboration of the argument for the liberty of conscience. As stated earlier, Madison argues in this document that the state may have no power over religion because society's illegitimate sectarian beliefs about the true religion will corrupt state judgments about the worth or value of religion. Such illegitimate political power degrades the reasonable moral independence that is essential to a community of principle among free people. Madison saw that the same argument justified a comparable protection for communicative independence because the state was familiarly inclined to make and enforce the same kinds of suspect judgments about the worth of speech and thus to compromise the communicative foundations of moral independence and of conscience itself. He saw the principle of free speech as directed at a comparable prohibition on the enforcement of these types of state judgments.

Certainly, Jefferson had stated the principle of religious liberty both in his Bill for Religious Freedom and in *Notes on the State of Virginia* in a way that correlatively protected religious speech ("it does me no injury for my neighbor to say . . ."[47]). However, Jefferson, unlike Madison, apparently did not extend this understanding beyond narrowly understood religious speech.[48] Madison's more expansive view of protection derives from the deeper and more critically elaborated conception of Lockean political legitimacy that he had already shown in his private correspondence with Jefferson over the latter's doctrinaire nineteen-year right of constitutional majoritarianism (see Chapter 4). Conscience, for both Madison and Jefferson, is an inalienable human right because it is the right that enables persons, on terms of equal respect, to be the sovereign moral critics of value in living. However, such values, Madison clearly saw, must, in principle, include political value like the

---

[44] Thomas Jefferson, *Notes on the State of Virginia* in William Peden, ed. (New York: W. W. Norton, 1954), p. 159.

[45] See *Madison's Report*, pp. 576–77; Richards *Toleration and the Constitution*, pp. 111–16.

[46] For Jefferson's quite restrictive conception of the scope of free speech (in contrast to his expansive protection of religious liberty), see Leonard W. Levy, *Jefferson and Civil Liberties: The Darker Side* (New York: Quadrangle, 1973), pp. 42–69.

[47] Jefferson, *Notes on the State of Virginia*, p. 159.

[48] See Levy, *Jefferson and Civil Liberties*, pp. 42–69.

legitimacy of government that was, for Locke (see Chapter 3), to be assessed and decided by the deliberative judgment of each and every free conscience. For Locke, the ultimate questions of legitimacy were addressed to such free and rational judgment—whether the government respected human rights and pursued the public good, and, if not, whether disobedience was warranted, including in extreme cases the right to revolt and revolution itself.[49] Both the American revolutionary and constitutional mind rested on that common principle of a free people's morally independent judgment to which all political power was accountable; Madison—who was a much better political theorist than Jefferson—was concerned that the principle's full demands of political integrity be fully understood and preserved among the foundations of American constitutionalism. In particular, the protections of speech—correlative to such protection of conscience—cannot be limited to narrowly understood religious speech. For Madison, then, the objection to the enforcement by the federal government of laws like the Alien and Sedition Acts is the way that these laws enforce a suspect judgment of the worth of speech (notably speech critical of government); such judgment interposes the government's self-protective beliefs about the legitimate scope of political criticism on the reasonableness of such criticism. For Madison, however, that kind of state judgment is guilty of the same kind of corruption that Jefferson, in his Bill for Religious Freedom, described in religious persecution:

> To restrain the profession of propagation of principles on supposition of their ill tendency is a dangerous falacy [sic], which at once destroys all religious liberty, because he being of course judge of that tendency will his opinions the rule of judgment, and approve or condemn the sentiments of others only as they shall square with or differ from his own.[50]

If anything, the state's temptation to engage in such corruption is greater with speech expressly critical of the state. Accordingly, speech should enjoy at least a comparable kind of protection to that of religious freedom.

Madison's argument of principle rests on the larger implications of the Lockean political theory, which is fundamental to American constitutionalism. He takes as axiomatic the inalienable right to conscience and then shows how the central place of that right—in Locke's overall theory of political legitimacy—requires a correlative scope to the right of free speech. Put simply, how can a state maintain the conditions of morally independent judgment of free people on the state's Lockean legitimacy without according them a correlative protection of the speech that is precisely most critical of the government, indeed of the constitution itself? Madison thus uses reasonable arguments of general political theory for a liberal interpretation of the free speech and press clauses. He rejects the way in which the Federalists parsed the clause because he found their linguistic arguments internally flawed (as in-

---

[49] Cf. Richards, *Toleration and the Constitution,* pp. 165–87.
[50] Boyd, ed., *Papers of Thomas Jefferson,* vol. 2, p. 546.

deed they are) and because he believed that the republican political theory already protected by much of the Constitution and Bill of Rights required, as a matter of principle, that the text and history be read in the way he proposes. In particular, he denied the authority of an appeal to the British common-law tradition of free speech—on which Federalists crucially depended—because the republicanism of the Constitution rejected the interpretive context (of British constitutional monarchy) that gave a sense to the limited guarantees of the British common law. Madison's argument of principle is precisely the argument we just investigated, namely, that the background right to conscience is most coherently understood, explicated, and defended to reasonable persons subject to coercive state power if the protection of conscience is correlatively extended to speech. Perhaps Madison believed as well that the power of his argument of principle might be justified by the way the community of principle he anticipated would over time gravitate around this argument. In fact, to a remarkable degree, that principle underlies much of the modern law of free speech.

An Interpretive Theory of the Modern Law of Free Speech

The current law of free speech in the United States first identifies an expanding class of communications protected by the free speech and press clauses of the First Amendment, and then forbids any state restriction on such communications aimed at what the communcations say (a content-based restriction on speech)[51] unless they present a clear and present danger of some imminent, rebuttable, and very grave harm.[52] The modern law of free speech is remarkable for both its expansion in the scope of protected speech and its highly demanding requirement that the law satisfy the clear and present danger test. Madison's argument of principles clarifies each development in this area.

We must begin by noting that the judiciary has sharply contracted the traditional range of communicative utterances (clearly "speech" in any reasonable sense of that term) that is exempt from protection by the values of free speech. The traditional list of unprotected speech included subversive advocacy,[53] fighting words,[54] libels of both groups and individuals,[55] obscenity,[56] commercial advertising,[57] and the like. The modern Supreme Court has now questioned and changed such traditional exemption of these forms of speech from free-speech protection: subversive advocacy[58] and group libel[59] are now

[51] See, e.g., *Chicago Police Department* v. *Mosley,* 408 U.S. 92 (1972); Kenneth I. Karst, "Equality as a Central Principle in the First Amendment," 43 *U. Chi. L. Rev.* 20 (1975).

[52] See, e.g., *Brandenburg* v. *Ohio,* 395 U.S. 444 (1969).

[53] See, e.g., *Gitlow* v. *New York,* 268 U.S. 652 (1925).

[54] *Chaplinsky* v. *New York,* 315 U.S. 568 (1942).

[55] See, e.g., *Beauharnais* v. *Illinois,* 343 U.S. 250 (1952).

[56] See *Roth* v. *New York,* 354 U.S. 476 (1957).

[57] See *Breard* v. *Alexandria,* 341 U.S. 622 (1951).

[58] See *Brandenburg* v. *Ohio,* 395 U.S. 444 (1969).

[59] See *Collin* v. *Smith,* 578 F.2d 1197 (1978), *cert. den.,* 439 U.S. 916 (1978).

fully protected, and much of what was traditionally fighting words,[60] obscenity,[61] or advertising[62] is now more fully protected than previously. We need to understand this development interpretively, and Madison's argument of principle meets this need.

Madison's Argument of Principle

Madison had argued that the protections accorded religious liberty could not be limited, as Jefferson believed, to narrowly understood religious speech; rather, Madison contended that state abridgments of speech based on its judgment of the value or worth of speech criticizing values in living, including political legitimacy, were objectionable for the same reason of principle, that is, they fail to respect the right of persons themselves to make such reasonable judgments. Therefore, he concluded that such speech should be similarly protected. The argument's interpretation is contextually responsive, as Madison's free-speech argument itself shows, to background conceptions of the legitimate scope of exercise of our reasonable moral powers.

In the area of religious liberty, for example, both Jefferson and Madison had expanded Lockean principles of toleration to Catholics and atheists precisely because background conceptions of ethics (i.e., the moral sense theory entertained by both the Virginians) could in their circumstances no longer reasonably exclude either group from the exercise of their critical moral powers about value in living.[63] Moral sense theory depended on a universally accessible, egalitarian sense of ethics that might be common to many religious and nonreligious moral tradtions and that might not be exhaustively defined by any one such tradition; indeed, for both Jefferson and Madison, part of the basic point of respect for conscience was to emancipate people's capacity responsibly to exercise their moral sense unencumbered by the sectarian orthodoxies the enforcement through law of which had enslaved the human mind to accept arbitrary hierarchy and privilege. The scope of toleration could not, for them, reasonably be narrowed to the measure of any orthodoxy that might compromise the reasonable freedom of inquiry, thought, and action. Although both Madison and Jefferson may have believed in some variant of Protestant Christianity, they realized that their beliefs were but one of many morally reasonable beliefs about value in living, and that the scope of universal toleration must expand to include all such beliefs (including Catholics and atheists).[64]

The reasonable justification over time to the community at large must, as we have seen (Chapter 4), be contextually sensitive to the various changes

---

[60] See, e.g., *Gooding* v. *Wilson*, 405 U.S. 518 (1972).

[61] See e.g., *Miller* v. *California*, 413 U.S. 15 (1973).

[62] See, e.g., *Virginia Pharmacy Board* v. *Virginia Consumer Council*, 425 U.S. 748 (1976). But see *Posadas de Puerto Rico Associates* v. *Tourism Company of Puerto Rico*, 106 S. Ct. 2968 (1986).

[63] See Richards, *Toleration and the Constitution*, pp. 126–27.

[64] See ibid.

that influence such justification (e.g., the interpretation of the powers of Congress over commerce must allow it to take into account the changing economic circumstances of the nation that influence the reasonable interpretation of these powers). The reasonable justification of inalienable rights of the person with contextual sensitivity to relevantly changed circumstances is a comparable imperative of the very legitimacy of constitutional argument. Each constitutional generation must, in the terms used earlier (Chapter 4), reasonably justify to all persons the distinction that is fundamental to the protection of the inalienable right to conscience—namely, between the positive conception of free public reason that is every person's right and the negative conception of orthodox religious, moral, and political truth that must be refused enforcement through law in order to give fair scope to the positive conception. The political distinction between these two conceptions of reason does not rest on philosophical skepticism in epistemology, metaphysics, or ethics, but on the kind of political skepticism about the corruptibility of political power that we have already examined at length (Chapter 2). Political power could not constitutionally extend to enforcement at large of ideological orthodoxies because of the ways such enforcement had subverted the competence of persons to know and claim their inalienable rights to reasonable moral, religious, and political self-government. Political power must accordingly be limited to the ends of a politics of public reason available and justifiable to all as persons capable of reasonable thought, deliberation, and action. In contrast, political power cannot extend to the enforcement of conceptions of orthodox truth (no matter how widely entertained) that are incapable of justification on the terms that alone respect our common and equal inalienable right to be treated as persons capable of reasonable self-government. The constitutional interpretation of this conception of a politics of public reason must change its contours consistent with an enlarged understanding of what could count as reasonable justification to all persons.

The American tradition of interpretation has thus not always construed the scope of universal toleration as liberally as Jefferson and Madison; furthermore, we may understand such shifts over time in terms of differing interpretations of the background context that influence reasonable justification in this arena. For example, the nineteenth-century American consensus on religion clause jurisprudence reflected an understanding of ethics that was closer to Locke's theological ethics than to Jefferson's moral sense theory. This is the consensus that Justice Joseph Story articulated when he appealed to the de facto establishment of Protestant Christianity in the United States, and thus justified state impositions of prayers and Bible reading in the public schools, blasphemy prosecutions, and excluding atheists from public office.[65] However, the nineteenth and twentieth centuries saw a number of developments in Bible criticism and in science, sharper demarcation of religion and ethical

---

[65] See Joseph Story, *Commentaries on the Constitution of the United States,* excerpted in Philip Schaff, *Church and State in the United States,* in *Papers of the American Historical Association,* vol. 2, no. 4 (New York: G.P. Putnam's Sons, 1886), pp. 128–30.

claims, and even criticism of religion on ethical grounds, which irretrievably undermined Justice Story's position. Story may have sensibly believed his views to be reasonably justifiable in his period, although even then Jefferson and Madison contested this interpretive judgment. His view make little sense today.

Effect of Historical Developments on the Interpretation of the Speech and Religion Clauses

To make a long and complex story short, the developments in historiography and Bible criticism have permanently eroded any monolithic conception of the essential beliefs and sources of Protestant Christianity[66]; indeed, there is reasonable metainterpretive disagreement over what these beliefs and sources are and how they should be understood, valued, and elaborated. Developments in science have further fueled criticism of the Bible, inspiring, for example, questions over how to reconcile the epistemic claims of science (such as evolution) with traditional Bible interpretation.[67] Correlative with the radical metainterpretive diversity regarding essential religious beliefs and sources of those beliefs, a more critical appreciation is accorded the autonomy of ethics from religion.[68] This appreciation is motivated by our need for a common ethical basis in the face of radical metainterpretive diversity; that is, it is motivated by our need for an ethics of equal respect centering on all-purpose general goods. Indeed, such an autonomous code of ethics may be required from an internally religious perspective if it better expresses, as it may, the ethical motivations of a religion in which our moral powers fully express themselves in an ethics of equal respect for all persons whose dignity is the image of God in us.[69] From this perspective, the ethical independence,

[66] See, e.g., Stephen Sykes, *The Identity of Christianity* (London: SPCK, 1984), Jerry Brown, *The Rise of Bible Criticism in America, 1800–1870* (Middletown, Conn.: Wesleyan Univ. Press, 1969); Stephen Neill, *The Interpretation of the New Testament 1861–1961* (New York: Oxford Univ. Press, 1966); Nathan Hatch and Mark Noll, *The Bible in America* (New York: Oxford Univ. Press, 1982); James Barr, *The Bible in the Modern World* (London: SCM Press, 1973). On the resulting divisions within Protestantism, see William Hutchison, *The Modernist Impulse in American Protestantism* (Cambridge, Mass.: Harvard Univ. Press, 1976); Marty Marty, *Righteous Empire* (New York: Dial Press, 1970); Ernest Sandeen, *The Roots of Fundamentalism* (Chicago: Univ. of Chicago Press, 1970); George Marsden, *Fundamentalism and American Culture* (New York: Oxford Univ. Press, 1980). On the erosion of distinctions between believers and unbelievers, see Martin Martin, *Varieties of Unbelief* (Garden City, N.Y.: Anchor, 1966); also his *The Infidel: Freethought and American Religion* (Cleveland: World Publishing, 1961).

[67] See, in general, Charles Gillispie, *Genesis and Geology* (Cambridge: Harvard Univ. Press, 1951); John Greene, *The Death of Adam* (Ames: Iowa State Univ. Press, 1959). On the response to Darwin by American religion, see Sidney Ahlstrom, *A Religious History of the American People* (New Haven, Conn.: Yale Univ. Press, 1972), pp. 766–72.

[68] See, in general, Gene Outka and John Reeder, eds., *Religion and Morality* (Garden City, N.Y.: Anchor, 1973); Paul Helm, ed., *Divine Commands and Morality* (Oxford: Oxford Univ. Press, 1981). Cf. Philip Quinn, *Divine Commands and Moral Requirements* (Oxford: Clarendon Press, 1978); Basil Mitchell, *Morality: Religious and Secular* (Oxford: Clarendon Press, 1980).

[69] Cf. Gordon Allport, *The Individual and His Religion* (New York: Macmillan, 1950).

even of the unbeliever, may better express the spirit of ethically prophetic religion than the attitude of the conventional religious believer whose views mirror, and do not ethically examine, the often callous inhumanity of conventional morality.[70]

Furthermore, some influential contemporary perspectives criticize religion itself as ethically repressive and claim that alternative nontheistic, or even atheistic, views are more expressive of realizing a community of equal respect.[71] Such a conception would, if true, turn the traditional exclusion of atheists from universal toleration on its head; advocacy of religion, not atheism, would be excluded from universal toleration.

None of these developments requires us to say that belief in God or in the truth of the Bible is false, or that any of the alternative propositions claimed is true. However, they do establish the general line of Jefferson's thought,[72] that persons may realize their personal and ethical dignity, and express their reasonable moral powers through belief in any of these propositions.[73] Our conception of reasonable metainterpretive diversity, in the exercise of a just freedom of conscience, has widened, if anything, beyond Jefferson's idea of reasonable arguments and sources. The scope of universal toleration must be correspondingly larger.

This kind of analysis clarifies how both the scope of universal toleration and cognate constitutional arguments about the meaning and application of the constitutional neutrality commanded by the religion clauses of the First Amendment have shifted over time. For example—consistent with the analysis proposed here—the antiestablishment clause has been interpreted to forbid any form of state-endorsed religious teaching such as prayers in the public schools,[74] or adaptation of the curriculum to sectarian religious belief (e.g., the creationism controversies[75]). An important thread of religion clause jurisprudence suggests that the central right protected by the religion clauses cannot be confined to conventional forms of theistic belief.[76]

The expansion in the scope of free-speech protection expresses the same kind of shift in the application of constitutional neutrality that was just examined in the area of religion clause jurisprudence; indeed, it is motivated by the same kind of interpretive argument of principle that Madison invoked when

[70] See, in general, Martin, *Varieties of Unbelief.*

[71] See, e.g., Kai Nielsen, *Ethics without God* (Buffalo, N.Y.: Prometheus Books, 1973). Cf. David Muzzey, *Ethics as a Religion* (New York: Frederick Ungar Publishing Co., 1951).

[72] See Richards, *Toleration and the Constitution,* pp. 126–27.

[73] See ibid.

[74] See, e.g., *Engel* v. *Vitale,* 370 U.S. 421 (1962); *Abington School Dist.* v. *Schempp,* 374 U.S. 203 (1963); *Wallace* v. *Jaffree,* 472 U.S. 38 (1985).

[75] See, e.g., *Epperson* v. *Arkansas,* 393 U.S. 97 (1968); *Edwards* v. *Aguillard,* 107 S.Ct.2573 (1987); *McLean* v. *Arkansas Board of Education,* 529 F. Supp. 1255 (E.D. Ark. 1982).

[76] See, e.g., *Torcaso* v. *Watkins,* 367 U.S. 488 (1961); *United States* v. *Seeger,* 380 U.S. 163 (1965); *Welsh* v. *United States,* 398 U.S. 333 (1970). *Gillette* v. *United States,* 401 U.S. 437 (1971) holds that the congressional refusal to exempt selective conscientious objectors (to some, but not all wars) is constitutional. It does not question the idea that religious and nonreligious conscience stand equal before the law. However, see *Wisconsin* v. *Yoder,* 406 U.S. 205 (1972).

he expanded principles of toleration beyond narrowly understood religious belief. No form of distinction among the various forms of conscience, religious or nonreligious, still appears consistent with the equal respect for moral independence; for the same reason, traditional exclusions from free-speech protection are inconsistent with the kind of equal respect for communicative integrity that constitutional values of free speech command in the service of the freedom of conscience itself.

American constitutional law now understands, for example, that neutrally applicable protections of free speech must include subversive advocacy[77] or group libel.[78] Suppression of subversive advocacy enforces the state's content-biased judgment about "dangerous" speech, which is precisely the kind of state judgment about which we have the most just grounds for skepticism, because the state thus unjustly controls the expression of ultimate social, political, and moral criticism that must remain independent of state power to assure the moral independence of the inalienable right to conscience itself.[79] Moreover, the enforcement of group libel laws involves the state in making and enforcing similar judgments, discriminating among legitimate and illegitimate expressions of conscientiously held and controversial views criticizing values in living. However, the state must not possess this power over one's conscience if it is to respect the moral sovereignty of each and every person to make his or her own judgments.[80]

Even the traditional scope of the obscene has, in my opinion, been eroded in light of the range of forms of legitimate moral pluralism in sexuality and life-styles. These life-styles were unthinkable in the morally homogeneous and sexually repressive society that dictated the way in which purity reformers in Britain and the United States enforced Victorian sexual morality through the use of antiobscenity laws, including, for example, suppression of contraceptive and abortifacient education, information, and advocacy.[81] If that sexual morality is now under legitimate conscientious debate in society at large (on the ground that it is immorally repressive and unjust[82]), then the tradi-

---

[77] See *Brandenburg v. Ohio*, 395 U.S. 444 (1969).

[78] See *Collin v. Smith*, 578 F.2d 1197 (1978), *cert. den.*, 439 U.S. 916 (1978).

[79] See, in general, Richards, *Toleration and the Constitution*, pp. 178–87.

[80] See, in general, ibid. pp. 189–93.

[81] See, e.g., *United States v. Chesman*, 19 F. 497 (E.D. Mo. 1881); *United States v. Bennett*, 24 F.Cas. 1093, No. 14,571 (C.C.S.D.N.Y. 1897); *Regina v. Bradlaugh*, 2 Q.B.D. 569 (1877), *rev'd on other grounds*, 3 Q.B.D. 607 (1878). The text of the substantive section of the Comstock Act Sec. 2, ch. 258, sec. 2, 17 Stat. 598, 599 (1873), *as amended*, 18 U.S.C. 1461 (1970), includes in its prohibitions of obscene matter "No obscene, lewd, or lascivious book, . . . or any article or things designed or intended for the prevention of conception or procuring of abortion."

[82] See, e.g., R.R. Bell, *Premarital Sex in a Changing Society* (Englewood Cliffs, N.J.: Prentice-Hall, 1966); James R. Smith and Lynn G. Smith, eds., *Beyond Monogamy* (Baltimore, Md.: Johns Hopkins Univ. Press, 1974); *The Wolfenden Report: Report of the Committee on Homosexual Offenses and Prostitution* (New York: Stein & Day, 1963); Dolores Klaich, *Woman and Woman* (New York: William Morrow, 1974). For related judicial decisions, see *Roe v. Wade*, 410 U.S. 113 (1973) (abortion); *Griswold v. Connecticut*, 381 U.S. 479 (1965) (contraception); *People v. Onofre*, 51 N.Y.2d 476 (1980), *cert. den.*, 451 U.S. 987 (1981) (consensual sodomy). However, cf. *Bowers v. Hardwick*, 106 S. Ct. 2841 (1986) (upholding state statute that criminalizes sodomy).

tional scope of obscenity must, like the traditional scope of religion clause jurisprudence, no longer be neutral. The constitutional constraints imposed on the scope of obscenity laws in *Roth* v. *United States*[83] and *Miller* v. *California*[84] reflect this transition.[85]

Correlative with the expanding scope of constitutionally protected speech, the Supreme Court has been increasingly demanding in the showing of a clear and present danger that is necessary for a content-based restriction on protected speech to be valid. The Court has thus moved from its highly deferential tendency test,[86] to a less deferential but still weak test of aggregate expectable harm,[87] to its current highly demanding requirements of very grave harms that are both highly probable and not rebuttable by the normal pattern of dialogue and discourse in society at large.[88] This modern interpretation of a clear and present danger is the same test for legitimate state action that was first stated by Jefferson in his Virginia Bill for Religious Freedom as a criterion for valid interference in religious liberty: "that it is time enough for the rightful purposes of civil government for its officers to interfere when principles break out into overt acts against peace and good order," and that the normal course for rebuttal of noxious belief—consistent with respect for the right to conscience—is "free argument and debate."[89] Indeed, the modern Supreme Court's rejection of its earlier highly deferential tendency test for free-speech abridgment strikingly echoes Jefferson's rejection of the state's self-validating judgments of "ill tendency."[90] Jefferson formulates this test as a way of ensuring that mere objection to a certain system of religious belief cannot of itself justify abridgment of exercise of that belief, because "that tendency will make his opinions the rule of judgment, and approve or condemn the sentiments of others only as they shall square with or differ from his own."[91] Accordingly, the state must limit any restrictions on religious belief to cases in which there are imminent secular harms (e.g., Locke's example of a religious ritual of child sacrifice[92]); otherwise, mere disturbances over what is said will be a proxy for imminent secular harms. However, the same pattern of intolerance familiar in unjust religious persecution also occurs, as Madison clearly saw, in the censorship of speech, and the modern Court has correctly understood that the same protections of moral independence that are fundamental to our Jeffersonian conceptions of religious liberty apply, as a matter of principle, to free speech as well. The lesson of the McCarthy witch-hunts is,

---

[83] 354 U.S. 476 (1957).

[84] 413 U.S. 15 (1973).

[85] For fuller explanatory and critical discussion of the expanding categories of protected speech, see Richards, *Toleration and the Constitution*, pp. 188–227.

[86] See *Schenck* v. *United States*, 249 U.S. 47 (1919); *Frohwerk* v. *United States*, 249 U.S. 204 (1919); *Debs* v. *United States*, 249 U.S. 211 (1919).

[87] *Dennis* v. *United States*, 341 U.S. 494 (1951).

[88] *Brandenburg* v. *Ohio*, 395 U.S. 444 (1969).

[89] Boyd, ed. *Papers of Thomas Jefferson*, vol. 2, p. 546.

[90] Ibid.

[91] Ibid.

[92] See John Locke, *Letter Concerning Toleration*, p. 33.

as the name suggests, precisely the common wrong of and remedy for religious and political persecution.[93]

It is not enough that a theory of free speech interpretively clarifies what the law is, although that is, of course, no small thing. It must also advance the critical thinking about the hard cases of constitutional interpretation and about defects in principle even in established law. That assessment may best be made against the benchmark of the important theories of free speech, including the standard utilitarian defenses of free speech, the argument of protecting democracy, and a recently proposed consequentialist theory of free-speech protection. There is good reason to be skeptical about the critical power of all these theories.

Why Speech?

Frederick Schauer has posed the central theoretical issue of the law of free speech as a query about the justification for the extraordinary degree of constitutional protection now accorded speech in contrast to nonspeech activities.[94] Schauer claims that the special constitutional protection of speech cannot be justified, as J.S. Mill argued,[95] by its distinctively innocuous character. Speech is often very harmful, indeed more harmful than many nonspeech activities, yet the state's burden of justification for the abridgment of speech is much greater than for other (less harmful) activities.[96] Schauer's answer to this puzzle is that, even conceding that speech is often very harmful, we have special reasons to be skeptical about the ways in which the state identifies and enforces its judgments of harm (e.g., its self-serving tendency to repress speech critical of state policies). This skepticism is, for Schauer, expressed by principles of tolerance with special force in the area of speech,[97] and he appears to believe that free speech not only combats the state's tendency—motivated by intolerance—to mistake useful criticism for dangerous sedition, but also the further harm that inheres in intolerance itself. Principles of free speech limit state power in order to combat both evils, and thus to secure a balance of political good over harm. Precisely because utilitarian argument appears unable to explain the special protection

---

[93] If, as has been suggested, the background right to conscience must today be interpreted to include all forms of conscience (theistic, agnostic, and atheistic), then suppression of Marxism is itself a kind of religious persecution in the constitutionally condemned sense: one of the great secular religions of the modern age is unjustly suppressed by law. On Marxism as a religion or heretical antireligion, see Joseph Needham, *Science in Traditional China* (Cambridge, Mass.: Harvard Univ. Press, 1981), pp. 122–31.

[94] Frederick Schauer, "Must Speech Be Special?" 78 *Northwestern U. L. Rev.* 1284, 1288–89 (1983).

[95] See John Stuart Mill, *On Liberty,* Alburey Castell, ed. (New York: Appleton-Century-Crofts, 1947), pp. 9–10.

[96] Offensive speech might, for example, inflict much more harm than a male high school student wearing his hair long, or having sex with his girl friend.

[97] See, e.g., Frederick Schauer, *Free Speech: A Philosophical Inquiry* (Cambridge: Cambridge Univ. Press, 1982), pp. 12, 68, 83, 106.

accorded speech,[98] Schauer understands such goods and harms and their importance as an intuitive balancing of pluralistic ends that are not reducible to Mill's
utilitarian terms of the "permanent interests of man as a progressive being."[99]
Presumably, comparable restrictions on action less often run amok in either of
the ways typical of state restrictions on speech, and so are entitled to greater
constitutional deference.

Lee Bollinger in a recent book conceives the puzzle and its remedy in ways
quite similar to Schauer.[100] Speech is often quite as harmful as Schauer suggests[101] (Bollinger is absorbed by the harms of chants of Nazis marching in the
heavily Jewish community of Skokie, Illinois[102]), but our constitutional grounds
for skepticism express wider constitutional worries about social and political
intolerance, worries about a generic problem of unjust majoritarian abridgments of both speech and action. So why do we fully protect only speech?
Bollinger agrees with Schauer that there are grounds for skepticism about how
the state identifies and enforces its judgments of harm in the area of speech
abridgment, but, unlike Schauer, he is analytically clearer that the same worries
infect state judgments abridging conduct, and that the best argument for our
principles of free speech gives greater weight to tolerance as a positive value
than to the likelihood that the state's judgments of harm are mistaken. His
argument at this point is instrumental: we insist on tolerance in the area of
speech, even when the state's judgments of harm are not mistaken (as with
fascist advocacy of racial genocide), because such tolerance has a focal causal
significance in promoting tolerance generally, or at least inhibiting the intolerance that pervades all exercises of state power. Indeed, it is precisely because
extremist speech like that of the Nazis in Skokie is so irredeemably harmful that
its constitutional protection is all the more powerful as a political symbol shaping a wider culture of tolerance.[103] The constitutional law of free speech veers in
a protective direction even of speech with much harm and no good because,
generally, it offsets the evil of pervasive intolerance. The argument is, like
Schauer's, a consequentialist one: his decisions about what is to be protected
rest on an intuitive weighing of various political harms and goods (e.g., the
good of tolerance versus the evil of fascist racism) in order to strike a balance
of goods over harms. Unsurprisingly, Bollinger, like Schauer,[104] can always

[98] See later in this text for criticism of the utilitarian theories of free speech of J.S. Mill and
Oliver Wendell Holmes. For Schauer's criticisms, see Schauer, *Free Speech*, pp. 33–34, 73–86.
[99] Mill, *On Liberty*, p. 11.
[100] See Lee C. Bollinger, *The Tolerant Society: Freedom of Speech and Extremist Speech in
America* (New York: Oxford Univ. Press, 1986).
[101] See, e.g., ibid., p. 198.
[102] See *Collin* v. *Smith*, 578 F.2d 1197 (1978), *cert. den.*, 439 U.S. 916 (1978); *Village of Skokie*
v. *National Socialist Party of America*, 69 Ill.2d 605, 373 N.E.2d 21 (1978).
[103] See, e.g., Bollinger, *Tolerant Society*, pp. 197–200.
[104] See Frederick Schauer, "Speech and 'Speech'—Obscenity and 'Obscenity,' " 67 *George-
town L.J.* 899 (1979). See also *Attorney General's Commission on Pornography: Final Report*
(Washington, D.C.: Department of Justice, July 1986), of which Schauer was the draftsman. For
criticism of his work, see David Richards, "Pornography Commissions and the First Amendment:
On Constitutional Values and Constitutional Facts," 39 *Me. L. Rev.* 275 (1987).

invoke harmful consequences to suspend this tolerance (e.g., in the obscenity area[105]).

The approach of Schauer and Bollinger reflects reasonable doubts about many of the existing important theories of free speech, for example, the standard utilitarian defenses of free speech or the argument of protecting democracy.[106] There *is* good reason to be skeptical about both of these theories.

Utilitarian Theory

Utilitarian arguments for free speech take a wide variety of forms, including John Stuart Mill's classically complex and nuanced arguments in *On Liberty*[107] and Oliver Wendell Holmes's crude appeal to Social Darwinian competition in his dissent in *Abrams* v. *United States*.[108]. These arguments justify the protection of free speech by a consequentialist appeal of a utilitarian sort, namely, maximizing the greatest net balance of pleasure over pain among all sentient creatures. However, these arguments afford no clear protection of free speech of the sort that American constitutional law now contemplates. The net aggregate of pleasure over pain is often advanced, not frustrated, by the abridgment of speech: large populist majorities often quite relish (hedonically speaking) the repression of outcast dissenters, the numbers and pains of dissenters are by comparison small, and there is rarely an offsetting future net aggregate of pain over pleasure to compensate for the difference. John Stuart Mill, of course, appeals to a complex history of moral and scientific cultural evolution in the West to show that the repression of dissent usually retards that evolution; in particular, it inhibits the emergence of moral, political, and scientific truths that advance "the permanent interests of man as a progressive being."[109] However, such a consequentialist invocation of the conditions of progress—contextually embedded in the optimism of Victorian technological advance—rings hollow from the vantage point of historical experience of the scientific barbarities of the twentieth century: for instance, the science of racial differences and the mass genocide it rationalized,[110] and the real threat of nuclear annihilation. Moral, political, and scientific truth do not, it appears, move in tandem in a way that would justify Mill's grand simplicities, nor can we have any confidence that truth per se is a just proxy for happiness. The role of free speech in yielding scientific truth might be better pursued by reserving the right of free speech to narrow technocratic elites; the moral truth-yielding role might similarly be served by a limited grant of free speech to other elites. Certainly, any realistic subversive threat to these truth-yielding institutions might, on utilitarian grounds, be repressed. If so, Holmes's more skeptical and less humane utilitar-

---

[105] See Bollinger, *Tolerant Society*, pp. 184–45.

[106] Indeed, Schauer's *Free Speech* is an extended criticism of these theories of free speech.

[107] Mill, *On Liberty*.

[108] 250 U.S. 616 (1919).

[109] Mill, *On Liberty*, p. 11.

[110] Cf. Hannah Arendt, *The Origins of Totalitarianism* (New York: Harcourt Brace Jovanovich, 1973).

ian vision may be closer to the consequentialist mark: free-speech values should only protect those "puny anonymities"[111] unlikely to harm anyone and from whom something might be learned. These values should not protect a more politically effective speaker whose danger but not benefit to existing institutions is clear. This approach, however, is not the current stance of free-speech protection under American constitutional law,[112] and rightly so.

Protection of Democracy as a Theory

The protection of democracy is equally puzzling as a basis of free speech.[113] The theory's intuitive force is that the kind of electoral choice that is fundamental to a working democracy requires that choice be exercised in the light of the widest range of critical views about how current state officials are performing. Free speech guarantees the electorate this kind of informed choice by limiting the capacity of state officials to censor critical debate about their performance. Such censorship is often motivated by a conscious or unconscious will to retain power.

However, the idea of democracy is essentially contestable in a way that dilutes the critical force of this justification for free speech. Observers differ as to what is and what is not essential to a well-functioning democracy, or, conversely, what counts as democratic "pathology" for purposes of special free-speech concerns.[114] They interpret the legitimate scope of democratic debate narrowly or broadly. The narrow interpretation limits legitimate debate to the issues directly in controversy among the main contenders for majoritarian political power[115]; the broader interpretation construes legitimate debate to include any issue of possible debate, including the very legitimacy of political power in general and democracy in particular.[116]

Neither of these interpretations provides a secure and convincing basis for the protection of speech. The narrow interpretation trivializes the scope of free speech to the measure of consensus politics, and thus excludes from free-speech protection the dissenting discourse most crucial to central issues of

---

[111] *Abrams* v. *United States,* 250 U.S. 624 (1919), at 629.

[112] See, e.g., *Brandenburg* v. *Ohio,* 395 U.S. 444 (1969); *Collin* v. *Smith,* 578 F.2d 1197 (1978), *cert. den.,* 439 U.S. 916 (1978).

[113] See, in general, Alexander Meiklejohn, *Political Freedom* (New York: Oxford Univ. Press, 1965).

[114] For a range of perspectives on the democratic pathologies that free speech should remedy, see, e.g., Vincent Blasi, "The Pathological Perspective and the First Amendment," 85 *Col. L. Rev.* 449 (1985); and Owen M. Fiss, "Free Speech and Social Structure," 71 *Iowa L. Rev.* 1405 (1986); idem, "Why the State?" 100 *Harv. L. Rev.* 781 (1987). For a recent controversy over these issues, see Vincent Blasi, "The Role of Strategic Reasoning in Constitutional Interpretation: In Defense of the Pathological Perspective," 1986 *Duke L.J.* 696; George Christie, "Why the First Amendment Should Not Be Interpreted from the Pathological Perspective: A Response to Professor Blasi," 1986 *Duke L.J.* 683.

[115] See Robert Bork, "Neutral Principles and Some First Amendment Problems," 47 *Indiana L.J.* 1 (1971).

[116] See Alexander Meiklejohn, "The First Amendment Is an Absolute," 1961 *Supreme Court Review* 245.

both justice and the common good. The broader interpretation seems itself to compromise democratic legitimacy, because it would protect attacks on the very foundations of such legitimacy, including attacks on free speech itself. If such attacks should be protected, as current law indeed requires,[117] then it seem rather strained to justify such protection on the grounds that they invariably advance democracy when they may sometimes self-consciously subvert it.[118] How can that view advance the protection of democracy? The argument here is at sea, unmoored by the very protection of democracy it claims to be its basis. We need a better theory of free speech, and Schauer and Bollinger clearly are in critical search of one. However, their approaches are deeply flawed.

Consequentialist Theories

Schauer's argument is structurally consequentialist at one remove. In his view, speech is quite as harmful as action, but we protect speech from harm-motivated state abridgment because state judgments of harm either inflict the harm of intolerance or mistakenly identify harms. However, the account does not explain its crucial terms, namely, its conception of harms, its reasons for skepticism about state judgments, or the way in which judgments of harm and good are to be weighed for purposes of deciding the crucial issues of free speech protection—its scope, its context, and the grounds for its justifiable abridgment. In short, the view is so deeply indeterminate that it is ultimately uncritical, because almost any conclusion about a controversial free-speech issue that is arrived at independently can be comfortably fitted into the theory. If we decide that some kind of communication is protected (e.g., advocacy of racial genocide), we ritualistically admit that it is harmful, but then concoct grounds for skepticism about the state's capacity to identify and enforce such judgments of harm.[119] On the other hand, we start with the conclusion that some speech is not protected (e.g., obscenity), and we then support that view by appropriately justifying our judgment of harm and explaining why we should have confidence in the state's capacity to make and enforce such

---

[117] For pertinent discussion, see Richards, *Toleration and the Constitution,* pp. 178–87.

[118] Suppose Socrates was an effective subversive critic of the Athenian democracy. See, e.g., I.F. Stone, *The Trial of Socrates* (Boston: Little, Brown, 1988). The repression of such subversive speech might plausibly be justified as a reasonable protection of fragile democratic institutions from an all too eloquent philosophical critic. The point is not that the argument for repression is clearly right (e.g., Stone argues that it was wrong in ways that ultimately impugned the legitimacy of the Athenian democracy), but that it is plausible, as a matter of principle, in ways that fail to capture the independent grounds for the protection of free speech against which we test the very idea of a legitimate democracy. Athens, for Stone, thus failed to respect its own intrinsically valuable commitment to free speech, and may be condemned for that reason; see idem, pp. xi, 197, 230. In fact, the founders of the Constitution regarded Athens as an unsound model for republican government precisely for that reason, among others, as Madison's argument in *The Federalist,* no. 10 makes quite clear.

[119] Bollinger offers grounds for skepticism in this spirit. See Bollinger, *Tolerant Society,* e.g., pp. 197–200.

judgments.[120] However, in each case, exactly the opposite position might be better justified with respect to both harms and an assessment of the impartiality of state judgments about such harms; indeed, the indeterminacy of the theory may lead to blatant misapplication of its principles. For example, the allegations of harm in obscene materials are notoriously controversial, even ideological; therefore, the state's action against these harms is often that of a partisan on one side of intractable moral controversies about sexuality and gender that divide reasonable people in the society at large. The state's prohibition of obscene materials should therefore trigger the classical skepticism about such state judgments that is required by the principles of free speech, and such statutes should, with due respect to Schauer, be constitutionally suspect.[121]

The problem is not only that Schauer's theory offers a general framework within which bad arguments can be made, in effect, misapplying the theory to a case like obscenity. Even when arguments set forth within the framework lead to intuitively plausible conclusions, Schauer's theory does not identify the right kinds of reasons for them. We do not need a theory of free speech that rests on an easily manipulated and question-begging consequentialist theory of harms, which has neither the clarity nor the critical force of utilitarian consequentialism. We need, rather, a critical theory not only of the legitimate interests protected by free speech, but also the range of legitimate interests that properly qualify the scope of protection of free speech, and we need a clear account of how free speech and these interests should be coordinated.

Bollinger's consequentialism is less philosophically sophisticated than Schauer's, but more forthright about the larger issues of principle that are central to free speech, namely, tolerance. However, tolerance is a value in search of a critical theory, especially when it is—as it is for Bollinger—the central normative term in the relevant consequentialism of free speech. Speech, he concedes, is often more harmful than action, but we protect even its most virulently harmful forms (e.g., advocacy of racial genocide) because that teaches a larger moral lesson about the value of tolerance, which inhibits the larger pattern of intolerance that unjustly oppresses both action and conduct. We accept such harmful speech because its protection is an indispensable instrument to the larger good of a community of liberal civility. But what is this larger ideal of democratic tolerance, and why does speech, in contrast to action, enjoy special protection? Why might not toleration of certain ac-

---

[120] Schauer has been a leading advocate of the position that obscene materials are not entitled to free speech protection. See Schauer, "Speech and 'Speech'—Obscenity and 'Obscenity'." Correspondingly, Schauer played a central role in drafting the *Attorney General's Commission on Pornography*, which I have discussed and criticized in "Pornography Commissions and the First Amendment." For Schauer's pivotal role on the commission, see Hendrik Hertzberg, *The New Republic*, July 14 and 21, 1986, p. 22. For views similar to those of Schauer, see Bollinger, *Tolerant Society*, pp. 184–85.

[121] For further development of this argument, see Richards, "Free Speech and Obscenity Law: Toward a Moral Theory of the First Amendment," 123 *U. Pa. L. Rev.* 45 (1974); idem, *Toleration and the Constitution*, pp. 203–9; idem, "Pornography Commissions and the First Amendment."

tions (e.g., consensual adult homosexuality) be even more focally important in developing social tolerance than toleration of speech? Even within the domain of speech the extent of the protection based on tolerance is left unexplained. Democratic societies certainly regard many actions motivated by racial hatred (e.g., racial discrimination in public rights and services[122]), as harmful and well beyond the pale of toleration, so why isn't advocacy of Nazi intolerance beyond the pale as well? Why doesn't tolerance require the protection of speech arguably less harmful than racist speech, namely, obscene speech?

If tolerance has this crucial normative force for the scope of protection of free speech, then we surely need a critical theory of tolerance to explain its nature and weight. Indeed, Bollinger believes the value extends only to a certain point (e.g., not to obscenity[123]), yet he offers no such critical theory. His consequentialism then is undoubtedly more complexly weighted than Schauer's but equally uncritical: the appropriate level of tolerance, which controls everything else in the theory, can be manipulatively adjusted to suit any result. For example, although Bollinger believes acceptable levels of tolerance are not exceeded by the Nazis of Skokie but are by hard-core pornography, equally forceful reasons would support exactly the converse levels of tolerance. Tolerance should be extended to speech but not in the same way to action, a bromide of classical liberalism that Mill's *On Liberty* forever exploded. Tolerance, for Bollinger, comes very close to some indeterminate conception of social acceptability or majoritarian common sense, which hardly reflects the principles of toleration of the First Amendment that set critical standards of critical morality against which majoritarian common sense must be assessed, criticized, and restrained.

A Critical Theory of Free Speech

Schauer and Bollinger fail to articulate clearly the central competing values in the law of free speech, to consider critically how they should be adjusted, and to connect these issues to the larger questions of both harm and tolerance that figure prominently in both their accounts. We begin with the question of why only speech is protected; then we examine both competing free-speech interests and potential harms from infringing these interests.

Schauer poses the issue of exclusive protection for speech, because he wishes to deny that the distinction between the protections of speech and the lesser protections of conduct can be explained, as John Stuart Mill claimed,[124] on the basis of the harm principle, namely, that the only ground for state interference is harm to others and never mere harm to oneself. Schauer does not challenge the harm principle, but rather its application to speech. Speech is often quite as harmful, if not more so, than action; therefore, we must

---

[122] See *Brown v. Board of Education,* 347 U.S. 483 (1954).
[123] See Bollinger, *Tolerant Society,* pp. 184–85.
[124] See, e.g., Mill, *On Liberty,* pp. 9–10.

inquire why our law specially protects speech. However, his theory neither explains these mistakes, nor the harms, nor how they should be weighed: almost any prior conception of what should or should not be protected can be manipulatively fitted into Schauer's account.

However, the theory of free speech, proposed here, explains quite straight-forwardly both the special priority of free speech and our grounds for skepticism about certain state abridgments of speech, that is, the core issues of free speech theory posed but not adequately answered by Schauer and Bollinger.

The priority of free speech is not coextensive with all speech, but with the communicative independence of willing speakers and audiences when they are exercising the critical moral powers of the inalienable right to conscience; that is, they are engaged in sincere discussion of the facts and values that is central to the exercise of our powers of reasonable thought, deliberation, and action.[125] Communications do not serve such communicative independence when they manipulatively bypass reflective capacities (e.g., subliminal advertising) or make claims about individuals known to be false (e.g., in fraud and knowing or reckless defamation), and the state may pursue legitimate secular interests like protection from consumer fraud and protection of reputation and privacy. There should accordingly be no objection, on free-speech grounds, to state regulations of deceit, fraud,[126] and individual defamation (suitably understood) and protections of privacy interests. Therefore, a theory of free speech—grounded in the communicative independence of our rational powers—should not be criticized for failing to give proper weight to such regulatory interests; on the contrary, the theory does give them proper weight.[127] Indeed, free speech has the priority we accord it only against a background of such regulatory principles (including fair time, place, and manner regulations[128]) that afford a supportive framework for communicative dialogue among free, rational, and equal persons.

Correspondingly, our skepticism about state power over speech is rooted not in a general fear of the state per se, but in more specific evils that our constitutional tradition identifies in the familiar patterns of persecutory state intolerance of moral and political criticism. This intolerance erodes the communicative independence that is essential to equal respect for our moral powers. The central principle of free speech thus forbids the state to abridge speech on content-based grounds because such enforceable views of the worth or value of speech justify censorship on grounds of sectarian beliefs in truth

---

[125] See, in general, Richards, *Toleration and the Constitution*, pp. 165–227.

[126] On the degree to which commercial speech should be regarded as protected speech, see ibid., pp. 209–15.

[127] It is for this reason, for example, that T.M. Scanlon abandons his autonomy-based theory of free speech in favor of an intuitionistic theory of various speaker, audience, and bystander interests. See, e.g., T.M. Scanlon, "Freedom of Expression and Categories of Expression," 40 *U. Pitt. L. Rev.* 519, 532 (1979); cf. idem, "A Theory of Free Expression," 1 *Phil. & Pub. Aff.* 204 (1972). If I am correct, this was not an adequate reason to abandon Scanlon's earlier theory, or some appropriately revised form of it.

[128] See, e.g., Richards, *Toleration and the Constitution*, p. 173.

and value, and thus usurp the inalienable right of a free people to engage in the full scope of reasonable discourse about critical values in living, including political legitimacy itself.[129]

It is not enough that a critical theory thus identifies the core free-speech interests and the main worries about its abridgment; it must also explain competing interests, how they should be balanced with the core free-speech interests, and what harms, if any, may justify the abridgment of speech. The focus of the theory of free speech proposed here is both a positive value of communicative independence and a negative worry about certain kinds of enforceable state judgments limiting such independence. Although these twin concerns specifically limit the kinds of interests that may count at all as countervailing interests, they do legitimate others.

As suggested earlier, the background principle of toleration puts normative focus on enforceable state judgments about the critical worth of public speech implicating values in living. Such condemned judgments include not only seditious libel laws that allow the state to condemn criticism of public policy and public officials,[130] but also laws that condemn either express or implied criticism of values in living.[131] Therefore, such condemned judgments must include state prohibitions of speech actuated by the offense taken by groups of citizens at the critical advocacy of values in living of other groups, because such prohibitions indulge the illegitimate state role of enforcing views believed to be true in the place of the play of the critical moral powers of free and equal people engaged in responsible discourse about these issues. It is this reason of principle that explains why group libel laws are currently constitutionally suspect in the United States.[132]

Bollinger, who is quite absorbed by the constitutional issues raised by the prospective Nazi marchers in Skokie,[133] grounds his argument in a larger conception of tolerance: we protect even the harms incident to Nazi speech because this protection serves a larger vision of a tolerant society. However, he has not explained how or why this is so. The issue of principle is that the kinds of enforceable state judgments, contemplated in group libel cases like Skokie and like those underlying obscenity laws, are illegitimate not because they are likely to be mistaken (they are, in the case of Skokie, and in contrast to obscenity, clearly correct), but because certain harms cannot be regarded as proper political grounds for the coercive abridgment of speech in the way Bollinger would allow. The principle of free speech, properly understood, discriminates among kinds of interests that may enjoy weight in the balance of political argument about free speech, and disentitles certain putative interests to any weight whatsoever. These include offense taken at the exercise of the

---

[129] See, e.g., ibid., pp. 166–87.

[130] See ibid., pp. 174–78.

[131] See, e.g., ibid., pp. 178–87.

[132] See *Collin* v. *Smith*, 578 F.2d 1197 (1978), *cert. den.*, 439 U.S. 916 (1978); Richards, *Toleration and the Constitution*, pp. 189–195.

[133] See, e.g., Bollinger, *Tolerant Society*, pp. 104–44, 197–200.

right of conscience itself. A consequentialism predicated on giving any weight to these latter interests is thus radically misconceived.[134]

The principle of toleration defines, as we have seen, a range of secular interests in the form of general goods that may, in contrast to sectarian values, be justly pursued by the state. The conception of such secular interests limits state interference in the right of conscience, allowing persons to define how or whether they will use these general goods in pursuit of the more ultimate aims defined by the independent exercise of their inalienable right to conscience.[135] Consistent with this conception, legitimate state purposes may neither include interests that violate the inalienable right to conscience itself nor consider harms defined by the frustration of forbidden interests.

However, Bollinger appeals to such "harms" in his argument about a Nazi rally in Skokie, Illinois. He defines "harms" in terms of the critical objection that offended people make to another's conscientious advocacy of certain values in living, and understands enforceable state judgments in terms of this sense of offense. Such state action not only deprives the condemned speakers of both conscientious expression of their views and the benefits of rebuttal by their equals but also deprives their opponents of the exercise of their critical moral powers in fair and free rebuttal. In other words, such repressive state action is, in principle, unacceptable state power, for the same reason that the equal moral independence of all is, in principle, immune from state power. Therefore, "harms" of this sort are excluded from the legitimate scope of state power, which is to say that John Stuart Mill may have made the correct point (albeit on inadequate utilitarian grounds[136]) when he denied that the repression of speech as offensively dangerous could fairly count as the kind of harm on which the liberal state may justly act.

All forms of conscientious objection to another's conscientious expression of views may be translated into a group libel action.[137] People often experience views with which they disagree as offensive, insulting, and even degrading of the values or interests of a group with whom they identify. Our long national experiment with commitment to principles of universal toleration teaches us that attempts to limit the scope of toleration (i.e., not extending it to Catholics, or atheists, or Communists, etc.) are familiarly justified on the ground that the intolerant have no claim of principle to the toleration of others.[138] However, the

---

[134] This disqualification is limited only to the theory of free speech, reserving to the state of more extensive regulatory role in basic education in democratic values and in combatting actions motivated by unjust forms of intolerance and prejudice. See Richards, *Toleration and the Constitution,* pp. 191–92.

[135] See, e.g., ibid., pp. 119–21; John Rawls, "Social Unity and Primary Goods," in Amartya Sen and Bernard Williams, eds. *Utilitarianism and Beyond* (Cambridge: Cambridge Univ. Press, 1982), pp. 159–85.

[136] Cf. Richards, *Toleration and the Constitution,* pp. 239–42.

[137] Cf. ibid., pp. 190–3.

[138] See, e.g., Robert Paul Wolff, Barrington Moore, Jr., and Herbert Marcuse, *A Critique of Pure Tolerance* (Boston: Beacon Press, 1965). Cf. pp. 216–21, John Rawls, *A Theory of Justice* (Cambridge, Mass.: Harvard Univ. Press, 1971) (criticizing the argument that toleration is not owed the intolerant).

principle of universal toleration respects persons as being equal and independent originators of value in living; such equal respect for persons means equal
respect for the independence of all speakers. This respect is most principled
when it guarantees the evaluative and expressive freedoms of the speakers
whose speech we most conscientiously reject and despise. Respect for these
liberties is consistent with and indeed requires the vigorous rebuttal of such
views, and is not abridged by constitutionally legitimate exercises of state
power to pursue valid aims such as antidiscrimination (e.g., prohibition of
harmful actions motivated by racial or religious hatred, or programs supportive
of racial and religious integration in the public schools[139]).

If, however, a critical theory of free speech delegitimizes a certain "harm"
as the ground for abridgment of speech, it allows, indeed legitimates a wide
range of other grounds. The theory proposed here focuses on a certain inad-
missible *ground* for state abridgment of speech, namely, an enforceable state
judgment about the worth or value of critical views of value in living that
deprives people of their inalienable right to express and rebut these critical
views. Therefore, group libel laws are invalid because they require this type of
forbidden state judgment. However, as was already suggested about manipulative advertising and willful misstatements of facts, people have a range of
interests that are as essential to their moral powers as conscience and free
speech, and the vindication of which does not infringe on the area protected
by the properly understood principle of universal toleration. This principle is,
as we have seen, preoccupied by the free play of general evaluative views
about value in living, and its protection does not structurally conflict (like
group libel laws) with the legitimacy of state purposes to maintain, for example, a reasonable protection of people's interests in their reputational integrity, in highly private facts and experiences, or in the security of a just system
of background property claims,[140] including those in products of their communicative labors (e.g., subject of copyright protections).

To the contrary, we base on these interests the constructive moral powers
we bring to living a valuable life. Our capacity to live well and humanely
requires protection from willfully false denigrations of our reputational self-
esteem as well as protection of resources of privacy and security of our just
property rights, including the communicative products of labor. Properly understood, the reasonable protection of this range of interests not only does not
infringe on the inalienable right of conscience, but also complements the
protection of the interests that are essential to personal integrity in the same
way that reasonable time, place, and manner regulations of speech enhance
the underlying values of equal respect. Accordingly, our interests in these
goods may be the legitimate basis of state protection, which is to say that the
state may protect us from harms defined by the frustration of such interests.

[139] See, e.g., *Brown v. Board of Education,* 347 U.S. 483 (1954).
[140] It is assumed that such a system of property claims must satisfy the background conditions
of a substantive theory of justice. See, e.g., Rawls, *Theory of Justice;* David Richards, *A Theory
of Reasons for Action* (Oxford: Clarendon Press, 1971); Ronald Dworkin, "What Is Equality?
Part 2: Equality of Resources," 10 *Phil. & Pub. Aff.* 283 (1981).

The promotion of complementarity among these interests should be the guiding principle in a reasonable understanding of how the pursuit of one of these interests should be adjusted to allow pursuit of another. To protect the underlying conception of a fair distribution of the resources essential to our moral powers, for example, one interest the core values of which are not at stake should yield to another interest that is threatened.[141] To illustrate, free speech protects core values of the free play of sincerely held and publicly articulated evaluative conceptions of value in living that are often critical of dominant moral and political orthodoxies. In contrast, reputational integrity serves our personal interests in controlling and vindicating fair factual representations of our lives and works against willful misrepresentation.[142] These values are usually not in conflict but are complementary. On the one hand, a libel action to protect a private person who cannot otherwise protect himself or herself against maliciously false factual statements vindicates the interest in reputational integrity and does not trench on core free-speech interests (the speech is willfully false about matters of hard fact). On the other hand, if the libel action is on behalf of a state official and depends on highly evaluative and sincerely critical conceptions of proper conduct and not on willful misstatements of fact, the libel action needlessly infringes on central free-speech interests (sincere expressions of critical conceptions of value in living) without securing core interests of reputational integrity (the libel action does not rest on willful factual misrepresentation nor does it protect private persons who cannot otherwise vindicate their reputations). Obviously, the appropriate adjustment among such values is subject to a wide range of reasonable disagreements, and bright-line rules may often be necessary to strike the balance in ways that are least prone to manipulative abuse.[143] The appropriate balance, however, is dictated by an underlying conception of a fair distribution of the complementary interests that permits the exercise of our constructive moral powers in a life well lived.[144]

That underlying conception is, of course, the principle of equal respect for conscience as an inalienable human right. A more analytically precise understanding of both this principle and its foundations enables us to move beyond the open-ended theory of harms of Schauer and Bollinger, the vagueness of their appeal to tolerance, and their impressionistic balancing among values that makes each of their theories so interpretively manipulative. A better critical theory may also improve our interpretive theory; that is, we may better under-

---

[141] Cf. Richards, *Toleration and the Constitution*, pp. 195–203.

[142] Cf. ibid.

[143] See, e.g., *Gertz* v. *Robert Welch, Inc.*, 418 U.S. 323 (1974), in which the Court for such reasons required negligence in libel actions by plaintiffs (who are not public figures) against media defendants. Because the free-speech interests are lowest with willfully false misstatements of fact, there is much to be said for a constitutionally compelled requirement that libel actions must show not just negligence, but willful falsity. This would require a radical expansion of *New York Times* v. *Sullivan*, 376 U.S. 254 (1964), in which the Court limited willful falsity to plaintiffs who are public figures against media defendants.

[144] Cf. Richards, *Toleration and the Constitution*, pp. 195–203.

stand troubling cases like group libel, and evaluate the kind of unprincipled incoherence in the way that Schauer and Bollinger treat obscenity.

In Defense of General Interpretive Theory

If these arguments have any force, then their interpretive methodology must have force as well. That methodology describes a general political theory of constitutional law. By exploring historically continuous common principles and structures in different areas of constitutional law (in this case, religious liberty and free speech), this theory advances the understanding of our constitutional tradition. We understand both general and specific structures of the law of religious liberty and free speech by the investigation of the kind of general arguments of principle proposed here. That is the kind of interpretive gain it would be folly to ignore. A person who ignores such interpretive gain might be motivated by another kind of general theory—a bad theory that does not explain the proper role of history or the text in the interpretation of an enduring written constitution.[145]

The earlier-proposed interpretive methodology yields substantial understanding of enumerated rights like those of religious liberty and free speech. Interpretation of our constitutional history (including the founders) focuses our attention on how to interpret the community of principle over time in ways that, if anything, deepen our interpretive grasp of contemporary interpretive practice. However, religious liberty and free speech, though controversial at the periphery, are in the core of what contemporary Americans mean by the protection of constitutional rights. It would be an even more remarkable tribute to the interpretive methodology advanced here if it could promote interpretive and critical understanding of constitutional rights that are controversial in their principle and not just in their applications. Today such rights certainly include unenumerated rights in general and the constitutional right to privacy in particular. We must turn our attention, therefore, to the interpretive and critical challenge posed by such rights.

[145] Cf. ibid., pp. 282–305.

6

Interpreting Unenumerated Rights: Constitutional Privacy

In 1986 the Supreme Court decided two important cases in the area of constitutional privacy, *Thornburgh* v. *American College of Obstetricians and Gynecologists*[1] (hereafter refered to as *Thornburgh*) and *Bowers* v. *Hardwick*[2] (hereafter referred to as *Bowers*). Both cases reflect deep doctrinal divisions within the Court and the nation at large over the nature, provenance, and justifiability of unenumerated constitutional rights in general and the constitutional right to privacy in particular. These disagreements relate to fundamental questions about the nature and justifiability of constitutional interpretation itself, including the role of text and history in interpreting constitutional rights both enumerated and unenumerated. The issue was well posed by Justice White in his dissent in *Thornburgh* and his majority opinion in *Bowers* as a question of constitutional legitimacy: "The Court is most vulnerable and comes nearest to illegitimacy when it deals with judge-made constitutional law having little or no cognizable roots in the language or design of the Constitution."[3] Indeed, more radical critics of constitutional privacy than Justice White have questioned, in principle, the very legitimacy of any such right at all[4]; one of them, Robert Bork—the nominee of President Reagan to the Supreme Court in 1987—was unsuccessful in part because he subscribed to such a view.[5] Bork's view rests on a more extreme version of Justice White's skepticism about essentially "judge-made" law with "little or no cognizable roots" in constitutional text or structure, namely, that the very inference of constitutional privacy is unprincipled because "the Constitution has not spoken."[6] Attorney

---

[1] 106 S. Ct. 2169 (1986).

[2] 106 S. Ct. 2841 (1986).

[3] *Bowers*, 106 S. Ct. at 2846; see also *Thornburgh*, 106 S. Ct. at 2194 ("When the Court ventures further and defines 'fundamental' liberties that are nowhere mentioned in the Constitution . . . it must, of necessity, act with more caution . . .").

[4] See, e.g., Walter Berns, *Taking the Constitution Seriously* (New York: Simon & Schuster, 1987), pp. 206, 225–28, 237–38.

[5] See Robert H. Bork, "Neutral Principles and Some First Amendment Problems," 47 *Ind. L.J.* 1, 7–11 (1971).

[6] Ibid., p. 9.

General Edwin Meese, Jr., who sponsored the Bork nomination, framed the critical issue in terms of "a jurisprudence of original intention."[7] Consistent with this perspective, constitutional privacy is unprincipled, in Bork's terms, when appropriately tested against "a demonstrable consensus among the framers and ratifiers as to a principle stated or implied by the Constitution."[8]

We need, as a constitutional community of principle, to come to terms with the interpretive and critical issues posed by the constitutional right to privacy, not only because the issue is so much at the center of constitutional controversy—both on and off the Supreme Court—but also because the issue raises larger questions about the very legitimacy of constitutional government itself, in particular, its fundamental commitment to the inalienable rights of the person.

In order to focus the dicussion, the argument of this chapter will examine these interpretive issues in the terms posed by the Supreme Court itself in 1986 and by the Bork nomination in 1987. In particular, the argument will critically examine both Justice White's claim about the limited scope of the constitutional right to privacy and Bork's more radical attack on the right itself in the terms in which they pose it, that is, from the perspective of an approach to constitutional interpretation and legitimacy. We naturally begin with the controversy within the Supreme Court itself reflected in *Thornburgh* and *Bowers,* and then turn to the larger issues of interpretive principle and legitimacy raised and debated by Robert Bork and those who opposed his nomination.[9]

The 1986 Privacy Cases

Thornburgh v. *American College of Obstetricians and Gynecologists*

In *Thornburgh,* in a five-to-four opinion delivered by Justice Blackmun, the Supreme Court invalidated six provisions of Pennsylvania's Abortion Control Act on the ground that they unconstitutionally burdened the exercise of the fundamental right of privacy.[10] The analytical issue in *Thornburgh* differs from that of *Roe* v. *Wade.*[11] *Roe* held that the state could not impose criminal sanctions on the access of a woman to abortion services in certain periods of her pregnancy, but *Thornburgh,* like many comparable post-*Roe* cases, dealt

[7] Edwin Meese, Jr., "Addresses—Construing the Constitution," 19 *U.C. Davis L. Rev.* 22, 26 (1985).

[8] Ibid., p. 26.

[9] The author was among these opponents and gave oral testimony against the nomination before the Senate Committee on the Judiciary on September 29, 1987, making a written submission to the same effect entitled, "Constitutional Privacy and Unenumerated Rights." His critical testimony is more fully elaborated in this chapter.

[10] 106 S. Ct. 2169 (1986).

[11] 410 U.S. 113 (1973).

with the permissibility of various regulations of abortion services (e.g., notice about medical risks and recordkeeping by physicians) that fell short of the outright prohibition at stake in *Roe*.[12] Many such regulations, like those in *Thornburgh,* had been struck down as constitutionally unreasonable limitations on exercise of the fundamental right to constitutional privacy at issue in *Roe*[13]; a few such regulations have, however, survived such scrutiny.[14] Commitment to the continuing authority of *Roe* did not, therefore, resolve the issue of these regulatory cases, and at least one justice (Powell) had maintained commitment to *Roe* and yet supported certain such regulations.[15] However, obviously, if one took the view that *Roe* was interpretively wrong, the validation of these regulatory cases must be wrong a fortiori. These cases have therefore been a natural forum for the debate within the Court on the validity of *Roe* v. *Wade* itself. Indeed, the interpretive interest of *Thornburgh* comes in the exchange between Justices Stevens and White on the issues of principle raised by *Roe* itself.[16]

Justice White's dissent goes beyond the specific facts in *Thornburgh* to what he views as the illegitimacy of *Roe*. His discussion of the latter issues begins with an argument that stare decisis does not bar the Supreme Court's reexamination of its own precedents,[17] and offers two arguments for overruling *Roe*. One argument focuses on the nature of the liberty interest at stake in *Roe*[18]; the other addresses the nature of the state interests that might justify state prohibitions of women's access to abortion services.[19]

Justice White's theory of stare decisis builds on a theory of interpretive mistake. When members of the Supreme Court critically recognize that the Court's prior decisions have departed from a proper understanding of the Constitution, they correct those mistakes by overruling the decisions. Such arguments are often not novel when they finally command governing majori-

---

[12] See, e.g., *Missouri* v. *Danforth,* 428 U.S. 52 (1976) (spousal and parental consent requirements for abortions); *Bellotti* v. *Baird,* 443 U.S. 622 (1979) (state regulations of minors' access to abortions); *H.L.* v. *Matheson,* 450 U.S. 398 (1981) (parental notice for minors' abortions); *Colautti* v. *Franklin,* 439 U.S. 379 (1979) (special regulations to protect "viable" fetuses); *Akron* v. *Akron Center for Reproductive Health,* 462 U.S. 416 (1983) (variety of regulations of abortions, including that second-trimester abortions take place in hospitals); *Planned Parenthood Ass'n of Kansas City* v. *Ashcroft,* 462 U.S. 476 (1983) (regulations of abortions, including that take place in hospitals and presence of second physician for abortions performed after viability).

[13] See, e.g., *Missouri* v. *Danforth,* 428 U.S. 52 (1976); *Bellotti* v. *Baird,* 443 U.S. 622 (1979); *Colautti* v. *Franklin,* 439 U.S. 379 (1979); *Akron* v. *Akron Center for Reproductive Health,* 462 U.S. 416 (1983).

[14] See, e.g., *H.L. Matheson,* 450 U.S. 398 (1981) (parental notice for abortions held valid); *Planned Parenthood Ass'n of Kansas city* v. *Ashcroft,* 462 U.S. 476 (1983) (requirement that abortions after twelve weeks of pregnancy be held in hospital held invalid, but requirement that abortions after viability be attended by second physician held valid).

[15] See, e.g., *H.L. Matheson,* 450 U.S. 398 (1981); *Planned Parenthood Ass'n of Kansas City* v. *Ashcroft,* 462 U.S. 476 (1983).

[16] *Thornburgh,* at 2185–90 (Stevens, J., concurring); idem at 2192–206 (J. White, dissenting).

[17] See *Thornburgh,* at 2192–93 (J. White, dissenting).

[18] Ibid., 2193–96.

[19] Ibid., at 2196–98.

ties of the Court; indeed, they were often anticipated by great judges in earlier cases.[20]

White makes clear that the idea of interpretive mistake requires a background understanding of constitutional interpretation itself. One possible view is that a decision like *Roe* v. *Wade* is interpretively wrong, and thus properly overruled, because "it is highly doubtful that the authors of any of the provisions of the Constitution believed they were giving protection to abortion."[21] White rejects that interpretation:

> As its prior cases clearly show, however, this Court does not subscribe to the simplistic view that constitutional interpretation can possibly be limited to the "plain meaning" of the Constitution's text or to the subjective intention of the Framers. The Constitution is not a deed setting forth the precise metes and bounds of its subject matter; rather, it is a document announcing fundamental principles in value-laden terms that leave ample scope for the exercise of normative judgment by those charged with interpreting and applying it. In particular, the Due Process Clause of the Fourteenth Amendment, which forbids the deprivation of "life, liberty, or property without due process of law," has been read by the majority of the Court to be broad enough to provide substantive protection against State infringement of a broad range of individual interests.[22]

However, the elaboration of such more abstract evaluative concepts may nonetheless be mistaken, and thus properly overruled, if the Court improperly identifies a fundamental right and/or fails to give proper weight to legitimate state interests. In White's view, *Roe* v. *Wade* is mistaken for both reasons.

Justice White concurred in *Griswold* v. *Connecticut,* [23] which elaborated the constitutional right to privacy and therefore the right of married couples to acquire and use contraceptives despite state criminal prohibitions. In *Thornburgh,* White does not sharply distinguish the liberty interest in *Griswold* from that in *Roe* v. *Wade:* "I can certainly agree with the proposition—which I deem indisputable—that a woman's ability to choose an abortion is a species of 'liberty' that is subject to the general protections of the Due Process Clause."[24] However, White denies that the weight to be accorded this liberty interest calls "into play anything more than the most minimal judicial scrutiny."[25]

White's position rests in part on the view that judicial protection of fundamental rights is most clearly justified "when the Constitution provides specific

---

[20] White adduces as relevant examples the dissents of Justices Harlan and Holmes in *Lochner* v. *New York,* 198 U.S. 45, 65–74 (1905) (J. Harlan, dissenting); idem at 74–76 (J. Holmes, dissenting) and Justice Harlan's dissent in *Plessy* v. *Ferguson,* 163 U.S. 537, 552–64 (1896).

[21] *Thornburgh,* at 106 S. Ct. 2193.

[22] Ibid., at 2193–94.

[23] 381 U.S. 479 (1965).

[24] *Thornburgh,* at 2194.

[25] Ibid.

textual recognition of their existence and importance."[26] Outside this area, the Court

> must, of necessity, act with more caution, lest it open itself to the accusation that, in the name of identifying constitutional principles to which the people have consented in framing their Constitution, the Court has done nothing more than impose its own controversial choices of value upon the people.[27]

Justice White notes two approaches to constraining judicial discretion in this area: first, that the liberties in question are implicit in the concept of ordered liberty, and second, that they are rooted in the nation's history and traditions.[28] Neither approach justifies making the right to abortion elaborated by *Roe* a fundamental liberty.

White's objection to any such inference relates largely to his second objection to *Roe*, namely, that the state's interest in fetal life quite overrides the decisive weight accorded a woman's liberty interest by the decision. The weighty and legitimate state interest in protecting biologically individual members of the human species overrides a woman's liberty interest in abortion:

> However one answers the metaphysical or theological question whether the fetus is a "human being" or the legal question whether it is a "person," one must at least recognize, first, that the fetus is an entity that bears in its cells all the genetic information that characterizes a member of the species *homo sapiens* and distinguishes an individual member of that species from all others, and second, that there is no nonarbitrary line separating a fetus from a child or, indeed, an adult human being.[29]

The state's interest in biological life makes the decision to terminate pregnancy "*sui generis*, different in kind from the others that the Court has protected under the rubric of personal or family privacy and autonomy."[30]

In a footnote, Justice White distinguishes the liberty interest in *Roe* from that in *Griswold* and other cases because the state interest in those cases was not on a par with the state's interest in fetal life.[31] The distinction bears not only on the comparative weight of the liberty interests in these cases, but on whether a fundamental liberty interest in terminating fetal life should even be acknowledged. He analogized the right to have an abortion to the right of parents to guide the upbringing of their children.

> No one would suggest that this fundamental liberty extends to assaults committed upon children by their parents. It is not the case that parents have a fundamental liberty to engage in such activities and that the State may in-

[26] Ibid.
[27] Ibid.
[28] Ibid.
[29] Ibid., at 2195.
[30] Ibid.
[31] *Thornburgh*, 106 S. Ct. at 2195 n.2.

trude to prevent them only because it has a compelling interest in the well-being of children; rather, such activities, by their very nature, should be viewed as outside the scope of the fundamental liberty interest.[32]

The termination of fetal life is as much a harm subject to state prohibitory power as the assault on a child, and just as a parent's right to raise a child does not justify child abuse, neither does a woman's liberty interest justify abortion.

Justice White faults the Court in *Roe* v. *Wade* for failing to show that either our concept of ordered liberty or our historical traditions extend to abortion. The division among Americans about *Roe* shows that the decision does not elaborate the nation's traditions, and the right is not implicit in ordered liberty because "it seems apparent to me that a free, egalitarian, and democratic society does not presuppose any particular rule or set of rules with respect to abortion."[33] White concludes that "in so denominating that liberty [as fundamental], the Court engages not in constitutional interpretation, but in the unrestrained imposition of its own, extraconstitutional value preferences."[34]

White also takes objection to the way in which the Court in *Roe* v. *Wade* identified a compelling state interest in preserving fetal life at the time of viability. Viability is irrelevant to the compelling state interest, which White identifies as "protecting those who will be citizens if their lives are not ended in the womb."[35]

Finally, Justice White argues that his interpretive theory is not a simple appeal to the founders' specific intention about abortion. Citing *Brown* v. *Board of Education*[36] (the decision that racial segregation in public schools violated the equal protection clause of the Fourteenth Amendment), he notes that the "founders" of 1868 (who may have accepted the constitutionality of racial segregation) may have been wrong about the way in which abstract constitutional principles should be applied in particular cases.[37] "Constitutional adjudication is a search for rights and institutions that are implicit (and explicit) in the structure of rights and institutions that the people have themselves created."[38] Ultimately, Justice White argues, it is "the will of the people that is the source of whatever values are incorporated in the Constitution."[39] He cited John Hart Ely's rejection of "clause-bound interpretivism" in support of both his reading of constitutionally legitimate interpretation and his rejection of *Roe*.[40] White concludes that *Roe* is wrong for the same reason that

---

[32] Ibid.

[33] Ibid., at 2196.

[34] Ibid., at 4631.

[35] Ibid.

[36] 347 U.S. 483 (1954) (racial segregation in the public schools held to be an unconstitutional violation of equal protection clause of the Fourteenth Amendment).

[37] *Thornburgh,* 106 S. Ct. at 2197 n.5.

[38] Ibid.

[39] Ibid.

[40] Ibid. See John Hart Ely, *Democracy and Distrust* (Cambridge, Mass.: Harvard Univ. Press, 1980), p. 12.

Lochner v. *New York*[41] was wrong, namely, *Lochner*—which invalidated a state labor regulation on substantive due-process grounds—"rested on the Court's belief that the liberty to engage in a trade or occupation without government regulation was somehow fundamental—an assessment of value that was unsupported by the Constitution."[42] *Roe* makes the same interpretive mistake by supposing that abortion is a constitutionally protected right.

Justice Stevens's remarkable concurring opinion in *Thornburgh* challenges each prong of White's argument, namely, the discussion of interpretive mistake, the relatively insubstantial weight of a woman's liberty interest in deciding whether to have an abortion, and the compelling state interest in preserving fetal life.[43] Justice Stevens finds that White's rhetorical appeal to the will of the people conflicts with White's conception of constitutional interpretation as the elaboration of abstract normative values over time.[44] For Justice Stevens, then, the issue turns solely on the cogency of White's analysis that neither a woman's liberty interest nor the absence of legitimate state interests justifies *Roe*.

Justice Stevens questions whether there can be any good argument of principle to reconcile Justice White's recognition of a weighty interest in *Griswold* and his refusal to recognize such an interest in *Roe:*

> For reasons that are not entirely clear, however, Justice White abruptly announces that the interest in "liberty" that is implicated by a decision not to bear a child that is made a few days after conception is *less* fundamental than a comparable decision made before conception.[45]

In either case, Stevens argues, the liberty of reproductive autonomy is infringed. The only possible ground for distinction between the cases is the state's burden of justification. Justice Stevens challenges the secularity of Justice White's claim that, for constitutional purposes, the fetus is indistinguishable from the living person she or he will be if not aborted and therefore eventually born: "I recognize that a powerful theological argument can be made for that position [i.e., the need for baptism], but I believe our jurisdiction is limited to the evaluation of secular state interests."[46] From a secular perspective, Justice Stevens finds compelling justifications for drawing distinctions in the status of the fetus during pregnancy:

> I should think it obvious that the state's interest in the protection of an embryo . . . increases progressively and dramatically as the organism's capac-

---

[41] 198 U.S. 45 (1905).
[42] *Thornburgh*, 106 S. Ct. at 2198 n.5.
[43] *Thornburgh*, at 2185–90.
[44] Ibid., at 2187 n.4.
[45] Ibid., at 2187 (emphasis in original).
[46] Ibid., at 2188.

ity to feel pain, to experience pleasure, to survive, and to react to its surroundings increases day by day.[47]

He accordingly finds that Justice White's appeal to biological individuality as the only constitutionally nonarbitrary line is motivated by a sectarian judgment that religious or moral personality exists throughout the period of pregnancy, a judgment that equates "the state interest in protecting the freshly fertilized egg" to "the state interest in protecting the 9-month-gestated, fully sentient fetus on the eve of birth."[48] However, Stevens argues, "recognition of this distinction is supported not only by logic, but also by history and by our shared experiences."[49]

Stevens conclude that Justice White's theory of interpretive mistake is wrong as applied to *Roe*. White himself remains committed to *Griswold* and other privacy cases, but he has not shown why these cases are justified and *Roe* is not. For Justice Stevens, *Roe* and its progeny correctly apply the important constitutional principle that "places the primary responsibility for decision in matters of childbearing squarely in the private sector of our society."[50]

Bowers v. *Hardwick*

In *Bowers*, Justice White, writing for a five-to-four majority, ruled that the privacy protections of the due-process clause do not extend to homosexual activity between consenting adults in the privacy of their homes.[51] The case was brought by Michael Hardwick, who had been charged with violating Georgia's sodomy statute.[52] Although the Georgia statute applied to both heterosexual and homosexual sex acts, including heterosexual cunnilingus, fellatio, and anal intercourse, Justice White focused exclusively on the application of the statute to homosexuals. This striking exclusion of heterosexuals from the majority's holding supports Justice Stevens's dissenting claim that the Georgia statute "is concededly unconstitutional with respect to heterosexuals."[53]

Justice White's argument for the majority focuses largely on the first prong in the analysis of constitutional privacy, namely, the identification of the underlying fundamental right itself. Reviewing the earlier cases in the privacy line, he concludes that they bear no resemblance to the *Bowers* case. "No connection between family, marriage, or procreation on the one hand and

[47] Ibid.
[48] Ibid.
[49] Ibid.
[50] Ibid., at 2189.
[51] *Bowers*, 106 S. Ct. 2841 (1986), 2842–47.
[52] Hardwick was never criminally prosecuted because the district attorney decided not to present the case to a grand jury. Ibid., at 2842.
[53] Ibid., at 2859 (J. Stevens, dissenting); see also *Post* v. *State*, 715 P.2d 1105, 1109–10 (Okla. Crim. App.) (holding law prohibiting consensual sodomy between adults unconstitutional as applied to heterosexual acts, but noting application of same law to homosexual conduct would present different question), *reh'g denied*, 717 P.2d 1151 (Okla. Crim. App.), *cert. denied*, 107 S. Ct. 290 (1986).

homosexual activity on the other has been demonstrated."[54] He argues further that cases in the privacy line "have little or no textual support in the constitutional language,"[55] and that, accordingly, in order to justify these rights as "more than the imposition of the Justices' own choice of values on the States and the Federal Government,"[56] the Court has required a showing that such rights are implicit in either the concept of ordered liberty or the nation's historical traditions. Any expansion of these rights—to homosexual activity, for example—requires such a showing. However, White argues, neither approach justifies expanding constitutional privacy to homosexual activity in view of the existence of criminal sodomy laws in all thirteen colonies at the time of ratification of the Bill of Rights, as well as in all but five of the thirty-seven states in 1868 when the Fourteenth Amendment was ratified. Accordingly, any such claim "is, at best, facetious."[57]

Justice White rejects "a more expansive view of our authority" because "The Court is most vulnerable and comes nearest to illegitimacy when it deals with judge-made constitutional law having little or no cognizable roots in the language or design of the Constitution."[58] He apparently regards the expansion of constitutional privacy to homosexual activity as the same kind of interpretive mistake as *Roe* v. *Wade,* invoking, in *Bowers,* the same historical precedent used in *Thornburgh:* "the face-off between the Executive and the Court in the 1930's, which resulted in the repudiation of much of the substantive gloss that the Court had placed on the Due Process Clause."[59]

Finding no fundamental right, Justice White's majority opinion pays little attention to the second prong of constitutional privacy analysis, namely, the nature and weight of the state purposes justifying the abridgment of a fundamental right. He assumes "that majority sentiments about the morality of homosexuality"[60] afford a sufficient rational basis for criminal prohibitions. He rejects the relevance of *Stanley* v. *Georgia,*[61]—which protected the use of obscene materials in the home from criminal prohibition—on the ground that *Stanley* "was firmly grounded in the First Amendment."[62] He points out that *Stanley* "itself recognized that its holding offered no protection for the possession in the home of drugs, firearms, or stolen goods,"[63] and further argues that the Court could not limit its *Bowers* holding to voluntary sexual conduct between consenting adults in their homes. Justice White claims that "it would be difficult, except by fiat, to limit the claimed right to homosexual conduct

[54] *Bowers,* 106 S. Ct. at 2844.
[55] Ibid.
[56] Ibid.
[57] Ibid., at 2846.
[58] Ibid.
[59] Ibid., at 2846.
[60] Ibid.
[61] 394 U.S. 557 (1969).
[62] *Bowers,* 106 S. Ct. at 2846.
[63] Ibid.

while leaving exposed to prosecution adultery, incest, and other sexual crimes even though they are committed in the home."[64]

In his opinion for the four dissenters, Justice Blackmun sharply questions the interpretive methodology of the majority and its analysis of both fundamental rights and compelling state purposes.[65] He contests, in particular, the decisive weight the majority places on history.

> Like Justice Holmes, I believe that "it is revolting to have no better reason for a rule of law than that so it was laid down in the time of Henry IV. It is still more revolting if the grounds upon which it was laid down have vanished long since, and the rule simply persists from blind imitation of the past."[66]

Rather, for Justice Blackmun, the issue relates to whether the normative values of constitutional privacy require that it be extended to homosexual activity.

In his view, the fundamental right identified by constitutional privacy has the decisional aspect of being able to make certain highly intimate decisions autonomously, and the heightened concern for the protection of such decisions when made in certain private places, like the home. Not all cases accorded protection by the constitutional right to privacy exemplify both aspects,[67] but all exemplify at least one, and some both.[68] Blackmun argues that the homosexual acts in *Bowers* merit protection under both aspects of constitutional privacy. Their sexual intimacy falls within the realm of intimate decisions, for

> the fact that individuals define themselves in a significant way through their intimate sexual relationships with others suggests, in a Nation as diverse as ours, that there may be many "right" ways of conducting these relationships, and that much of the richness of a relationship will come from the freedom an individual has to *choose* the form and nature of these intensely personal bonds.[69]

Furthermore, the sex acts in question occur in the home, the locus for heightened protection by the constitutional right to privacy. Blackmun rejects White's narrow reading of *Stanley,* because it fails to give weight to the *Stanley*

---

[64] Ibid.

[65] Ibid., at 4923–7.

[66] Ibid., at 2848 [quoting Oliver Wendell Holmes, "The Path of the Law," 10 *Harv. L. Rev.* 457, 469 (1897)].

[67] In *Roe* v. *Wade,* 410 U.S. 113 (1973), for example, a woman's right to abortion services is not limited to the home, but extends to any place (e.g., clinics or hospitals) where such services are available.

[68] *Griswold* v. *Connecticut,* 381 U.S. 479 (1965), for example, clearly involves both elements: the intimate decision to use contraceptives and their use in the privacy of one's home.

[69] *Bowers,* 106 S. Ct. at 2851 (emphasis in original).

Court's invocation of Brandeis's views of the inviolable rights of a free person that are essentially cultivated in the privacy of the home.[70]

Justice Blackmun also criticizes the purposes offered by the state in support of the Georgia statute. He analyzes the purported state purposes in the way Justice Stevens analyzed state purposes in *Thornburgh*,[71] distinguishing sectarian and secular justifications. For Justice Blackmun, the very statement of the state's moral purpose refutes it as a sufficient justification for abridging fundamental rights.

> The assertion that "traditional Judeo-Christian values proscribe" the conduct involved . . . cannot provide an adequate justification. . . . That certain, but by no means all, religious groups condemn the behavior at issue gives the State no license to impose their judgments on the entire citizenry. The legitimacy of secular legislation depends instead on whether the State can advance some justification for its law beyond its conformity to religious doctrine.[72]

Blackmun answers White's line-drawing argument by identifying plausible secular interests that might justify criminal prohibitions on incest, adultery, and the like.[73] Furthermore, he rejects the state's alternative argument about protection of the moral environment because the conduct at issue in *Bowers* took place entirely in private.[74]

These disagreements within the Supreme Court on the interpretive legitimacy of constitutional privacy in general, and its application to abortion and homosexual activity in particular, relate to larger disputes about the nature and legitimacy of constitutional interpretation. We must therefore assess them from that perspective.

The Interpretive Legitimacy of Constitutional Privacy:
Griswold v. *Connecticut*

As in many areas of public law, argument over constitutional privacy centers on the principled articulation of a rule of law that justifies both the inference

---

[70] Ibid., at 2852. The *Stanley* Court quoted Brandeis on the Fourth Amendment's special protection for the individual in the home as follows:

> "The makers of our Constitution undertook to secure conditions favorable to the pursuit of happiness. They recognized the significance of man's spiritual nature, of his feelings and of his intellect. They knew that only a part of the pain, pleasure and satisfactions of life are to be found in material things. They sought to protect Americans in their beliefs, their thoughts, their emotions and their sensations."

> These are the rights that appellant is asserting in the case before us. He is asserting the right to read or observe what he pleases—the right to satisfy his intellectual and emotional needs in the privacy of his own home. [*Stanley* v. *Georgia*, at 564–565, quoting *Olmstead* v. *Unites States*, 277 U.S., at 478 (J. Brandeis, dissenting)].

[71] 106 S. Ct. at 2185–90 (J. Stevens, concurring).
[72] *Bowers*, 106 S. Ct. at 2854–55 (quoting petitioner's brief).
[73] Ibid., at 2853–54 n.4.
[74] Ibid., at 2855.

and elaboration of the right in question. Such a debate dates from the initial recognition of the constitutional right to privacy in *Griswold* v. *Connecticut.*[75] Justice White concurred in *Griswold's* elaboration of constitutional privacy and its application to contraceptive use,[76] but, as we have seen, he objects to expanding constitutional privacy to abortion and consensual adult homosexual activity. Robert Bork is more radical than Justice White, attacking the interpretive principle of constitutional privacy, including *Griswold.*[77] My discussion of these issues begins by focusing in this section on the interpretive legitimacy of *Griswold* itself, which is a rather more troubling case than is usually supposed. If we treated *Griswold* as a harder case than we usually do, and resolved our interpretive doubts about its legitimacy by more critically focused arguments, we would not be quite so anxious about expanding the scope of the constitutional right to privacy. Accordingly, it is my intention first to explore my own views of *Griswold's* various difficulties, and then to examine and criticize Bork's version of these difficulties. Bork's attack on *Griswold* is, in my opinion, mistaken on each of the grounds he offers against its interpretive legitimacy, namely, text, history, republican political theory, and judicial reasoning and role. That criticism makes possible an alternative constructive account of the principle of constitutional privacy, which will later be used in this chapter to criticize the theory of interpretive legitimacy Justice White puts forward in *Thornburgh* and *Bowers.*

Critical Difficulties

In *Griswold* v. *Connecticut,*[78] the Supreme Court announced that the constitutional right to privacy protected married couples from criminal liability based on the acquistion and use of contraceptives. *Griswold* raises two interpretive issues of principle: first, the nature, and scope of the constitutional right to privacy itself, and second, the appropriate burden of justification that the state must satisfy in order to abridge this right.

THE FUNDAMENTAL RIGHT

Griswold placed great weight on two separate aspects of the use of contraceptives in question: use by married couples and use in the privacy of the home. The Court noted that the marriage relationship itself is a locus of constitutional rights worthy of protection.

> Marriage is a coming together for better or for worse, hopefully enduring, and intimate to the degree of being sacred. It is an association that promotes a way of life, not causes; a harmony in living, not political faiths; a bilateral

---

[75] 381 U.S. 479 (1965).
[76] Ibid., at 502.
[77] Bork, "Neutral Principles."
[78] 381 U.S. 479 (1965).

loyalty, not commercial or social projects. Yet it is an association for as noble a purpose as any involved in our prior decisions.[79]

Later cases, however, have expanded the principle in *Griswold* to include unmarried adults[80] and even adolescents.[81] Furthermore, neither *Roe* v. *Wade*[82] nor *Stanley* v. *Georgia*[83] relied on marriage when extending the protections of constitutional privacy to include, respectively, abortion and the possession of pornography in the home.

The Court in *Griswold* also emphasized that the activity in question occurred in the privacy of the home. In particular, Justice Douglas noted the threat to Fourth Amendment values that criminal prosecutions for contraceptive use would require, querying, "Would we allow the police to search the sacred precincts of marital bedrooms for telltale signs of the use of contraceptives?"[84] Not all later elaborations of constitutional privacy, however, involve situations that threaten such violations; abortion services, for example, are generally performed outside the home.

There are many puzzles here. First, why marriage? The right to marriage is not textually specified, so its existence must depend on a conception of unenumerated reserved rights of the sort referred to in the Ninth Amendment, the privileges and immunities clause of Article IV, and the privileges and immunities and due-process clauses of the Fourteenth Amendment.[85] As we shall later see, the founders contemplated that the express protections of human rights in the Constitution should be supplemented by implied protections of other basic rights of the person.[86] We must, then, ask why the marriage relationship should be regarded as one of these basic rights. Marriage is a highly regulated legal institution in which the state has traditionally asserted a wide range of legitimate interests. Any constitutional inhibition on state power would have to rebut this long historical tradition.

Second, why beyond marriage? A natural explanation that appears to fit much of the case law is Justice White's suggestion in *Bowers* v. *Hardwick*[87] that constitutional privacy protects decisions whether or not to reproduce and how otherwise to control one's relations to biological offspring. This approach certainly explains the protected right to use contraceptives in and outside marriage, and connects those decisions to *Roe* and other decisions.[88] However,

[79] Ibid., at 486.
[80] See *Eisenstadt* v. *Baird*, 405 U.S. 438 (1972).
[81] See *Carey* v. *Population Services*, 431 U.S. 678 (1977).
[82] 410 U.S. 113 (1973).
[83] 394 U.S. 557 (1969).
[84] *Griswold*, 381 U.S. at 485.
[85] Cf. Ely, *Democracy and Distrust*, pp. 22–30 (discussing proper interpretation of privileges and immunities clause of Fourteenth Amendment).
[86] See ibid.
[87] 106 S. Ct. 2841, 2843–44 (1986).
[88] It would explain, for example, the decisions that protect parental rights to control the upbringing of their children. See, e.g., *Moore* v. *City of East Cleveland*, 431 U.S. 494 (1977) (upholding right of grandmother to share her home with two nonsibling grandchildren); *Pierce* v.

what is it about the control of biological reproduction and its consequences that entitles it—as a matter of principle—to constitutional protection? Can Justice White's proposal be articulated as a principle that corresponds to a basic right of the person that could reasonably justify appropriate limitations on the coercive power of law? It cannot, because his view of privacy is problematically unprincipled.

On the one hand, control of biological reproduction is unreasonably underinclusive. Why does the issue relate to a control of biological reproduction and not control of other biological process—like breathing and eating and elimination—that bear more directly on survival of the person herself or himself? Why does survival of the species enjoy primacy over individual conditions of biological survival? Why think of the impersonal facts of biological reproduction as the issue at all instead of the diverse range of reasonable interpretations persons bring to intimate personal life? Control of biological reproduction is, to say the least, artificially truncated as a principle of law; it does not correspond to any sensibly coherent theory of reasonable freedom that could be justified in the required way.

On the other hand, identification of biological reproduction as the essential moral basis of the right to marriage is also overinclusive in that it treats biological reproduction as the primary personal value of marriage. If the right in question includes the right of married couples to use contraceptives, then it must include their right either not to engage in biological reproduction at all or not to make it the organizing center of the relationship; indeed, that is perhaps the point of a case like *Griswold,* which repudiated state enforcement of a rigidly pronatalist conception of marriage.[89] How can biological reproduction be the point of a right that precisely empowers married couples to choose not to reproduce? Certainly, many people today reject biological reproduction as the central value of marriage,[90] not because they do not have interests in having and raising offspring, but because they believe that an exclusive focus on that aspect of marriage degrades the personal bonds between spouses that nourish the continuing value of the relationship in all areas, the nurturing of the wide range of common interests and projects that the relationship supports throughout a shared life. The right to use contraceptives—the right established by *Griswold*—is one of the core liberties that has enabled couples to identify and explore the value of marriage as a personal and ethical relationship in and of itself. In particular, contraceptive use has enabled many

---

Society of Sisters, 268 U.S. 510 (1925) (upholding right of parents to send their children to parochial and private schools); *Meyer* v. *Nebraska,* 262 U.S. 390 (1923) (upholding right of parents to have their children instructed in foreign languages).

[89] On the pronatalist conception of marriage, see, e.g., Augustine, *The City of God,* Henry Bettenson, trans. (Harmondsworth, Middlesex, England: Penguin, 1972), pp. 577–94; Thomas Aquinas, *On the Truth of the Catholic Faith: Summa Contra Gentiles,* Vernon Bourke, trans. (New York: Image, 1956), pt. 2, ch. 122(9), p. 146.

[90] See, e.g., Irenaus Eibl-Eibesfeldt, *Love and Hate* G. Strachen, trans. (New York: Holt, Rinehart & Winston, 1972); William H. Masters and Virginia Johnson, *The Pleasure Bond* (Boston: Little, Brown, 1975).

women—perhaps for the first time in human history—to construct and define new conceptions of reproductive autonomy, unburdened by a sense of mandatory procreative function within an unquestionable gender hierarchy of domination and submission, and to integrate them into larger agendas of personal and ethical fulfillment.[91] It is inherently unreasonable and unconvincing to justify *Griswold* to such women on the ground of the universal value of biological reproduction when it is precisely the legitimacy of disagreements over that value that *Griswold* expresses. In short, the very reasonable controversial nature of biological reproduction as the constitutive value of marriage debars it as the neutrally justifiable principle embodied in *Griswold*.

The requirement that constitutional interpretations be principled is rooted, as suggested earlier, in the Lockean theory of political legitimacy of the reasonable justification of state coercion of free and equal persons on terms of equal respect for rights and pursuit of the common interests of all. Such justification must be faithful to the history of a constitutional provision over time and justify its further elaboration with contextual sensitivity to the circumstances that bear on the reasonable justification to all that is constitutive of a community of principle. Biological reproduction fails to meet this standard because it underinclusively fails to elaborate a reasonable value of the appropriate sort, and overinclusively imputes to marriage a value that reasonable people contest in ways that *Griswold* itself protects. *Griswold* may protect an essential right of free, rational, and equal persons, but biological reproduction is not that value.

BURDEN OF JUSTIFICATION

If it is relatively clear from *Griswold* that anticontraception laws abridge the fundamental right to marital intimacy, then it is much less clear why the state's justification for the law does not meet the constitutionally acceptable burden of justification for the abridgment of this type of fundamental right. Several concurring justices in *Griswold* discuss the issue as if anticontraception laws could only be justified by the state's policies against premarital or extramarital sex.[92] If these were the only possible legitimate purposes for the statute, then the statute's abridgment of a fundamental right could not stand, of course, because its application to married couples is irrationally overinclusive. These laws might, however, plausibly be regarded as resting on another kind of state purpose altogether, namely, that any form of contraception is immoral per se because it frustrates the essential purpose of sexuality, namely, procreation.

---

[91] See generally James Reed, *The Birth Control Movement and American Society* (Princeton, N.J.: Princeton Univ. Press, 1978).

[92] See *Griswold*, 381 U.S. at 486–98 (J. Goldberg, concurring); idem, at 502–07 (J. White, concurring). In contrast, Justice Harlan's concurring opinion identifies larger moral purposes that the anticontraception statute might serve; he does not, however, explain why those purposes are not justly enforceable in this case as they are in other cases like adultery and homosexuality. Idem, at 499–502.

Both Augustine[93] and Thomas Aquinas,[94] for example, condemn this evil as an independent moral wrong. Combatting nonprocreative sexuality is a purpose pursued quite rationally by the statute, because marital sexuality is subject to the evil. Why is such a moral purpose not constitutionally acceptable?

The question is, either implicitly or explicitly, at the very heart of all serious debate over constitutional privacy. It poses, for example, the sharpest conflict of principle with the much-proclaimed overruling of *Lochner* v. *New York*.[95] If *Griswold* implicitly rules certain substantive moral purposes constitutionally unacceptable, then *Griswold*'s holding looks very much like the *Lochner* Court's implicit refusal to accept the equalization of bargaining power between employers and employees as a legitimate state purpose.[96] What is it about the moral purpose invalidated in *Griswold* that makes it constitutionally unacceptable?

Three arguments are plausible.[97] First, most Americans no longer believe in such moral purposes, and the judiciary may invalidate them on that majoritarian ground. Second, the acts in question neither harm third parties, nor the parties themselves, and thus the moral purposes at issue are invalid because they do not meet some required threshold showing of harms to oneself or others. Third, the substantive moral values in question here are today sectarian values not believed by all reasonable people. The enforcement of such sectarian values through criminal laws violates the establishment clause, and thus such values cannot enjoy the force of law.[98]

Each of these arguments is not without its difficulties. Why, for example, should the judiciary act on the first, allegedly majoritarian ground, when such majoritarian sentiments could easily have harnessed the democratic process to accomplish their aims? We usually think of judicial review as most appropriate when it vindicates the rights of minorities who, by virtue of their minority status, could not otherwise vindicate their rights. However, justifying *Griswold* on majoritarian grounds inverts the rationale behind judicial review, because, on this rationale, the judiciary should protect minorities and not contraceptive-using majorities. Furthermore, the majoritarian argument does not vindicate an interpretive understanding of historical principles against

---

[93] For Augustine, procreation was the only legitimate function of sexuality. The classic statement of his view is Augustine, *City of God,* pp. 577–94.

[94] Aquinas is in accord with Augustine's view. Of the emission of semen apart from procreation in marriage, he wrote, "After the sin of homicide whereby a human nature already in existence is destroyed, this type of sin appears to take next place, for by it the generation of human nature is precluded" (Aquinas, *On the Truth of the Catholic Faith,* p. 146).

[95] 198 U.S. 45 (1905). On the decline of the *Lochner* doctrine, see, e.g., *West Coast Hotel Co.* v. *Parrish,* 300 U.S. 379 (1937) (sustaining minimum wage for women); *Nebbia* v. *New York,* 201 U.S. 502 (1934) (upholding state control of milk prices).

[96] For an explicit constitutional repudiation of the state purpose of equalizing bargaining power, see *Coppage* v. *Kansas,* 236 U.S. 1 (1915).

[97] These arguments are explored at greater length in David Richards, *Toleration and the Constitution,* (New York: Oxford Univ. Press, 1986), pp. 234–54.

[98] Cf. Louis Henkin, "Morals and the Constitution: The Sin of Obscenity," 63 *Col. L. Rev.* 391 (1961).

transient contemporary majorities but rather upholds majoritarian sentiment against anachronistic tradition. If *Griswold* rests only on this justification, then its legitimacy is in real doubt.

The second rationale for *Griswold* is more analytically promising. On this view, *Griswold* is justified because a criminal prohibition of the sale and use of contraceptives does not fit within the limiting principle of substantive criminal liability—the harm principle.[99] Contraceptives do not harm their users but rather enable them better to integrate reproductive aims with other personal and ethical aims; they do not harm others, but rather advance larger social aims of population control. However, the harm principle—regardless of its plausibility as liberal political theory—does not explain why contraception, and not all behavior that fails to satisfy the harm principle, should be the locus of special constitutional scrutiny. Nor does it explain how or why the harm principle is embedded in American constitutional traditions in a way that would justify its elaboration in *Griswold* and later cases.

The third rationale is a variant of the harm principle, but it, unlike the harm principle, explains why secular harms might be the sine qua non of constitutionally justifiable state action. On this view, *Griswold* properly upholds the principle that the state may not enforce a criminal statute that today rests only on a sectarian ground (sex must always be used for procreation) that some people no longer find to be a reasonable basis for laws. However, arguments of this kind do not explain how or why we should distinguish illegitimate sectarian purposes from legitimate moral purposes. Certainly, religiously motivated groups have often significantly advanced public understanding of human rights—for example, the abolition of slavery and advancement of civil rights in general[100]—and some religion-influenced conceptions of moral values are not without justifiable public appeal.[101] The question, then, is when and how we should distinguish the proper from the improper appeal to such conceptions.

Even if *Griswold* might be regarded as satisfying one of these three arguments, however, the later privacy cases are arguably more troubling. The morality of abortion at the time of *Roe* may not have commanded the same kind of majoritarian consensus as the morality of contraception at the time of *Griswold*. Furthermore, even if the harm principle were a principle of constitutional law, then arguably abortions do inflict harms by terminating life. Nor is

---

[99] See, e.g., John Stuart Mill, *On Liberty* Alburey Castell, ed. (New York: Appleton-Century-Crafts, 1947), pp. 55–118. An important contemporary restatement of Mill's argument is Joel Feinberg's four-volume work, *The Moral Limits of the Criminal Law*. See J. Feinberg, *Harm to Others* (New York: Oxford Univ. Press, 1984); idem, *Offense to Others* (New York: Oxford Univ. Press, 1985); idem, *Harm to Self* (New York: Oxford Univ. Press, 1986); idem., *Harmless Wrongdoing* (New York: Oxford University Press, 1988).

[100] See John P. Diggins, *The Lost Soul of American Politics* (New York: Basic Books, 1984), pp. 277–333; Richard J. Neuhaus, *The Naked Public Square* (Grand Rapids, Mich.: William B. Eerdmans, 1984).

[101] Conceptions of environmental ethics, including preservation of species, may be values of this kind. See, e.g., Kent Greenawalt, *Religious Convictions and Political Choice* (New York: Oxford Univ. Press, 1988), pp. 98–114.

the conclusion that abortion is the taking of life an exclusively sectarian value, because secular biologists can also accept it.

Doubts of these kinds have led some constitutional scholars, notably John Hart Ely, to challenge the privacy cases in general and the abortion cases in particular.[102] Ely concedes that the constitutional right to privacy has a sound basis in the text, history, and political theory of natural rights that are fundamental to the Constitution.[103] He then objects to the extension of privacy to *Roe,* because *Roe* was based on open-ended textual language, rather than the more specific language of the Fourth Amendment that is central to *Griswold.*[104] Furthermore, according to Ely, *Roe* is not defensible on the ground of aiding traditionally disenfranchised minorities; to the contrary, fetuses are arguably the most insular of disenfranchised minorities.[105]

Ely notwithstanding, it is not clear that even *Griswold* is a legitimate construction of the text of the Constitution. Certainly, the Fourth Amendment considerations that Ely adduces in its support explain nothing, because much conduct that takes place in the home (e.g., murder, rape, spouse and child abuse) is not and should not be protected from substantive criminal liability. We must face squarely the legitimacy of the very principle of constitutional privacy, and there is no better way to do so than by addressing the radical skepticism of Robert Bork.

Bork's Skepticism

Bork's critical views on the very inference of the constitutional right to privacy are at the core of his interpretive philosophy. In particular, Bork took *Griswold* as a kind of model of constitutionally illegitimate interpretive mistake. The *Griswold* Court thus failed to "stick close to the text and the history"[106] of the Constitution, violated the democratic political theory of the Constitution by failing "to let the majority have its way,"[107] and abandoned judicial reasoning and role by imposing its own views that the "sexual gratification" of contraceptive users is "more worthy than [the] moral gratification"[108] of democratic majorities. His arguments raise reasonable doubts about whether Bork understands the traditional role of the judiciary in the protection of the inalienable rights of a free people. The protection of rights cannot reasonably or responsibly be left to any such doubt.

Bork's attack on the inference of constitutional privacy fails on each of the grounds he specifies, namely, text, history, democratic political theory, and judicial reasoning and role.

---

[102] See Ely, *Democracy and Distrust,* at p. 248 n.52; idem, "The Wages of Crying Wolf: A Comment on *Roe* v. *Wade,*" 82 *Yale L.J.* 920 (1973).

[103] See Ely, "Wages of Crying Wolf," at pp. 928–29.

[104] See ibid., pp. 929–33; Ely, *Democracy and Distrust,* p. 221 n.4.

[105] See Ely, "Wages of Crying Wolf," pp. 933–35.

[106] Bork, "Neutral Principles," at p. 8.

[107] Ibid., p. 10.

[108] Ibid.

TEXT AND HISTORY: UNENUMERATED RIGHTS

The Constitution of 1787 and the Bill of Rights of 1791 form a constitutional unit, because the ratification of the one was—in the view of leading ratifying states like Massachusetts, Virginia, and New York—premised on the promise of the ratification of the other. These founding documents of American constitutionalism were deemed acceptable not because they exhausted the protection of basic rights but precisely because—in the view of the founders—they expressly protected unenumerated rights as well. Indeed, agreement that unenumerated rights are fully protected is at the very center of the deliberative argument offered and accepted for ratification of the Constitution, and rests on the deepest convictions of the founders about the legitimacy of a written constitution, namely, that rights are not given by the Constitution, but that the Constitution's authority rests on its respect for and protection of the inalienable rights that persons have as free and rational persons capable of moral self-government.

One of the most important and cogent challenges of the anti-Federalists to the 1787 Constitution was its lack of a Bill of Rights.[109] The standard answer to this objection in the ratification debates over the 1787 Constitution was made by leading founders like Wilson[110] and Madison[111] at their respective constitutional conventions (Pennsylvania and Virginia), and by Hamilton in *The Federalist*.[112] They argued that the theory of the 1787 Constitution, in contrast to the British constitution, was republican; any powers not expressly granted to the federal government by the Constitution were reserved for the people, including the wide range of inalienable human rights that could not, in principle, be surrendered to the state. Indeed, a Bill of Rights would, on this view, undermine the protection of inalienable human rights, because the express protection of certain rights would justify the inference that rights not expressly protected were subject to the illimitable power of the federal Leviathan; in effect, any gain in protection of rights from a Bill of Rights would be lost by this negative inference.

The point was not merely that it would be insuperably difficult, as Wilson had argued,[113] to specify all such inalienable rights of the person as they were understood in 1787 and 1791. The founders framed the Constitution to "se-

---

[109] *Federalist Farmer,* one of the best of the antifederalist tracts, puts the argument with particular force. See, e.g., pp. 56–59, 79–86, Herbert J. Storing, ed., *The Anti-Federalist,* abridged ed. (Chicago: Univ. of Chicago Press, 1985).

[110] See, e.g., Merrill Jensen, ed., *The Documentary History of the Ratification of the Constitution,* vol. 2 (Madison: State Historical Society of Wisconsin, 1976), pp. 388, 470–71.

[111] See, e.g., Jonathan Elliot, ed. *Debates in the Several State Conventions on the Adoption of the Federal Constitution,* vol. 3 (Philadelphia: Lippincott, 1836), pp. 620, 626–27.

[112] See *The Federalist,* no. 84.

[113] Wilson observed, of the attempt to specify all reserved rights: "I consider there are very few who understand the *whole* of these rights. All the political writers, from Grotius and Puffendorf down to Vattel, have treated on this subject; but in no one of those books, nor in the aggregate of them all, can you find a complete enumeration of rights, appertaining to the people as men and as citizens" (Jensen, ed., *Documentary History,* vol. 2, p. 470).

cure the blessings of liberty to ourselves and our posterity,"[114] and they were as much concerned by the effects of such an enumeration of rights on the legitimacy of the Constitution in future generations. The most prophetic expression of the founders' fears about a Bill of Rights not protecting unenumerated rights as well is Iredell's argument at the North Carolina ratifying convention:

> A bill of rights, as I conceive, would not only be incongruous, but dangerous. No man, let his ingenuity be what it will, could enumerate all the individual rights not relinquished by this Constitution. Suppose, therefore, an enumeration of a great many, but an omission of some, and that, long after all traces of our present disputes were at an end, any of the omitted rights should be invaded, and the invasion complained of; what would be the plausible answer of the government to such a complaint? Would they not naturally say, "We live at a great distance from the time when this Constitution was established. We can judge of it much better by the ideas of it entertained at the time, than by any ideas of our own. The bill of rights, passed at that time, showed that the people did not think every power retained which was not given, else this bill of rights was not only useless, but absurd. But we are not at liberty to charge an absurdity upon our ancestors, who have given such strong proofs of their good sense, as well as their attachment to a liberty. So long as the rights enumerated in the bill of rights remain unviolated, you have no reason to complain. This is not one of them." Thus a bill of rights might operate as a snare rather than a protection.[115]

How, despite such prophecies, did the best anti-Federalist arguments persuade the people that the 1787 Constitution required a complementary Bill of Rights? *Federal Farmer,* a leading anti-Federalist publication, argued that any negative inference drawn from enumeration of certain rights could be expressly rebutted (e.g., by a provision like the Ninth Amendment), and then pointed to the inestimable value of a Bill of Rights:

> We do not by declarations change the nature of things, or create new truths, but we give existence, or at least establish in the minds of the people truths and principles which they might never otherwise have thought of, or soon forgot. If a nation means its systems, religious or political, shall have duration, it ought to recognize the leading principles of them in the front page of every family book. What is the usefulness of a truth in theory, unless it exists constantly in the minds of the people, and has their assent . . . —Men, in some countries do not remain free, merely because they are entitled to natural and inalienable rights; men in all countries are entitled to them, not because their ancestors once got together and enumerated them on paper, but because by repeated negociations [sic] and declarations, all parties are brought to realize them, and of course to believe them to be sacred.[116]

---

[114] U.S. Constitution, Preamble.

[115] See Elliot, ed., *Debates,* vol. 4, p. 149. The same argument was made by Yeates at the Pennsylvania ratifying covention. See Jensen, ed., *Documentary History,* vol. 2, p. 437.

[116] Storing, ed., *Anti-Federalist,* pp. 80–1.

Paradoxically, *Federal Farmer* shared Iredell's worries that later generations living under an enduring written republican constitution would lose faith with the principles of republican morality. In contrast to Iredell, however, *Federal Farmer* perceives a bill of rights as a way of preserving these values and of reminding each generation of the arguments of principle through which they acknowledge one another as free and equal members of a cooperative community. If the point of a written constitution was, as Madison argued,[117] to use the deeply human sense of historical tradition in service of republican values, then a bill of rights would, as *Federal Farmer* cogently argued, naturally complement and advance this end. Thus Madison, despite earlier reservations,[118] was not unnaturally the central leader in the drafting and passage of the Bill of Rights.[119]

A number of ratifying states in 1787–1788 were persuaded by the anti-Federalist arguments. Much concerned at the absence of a bill of rights, they ratified the Constitution only on the understanding that a bill of rights would shortly be added, one that included a general provision that there should be no negative inference from the express protection of certain rights that unenumerated rights are not also protected.[120] The consequences of this debate is the first ten amendments to the 1787 Constitution—namely, the 1791 Bill of Rights (including the Ninth Amendment[121])—which expressly rebuts the negative inference so feared by many founders.[122] Indeed, the ratification debates and relevant texts make it clear that all these rights, both enumerated and unenumerated, are *textually* protected.[123] Neither history nor text sustains the claim that these rights are "nontextual." It is one of the remarkable facts about contemporary views of constitutional interpretation that this claim should be so uncritically espoused, not least by members of the Supreme Court.[124]

---

[117] See *The Federalist*, no. 49.

[118] See, e.g. Elliot, ed., *Debates*, vol. 3, pp. 620, 626.

[119] See Bernard Schwartz, *The Great Rights of Mankind* (New York: Oxford Univ. Press, 1977), pp. 160–91.

[120] For general studies of the call of ratifying conventions for a bill of rights, see Schwartz, *Great Rights of Mankind,* pp. 119–59; Robert A. Rutland, *The Birth of the Bill of Rights 1776–1791,* rev. ed. (Boston: Northeastern Univ. Press, 1983). See, also, the Massachusetts' recommendations, pp. 177–78, Elliot, *Debates,* vol. 2; and Virginia's recommendations, pp. 657–61, idem, vol. 3.

[121] The Ninth Amendment reads: "The enumeration in the Constitution, of certain rights, shall not be construed to deny or disparge others retained by the people" (U.S. Constitution, Amendment IX).

[122] See, e.g., Schwartz, *Great Rights of Mankind,* pp. 165–68, 177, 199–200; Ely, *Democracy and Distrust,* pp. 22–30, 34–41.

[123] *Cf.* Ely, *Democracy and Distrust,* pp. 34–41, 22–30 (noting that in addition to Ninth Amendment, textual support for unenumerated rights can be found in privileges and immunities clause of Ariticle IV and in privileges and immunities and due process clauses of Fourteenth Amendment).

[124] "Among such cases are those recognizing rights that have little or no textual support in the constitutional language. *Meyer, Prince,* and *Pierce* fall in this category, as do the privacy cases from *Griswold* to *Carey.*" *Bowers* v. *Hardwick,* 106 S. Ct. 2841, 2844 (1986) (J. White).

It is, of course, supremely paradoxical that Bork, who was so allegedly absorbed by text and history as well as fidelity to the founders, should do them such injustice by supposing that the Constitution does not fully protect unenumerated rights of the person. The capacity of the Bill of Rights to meet *Federal Farmer's* hopes and quell Iredell's fears obviously relates to whether guarantees of rights—enumerated and unenumerated—are responsibly interpreted by each generation in service of enduring republican principles (establishing "in the minds of the people truths and principles they might never otherwise have thought of, or soon forgot"[125]). Bork, in contrast, is Iredell's nightmare, a prospective judge on the highest court of the land who would read the constitutional protections of enumerated rights in precisely the way that Iredell fearfully anticipated, namely, that "we can judge of it much better by the ideas of it entertained at the time, than by any ideas of our own,"[126] and therefore the Constitution protects no other rights.

We need then to make the best interpretive sense we can of the idea of unenumerated rights of the person if we are to remain faithful to an enduring written constitution, a constitution based on a theory of republican legitimacy (i.e., the reservation of all inalienable human rights from state power). How should we understand these rights, and does the constitutional right to privacy appear among them?

HISTORY AND POLITICAL THEORY: CONSTITUTIONAL PRIVACY

As we saw earlier (Chapters 2–4), the American constitutional experiment was distinguished from classical republicanism by the conception of both substantive and procedural guarantees that created a larger republican conception of self-government on terms of respect for rights and the pursuit of the public good. Constitutional guarantees not only define and regulate independent spheres of political self-government (i.e., federalism, separation of powers, and judicial review) in ways oriented to secure the impartial exercise of republican political rights consistent with respect for all rights and the public good, but they also define substantive spheres of moral self-government that are wholly immune from certain exercises of state power. Indeed, the U.S. Constitution defined the very legitimacy of political power in terms of respect for the inalienable rights of the person—both rights enumerated and unenumerated in the 1787 Constitution, 1791 Bill of Rights, and the 1868 Fourteenth Amendment. Constitutional protection of rights defines private spheres of reasonable self-government in terms of equal respect for all persons living in a cooperative community as democratic equals. Indeed, the very legitimacy of political power is tested against arguments of principle that reasonably justify this power to all in the required terms of respect for equal rights and pursuit of the common interests of all. For example, both the equal liberties of conscience and speech—essential to any plausible understanding of the enumerated rights guaranteed against the federal government by the First Amendment and

---

[125] *Federal Farmer*, p. 80.
[126] Elliot, ed., *Debates*, vol. 4, p. 149.

against the states by the Fourteenth Amendment—define essential spheres of independence from the state-enforced sectarian judgments of moral and political orthodoxy that had historically deprived both persons and communities of their natural right to reasonable judgment about personal and ethical value in living.[127] The constitutional thought of the American founders was thus very much at the cutting edge of the long-standing emancipatory and democratic project of European humanists to identify the oppressive uses of political power that had entrenched arbitrary structures of power and privilege. No such oppression had, in their judgment, been more debilitating and corrupting than the enforcement by the state of religious, moral, and political orthodoxies that deprived people of both their moral competence for reasonable self-government as ethical beings and their political competence to hold the state accountable to such reasonable judgment. Constitutional protection of independent spheres—through textual guarantees of both enumerated and unenumerated rights—thus enshrines a larger conception of the democratic accountability and justifiability of state power to the reasonable conscience of a self-governing people. Such morally independent self-government was, for the founders, a main object of the construction of constitutional government.

This larger conception of essential spheres of moral independence naturally included protection of the unenumerated right of intimate association[128] that underlies the traditional understanding of a fundamental right to marriage, which was clearly assumed by the founders.[129] For example, Witherspoon—Madison's teacher at Princeton—follows Hutcheson[130] in denominating marriage as a fundamental right of a free people, linking it to a more general right of

---

[127] See Richards, *Toleration and the Constitution*, pp. 67–227.

[128] See Kenneth I. Karst, "The Freedom of Intimate Association," 89 *Yale L.J.* 624 (1980).

[129] For example, leading statesmen at the state conventions ratifying the Constitution, both those for and against adoption, assumed that the Constitution could not interfere in the domestic sphere. Thus, Hamilton of New York denies that federal constitutional power does or could "penetrate the recesses of domestic life, and control, in all respects, the private conduct of individuals" (p. 268, Elliot, *Debates*, vol. 2). And Patrick Henry of Virginia speaks of the core of our right to liberty as the sphere where a person "enjoys the fruits of his labor, under his own fig-tree, with his wife and children around him, in peace and security" (p. 54, Elliot, idem, vol. 3). And a leading founder, Oliver Ellsworth of Connecticut, in rebutting the antifederalist argument that the Constitution of 1787 did not protect a free press, referred to other reserved rights, including the right to marriage, that could not be abridged: "Nor is [there a declaration preserving] liberty of conscience, or of matrimony, or of burial of the dead; it is enough that congress have no power to prohibit either, and can have no temptation" [*To the Landholders and Farmers, Conn. Courant*, Dec. 10, 1787, reprinted in 14 *The Documentary History of the Ratification of the Constitution: Commentaries on the Constitution*, John P. Kaminski and Gaspare J. Saladino, eds. (Madison: State Historical Society of Wisconsin, 1983), pp. 398, 401—hereafter referred to as *Commentaries*]; see also *To the Holders and Tillers of Land, Conn. Courant*, Nov. 19, 1787, reprinted in 14 *Commentaries*, pp. 139, 401 (referring to rights of personal liberty "more sacred than all the property in the world, the disposal of your children"). It is striking that the arguments of both leading proponents (Hamilton, Ellsworth) and opponents (Henry) of adoption of the Constitution converge on this private sphere of domestic married life.

[130] See Francis Hutcheson, *A System of Moral Philosophy* (New York: Augustus M. Kelley, 1968), p. 299.

associational liberty.[131] It is not difficult to interpret that historical understanding as a coherent expression of a basic principle of protected moral independence worth carrying forward in the community of principle that underlies the American commitment to an enduring written constitution.

The understanding of an unenumerated right to marriage—as expressed in the historical understanding—reflects a larger historical conception of companionate marriage,[132] marriage as a voluntarily formed association of intimate friendship and love through which persons realize the complementary fulfillment of essential needs for the mutual support, companionship, and understanding that is often the very basis for sustaining enduring personal and ethical values in living a complete life. That new conception of marriage was rooted in a larger republican conception of self-governing people guaranteed the moral independence on reasonable terms to form the range of communities that are essential to the integral expression of their moral powers.[133] Certainly, the relationships of intimate personal life cannot reasonably be isolated from more general ethical relationships and from the emancipatory consequences for ethical thought and practice of the democratic reason that are central to the larger republican project. Marriage was thus correctly characterized by Witherspoon as an instance of a larger republican right of democratic association because marriage—as much as religious, political, or other associations—is one of the associations essential to sustaining the moral independence in living a complete life that is required for republican self-rule. Accordingly, for republican Americans, "the very concept of citizenship developed in the revolutionary period, was—like love—based on consent, not on descent, which further blended the rhetoric of America with the language of love and the concept of romantic love with American identity."[134] State abridgment of such associational liberties of marital intimacy on constitutionally inadequate grounds usurps the essential intellectual and emotional resources of the moral independence at the very foundation of republican respect for a self-governing people. It is no accident that modern totalitarianism has warred on the value of republican self-rule in terms of the illegitimacy of private life: "There is no such thing as a private individual in National Socialist Germany."[135]

---

[131] Witherspoon lists, as a basic human and natural right, "a right to associate, if he so incline, with any person or persons, whom he can persuade (not force)—under this is contained the right to marriage" [John Witherspoon, *Lectures on Moral Philosophy,* Jack Scott, ed. (East Brunswick, N.J.: Associated Univ. Presses, 1982), p. 123].

[132] See, e.g., Lawrence Stone, *The Family, Sex and Marriage* (New York: Harper & Row, 1977), pp. 325–404.

[133] See, in general, ibid., (tracing historical development of marriage from deferential patriarchy to expression of autonomous individual affection). On Locke's attack on patriarchal political morality, see David Richards, "The Individual, the Family, and the Constitution: A Jurisprudential Perspective," 55 *N.Y.U. L. Rev.* 1, 14–15 (1980).

[134] Werner Sollors, *Beyond Ethnicity: Consent and Descent in American Culture* (New York: Oxford Univ. Press, 1986), p. 112.

[135] E.K. Bramstedt, *Dictatorship and the Political Police* (New York: Oxford Univ. Press, 1945), p. 178.

Suppose a society protected liberties of association for politics, religion, and the like, but extended no comparable protection to intimate relations like marriage. People could form alternative political and religious groups that dissented from reigning majoritarian orthodoxies and the structures of arbitrary hierarchy and privilege that they have often sanctified, but not alternative conceptions of personal intimacy that challenge structures of "natural" hierarchy and domination in personal life. In effect, a majoritarian sectarian orthodoxy in intimate relations would be enforceable by law in a way it is not in the public sphere of political and religious debate. However, the resources of moral independence—centrally protected by both political and religious liberties—cannot be truncated in this way; public life in politics or religion is a dry and shriveled desert without natural moral feeling or depth or integrity when it is a dichotomously disengaged from any comparable moral independence for reasonable deliberation about more just and satisfying forms of private life and the nourishing springs of personal intimacy.[136] For many, much of the value of life is centered in the personal and ethical values of private life; moral independence in the reasonable conduct of that life is foundational in the lives of free people. Indeed, the traditional terms of private life are so much in serious moral, political, and religious controversy today that the wall separating the political or the religious from intimate personal life has collapsed.[137] Accordingly, the moral resources of private life may require as much protection as politics or religion against oppressive, majoritarian orthodoxies. Thus, both our historical understanding and political theory of enumerated and unenumerated rights converge on intimate relations as a fully protected unenumerated right.[138]

Bork thus improperly invokes democratic political theory against the constitutional right to privacy, because the very point of American constitutionalism was to limit the scope of majority rule on terms of arguments of principle that would respect the inalienable rights of the person. The issue of principle here is whether, in contemporary circumstances, factionalized majoritarian views impose significant coercive threats to the right of the person to a reasonable private life, and, if so, whether the judiciary plays an appropriate role in vindicating such rights.

JUDICIAL REASONING AND ROLE

We need to remind ourselves of our earlier discussion of both Madison's despair at the constitutional convention's failure to agree on a federal negative and council of revision and his initial opposition to a bill of rights (see Chapter 3). No one among the founders took more seriously the protection of inalienable human rights than Madison, but he had supposed that the only effective protection of such rights was a federal negative in Congress that

---

[136] Cf. Karst, "Freedom of Intimate Association."

[137] See, e.g., Kate Millett, *Sexual Politics* (Garden City, N.Y.: Doubleday, 1970).

[138] See Karst, "Freedom of Intimate Association" pp. 652–66 (arguing right to intimate association has doctrinal bases in First Amendment, equal protection, and substantive due process).

could invalidate state laws that were inconsistent with such rights and a council of revision that could monitor Congress's violations of rights. Once the convention failed to agree on either the federal negative or council of revision, Madison initially saw little point in a bill of rights. In response to Jefferson's criticism of the omission of a bill of rights in the 1787 Constitution,[139] Madison wrote that his "own opinion has always been in favor of a bill of rights; provided it be so framed as not to imply powers not meant to be included in the enumeration," but

> I have not viewed it in an important light 1. because I conceive that in a certain degree, though not in the extent argued by Mr. Wilson, the rights in question are reserved by the manner in which the federal powers are granted. 2. because there is great reason to fear that a positive declaration of some of the most essential rights could not be obtained in the requisite latitude . . . 3. because the limited powers of the federal Government and the jealousy of the subordinate Governments, afford a security which has not existed in the case of the State Governments, and exists in no other. 4. because experience proves the inefficacy of a bill of rights on those occasions when its controul [sic] is most needed. Repeated violations of these parchment barriers have been committed by overbearing majorities in every State.[140]

Jefferson answered Madison's objections first by noting that "in the arguments in favor of a declaration of rights, you omit one which has great weight with me, the legal check which it puts into the hands of the judiciary,"[141] and then answered his objections point by point:

> 1. That the rights in question are reserved by the manner in which the federal powers are granted. Answer . . . in a constitutive act which leaves some precious articles unnoticed, and raises implications against others, a declaration of rights becomes necessary by way of supplement . . . 2. A positive declaration of some essential rights could not be obtained in the requisite latitude. Answer. Half a loaf is better than none . . . 3. the limited powers of the federal government & jealousy of the subordinate governments afford a security which exists in no other instance. Answer . . . those governments are only agents. They must have principles furnished them whereon to found their opposition. The declaration of rights will be the text whereby they will try all the acts of the federal government. In this view it is necessary to the federal government also: as by the same text they may try the opposition of the subordinate governments. 4. Experience proves the inefficacy of a bill of rights. True. But tho it is not absolutely efficacious under all cirumstances, it is of great potency always. . . . The inconveniencies of the want of a Declaration are permanent, afflicting & irreparable: they are in constant progression from bad to worse. . . . The tyranny of legislatures is the most formidable

[139] Robert A. Rutland et al., eds., *The Papers of James Madison, 1788–1789* (Charlottesville: Univ. Press of Virginia, 1977) pp. 212–13.

[140] Ibid., p. 297.

[141] Charles F. Hobson et al., eds., *The Papers of James Madison, 1789–1790*, vol. 12 (Charlottesville: Univ. Press of Virginia, 1979), p. 13.

dread at present, and will be for long years. That of the executive will come in it's turn, but it will be at a remote period. . . . The rising race are all republicans. We were educated in royalism: no wonder if some of us retain that idolatry still. Our young people are educated in republicanism.[142]

Jefferson was, like *Federal Farmer* and Iredell, concerned not only with the importance of a bill of rights in supplying appropriate critical standards for contemporary political debate, but also with its role in what he had earlier called "a time, and that not a distant one, when corruption in this, as in the country from which we derive our origin, will have seized the heads of government, and be spread by them through the body of the people."[143] American constitutionalists, including Madison,[144] came to regard the Bill of Rights, including the Ninth Amendment, as fundamental in maintaining allegiance to the essential principles of constitutional legitimacy over time, namely, respect for inalienable human rights. *Federal Farmer* had put the point as well as anyone: there would be a continuing need to "at least establish in the minds of the people truths and principles which they might never otherwise have thought of, or soon forgot," because "men . . . do not remain free, merely because they are entitled to natural and inalienable rights."[145]

However, as Jefferson clearly saw and Hamilton had argued in *The Federalist*,[146] the judiciary would (under American Lockean constitutionalism) play a central role in maintaining the integrity of the contextually sensitive reasonable arguments of principle that are necessary to respect for such inalienable rights of the person over time. Indeed, the work of the judiciary would importantly be tested against its deliberative performance in advancing the understanding of its own generation about the kind and quality of reasonable justification for political power that is required by constitutional legitimacy. To be adequate to its institutional mission, the judiciary must advance and deepen public understanding of the just demands of constitutional principle in contemporary circumstances. *Griswold* v. *Connecticut* did just that.

The Fundamental Right

The Supreme Court thus properly inferred the constitutional right to privacy in *Griswold* because Connecticut's coercive intrusion into marital sexuality (i.e., that married couples could neither buy nor use contraceptives) inhibited one of the decisions that is central to companionate marriage—that is,

---

[142] Ibid., pp. 13–15.

[143] Thomas Jefferson, *Notes on the State of Virginia*, in William Peden, ed. (New York: W. W. Norton, 1954), p. 121.

[144] Indeed, by the time of Jefferson's letter, Madison had come to see that a bill of rights would be necessary to secure support for the Constitution, anticipating his own central role in the drafting and ratification of the Bill of Rights. See Rutland et al., eds., *Papers of James Madison 1788–1789*, pp. 382–83, 416. Madison's original letter to Jefferson, quoted earlier, had anticipated this development in his thought: "I have favored it [a bill of rights] because I supposed it might be of use, and if properly executed could not be of disservice" (idem, p. 297).

[145] Storing, ed., *Anti-Federalist*, pp. 80–81.

[146] See *The Federalist*, no. 78.

whether and when one will have offspring. The constitutional right to privacy emerged in a case that concurrently involved privacy in another sense, namely, the egregious violation of the informational privacy interests protected by the Fourth Amendment that criminal prosecutions of contraception use would require (i.e., bugging the marital bedroom).[147] However, as the Court recognized in *Griswold* and clarified later, the pertinent constitutional violation is independent of the Fourth Amendment because it relates to coercive intrusion into the liberty of association that is traditionally associated with marriage in a way unsupported by the constitutionally required burden of justification.

Burden of Justification

Because of the state purpose that it involved—that all sexuality must be procreative, and that the use of contraceptives may thus be forbidden— *Griswold* should be regarded as a more difficult case then it is usually supposed to be. Why is such a state purpose constitutionally dubious? We must bring to this question the larger principle of constraint on state power that pervades many textually guaranteed constitutional rights. In my opinion, the key is that state power that intrudes into one of the essential spheres of moral independence—a sphere protected by both enumerated and unenumerated rights—must satisfy a heavy burden of justification; it must be of indispensable necessity in protecting the general goods of life, liberty, and property.[148]

The point is well illustrated by the burden of justification that religion clause jurisprudence requires for the abridgment of the inalienable right to conscience. As we have seen (Chapter 5), one principle of that jurisprudence is that the state may not forbid people to engage in the religious beliefs or rituals of their choice, because such coercion usually relates to state objection to one kind of religious or irreligious belief.[149] However, the state might constitutionally interfere by forbidding religious rituals that cause serious secular harm, like human sacrifice.[150]

---

[147] On such arguments analogizing these rights, see David Richards, *Sex, Drugs, Death and the Law* (Totowa, N.J.: Rowman & Littlefield, 1982), pp. 33–34, 61–63.

[148] See Richards, *Toleration and the Constitution*, pp. 244–47. General goods, thus understood, are all-purpose resources that rational and reasonable purposes need to define and pursue their ultimate personal and ethical aims. See Rawls, "Social Unity and Primary Goods," in Amartya Sen and Bernard Williams, eds., *Utilitarianism and Beyond* (Cambridge: Cambridge Univ. Press, 1982), pp. 159–85.

[149] See, e.g., *Board of Educ.* v. *Barnette.* 319 U.S. 624 (1943) (striking down public school requirement that students salute the flag); *Sherbert* v. *Verner*, 374 U.S. 398 (1963) (striking down unemployment insurance eligibility requirements excluding workers fired for not working on their religious day of rest).

[150] In his first *Letter Concerning Toleration,* John Locke quite clearly exempts from universal toleration the case "if some congregation should have a mind to sacrifice infants" [p. 33, in *Works of John Locke,* vol. 6 (London: Thomas Tegg, 1823)]. The Supreme Court once suggested an absolute distinction between belief and action: conscientious beliefs were immune from state regulation, but conscientiously motivated actions could be regulated without limit. See *Reynolds* v. *United States,* 98 U.S. 145 (1878). The governing view today is that conscientiously motivated actions are not wholly exempt from constitutional scrutiny, but state regulation must advance a

The idea—stated clearly by Locke in his classic defense of toleration[151]—is that republican political theory forbids the state from engaging in sectarian choices among religious beliefs. However, the republican contract permits the state to protect life, liberty, and property in a nonsectarian manner. This protection allows just scope to moral independence because it ensures all-purpose goods that people may then interpret and weight in widely varying ways, depending on how they define the ultimate aims of their personal and ethical lives. The state may accordingly justify even the abridgment of a fundamental right like conscience if necessary to protect life, liberty, and property, because the just role of the republican state is to ensure the general conditions of life and security.

Of course, in most areas, the legitimate scope of state power is more ample because fundamental rights are not abridged in the way that triggers this heavy burden of justification. This power may include state regulation that does not directly protect general goods, but only bears a rational relationship to their protection. Animals or the irretrievably comatose, for example, may not be bearers of rights, but the state may have a rational basis for prohibiting cruelty to animals and limiting termination of the lives of the irretrievably comatose because of the ways in which such prohibitions bear on attitudes condemnatory of wanton cruelty and supportive of respect for life.[152] People may make such points in quite sectarian religious terms, to which there is no objection on the view taken here. The heavy burden of justification is triggered only when fundamental rights, like the right to conscience, are in jeopardy.

The constitutional right to privacy is a right of such weight because—as was argued earlier—it is one of the spheres of moral independence that is protected by the textual guarantees of unenumerated rights in the U.S. Constitution (e.g., the privileges and immunities clause of Article IV, the Ninth Amendment, the privileges and immunities and due-process clauses of the Fourteenth Amendment). Accordingly, the coercive abridgment of the right of marriage on the facts of *Griswold* naturally triggered the heavy burden of justification required for the curtailment of such weighty rights. The only state interest that could have justified such an incursion—namely, the prohibition of nonprocreational sexuality—could not do so. The condemnation of nonprocreational sexuality, including that involving marriage, was originally ex-

---

compelling secular state purpose. See, e.g., *Cantwell v. Connecticut.* 310 U.S. 296 (1940); *Sherbert v. Verner.* 374 U.S. 398 (1963).

[151] Locke defined the limits of state power in terms of "civil interests," which he defined as follows: "Civil interest I call life, liberty, health, and indolency of body; and the possession of outward things, such as money, lands, houses, furniture, and the like" (pp. 9–10, Locke, *Letter Concerning Toleration*). Futhermore, he naturally appealed to such "civil interests" in defining when the state may and may not restrict or regulate conscience: the state may require that babies be washed for health reasons, but it may not do so if the aim is compulsory baptism; the state may not stop a person from killing a calf in a religious ritual, but it may forbid the taking of a child's life in such a ritual. See idem, pp. 30–31, 33–34.

[152] See Richards, *Toleration and the Constitution,* pp. 265–67.

pressed by Thomas Aquinas as a kind of homicide against the child who would otherwise have been conceived.[153] Perhaps in a period of high infant and adult mortality, when children were needed to fuel a largely agrarian economy, the prohibition on contraception made some secular sense. However, today, in circumstances of legitimate public concerns about ways of limiting population growth, our context differs. In contemporary circumstances, the enforcement of Aquinas's prohibition on society at large cannot be justified in the required way. People's reasonable moral freedom in intimate matters is coercively abridged on grounds of a sectarian moral orthodoxy the enforcement through law on dissenters of which fails to address them as reasonable members of the community of principle. Such political action is—in the founders' sense—an expression of faction, the substitution of force for reason; in effect, dissenters to the moral orthodoxy are treated as contemptible exiles from reasonable moral community. For this reason, the Supreme Court properly protected the community of principled public reason by striking down the enforcement through law of such a model of marital sexuality, abridging, as it did, an aspect of the right to companionate marriage (namely, whether and when one will have offspring) on the basis of a sectarian conception of value.

The point was put forward earlier in the following way: contraceptive use in marriage harms no third party, but rather advances the public good of population control; furthermore, it does not harm the married couple, but rather enables them to control better their reproductive aims consistent with other personal and ethical aims, including the expression of marital sexuality as an end in itself, an expression of natural affection and mutual love. Indeed, such enlargement of human freedom—so far from harming or degrading agents—has enabled women in particular to define conceptions of marital sexuality more expressive of personal aspirations and needs and more consistent with a wider range of responsible exercises of their moral powers in complex patterns of both private and public life. Indeed, the right to such contraceptive use has dignified women, enabling them to disencumber themselves from a rigidly stereotypical conception of gender hierarchy and mandatory procreational role.[154]

We may now see these arguments as wholly proper, because they are grounded in a constitutional burden of justification that is required for the abridgment of fundamental rights. The state may no more indulge its sectarian preferences among forms of marital sexuality than it may among forms of conscience or speech, because a morally independent people must be accorded their just equal liberties when the state's grounds for abridgment reflect no acceptable theory of secular harms.

On this view, our conception of the just scope of many constitutional rights, including the constitutional right to privacy, crucially relates to contex-

---

[153] Of the emission of semen apart from procreation in marriage, Thomas Aquinas wrote: "After the sin of homicide whereby a human nature already in existence is destroyed, this type of sin appears to take next place, for by it the generation of human nature is precluded" (Aquinas, *On the Truth of the Catholic Faith,* p. 146).

[154] See Richards, *Toleration and the Constitution,* pp. 256–61.

tually sensitive elaborations of background constitutional principles, for example, that in contemporary circumstances the prohibition of the purchase and use of contraceptives by married couples cannot satisfy the required burden of public justification. We noted earlier that the contextually sensitive elaboration of constitutional principles expresses the community of principle that is essential to the American commitment to an enduring written constitution, and we now should connect that larger point to *Griswold's* elaboration of the constitutional right to privacy. *Griswold* elaborates the historical understanding of textually guaranteed unenumerated rights in precisely the way that our commitment to a community of principle requires. We see today that constitutional privacy protects married couples against anticontraception laws because these laws cannot be publicly justified to those couples subject to them in the required way, namely, public justification to free, rational, and equal persons. The background constitutional right has expanded as the legitimacy of the justification for limiting the right has contracted.

The American constitutional tradition reflects a deep consensus on fundamental unenumerated rights.[155] The idea that unenumerated rights are foreign to the Constitution thus distinguishes neither liberal nor conservative constitutional jurisprudence because this idea itself is quite foreign to the text, history, political theory, and continuous judicial tradition of American public law. It is, in the worst sense, radical, because it is outside the deep constitutional consensus on values of Americans as free people under the rule of law. It is quite paradoxical that such a claim should have been sponsored by the founders' intent, because the best reading of that intent is undoubtedly that unenumerated rights are at the core of the American conception of constitutionalism.

When it considered the Bork nomination, the U.S. Senate had both the right and the duty to demand more of a prospective justice to the Supreme Court than a rigid interpretive attitude that, against the weight of so much argument and authority, could dismiss unenumerated rights as enduring values of American constitutionalism. That view was driven by a kind of self-blinding ideology that showed no respect for text, history, political theory, or judicial role, because it would either uproot constitutional privacy entirely or narrow the doctrine in unprincipled ways.[156] In effect, Bork construed the founders as Filmerian positivistic patriarchs: they rule us from their graves, and in those cases in which they do not rule us the democratic majorities do. However, the founders were Lockean constitutionalists who did not operate in Bork's morally vacuous universe. They had fought a revolution and constructed a constitutional order for the fullest defense of enumerated and unenumerated human

---

[155] Justice Harlan's concurring opinion in *Griswold* reflects this consensus. See *Griswold,* 381 U.S. at 499–502.

[156] See, e.g., *Franz v. United States,* 707 F.2d 582, Addendum to the Opinion for the Court, 712 F.2d 1428 (D.C. Cir. 1983) (Tamm, Edwards, and Bork, concurring and dissenting), in which then Judge Bork refused to give any constitutional protection to a father's powerful biological, emotional, and legal connection with his children because the Supreme Court had not specifically addressed this situation.

rights under the strongest rule of law that had yet graced human history, and they thought of their own authority as properly used only in service of a more reasonable elaboration of constitutional principles over time. Bork's skepticism about rights prevents him from understanding the founders' project and the role of the judiciary in making principled sense of it, because he cannot—within the framework of his sterile positivism—make sense of what alone gives value and sense to the entire historical project, namely, the protection on fair terms of all inalienable rights of the person.

Justice White on Abortion and Homosexuality: A Critical View

Justice White argues in *Thornburgh* and *Bowers* that the right of constitutional privacy, though correctly applied to contraceptive use in *Griswold,* is not properly elaborated to either abortion or consensual adult homosexual relations. In both cases, he makes his point in terms of constitutional legitimacy. According to Justice White, rights like constitutional privacy "have little or no textual support in the constitutional language,"[157] and there should thus be great resistance to protecting these rights under the due-process clause. For Justice White, the claimed rights in both cases "fall short of overcoming this resistance."[158]

My position has already been argued that *Griswold* is a rather harder case than Justice White supposes. Its justification cannot be resolved on either the basis of a fundamental right to biological reproduction or an appeal to majoritarian consensus. If Justice White is correct about the illegitimacy of extending constitutional privacy to abortion and consensual homosexuality, *Griswold* would be equally illegitimate. We need to ask what Justice White means by constitutional legitimacy and whether his theory of legitimacy is defensible.

Justice White justifies his claim that extending constitutional privacy is illegitimate by arguing that the cases involve either no weighty right (*Thornburgh*) or no right at all (*Bowers*). In *Thornburgh,* he concedes that it is "indisputable—that a woman's ability to choose an abortion is a species of 'liberty' that is subject to the general protections of the Due Process Clause,"[159] but he later denies that such a right has any weight when placed against the state's interest in the survival of a biologically individual "member of the species *homo sapiens.*"[160] In *Bowers,* he dismisses the claim of any fundamental right as "at best, facetious."[161]

Justice White's dissent in *Thornburgh* examines the question of the state's burden of justification. The scope of constitutional privacy often relates to the nature and weight of the state's prohibitory interests. However, Justice White

---

[157] *Bowers,* 106 S. Ct. at 2844.
[158] Ibid., at 2846; see also *Thornburgh,* 106 S. Ct. at 2194 (J. White, dissenting).
[159] *Thornburgh,* 106 S. Ct. at 2194 (J. White, dissenting).
[160] Ibid., at 2195.
[161] 106 S. Ct. at 2846.

likens the termination of fetal life—"protecting those who will be citizens if their lives are not ended in the womb"[162]—to murder. To the contrary, a state's interest in protecting fetal life is, as Justice Stevens notes,[163] fundamentally different from the state's interest in forbidding murder of a person. Justice White confuses a biological question with a moral one, resting his opinion on questionable sectarian assumptions that cannot provide adequate justification for abridging a woman's fundamental rights to reproductive autonomy.[164]

The abridgment of fundamental rights requires a heavy burden of justification that has been characterized by me in terms of indispensable necessity in the protection of general goods. In principle, general goods are those goods the nature and relative value of which are free of sectarian disagreements so that all persons, irrespective of religious or philosophical convictions, could reasonably agree that the criminal law should protect those goods from harm. However, because there is no reasonable consensus about fetal life (quite the opposite), it is not reasonably understood as a "good" in this sense, that is, as a good the protection of which is an adequate justification for the application of criminal law to choices protecting reproductive liberty. Although the matter is not free from doubt, even the not irrational belief in the moral personality of a fetus can no more be equated with such general goods than can sectarian beliefs in, for example, the presence of moral personality in animals, trees, or rocks.[165] Many reasonable people can no more regard fetal life as a moral person than animals, trees, or rocks. Today the assignment of moral personality in all such cases is the product of sectarian conceptions of fact and value that are unsupported by a reasonable common ground shared by all and thus cannot enjoy the force of law as the justification for the coercive abridgment of fundamental rights.[166] The nature of the moral debate over abortion is as profoundly sectarian as the comparable debate over contraception. In both cases, condemnation derives from a traditional conception of both sexuality and gender roles, one in which value in living is viewed through the sectarian prism of exclusively procreational sexuality and woman's ordained role as selflessly devoted mother with no other aims or aspirations.[167] Because

[162] *Thornburgh,* 106 S. Ct. at 2195 & n.2.

[163] Ibid., at 2188 (J. Stevens, concurring).

[164] For fuller discussion, see Richards, *Toleration and the Constitution,* pp. 261–69; *Thornburgh,* 106 S. Ct. at 2188 (J. Stevens, concurring).

[165] For an argument that, in this area, nonrational (though not irrational) convictions—religious or nonreligious—should suffice as a permissible ground for state power and that *Roe* v. *Wade,* 410 U.S. 113 (1973), is for this reason wrong, see Kent Greenawalt, "Religious Convictions and Lawmaking," 84 *Mich. L. Rev.* 352, 371–80 (1985). Greenawalt argues, however, that there is no rational, secular argument for the application of criminal law to consensual homosexuality, and that such laws therefore violate the requirement of constitutional neutrality (idem, pp. 362–64). It is of interest that accounts of constitutional neutrality bearing a family resemblance to my own (like Greenawalt's) reach different results in a case like *Roe* and yet demand a similar condemnation of a case like *Bowers.* See also Greenawalt, *Religious Convictions and Political Choice* (similar argument, but without using a theory of rationality, to same effect).

[166] See Richards, *Toleration and the Constitution,* pp. 262–65.

[167] See Kristin Luker, *Abortion and the Politics of Motherhood* (Berkeley: Univ. of California Press, 1984).

there is no reasonable consensus on any of these issues, a sectarian interpretation of these matters cannot satisfy the burden of justification. Only clearly secular harms can justify the coercive abridgment of such essential spheres of moral independence. The absence of constitutionally neutral justification for these laws explains why women have a right to define their relationship to childbearing in the same way that men and women have a right to define and control the reproductive nature and consequences of their sexual relations. The consequence is that women are and should be free to define their relationship to childbearing in accord with their constructive moral powers of value in living in a complete, varied, and multiply fulfilled life.[168]

Justice White's argument in *Bowers* is more analytically remarkable than his argument in *Thornburgh,* because in *Bowers* he denies that the case involves anything even resembling a fundamental right. He thus engages in no examination whatsoever of the state's burden of justification, other than a cursory reference to the "belief of a majority of the electorate in Georgia that homosexual sodomy is immoral and unacceptable."[169] The gravamen of White's argument is an appeal to history:

> Proscriptions against that conduct [consensual sodomy] have ancient roots. . . . Sodomy was a criminal offense at common law and was forbidden by the laws of the original thirteen States when they ratified the Bill of Rights. In 1868, when the Fourteenth Amendment was ratified, all but 5 of the 37 States in the Union had criminal sodomy laws. In fact, until 1961, all 50 States outlawed sodomy, and today, 24 States and the District of Columbia continue to provide criminal penalties for sodomy performed in private and between consenting adults. . . . Against this background, to claim that a right to engage in such conduct is "deeply rooted in this Nation's history and tradition" or "implicit in the concept of ordered liberty" is, at best, facetious.[170]

It is difficult not to regard this appeal to history as anything but disingenuous, because the Court's previous work in the area of constitutional privacy and almost all of its work elsewhere disavow such an anachronistic and indeed ahistorical way of interpreting history. Even Justice White made clear in *Thornburgh* that he rejects the appeal to the founders' denotations as the decisive method of constitutional interpretation.[171] He recognizes that constitutional interpretation often properly revises the founders' denotative understanding in order to serve the more abstract values intended by constitutional principles.[172] However, his appeal is precisely such a simplistic tracking of the founders' denotations.

[168] See generally Beverly Harrison, *Our Right to Choose* (Boston: Beacon, 1983).

[169] *Bowers,* 106 S. Ct. at 2846.

[170] Ibid., at 2844–46 (quoting *Moore* v. *City of East Cleveland,* 431 U.S. 494, 503 (1977) ("deeply rooted in this Nation's history and tradition") and *Palko* v. *Connecticut,* 302 U.S. 319, 325 (1937) ("implicit in the concept of ordered liberty")).

[171] *Thornburgh,* 106 S. Ct. at 2193 (J. White, dissenting).

[172] Ibid., at 2197 n.5 [citing *Brown* v. *Board of Education,* 347 U.S. 483 (1953)].

The issue of principle is not how a previous generation, by its own factual and normative lights, failed to apply any guarantee of fundamental rights (e.g., free speech to seditious libel, equal protection to segregation, privacy to contraception or abortion), but how such fundamental rights should be read in which they remain consistent with the most sound *current* interpretation of the principles of an enduring written constitution. Why should the extension of constitutional privacy to adult homosexual relations not be treated in this way?[173] Apparently, Justice White believes that there is some principled difference between an already protected right, like marriage, and a right not historically recognized, like homosexual relations. He posed the difference, as we have seen, in terms of constitutional illegitimacy: "The Court is most vulnerable and comes nearest to illegitimacy when it deals with judge-made constitutional law having little or not cognizable roots in the language or design of the Constitution."[174]

What can White mean by constitutional illegitimacy in this context? Presumably, a claim of constitutional legitimacy or illegitimacy is a claim about the proper exercise of authority, that is, about whether the reasons offered in support of an exercise of authority are adequate.[175] The Supreme Court's constitutional interpretation is legitimate if so supported and illegitimate if not. Constitutional legitimacy in the United States must relate to the special normative demands for justification that are required by constitutional democracy, namely, whether power can be appropriately justified to the people as democratic equals. However, justifiable or unjustifiable to whom? To democratic majorities? Democratic majorities may have supposed *Brown* v. *Board of Education*[176] and many other clearly correct cases to be illegitimate; they perceived constitutional law through the distorting prism of unexamined and insular assumptions about fundamental constitutional rights they have always pridefully enjoyed but—because they are in the self-consciously dominant majority—have never coherently extended, on terms of principle, to minority outsiders. Such unreflective majoritarian suppositions cannot be the measure of actual illegitimacy; rather, their very majoritarian insularity sets the terms of the central problem defined and addressed by the founders, namely, the failure of democratic majorities to exercise the public reason necessary to realize the abstract terms of a community of principle fundamental to the legitimacy of political power under American constitutionalism. The role of judicial independence in the American constitutional system is, as we have seen, precisely to ensure an impartial arbiter of issues of the constitutional interpretation of matters of principle that must, in order to be adequate to this mission, not themselves be beholden to factionalized majoritarian views.

Or, perhaps a judicial expansion of constitutional privacy on the facts of *Bowers* is illegitimately antidemocratic not for majoritarian reasons, but be-

---

[173] See Richards, *Sex, Drugs, Death and the Law*, pp. 29–83; idem, *Toleration and the Constitution*, pp. 269–80.

[174] *Bowers*, 106 S. Ct. at 2846.

[175] See Joseph Raz, *The Morality of Freedom* (Oxford: Clarendon Press, 1986), pp. 1–105.

[176] 347 U.S. 483 (1953).

cause it is not required by what Justice White may consider to be the best political theory of constitutional legitimacy, namely, it is not representation-reinforcing in Ely's sense.[177] In *Thornburgh,* Justice White appealed to Ely's theory of judicial review in defense of his argument of interpretive illegitimacy.[178] He also expressed fears of repeating the judicial mistake of enforcing "nonconstitutional values" against democratic majorities.[179] However, the protection of homosexuals, a stigmatized minority, is probably closer to the spirit of Ely's concern for the protection of minorities[180] than the protection accorded contraceptive-using majorities in *Griswold,* and the Fourth Amendment privacy concerns are at least as weighty. Furthermore, Ely's theory itself rests on a highly controversial political theory of democratic legitimacy. It edits out important historical strands of the American political tradition[181]; it may not even adequately identify and protect the stigmatized minorities whose protection is so crucial to Ely's theory of legitimate judicial review.[182]

Perhaps Justice White believes that the legitimate scope of constitutional privacy is limited to the claims of those traditionally protected (e.g., married couples), and that protection of the privacy claims of homosexuals is illegitimately antidemocratic because it is not sanctioned by traditions. However, as we have seen, the principled meaning of the protection of the right to marriage was its protection of an essential sphere of moral independence, namely, companionate marriage, as an intimate association in which the moral independence of pursuing value in living was essentially fostered. However, that is an issue of principle, as Justice Blackmun argues in his dissent in *Bowers,*[183] centrally in play in the criminal prohibition of homosexual activity and the intimate personal relationships among homosexuals. Indeed, if the traditional condemnation of homosexual activity is today as nonneutrally unjustified as the comparable condemnation of contraception use and access to abortion services (see following discussion), the protection of the resources of intimate personal life for homosexuals may be one of the most exigently needed elaborations of the constitutional right to privacy, because they—certainly more than the contraceptive-using heterosexual majority—are in desperate human need of the protection of minimal resources of moral independence to define and construct the relationships that are essential to their finding and exploring reasonable communities of value in living. Traditional moral condemnation of homosexuality has subverted the most intimate resources of imaginative, emo-

---

[177] See Ely, *Democracy and Distrust,* pp. 135–79.

[178] See *Thornburgh,* 106 S. Ct. at 2197 and n.5.

[179] Ibid., at 2197 n.5 [citing *Lochner* v. *New York,* 198 U.S. 45 (1905)].

[180] See Ely, *Democracy and Distrust,* pp. 135–37.

[181] Ely concedes that much of the text of the Constitution contemplated the inference of fundamental rights not specified in the Bill of Rights. See ibid., at pp. 22–30. He nonetheless rejects what are textually and historically sustainable inferences from the "more indeterminate phrases" of the written Constitution (idem, at p. 221 n.4), when they are inconsistent with his view of the best political theory of constitutional democracy. See idem, at pp. 56–60.

[182] See Lawrence Sager, "Rights Skepticism and Process-Based Responses," 56 *N.Y.U. L. Rev.* 417, 426–32 (1981); Richards, *Toleration and the Constitution,* pp. 14–19, 296–303.

[183] *Bowers,* 106 S. Ct. at 2851–52.

tional, and intellectual freedom through which homosexuals can construct a personal and ethical life on the only terms that generate reasonable value in living. That erosion of just moral independence is not at the periphery of the historical meaning of the protection of constitutional privacy as an unenumerated right; it is at its very core.

It is paradoxical indeed to truncate the scope of protection of unenumerated rights like the right of intimate association precisely at the point at which the right would protect not contraceptive-using majorities but a traditionally despised and powerless minority whose awakened and awakening interests in the just moral independence of a private life are crucially at stake. Such judicial treatment realizes the worst fears of Iredell and other founders about the abuse of textually enumerated rights as an argument against defense of textually unenumerated rights, namely, the inability to interpret basic guarantees of spheres of moral independence in a way reasonably justifiable in contemporary circumstances, anachronistically indulging Iredell's fear: "We live at a great distance from the time when this Constitution was established. We can judge of it much better by the ideas of it entertained at the time, than by any ideas of our own."[184] Such interpretation betrays as well the clear intent of the founders that an enduring written constitution, containing guarantees of both enumerated and unenumerated rights, be reasonably justified to all persons over time as a community of principle that respects the essential spheres of moral independence guaranteed to all persons on equal terms. That historical purpose of a written constitution and its bill of rights makes the exercise of judicial power most justifiable when it holds factionalized democratic majorities to arguments of principle, establishing "in the minds of the people truths and principles which they might never otherwise have thought of, or soon forgot,"[185] namely, that equal rights must fairly be extended to the most stereotypically despised minority outsiders. That purpose of the written constitution is betrayed when the judiciary fails to respect the right of homosexuals to the moral independence of a private life that is the acknowledged right of heterosexuals.

The basic terms of the Constitution—whether the commerce clause, the Fourth Amendment, or the equal protection clause—have been interpreted to reject the founders' denotations in the interest of a more principled elaboration of constitutional values and a corresponding critical evaluation of constitutional facts. For example, was we shall see (Chapter 7), current interpretation of the equal protection clause rejects theories of racial differences because it has become clear that they serve as uncritical rationalizations for existing patterns of unjust racial domination. The reasonable justification of basic constitutional guarantees over time must observe the highest standards of public reason, which must include debunking stereotypical factual and normative orthodoxies the enforcement through law of which has unjustly stunted the scope of reasonable moral freedom.

There is voluminous critical literature today—both normative and factual—

---

[184] See Elliot, ed., *Debates,* vol. 4, p. 149.
[185] See Storing, *Anti-Federalist,* pp. 79–80.

about such injustices underlying traditional condemnatory conceptions of sexual preference as a disease or a moral vice.[186] Homosexual preference per se cannot reasonably be regarded as a disease,[187] and is often embedded in a larger pattern of a life that has as much personal and ethical value as other life patterns.[188] Much of the traditional condemnation of homosexuality interprets sexual preference in the same distorted way that nineteenth-century theories of racial differences interpreted race, stereotypically associated homosexuality with Manichean images of incompetence, immaturity, licentiousness, and animalistic immorality.[189] However, these images are themselves the cultural artifacts of a long history of uncritical common sense about proper sexuality,[190] a common sense that required sex to be procreational[191] or to follow the pattern of masculine dominance and feminine submission.[192]

---

[186] See, e.g., *The Wolfenden Report: Report of the Committee on Homosexual Offenses and Prostitution* (New York: Stein & Day, 1963); Alan P. Bell and Martin S. Weinberg, *Homosexualities* (New York: Simon & Schuster, 1978); Alan P. Bell, Martin S. Weinberg, and Sue Kiefer Hammersmith, *Sexual Preference* (New York: Simon & Schuster, 1978); Philip Blumstein and Pepper Schwartz, *American Couples: Money, Work, Sex* (New York: Morrow, 1983); Wainwright Churchill, *Homosexual Behavior among Males* (New York: Hawthorn, 1967); Martin Hoffman, *The Gay World* (New York: Bantam, 1968); William H. Masters and Virginia Johnson, *Homosexuality in Perspective* (Boston: Little, Brown, 1979); C.A. Tripp, *The Homosexual Matrix* (New York: McGraw-Hill, 1975); D.J. West, *Homosexuality* (Chicago: Aldine, 1968); John J. McNeill, *The Church and the Homosexual* (Kansas City, Mo.: Sheed, Andrews & McMeel, 1976); Derrick Sherwin Bailey, *Homosexuality and the Western Christian Tradition* (New York: Longmans, Green, 1955); John Boswell, *Christianity, Social Tolerance and Homosexuality* (Chicago: Univ. of Chicago Press, 1980). See also Richards, *Sex, Drugs, Death and the Law*, pp. 29–83; idem, "Unnatural Acts and the Constitutional Right to Privacy," 45 *Ford. L. Rev.* 1281 (1977); idem, "Sexual Autonomy and the Constitutional Right to Privacy," 30 *Hastings L.J.* 957 (1979).

[187] See *Wolfenden Report*, pp. 31–33; E. Hooker, "The Adjustment of the Male Overt Homosexual," 21 *J. of Projective Techniques* 18 (1957). Both the American Psychiatric Association and the American Psychological Association no longer regard homosexuality as a manifestation of psychological problems. See Blumstein and Schwartz, *American Couples* (1983), p. 44; J. Marmor, "Homosexuality and Sexual Orientation Disturbances," p. 1510, in 2 *Comprehensive Textbook of Psychiatry*, Alfred M. Freedman, Harold I. Kaplan, and Benjamin J. Sadock, eds., 2d ed. (Baltimore, Md.: Williams & Wilkins, 1975).

[188] Apart from sexual preference, exclusive homosexuals are indistinguishable from the general population. See Bell and Weinberg, *Homosexualities*, pp. 195–231; Churchill, *Homosexual Behavior among Males*, pp. 36–59.

[189] See, e.g., Roger Magnuson, *Are Gay Rights Right?* (Minneapolis: Straightgate Press, 1985), pp. 11–29.

[190] See, e.g., Bailey, *Homosexuality and the Western Christian Tradition;* Boswell, *Christianity, Social Tolerance and Homosexuality;* McNeill, *Church and the Homosexual.*

[191] See, e.g., Augustine, *City of God*, pp. 464–76.

[192] That is, it would be self-degradation for men to allow themselves to make love to, or to be made love to, by a man. This conception is also implicit in the idea, pervasive in the ancient Greek and Roman worlds, that while homosexuality per se was not wrong, to allow oneself to be the passive partner (i.e., the woman) was shameful and degrading. The aggressively bisexual Julius Caesar, thus, was criticized not for his homosexual connections, but for permitting himself at one time to be the passive partner. See *Catullus* 57, where Caesar is insulted by being called "morbosus," that is, passive (equivalent to the Greek "pathicus"). See Thorkil Vanggaard, *Phallos* (New York: International Universities Press, 1972), pp. 87–99; Boswell, *Christianity, Social Tolerance and Homosexuality*, pp. 74–75. This interpretation of the condemnation of

But for *Bowers,* modern constitutional law now rejects the idea that such conceptions of sexuality are enforceable through law. Certainly, they cannot be enforced on heterosexual activity through anticontraception and antiabortion laws, or through discrimination against persons on grounds of gender.[193] Why then can such conceptions be enforced against homosexual activity? If the principle of these cases is the right of heterosexuals to engage in sexual relations that do not produce offspring, then the same right should be accorded homosexuals. We acknowledge the right of heterosexual persons to disencumber their personal and ethical lives of deforming sexual stereotypes of masculinity and femininity—of dominance and submission—in favor of reciprocity and equality, and to explore a range of sexual relationships unencumbered by enforceable conceptions of mandatory procreational role and duty, including, as Justice Stevens notes in his *Bowers* dissent,[194] nonprocreational sex acts like fellatio, cunnilingus, and sodomy.[195] How, as a matter of

---

homosexuality (degrading a man into a woman) explains why lesbianism was never condemned with the force that was directed against male homosexuality. The Old Testament prohibitions clearly seem to be directed against men. See *Leviticus* 18:22; idem, 20:13. Note that lesbianism carried far lighter penalties than did male homosexuality under later rabbinical law. See Bailey, *Homosexuality and the Western Christian Tradition,* pp. 61–63. For a similar view of the extreme condemnation of male homosexuality, see McNeill, *Church and the Homosexual,* pp. 83–87.

[193] See, e.g., *Craig* v. *Boren,* 429 U.S. 190 (1976) (striking down state laws that prohibited sale of alcoholic beverages to eighteen- to twenty-year-old men, but permitted sale to women of same age); *Frontiero* v. *Richardson,* 411 U.S. 677 (1973) (husband of military officer constitutionally entitled to same medical benefits as similarly situated wives of military officers).

[194] See *Bowers,* 106 S. Ct. at 2857–58; see also *Oklahoma* v. *Post,* 107 S. Ct. 290 (1986) (refusing to review Oklahoma state court decision holding unconstitutional criminal law prohibiting consensual sodomy between adult heterosexuals).

[195] The classic Kinsey and later studies make clear that large and growing numbers of heterosexual women and men regard forms of oral and anal sex as important options of sexual fulfillment central to the integrity of their intimate relationships. The early Kinsey studies found, for example, that 15 percent of high school-educated men engaged in cunnilingus or experienced fellatio in marriage, and 45 percent of college-educated men engaged in cunnilingus and 43 percent experienced fellatio [A.C. Kinsey et al., *Sexual Behavior in the Human Male,* p. 371 (Philadelphia: W.B. Saunders, 1948)], and that 50 percent and 46 percent of high school-educated women experienced cunnilingus or engaged in fellatio, respectively, in marriage, and 58 and 52 percent of college-educated women, respectively [A.C. Kinsey et al., *Sexual Behavior in the Human Female* (Philadelphia: W.B. Saunders, 1953) p. 399]. By 1974, 56 and 54 percent of high school-educated men engaged in cunnilingus and fellatio, respectively, in their marriages; and 66 and 61 percent of college-educated men, respectively; 58 and 52 percent of high school-educated women engaged in cunnilingus and fellatio, respectively, in marriage; 72 percent of college-educated women engaged in both [Morton Hunt, *Sexual Behavior in the 1970's* (Chicago: Playboy Press, 1974), p. 198]. By 1983, the percentages of heterosexual couples reporting fellatio were as follows: 5 percent every time they had sex, 24 percent usually, 43 percent sometimes, 18 percent rarely, 10 percent never; the percentage reporting cunnilingus were: 6 percent every time, 26 percent usually, 42 percent sometimes, 19 percent rarely, 7 percent never (Blumstein and Schwartz, *American Couples* p. 236). In the same study, heterosexual men who received oral sex are happier with their relationships in general (idem, pp. 231–33); women report no comparable increment (idem, pp. 233–37). The Kinsey studies found heterosexual anal sex quite infrequent [A.C. Kinsey et al., *Sexual Behavior in the Human Male,* p. 579; P.H. Gebhard and A.B. Johnson, *The Kinsey Data,* (Philadelphia: W.B. Saunders, 1979) pp. 304, 383]. By 1974, half of the younger married respondents reported finding forms of it acceptable in love (Hunt, *Sexual*

principle, can homosexual activity be treated differently when it explores the same personal continuum of imaginative and emotional sexuality?[196]

Justice White's sense of homosexuals as "different"—the clear and unseemly premise of the majority opinion[197]—is not principled, because he offers no reasonable argument of principle that even attempts to justify their different treatment. His argument actually parodies an argument of principle, for example, in the way he avoids examining why constitutional privacy extends to the nonprocreative sex acts of heterosexuals but not to the comparable nonprocreative sex acts of homosexuals. It is not an argument of principle to dismiss plausible arguments about the right to a morally independent private life as "facetious."[198] That is a conclusive expression of factionalized majority sentiment, a repetition of unreflective taboos and not the reasonable arguments of public law Americans legitimately demand of their highest court of law.[199] We are left then with the unprincipled remnant of sexist stereotype—no longer given coercive expression through law against heterosexuals—but allowed its full uncritical ferocity against the sexual minority most vulnerable to its moralistic force. In effect, homosexuals are normatively exiled from the community of principle as nonpersons without the right to a private life accorded other persons. There is no argument of principle here, for there is no attempt to take seriously the demand of reasonable justification to all and the pressure to abstractness (a right of intimate personal life available to all) that expresses that demand of principle. Indeed, Justice White's invocation of constitutional "illegitimacy" is a kind of interpretive "Newspeak," inverting the very conception of constitutional legitimacy, the true measure of which is based on reasonable arguments of principle. This rhetoric of legitimacy gives the majority opinion a style of high constitutional self-righteousness when its substance is a willful failure of reasonable constitutional justification.[200]

The real weight of White's argument for the majority is not its fundamental rights analysis, but its quite transparent worries about according any de-

---

Behavior 1970's pp. 199–200). Other, more informally gathered samples confirm all these trends in the data. See, e.g., Shere Hite, *The Hite Report* (New York: Macmillan, 1976); Anthony Pietropinto and Jacqueline Simenauer, *Beyond the Male Myth* (New York: New York Times Books, 1977); Carol Tavris and Susan Sadd, *Redbook Report on Female Sexuality* (New York: Delacorte, 1975); Shere Hite, *The Hite Report on Male Sexuality* (New York: Ballantine, 1981); Linda Wolfe, *Cosmo Report* (New York: Arbor House, 1981).

[196] For the continuities in the nature of sexual experience, see, especially, Masters and Johnson, *Homosexuality in Perspective*. For continuities in both sexual experience and bonding, see Blumstein and Schwartz, *American Couples*.

[197] Justice Blackmun calls attention to the majority's "obsessive focus on homosexual activity" [*Bowers*, 106 S. Ct. at 2849 (J. Blackmun, dissenting)].

[198] Ibid., at 2846.

[199] For a similar outburst of unprincipled bad temper, see Berns, *Taking the Constitution Seriously* pp. 225–28, 237–38. Such outbursts are, in Berns's case, unlike Justice White's, all the more ad hoc and unprincipled, because Berns takes a view of the Constitution that gives fundamental weight to both its protection of rights and spheres of private life.

[200] La Rochefoucauld, a perceptive student of the abuses of power that flow from self-righteousness, wrote, "Hypocrisy is a tribute vice pays to virtue" (La Rochefoucauld, *Maxims*, L. Tancock, trans. (Harmondsworth, Middlesex, England: Penguin, 1959), at p. 65).

manding level of constitutional scrutiny to the moral arguments used to justify
the criminalization of homosexual acts. His attitude toward acceptable state
purposes is, as we saw earlier in his *Thornburgh* dissent, deferential to arguments of traditional moral purposes, however controversial, that enjoy some
level of continuing public support. Justice White's concurrence in *Griswold*
presumably reflects that the level of public support for the traditional moral
arguments against contraceptive use had collapsed; his dissent in *Roe* and
majority opinion in *Bowers* reflect continued public support for the relevant
moral condemnations. Such public support strains, for Justice White, the
ability of the Court to intervene legitimately. Under White's approach to
constitutional privacy, the relevant constitutional issue is whether the current
moral arguments for the criminalization of any area of sexual intimacy are
sufficiently majoritarian. That, as was already suggested, is a threadbare and
paradoxical conception of constitutionally legitimate judicial review that confuses factionalized majoritarian views with constitutionally reasonable justification to all persons as equals on terms of principle.

Justice White's invocation[201] of the Supreme Court's jurisprudence in the
era of *Lochner* v. *New York*[202] does not support his truncated reading of the
right to constitutional privacy. The mistake of *Lochner* was that the Court
invalidated, on inadequate constitutional grounds, a substantive state purpose
(i.e., equalizing bargaining power) that was consistent with and complementary to constitutional values of respect for rights (including a right to work).[203]
Nothing in the Constitution forbids, as the *Lochner* Court wrongly supposed,
regulations of hours of work reasonably aimed—in the relevant historical
circumstances—at securing a more nearly just distribution of power and resources between employers and employees in order to have a more equitable
overall framework for exercise of their liberties. Indeed, this type of legislation
may advance deeper constitutional values of equal respect. Constitutional privacy, in contrast, is rooted in the reasonable elaboration of a long-standing
constitutional tradition that limits the coercive enforcement of sectarian values
into essential spheres of reasonable moral self-government. The sodomy laws
at issue in *Bowers* are constitutionally dubious because the force of the traditional moral condemnation of these sex acts can no longer be justified in the
required way.[204]

---

[201] *Bowers,* 106 S. Ct. at 2846 (discussing "the face-off between the Executive and the Court in
the 1930's which resulted in the repudiation of much of the substantive gloss that the Court had
placed on the Due Process Clause").

[202] 198 U.S. 45 (1905).

[203] Cf. Richards, *Toleration and the Constitution,* pp. 215–19 (arguing that attempting to
equalize power of speech by limiting campaign spending is consistent with constitutional values).

[204] The traditional moral condemnation of oral and anal sex in our culture may be traced to a
number of beliefs: (1) that homosexual forms of such sexual expression undermine—particularly
in men—desirable masculine character traits (e.g., courage and self-control); (2) a general conception that sexuality has one proper purpose alone (procreation), and any other form of sexual
expression—disengaged from procreation—is shamefully wrong (including contraceptive use);
(3) an empirical belief that prohibitions of homosexual forms of such sexual expression combatted
pestilence, plague, and natural disaster; (4) a theological conception that relevant passages in the

Justice White pursues a false analogy when he likens *Bowers* to *Lochner* and to other paradigms of interpretive mistake.[205] As we have seen, these interpretive errors—whether narrow interpretations of the commerce clause, the Fourth Amendment, or the Fourteenth Amendment—are mistakes precisely because they fail to read constitutional guarantees in ways sufficiently sensitive to contextually relevant facts and values. Attention to context is necessary in order publicly to justify these guarantees on grounds of principle in contemporary circumstances. Failure to provide such a contextually sensitive constitutional reading is, paradoxically, the interpretive mistake of *Bowers*.

In contrast, Justice Blackmun's argument for the four dissenters is clear about arguments of principle regarding the fundamental right in question (namely, a right of morally independent intimate personal association) because he brings to the analysis of legitimate state purposes not Justice White's uncritical deference, but a searching scrutiny of the state purposes used to justify the traditional moral condemnation of homosexuality.[206] For Justice Blackmun, sectarian moral views are no more adequate justification for criminalization of homosexuality[207] than they are for racist degradation of blacks by antimiscegenation laws.[208] In both cases, criminal sanctions can no longer be reasonably justified in nonsectarian terms. In *Bowers*, four justices of the Supreme Court thus adopt a view of legitimate state purposes—similar to that urged by Justice Stevens in his *Thornburgh* concurrence[209]—that draws a constitutional distinction between sectarian and nonsectarian moral purposes as justifications for abridging fundamental rights.

From this perspective, criminal prohibitions bearing on the right of constitutional privacy require a heavy burden of justification, but a burden that can, in principle, be met. There would be, for example, no constitutional objection to the application of neutral criminal statutes to intrafamilial murders, wife or husband beatings, or child abuse, no matter how rooted in intimate family life and sexuality; nor should there be any objection to rape laws if applicable to married or unmarried sexual intimacies. In these cases, the constitutional burden of justification is met, because countervailing rights of persons justify coercive interference into intimate relations. The relevant ethical approach is

---

Old and New Testaments condemned such acts; (5) various empirical beliefs about the inhumanly exceptional choice of sexual propensities and the evil consequences of their exercise to the agent and others (child molestation); and (6) a political conception that such acts constitute a form of willful heresy or treason against the stability of social institutions. None of these beliefs can today reasonably sustain the application of coercive sanctions to oral and anal sex: they rest on either demonstrably false factual premises, or normative assumptions no longer reasonably enforced elsewhere on the community at large and no longer justly enforceable here.

For a more lengthy discussion of these six traditional beliefs and why they fail reasonably to justify the criminal prohibition of homosexual activity, see Richards, *Toleration and the Constitution*, pp. 275–80.

[205] *Bowers*, 106 S. Ct. at 2843–44.
[206] Ibid., at 2848–56.
[207] Ibid., at 2854–55.
[208] Ibid., at 2854 n.5.
[209] 106 S. Ct. at 2188–89.

to treat other persons as one would oneself want to be treated as a free and self-governing moral agent. Such an ethical approach expresses itself in a constitutional commitment to the liberties that are essential to the moral individuality of a free and equal people.[210] These constitutional liberties can only be guaranteed if the state is required to be tolerant among forms of conscience, speech, and ways of life unless there is a compelling showing of a clear and present danger of secular harms.

Ethical principles can dictate prohibitions and regulations of certain types of sexual conduct. For example, respect for the developmental rights of the immature requires that various liberties that are guaranteed to adults not be extended to children who lack developed rational capacities. Neither is there any objection to the reasonable and neutral regulation against obtrusive sexual solicitation nor, of course, against forcible forms of intercourse of any kind. In addition, forms of sexual expression can be limited by other ethical principles, namely, principles of not killing, harming or inflicting gratuitous cruelty (nonmaleficence),[211] principles of fidelity,[212] and principles of paternalism in narrowly defined circumstances.[213]

Consistent with these principles, statutes that absolutely forbid oral and anal intercourse cannot be justified. These statutes are not limited to forcible or public forms of sexual intercourse, or sexual intercourse by or with children. They extend to private, consensual acts between adults. The argument that such laws are justified because they indirectly prevent homosexual intercourse by or with children is as absurd as the claim that absolute prohibitions on heterosexual intercourse could be so justified. There is no reason to believe that homosexuals as a class are any more involved in offenses with the young than heterosexuals.[214] Nor is there any reliable evidence that such laws inhibit children from being naturally homosexual who would otherwise be naturally heterosexual. Sexual preference is settled—largely irrever-

---

[210] See Richards, *Toleration and the Constitution,* pp. 244–47.

[211] See David Richards, *A Theory of Reasons for Action* (Oxford: Clarendon Press, 1971), pp. 176–85.

[212] See ibid., pp. 148–75 (arguing obligation to keep promises is principle of fairness essential to contractualist morality).

[213] See ibid., at pp. 192–95 (arguing it is consistent with contractualist morality to prevent incompetent persons from irrationally acting to their own detriment).

[214] See the classic Kinsey Institute study of sex offenders, P.H. Gebhard et al., *Sex Offenders* (New York: Bantam, 1965); Hoffman, *Gay World,* pp. 89–92. In general, seduction of the young appears to be more centered on heterosexual rather than homosexual relations. See Bell and Weinberg, *Homosexualities,* p. 230. Importantly, the failure to note the distinction between homosexuality and pedophilia is deplored by the majority of homosexual people who "do not share, do not approve, and fear to be associated with pedophiliac interests" (West, *Homosexuality,* p. 119). One recent study summarizes the pertinent empirical literature as follows: "these men are much more likely to have a heterosexual history and orientation than a homosexual one. Contrary to public belief, homosexual adult males rarely molest young male children," R.L. Geiser, *Hidden Victims: The Sexual Abuse of Children* (Boston: Beacon, 1979), p. 75.

sibly[215]— in very early childhood,[216] well before laws of this kind have any effect.

Other moral principles fail to justify absolute prohibitions on homosexual oral and anal sex. Prohibitory statutes cannot be justified by a moral principle of harm prevention because there is no convincing evidence that sexual acts by their nature harm the participants.[217] These statutes do not correspond to any just purpose the state might have in enforcing principles of fidelity, because the acts often occur in the context of long-standing relations in which sexual intimacy is both integral and stabilizing.[218]

Consistent with the Court's previous applications of constitutional privacy, blanket prohibitions on homosexual activity fail to satisfy the burden required for abridging the constitutional right to privacy. Like anticontraception laws, the bans on homosexual sex force people to refrain from nonprocreative sex. The interest in autonomy in intimate relations is here at least as strong as that in the reproductive autonomy of abortion decisions. Moreover, the evidence of harms to the rights of other persons is even more controversial and speculative.

From this perspective, the *Bowers* majority's appeal only to "morality"[219] begs the central question. The Court supposes precisely the kind of homogeneity in moral values that both the history of western ethics and specific history of constitutional privacy belie. It is a valued and admirable distinction of western ethics and law that they have changed—open to critical reflection on their own history and open to new empirical and normative perspectives. Indeed, as we have seen, American constitutionalism itself was at the cutting edge of a larger humanist project of that sort. Using critical reflection, the founders created a new kind of community of principle that used heterogeneity to advance a deeper vision of equality. That project rested on the critical

---

[215] See Churchill, *Homosexual Behavior among Males,* pp. 283–91; Tripp, *Homosexual Matrix,* pp. 251–54; West, *Homosexuality,* p. 266.

[216] See, e.g., John Money and H. Ehrhardt, *Man & Woman Boy & Girl* (Baltimore, Md.: Johns Hopkins Univ. Press, 1972), pp. 153–201. One study hypothesizes that gender identity and sexual object choice coincide with the development of language, that is, form eighteen to twenty-four months of age. See J. Money, J.G. Hampson and J.L. Hampson, "An Examination of Some Basic Sexual Concepts: The Evidence of Human Hermaphroditism," 97 *Bull. Johns Hopkins Hosp.* 301 (1955). Cf. Bell *Sexual Preference* (1981).

[217] For example, any general coercive statute, allegedly directed against sexual activity likely to minimize AIDS health risks to the agent, would be grossly overinclusive, condemning the many acts not subject to these risks at all and other such acts in which risks can be reduced by appropriate prophylactic measures. Indeed, it is the criminalization of sexual activities that leads to their secretive and clandestine nature uninformed of possible health risks, and discourages the kind of candid access to medical information and services that might enhance and respect people's judgment and capacity to decide how to mitigate health risks. See Note, "The Constitutionality of Laws Forbidding Private Homosexual Conduct," 72 *Mich. L. Rev.* 1613, 1631–33 (1974). Criminalization and larger patterns of discrimination also make difficult the formation of the kinds of stable relationships that would both minimize health risks and humanely deal with health problems when they occur. See idem; Richard D. Mohr, "AIDS, Gay Life, State Coercion," 6 *Raritan,* Summer 1986, at p. 38.

[218] See generally Blumstein and Schwartz, *American Couples.*

[219] 106 S. Ct. at 2846.

conviction that the political power of much traditional moral, religious, and political orthodoxy rested on corrupt foundations that had undermined the very capacity of human nature reasonably to know and understand its natural rights to freedom and self-government. Constitutional argument rested, for the founders, on the protection of such rights against such political oppressions. Their legacy to us is the constitutional demand for the justification of political power by public reason that requires of us, as it did of them, the progressive elaboration of the same vision of basic rights of the person in the same spirit of skepticism about the political enforcement at large of views that, on examination, rest on corrupt political foundations of sectarian insularity and faction.

The principle of constitutional privacy is fundamental to the founders' critical emancipatory project, requiring the same searching analysis of oppressive orthodoxies of intimate personal life as of those of religion or politics or ethics more generally. It stultifies that enterprise to appeal to "morality" as the measure of such rights when the unreasonable majoritarian force of that appeal states the terms of what the cumulative argument of this book shows to be (both for the founders and ourselves) the most fundamental of constitutional evils and the one most amenable to constitutional remedy—namely, the enforcement at large of any politically entrenched orthodoxy whose force depends on stunting the moral powers of people reasonably to know and understand the rights of their human nature, which, in this case, is the right of free persons to conduct their own intimate personal lives on reasonable terms. The scope of the right to privacy must, like other basic rights of the person, be contextually responsive to the ways in which the enforcement of traditional values may no longer express the reasonably acceptable arguments that may constitutionally be imposed on all persons. Certainly, the enforcement of such views on people at large should not be based on values that are reasonably authoritative in contemporary circumstances for only some adherents to certain traditions; and it is, of course, a grotesque distortion of anything arguments of principle could be reasonably taken to mean to allow such views to be enforced only against the group most vulnerable to and victimized by such factionalized moral majoritarianism.

Enforcement of such perspectives on the community at large is the functional equivalent of a heresy or treason prosecution.[220] Homosexuals are a popular object of social contempt and scorn. In this popular view, they are, and must remain, exiles from the family. Their heresy or treason is their rejection of heterosexual family life, an institution that is so central to some people's moral integrity that homosexuals, as a class, are the ultimate rebels against essential values in living.[221] We can see the ugly reality of these attitudes when allowing homosexuals to teach in schools is equated with homosex-

---

[220] The English legal scholar, Tony Honoré, observed of the contemporary status of the homosexual: "It is not primarily a matter of breaking rules but of dissenting attitudes. It resembles political or religious dissent, being an atheist in Catholic Ireland or a dissident in Soviet Russia" [Tony Honoré, *Sex Law* (London: Duckworth, 1978), p. 89].

[221] See, e.g., Magnuson, *Are Gay Rights Right?* pp. 11–29.

ual seduction of their students, and when the heartrending tragedy of the deaths of many young homosexual men in a health crisis is transformed into an aggressive attack on the victims themselves. These imaginative perversions of reality are revealing because they create aggressors out of victims and invert morality in service of the ideological need to crush a perceived threat from these heretics against the family.

Of course, these perceptions create the thing on which they feed, because they exile homosexuals from security in a private life by imposing criminal sanctions on their sexuality, and by denying them child custody, the legal protections of marriage, and the antidiscrimination protections that are essential to a secure personal life. That is why, in my judgment, homosexuals as a group so clearly require, as a minimum measure of constitutional decency, the protection of the constitutional right to privacy.

Because the criminal prohibitions of homosexuality can no longer be acceptably justified, homosexuals have the basic constitutional right of moral independence to construct conceptions of personal relationships and of community in accord with their reasoned convictions of permanent value in living. They must be permitted to present these conceptions as one among the competing pluralistic visions of value in living that enrich the range of imagination and intelligence of free people. These conceptions can enrich the social imagination of us all, as homosexual couples demonstrate that the redemptive force of personal love is an inalienable right of the human soul in which gender plays no role.

Arguments of principle significantly preoccupy American public law. We know the importance of this normative requirement by the consequences of its absence. Precisely because they so perspicuously display the quality of bad argument that is required to reach the results least threatening to majoritarian common sense, cases like *Bowers* illustrate what principles are, and the kinds of price we pay as a constitutional community when these principles are not reasonably explained or elaborated. That price is not only a gratuitous insult to and branding of aggrieved minorities as heretical outlaws to essential values in living (indeed, as exiles from the constitutional community of principle), but also an erosion of the sense of ourselves as a reasonable community of law, not of will. It is the bitterest of betrayals to abandon the great work of collective democratic decency that is the Constitution of the United States in the name, as we have seen, of wholly specious conceptions of the founders' intent or of text or of political theory, because—on examination—it is the founders' intent, their text, and their republican political theory of an enduring community of principle that are thus mocked.

7

Interpreting Equal Protection

We have used the interpretive methodology of this book to analyze the constitutional structures and doctrines of both the Constitution of 1787 and the Bill of Rights of 1791, including federalism, the separation of powers, judicial review, the enumerated rights of religious liberty and free speech, and the unenumerated constitutional right to privacy. Our analysis of all these concepts was largely a matter of making interpretive sense of the documents of 1787 and 1791 however expanded in scope of application by later constitutional amendments.

We turn now to a different interpretive task, one that is directed at the equal protection clause of the Fourteenth Amendment. The equal protection clause, as a doctrinal innovation, was, as we shall see, importantly anticipated by various features of the 1787–1791 Constitution. As was suggested earlier (Chapter 4), the "founders" of 1868 (i.e., the Congress that proposed and the states that ratified the Fourteenth Amendment) acted very much in the spirit of the founders of 1787 and 1791, bringing to them and the interpretation of their work by succeeding generations a critical interpretive stance very like that the 1787–1791 founders applied to their predecessors. Regarding the view of the 1787–1791 founders that is taken here, it can be said that they left as their essential constitutional legacy these historically self-conscious critical and interpretive procedures, which constituted the only kind of legitimate authority that they could have for the later generations of Americans whose interpretive work would center on them as founders. For this reason, we best honor their work when we interpret it in our circumstances, as was argued in Chapters 4–6, with the same integrity of argument that they brought to the reasonable justification of their work in their circumstances. However, an even more profound tribute to the 1787–1791 founders would be to bring to the criticism and reform of their own work the kind of procedures they applied, often imperfectly, to their own. That was, in my judgment, the enduring achievement of the Reconstruction amendments.

As we have seen, American interpretation of the written constitution naturally gives weight to the arguments of the founders that center on an enduring community of principle, but any reasonable attention to these arguments shows ways in which the 1787 Constitution and 1791 Bill of Rights—

remarkable achievements that they are—contain compromises over and even sacrifices of republican principles of which the founders were themselves all too painfully aware. Madison himself, for example, regarded equal representation of states in the Senate as in clear violation of basic republican principles of justice in voting,[1] advocated a federal negative over state laws that violated rights of the person or compromised the interests of the nation,[2] would have preferred a guarantee of religious liberty and free speech that extended to both the states and the federal government,[3] and knew—as did many of the founders—that the institution of slavery in the southern states was an obscene violation of the republican equal liberty of all persons.[4] Some constitutional compromises were perhaps not as disastrous in fact as the founders feared, but the evil of blatant sacrifices of principle—like the legitimation of slavery and the absence of a federal constitutional inhibition on the power of states to deprive persons of basic rights—worsened with cumulative historical experience. The founders' sense of basic flaws in the community of principle was confirmed, and—in the wake of the Civil War—many of them were expressly addressed by the Reconstruction amendments.

The "founders" of the Reconstruction amendments brought to their work the same kind of interpretive sense of history that we saw earlier in the founders of the 1787 Constitution, namely, an attempt to learn from past republican and federal mistakes in institutional design, including in this case the Constitution and Bill of Rights themselves.[5] However, they are not institutional innovators in the sense of the 1787 founders, because their interpretive sense of history importantly accepts, indeed elaborates, many of the substantive and procedural constraints of the 1787 Constitution and 1791 Bill of Rights. Of course, they address central defects in the earlier constitutional design: the Thirteenth Amendment (1865) abolishes slavery, the Fourteenth Amendment (1868) extends guarantees of basic rights against the states,[6] and

[1] See, e.g., Max Farrand, ed., *Records of the Federal Convention*, (New Haven, Conn.: Yale Univ. Press, 1966), pp. 151–52.

[2] The fullest statement of Madison's views on this question appears in his October 24, 1787 letter to Jefferson, criticizing the failure of the constitutional convention to adopt the federal negative. See Robert A. Rutland et al., eds., *The Papers of James Madison, 1787–1788* (Chicago: Univ. of Chicago Press, 1977), pp. 209–14.

[3] Madison originally proposed to the House of Representatives the following amendment to the 1787 Constitution: "No state shall violate the equal rights of conscience, or the freedom of the press, or the trial by jury in criminal cases" [Leonard Levy, *Judgments* (Chicago: Quadrangle, 1972), p. 179]. The proposed amendment was not adopted.

[4] At the constitutional convention, Madison observed that the mention of the slave trade "will be more dishonorable to the National character than to say nothing about it in the Constitution." Farrand, ed., *Records of Federal Convention*, vol. 2, p. 415.

[5] My understanding of these issues is indebted to the recently published book of my colleague William E. Nelson, *The Fourteenth Amendment: From Political Principle to Judicial Doctrine* (Cambridge, Mass.: Harvard University Press, 1988).

[6] See, e.g., Michael Kent Curtis, *No State Shall Abridge: The Fourteenth Amendment and the Bill of Rights* (Durham, N.C.: Duke Univ. Press, 1986), pp. 57–91, 131–53. The only significant contrary historical evidence rests on the failure of several ratifying states at the time or thereafter fully to comply with the Bill of Rights. See, e.g., Charles Fairman, "Does the Fourteenth

the Fifteenth Amendment (1870) prohibits racial discrimination in voting. However, these changes do not innovate principles as much as they elaborate the scope of application of standing constitutional principles in ways often defended by the 1787 founders themselves. For example, when the Fourteenth Amendment extends guarantees of basic rights against the states, it does not innovate new rights but rather takes standing guarantees of the 1791 Bill of Rights and expands them from the federal government to the states, a point that Madison had abortively advocated both at the constitutional convention (the federal negative importantly incorporated this idea[7]) and in proposals for the Bill of Rights (religious liberty and free speech were to apply to the states[8]); one of the great lacunae in the Constitution's protection of basic rights was thus filled. Furthermore, the abolition of slavery in similar fashion expands the scope of application of republican principles of inalienable human rights in the way that those principles clearly require.

The legitimation of slavery was the one unpardonable lapse from the founders' republican principles of the inalienable rights of liberty of all persons—unpardonable because the founders so clearly knew it to be a vicious lapse from the republican principles that are fundamental to political legitimacy. For example, when Madison explicated the general theory of faction for the constitutional convention, he made it quite clear that slavery rested on the most morally malign of political factions:

> Why was America so justly apprehensive of Parliamentary injustice? Because G. Britain had a separate interest real or supposed, & if her authority had been admitted, could have pursued that interest at our expense. We have seen the mere distinction of colour made in the most enlightened period of time, a ground of the most oppressive dominion ever exercised by man over man. What has been the source of those unjust laws complained of among ourselves? Has it it not been the real or supposed interest of the major number? . . . The lesson we are to draw from the whole is that where a

---

Amendment Incorporate the Bill of Rights?: The Original Understanding," 2 *Stan. L. Rev.* 5, 81–126 (1949). However, such historical data are compatible with an abstract commitment to selective incorporation of the Bill of Rights that takes the view that certain rights—on the proper account of when such rights are selectively incorporated—are not incorporated. The evidence of the abstract commitment to incorporation is, as Curtis argues, quite clear. In fact, much of the later interpretive debate has been over the best theory of selective incorporation, and an appeal to the founders' denotations in this matter (which Fairman erroneously takes to be dispositive) has been no more decisive here than it is anywhere else in constitutional interpretation. See, e.g., *Duncan* v. *Louisiana*, 391 U.S. 145 (1968) (Sixth Amendment requirement of criminal jury held applicable to states under Fourteenth Amendment); *Williams* v. *Florida*, 399 U.S. 78 (1970) (holding, however, twelve-person criminal jury requirement, historically required in federal criminal prosecutions, not required for state criminal prosecutions).

[7] Madison's conception of the federal negative incorporated a power to negative not only state laws inconsistent with Congress's views of the national interest but also all such laws inconsistent with Congress's views of human rights. His October 24, 1787 letter to Jefferson makes both points quite clear. See Rutland et al., eds. *Papers of James Madison 1787–1788*, pp. 209–14.

[8] See note 3, above.

majority are united by a common sentiment and have an opportunity, the rights of the minor party become insecure.[9]

Slavery was, in Madison's view, the most extreme example of the depths of political depravity to which a factionalized majority with untrammeled political power could fall. The natural inference should be—consistent with the larger fabric of Madisonian constitutionalism—that appropriate structures and doctrines must limit both the power and opportunity of such factions to work their will. However, when it came to justifying the work of the convention in *The Federalist,* Madison self-consciously limited the operative scope of the theory of faction to "a number of citizens" oppressing "the rights of other citizens,"[10] a scope of constitutional concern he expressly distinguished from noncitizens like slaves, euphemistically called "an unhappy species of population abounding in some of the States."[11] In short, the proper moral and political scope of the theory of faction, as it was clearly understood by Madison and other founders, was arbitrarily truncated constitutionally[12]: the terrible republican injustice done to slaves was, as it were, made invisible constitutionally. Slaves were, as a matter of basic constitutional law and theory, politically dead persons.[13]

The Reconstruction amendments addressed these defects in the original Constitution by both less and more radical constitutional innovations. The less radical innovation was the expansion of basic constitutional rights in a more principled way, including both the expansion of federal guarantees of basic rights to limit state as well as federal political abuses, and the expansion of basic republican principles of liberty to all persons (i.e., the abolition of slavery). The more radical doctrinal innovation was the equal protection clause of the Fourteenth Amendment.

My concern in this chapter is to use the general interpretive methodology of this book to examine the issue of equal protection. The first task of this chapter is to criticize the dominant procedural approach to equal protection analysis and then to develop a constructive alternative approach in the course of that discussion. The latter approach is then elaborated by using it to shed light on central interpretive issues in the law of equal protection, including the unconstitutionality of racial segregation and related issues about affirmative action and the expansion of equal protection analysis to nonracial classifications like gender. A central aspect of the interpretive analysis of these issues must be a further elaboration of my earlier discussions (Chapters 1 and 4) of the appropriate kind of meaning (e.g., denotative exemplars, concrete versus abstract connotations, less versus more abstract connotations) to be ascribed to the constitutional text.

[9] Farrand, ed., *Records of Federal Convention,* vol. 1, pp. 135–36.

[10] *The Federalist,* p. 57.

[11] Ibid., p. 294.

[12] For useful commentary on these points, see Morton White, *Philosophy, The Federalist, and the Constitution* (New York: Oxford University Press, 1987) pp. 168–71.

[13] On the wider importance of this concept in the understanding of slavery historically, see Orlando Patterson, *Slavery and Social Death* (Cambridge, Mass.: Harvard Univ. Press, 1982).

Procedural versus Substantive Models of Equal Protection

We noted earlier (Chapter 6) the impact of John Hart Ely's theory of judicial review on the way Justice White thought about the interpretive elaboration of the constitutional right to privacy in the 1986 cases of *Thornburgh* and *Bowers*. Ely's views about constitutional privacy derive from his more general theory of constitutional legitimacy, which arises, in turn, from his influential procedural model of equal protection analysis.[14] My analysis of Ely's theory of equal protection begins with his more general views of interpretive legitimacy, and then turns to the critical examination of his views of equal protection.

Ely's theory is in two ill-fitting parts. First, he offers the interpretivist theory, which outlines the full range of rights protected by constitutional texts in light of reasonable historical inferences about the intentions that are expressed by those texts. These rights would include a full range of both enumerated and unenumerated rights, including the expansive elaboration by our law of the constitutional right to privacy. Second, however, Ely proposes a critical theory of the values of political democracy as a legitimate and defensible form of government, and then asks, in light of the critical theory, whether and to what extent the interpretivist theory can reasonably be pursued. Ely concludes that the full scope of rights protected by interpretivist theory cannot reasonably be pursued; in particular, the elaboration of constitutional privacy to include abortion—however much required by text and history—was a mistake.

Ely's appeal to critical political theory is a familiar move in constitutional thought, and often leads to even more radical skepticism about rights per se (e.g., Bork's skepticism[15]). However, to perform such a critical function properly, the political theory in question must presumably be independently justifiable as the best account of the values of constitutional democracy. Does Ely's theory meet this test?

Ely advances a political theory that, in contrast to rights-based theories, is allegedly nonsubstantive, resting on a procedural theory of democracy that does not appeal to the controversial substantive premises that Ely thinks is virtuous to avoid. He argues that the best way to understand the value of democracy is in terms of an ideal democratic procedure, in which all the interests of the persons affected by the democratic polity are both fairly represented and given influence by the democratic process. It follows that constitutional law and interpretation are valid as long as they are representation-reinforcing—that is, to the extent that judicial review is necessary to ensure that democratic politics gives weight to and represents interests in the required way. For example, laws that use racial classifications, giving racist stereotypes the force of law, are the paradigmatic case of Ely's representational unfairness. The imposition of these racial classifications not only does not represent the blacks affected,

---

[14] See, in general, John Hart Ely, *Democracy and Distrust* (Cambridge, Mass.: Harvard Univ. Press, 1980).

[15] For a similar skepticism about rights, see Learned Hand, *The Bill of Rights* (New York: Atheneum, 1968).

but also is inimical to the giving of proper weight to their interests.[16] Accordingly, these racial classifications are the just object of condemnation under the equal protection clause, which denies validity to laws that rest on such a representationally unfair process. The use of racial classifications in affirmative action programs, however, is not subject to constitutional invalidation. These classifications give proper representational influence to the interests of blacks—consistent with undoing and making reparation for the long heritage of unfair treatment dealt them in the past—and therefore are not the proper subject of judicial invalidation.[17]

Ely objects to the elaboration of the constitutional right to privacy in *Roe v. Wade*[18] because the laws invalidated on this ground do not—unlike the anticontraception laws invalidated in *Griswold* v. *Connecticut*[19]—protect the privacy interests in the home that are guaranteed by the Fourth Amendment, nor are they the product of representational unfairness; instead they rest on a substantive ground independent of either such specifically protected constitutional interests or procedural defects. Indeed, *Roe* fails to accord appropriate representational value to fetuses.[20] However, judicial review has, in Ely's view, no proper role outside the interpretation of specifically guaranteed enumerated rights or the fairness of the underlying process of representation leading to legislation—a task in which courts are uniquely competent. In particular, the judicial elaboration of an unenumerated right like constitutional privacy to include abortion—however required by text and history—cannot legitimately be pursued if it cannot be justified by specific guarantees like the Fourth Amendment or by rectifying representational unfairness.

This argument has two dubious features. First, Ely's critical theory of democracy does not explain why even specific textual guarantees should have interpretive force at all. Why doesn't reinforcing representation simply occupy the entire field? Second, Ely's argument depends crucially on the accuracy of his characterization of his critical theory as a *procedural* theory of fair democratic process. Proper judicial actions correct unfair procedures; an improper judge acts on substantive values. Yet Ely's appeal to procedure itself actually masks a highly controversial appeal to substantive values.

Thus, one plausible criticism of Ely's arguments asks exactly how we know that a democratic process has been, in Ely's sense, unfair. The underlying test for the fairness of the process is, on this interpretation, some form of utilitarianism.[21] A process is unfair to the degree to which it does not give certain

---

[16] See Ely, *Democracy and Distrust*, pp. 135–70.

[17] Ibid., pp. 170–72.

[18] 410 U.S. 113 (1973).

[19] 381 U.S. 479 (1965).

[20] See John Hart Ely, "The Wages of Crying Wolf: A Comment on *Roe* v. *Wade*," 82 *Yale L. J.* 920 (1973).

[21] Ely has denied this utilitarian interpretation of his views. See John Hart Ely, "Professor Dworkin's External/Personal Preference Distinction," 1983 *Duke L.J.* 959. It is, however, a quite plausible interpretation of the argument; see, e.g., Paul Brest, "The Fundamental Rights Controversy: The Essential Contradictions of Normative Constitutional Scholarship," 90 *Yale L.J.* 1063 (1981).

interests weight or it actively prejudices them. If democratic politics fails to advance these interests or actively frustrates them, then it fails to maximize the aggregate of satisfaction over frustration of interests, and judicial review assures that the interests are given their proper utilitarian weight. Once one sees that utilitarianism guides Ely's political theory, the theory cannot be represented as process-based at all, because the judgment of representational fairness rests on a judgment of substance, namely, the utilitarian principle. If utilitarianism motivates the critical political theory, then one surely needs some defense of it against the many forms of rights-based theories current in the philosophical field. Ely, however, simply dismisses all such theories because there is controversy about relative adequacy. However, nothing can be more certain than that controversy also exists about the inadequacy of utilitarianism, especially in its classical forms, as a moral and political theory.[22] Ely's account rests on an inadequately defended substantive political theory.

A related analysis of Ely's argument might take note that utilitarianism can hardly do justice to the judicial decisions that Ely regards as paradigmatically just, particularly cases in which despised minorities are subjected to prejudice through the political process.[23] If the minority is sufficiently small and despised and the majority sufficiently large and cohesive, then the pleasures of group solidarity and domination gained by the majority may be much greater than the frustrations inflicted on the minority. Such oppressive political action would, then, on utilitarian grounds, be justified. If the intuitive spirit of Ely's argument would still condemn the procedural unfairness of such actions, then some underlying substantive argument of justice must explain why they are unacceptable. The very concept of procedural unfairness requires an underlying, nonutilitarian, perhaps rights-based substantive political conception. Yet, it is precisely such conceptions that Ely earlier dismissed. Again, the critical issues of democratic political theory are not adequately examined and defended.[24]

We need to look more closely at equal protection as an interpretive question in its own right. Ely's general constitutional theory may be wrong precisely because he ignores the substantive values that actuate equal protection, and he may have taken this interpretive wrong turn because his interpretive methodology has not taken sufficiently seriously the larger fabric of constitutional structures and principles that the 1868 "founders" both interpreted and criticized when they innovated the constitutional protection of equal protection in the Fourteenth Amendment. Precisely because it conceives constitutional interpretation in terms of the larger humanist critical, interpretive, and historical methodologies assumed by the founders, the interpretive methodology advocated here may, in contrast, fruitfully advance the interpretive under-

---

[22] Cf. Brest, "Fundamental Rights Controversy," pp. 1102–4.

[23] See, e.g., Lawrence G. Sager, "Rights Skepticism and Process-Based Responses," 56 *N.Y.U. L. Rev.* 417 426–32 (1981).

[24] Cf. Erwin Chemerinsky, *Interpreting the Constitution* (New York: Praeger, 1987), pp. 6–11.

standing of equal protection because it takes seriously the innovation of equal protection as both an interpretive and critical act.

Whereas the equal protection clause is a relatively late addition to our constitutional history, the underlying moral ideal of the equality of all persons is not. This is evident not only in the solemn aspirations of the Declaration of Independence, but also in the theory of Lockean political legitimacy that is fundamental to the design, justification, and ratification of both the Constitution and the Bill of Rights. In this connection, Ely has made much of the anticipation of equal protection by the privileges and immunities clause of Article IV.[25] However, interpretive weight must be accorded as well to the protection of equal rights by the kinds of guarantees of both enumerated and unenumerated rights we have already examined at length. Madison, who was the chief architect of the First Amendment, regarded guarantees of religious freedom as a form of equal liberty. His great *Remonstrance* is clear on the point that such guarantees protect "every Citizen in the enjoyment of his Religion with the same equal hand which protects his person and his property, by neither invading the equal rights of any Sect, nor suffering any Sect to invade those of another."[26] This kind of equality principle, like the other guarantees of enumerated and unenumerated rights of the person, does not lend itself to the interpretation of representational unfairness that Ely plausibly imputes to the privileges and immunities clause of Article IV (And then overgeneralizes to equal protection jurisprudence, and finally to legitimate constitutional interpretation per se).

A violation of our constitutionally protected liberties of conscience or speech does not necessarily have to be representationally unfair in the sense of Article IV. Representational unfairness arises from the unequal burdens that a state law imposes on nonresidents, who are not themselves represented in the decision leading to the law in question.[27] The unfairness is the kind of burden imposed without the relevant opportunity to have a democratically appropriate voice and influence in a decision that thus affects one's life. However, violations of equal liberties of conscience and speech are often the product of representationally fair procedures in this sense. All relevant persons have a fair voice and influence in the decision to pass constitutionally nonneutral violations of conscience or speech. Furthermore, representationally unfair procedures often do not threaten constitutional liberties, indeed, on some views, may secure them.[28] It is not representational unfairness

---

[25] See Ely, *Democracy and Distrust,* pp. 83–88. The pertinent text is U.S. Constitution, Article IV, section 2: "The citizens of each state shall be entitled to all privileges and immunities of citizens in the several states."

[26] James Madison, *Memorial and Remonstrance against Religious Assessments,* in Robert A. Rutland et al., eds., *The Papers of James Madison 1784–1786* vol. 8, p. 302.

[27] See, e.g., *Baldwin v. Montana Fish and Game Commission,* 436 U.S. 371 (1978).

[28] John Stuart Mill's advocacy of weighted voting rests, in part, on such a view. See John Stuart Mill, *Considerations on Representative Government,* Currin V. Shields, ed. (Indianapolis, Ind.: Bobbs-Merrill, 1958), p. 135 ff. Mill would not, of course, have regarded such a representative procedure as unfair.

that is at issue in the kind of unjust inequality that Madison condemned as violations of equal liberties of conscience and speech. It is rather the failure of the law in question, whatever its provenance, to respect the inalienable right of the equal dignity of all consciences and speakers.

A failure to respect equal rights is simply not the same kind of political injustice as the failure to give all persons affected by state decisions appropriate democratic influence in the deliberative procedure leading to the decision. Unequal respect does a wrong of a different and more serious kind than does the procedural defect of undemocratic influence. A procedural defect puts no constraint on the output other than certain kinds of inputs. In contrast, violating the principle of equal respect—central to the liberties of the First Amendment and related constitutional guarantees—permits laws that undermine the equal dignity of conscience and speech, which is a forbidden output.

The difference between these two kinds of injustice cannot be defensibly explained in terms of the acceptably procedural character of representational unfairness and the unacceptably substantive nature of unequal respect. First, we worry about representational unfairness as a constitutional matter because of substantive considerations, often considerations of equal liberty itself. Second, equal respect for conscience and speech forbids content bias for reasons of justice that may be defended on grounds more acceptably procedural than representational unfairness. Each point should be expanded as a preface to my alternative interpretation of equal protection.

First, as Ely's critics have been at pains to emphasize, only because representational unfairness preserves certain substantive values can it be itself a wrong.[29] As was suggested earlier, if these substantive values are utilitarian, then we have the vicious circularity of an attack on substantive political theories that itself rests on an unexamined and probably even more controversial political theory. In contrast our concern for forms of representational unfairness is often actuated by a nonutilitarian concern for equal liberty itself. For example, a more nearly equal liberty in the political rights to vote and participate in government is as much subject to the mandates of equal respect as the rights of conscience, free speech, and privacy discussed earlier (Chapters 5 and 6). Thus, the reapportionment mandate—one person one vote[30]—reflects a concern for a more nearly equal weighting of the power of voting as a central equal liberty of political voice and participation in a community of persons who are understood to be free and equal.[31] Understanding representational unfairness as a constitutional value may thus require a background theory of equality, which guided our interpretation of how this value should be coordinated with other constitutional values of equal dignity. However, the claim that representational unfairness is the exclusive value of constitutional legitimacy is then subverted; the very point and place of the value is guided by

[29] See, e.g., Ronald Dworkin, "The Forum of Principle," in *A Matter of Principle* (Cambridge, Mass.: Harvard Univ. Press, 1985), pp. 33–71.

[30] See, e.g., *Reynolds* v. *Sims,* 337 U.S. 533 (1964).

[31] See John Rawls, *A Theory of Justice,* (Cambridge, Mass.: Harvard Univ. Press, 1971), pp. 222–23.

substantive values in which it is understood as one important value integrated with others of equal dignity.

Second, constitutional guarantees of equal liberty of conscience, speech, and private life (properly understood) themselves express a procedural conception at a deeper and less question-begging level than that invoked by representational unfairness.[32] This procedural conception expresses the Lockean view of the only legitimate exercises of political power, namely, that political power must be conducted in ways that can be reasonably justified to all persons subject to it on terms that respect their powers of moral self-government. Both substantive and procedural guarantees of constitutional government frame the scope and uses of political argument in ways that give expression to a political community of free and equal persons. Our observance of the constitutional neutrality required by the First Amendment is procedural in this deeper sense. We conduct the procedures of our common political life—the kinds of arguments we make and demands we exact—in ways that make each of us ultimately responsible for the reasonable conduct of our personal and moral lives; we remit to each person reasonable deliberation over the ways their thought, speech, and lives will weigh and order the general goods that our cooperative community makes possible (e.g., a flourishing and varied religious, artistic, and commercial life). We thus rule out, as procedurally unfair abuses of political power, state coercion or endorsement of constitutionally nonneutral conceptions of what to think or say or how to live, because this type of state action fails to accord equal respect for our powers of personal and moral self-government.

Ely's theory of equal protection, like many other similar theories,[33] assumes a pluralist normative model of American constitutional democracy. This model postulates that groups have interests exogenous to the political process, and that the democratic process satisfies or aggregates these interests in an acceptably utilitarian way. However, the model is, at best, a very partial and incomplete account of American constitutional processes. Of course, American representative democracy does, as it was framed to do, make government responsive to the interests of the electorate, and elected officials are often properly assessed in terms of how, over time, they give appropriate weight to the common interests of all. However, the proper democratic scope of the domain of preference is not, as pluralist models assume, the proper measure of the equally important domain of principle that is fundamental, as we have seen, to the very political legitimacy of constitutional government. As the founders quite clearly understood, some things that the electorate might want to achieve through politics are not politically legitimate ends of the politics of a community of free and equal persons. The political community must be appropriately structured and limited so that legitimate ends are pursued in fact. The salience of the theory of faction in the founders' constitutional thought expresses both this fundamental truth of human nature in

---

[32] On these deeper conceptions of procedural justice, see ibid., pp. 83–90.

[33] See, e.g., Bruce A. Ackerman, "Beyond *Carolene Products*," 98 *Harv. L. Rev.* 713 (1985).

politics and the imperative of legitimate government to take it seriously. Factionalized ends—those that by definition take seriously neither the rights nor ends of outsiders to the faction—were illegitimate political ends. They could not be justified in terms of the deeper value of equality that is fundamental to constitutional government, namely, that political power must be reasonably justifiable to all persons as respecting their rights and serving the common interests of all. In effect, constitutional guarantees define principles and structures of public argument that delimit the force of purely private group interests as the fundamentally legitimating force of democratic politics. The pluralist normative model, however, gives such interests precisely such a pivotal and dispositive place in its theory of politics. A theory of constitutional legitimacy or of equal protection that rests on such a normative model is, therefore, fundamentally misconceived.

The constitutional command of equal protection of the laws—in the Fourteenth Amendment—builds on, consolidates, and elaborates these familiar American constitutional concerns. In contrast to Ely, these concerns are not properly understood exclusively as ideals of representational fairness. Rather, both substantive and procedural guarantees of the Constitution and Bill of Rights express, on examination, a background conception of the procedures for the exercise of political power of a community of free and equal persons. It is therefore a historical, interpretive, and critical mistake to suppose that the equal protection clause can be circumscribed to forms of procedural unfairness. On the contrary, the equal protection clause takes all that is best in the egalitarian ideals of the Constitution and Bill of Rights, consolidates and elaborates them with the force and remedies of federal law by its abstract command that all exercises of state political power must be reasonable. The clause decisively repudiates those betrayals of these ideals in the Constitution that had permitted slavery to coexist with a Constitution based on the inalienable equal rights of persons. The equal protection clause, in short, decisively announces the most abstract ideal of constitutional government (namely, the reasonable justification of political power to all on terms of respect for rights and pursuit of the public good), and aligns the political power of the states with this ideal.

Some aspects of equal protection jurisprudence (in particular, the fundamental rights aspect of strict scrutiny under the equal protection clause) were already anticipated by the equality principles of the Constitution, as in the First Amendment.[34] Constitutional arguments of a content-biased regulation of speech under the free-speech clause may be made to precisely the same effect under this mode of equal protection scrutiny.[35] Ely argues that the novel concerns of the equal protection clause (which he characterizes as unfairness to unrepresented minorities) are the exclusive measure of constitutional legiti-

---

[34] On both fundamental rights and suspect classification analysis, see "Developments in the Law—Equal Protection," 82 *Harv. L. Rev.* 1065 (1969). See also Polyvios G. Polyviou, *Equal Protection of the Laws* (London: Duckworth, 1980).

[35] See, e.g., *Erznoznik* v. *Jacksonville*, 422 U.S. 205 (1975).

macy. However, the general view of constitutional interpretation developed here illuminates the independent grounds of other features of constitutionally legitimate government, including, as we have seen, respect for religious liberty, free speech, and constitutional privacy, as well as aspects of equal protection jurisprudence (fundamental rights analysis) that are otherwise inexplicable.

Ely is also mistaken in his view of the constitutionally novel concerns of the equal protection clause. These concerns focus on the oppression of stigmatized minorities and are directed at the kind of stigma that thus oppressively enjoys the force of law.[36] These worries are not new to our constitutional law. Furthermore, to the extent that they are new, they cannot be explained on the model of representational unfairness, which is only a symptom of the deeper moral evil condemned by the constitutional command of the reasonable justification of political power to all.

Madison's theory of faction itself suggests these concerns. One of Madison's central examples of faction, sectarian religious groups,[37] displays an insightful understanding of the social psychology of intolerance, which has its roots in the limitation of moral reasoning to one's reference group and the distorted perception and denigration of the claims of those outside one's group. Indeed, the central moral conception motivating the political tradition of respect for conscience that Madison elaborated was precisely the sense of how sectarian conscience had corrupted both ethics and religion. That corruption is (and was so understood by Jefferson and Madison) of our moral sense, our capacity to see the conscience, the speech, and the lives of others as consistent with a fair-minded respect for them as persons.

Recent accounts of the Madisonian theory of faction often distinguish it, in a way Madison did not, from the kinds of degrading stereotypes that are central to the equal protection clause's concerns for suspect classifications.[38] The moral corruption of sectarian conscience, at the heart of Madison's worries about faction, is itself a kind of stereotyped thinking: the tendency to see others through the lenses of one's sectarian perceptions of a world divided into those that agree and disagree with these perceptions, as though civic virtue and vice track sectarian belief and disbelief. The arguments for toleration in Locke and Bayle—which American constitutional principles elaborate—were acutely conscious of the political evil to which this kind of circular thinking leads, creating stereotypes of good and evil that remake moral reality in their own Manichean image. Such intolerance, both Locke and Bayle insist, itself creates moral disorder, oppression, and resistance, which it claims to combat.[39] The political wrong in this case expresses the stereotyped Augustinian contempt for the

---

[36] See, e.g., *Brown v. Board of Education,* 347 U.S. 483 (1954).

[37] See *The Federalist,* pp. 58–59, 61, 64–65, 351–52.

[38] See, e.g., Robert Cover, "The Origins of Judicial Activism in the Protection of Minorities," 91 *Yale L.J.* 1287, 1294 (1982).

[39] See, e.g., John Locke *A Letter Concerning Toleration,* in *The Works of John Locke,* vol. 6 (London: Thomas Tegg, 1823), pp. 6–9; Pierre Bayle, *Philosophique Commentaire sur ces paroles de Jesus Christ "Contrain-les d'entree,"* in *Oeuvres Diverses de Mr. Pierre Bayle,* vol. 2 (A la Haye: Chez P. Husson et al., 1727), pp. 415–19.

moral powers of those with whom one conscientiously disagrees, as if all such disagreement must reflect a wantonly irrational and even diabolic will. This contempt itself creates the justification on which it feeds. However, this kind of contempt is the political evil that is combatted by both the substantive guarantees of the First Amendment and the constitutional structures shaped by the theory of faction, and is continuous with the forms of contempt expressed by the stigma condemned by the equal protection clause. Religious intolerance is, to this extent, the first suspect classification known to American law, and we best understand the equal protection clause when we connect it to the earlier historical tradition it assumes, elaborates, and, as we must now see, criticizes.

As was observed earlier, there was no more unpardonable breach of political republican faith by Madison and other founders than their failure to give expression to the principled constitutional scope of the theory of faction. The historian Edmund Morgan has suggested a disturbing analysis of this failure with particular relevance to distinguished Virginian constitutionalists (like Madison and Jefferson), namely, that Virginian republican

> ardor was not unrelated to their power over the men and women held in bondage. In the republican way of thinking as Americans inherited it from England, slavery occupied a critical, if ambiguous, position: it was the primary evil that men sought to avoid for society as a whole by curbing monarchs and establishing republics. But it was also the solution to one of society's most serious problems, the problem of the poor. Virginians could outdo English republicans as well as New England ones, partly because they had solved the problem: they had achieved a society in which most of the poor were enslaved.[40]

If so, Virginia republicans, even of the stature of Madison, remained too much under the sway of the classical republicanism they had otherwise thoroughly rejected as a model for American republican constitutionalism (see Chapter 2). Slavery was, of course, fundamental to the classical republics of the ancient world, and the thinking of Madison about their defects and the American alternative did not sufficiently address the need to construct a structure of arrangements free of this taint.[41] On the other hand, at the level of republican theory, Madison could not have made more clear to the constitutional convention that not only was slavery a political expression of faction but that it also expressed the worst such form; his words bear repeating yet again:

---

[40] Edmund S. Morgan, *American Slavery American Freedom: The Ordeal of Colonial Virginia* (New York: W.W. Norton, 1975), p. 381.

[41] Jefferson and Madison developed an essentially agrarian ideal of republican independence hostile to Hamilton's conception of a more diverse range of economic structures. See Lance Banning, *The Jeffersonian Persuasion: Evolution of a Party Ideology* (Ithaca, N.Y.: Cornell Univ. Press, 1978). The agrarian model may have blinded them to the structures of servile dependencies on which their model depended and the need to think about a more diverse range of economic alternatives not requiring such antirepublican structures. Certainly, abolitionist thought had focused on a broader conception of the economic structures supportive of republican ideals. See, in general, Eric Foner, *Free Soil, Free Labor, Free Men* (London: Oxford Univ. Press, 1970).

"We have seen the mere distinction of colour made in the most enlightened period of time, a ground of the most oppressive dominion ever exercised by man over man."[42] The "founders" of the Reconstruction amendments—by including the equal protection clause of the Fourteenth Amendment—brought to their task the republican political morality of the antebellum abolitionists that regarded slavery as an inexcusable breach of the very foundations of republican political legitimacy, namely, respect for the equal inalienable rights of all persons subject to power.[43] Their tone was certainly not that of Madison's measured political rationalism, but their republican political theory was the same and their analysis of the depth of the political problem more incisive and probing. John A. Bingham—the author of the equal protection clause as it appears in section 1 of the Fourteenth Amendment[44]—argued that the amendment was needed in order to protect "the inborn rights of every person,"[45] reflecting the views of other abolitionist Americans that "a *just* God, can't permit a nation to [reject?] these just inalienable rights, without measuring but sooner or later the *penalty.*"[46] As Illinois Senator Richard Yates argued in debate, the Declaration of Independence, the cornerstone of American government, "proclaimed the great doctrine which we stand maintaining to-day, that all men are created, not by man but by God himself, equal and entitled to equal rights and privileges."[47] Pursuant to this doctrine, rights and privileges under the Constitution could not be

> accorded only to citizens of "some class," or "some race," or "of the least favored class," or "of the most favored class," or of a particular complexion, for these distinctions were never contemplated as possible in fundamental civil rights, which are alike necessary and important to all citizens.[48]

The 1868 "founders" applied Madisonian political morality not only to the analysis and rectification of the unconscionable wrong of slavery, but also to the noxious political attitudes that had grown up around its constitutional legitimation in succeeding generations of Americans. Founders of Madison's generation may have accepted a theory of racial differences in talents of the sort that Jefferson had tentatively suggested in *Notes on the State of Virginia,*[49]

---

[42] Farrand, ed., *Records of Federal Convention,* vol. 1, p. 135.

[43] See, for illuminating discussion, Nelson, *The Fourteenth Amendment,* pp. 13–39, 64–90.

[44] U.S. Constitution, Amendment XIV, section 1 states: "All persons born or naturalized in the United States, and subject to the jurisdiction thereof, are citizens of the United States and of the state wherein they reside. No state shall make or enforce any laws which shall abridge the privileges or immunities of citizens of the United States; nor shall any state deprive any person of life, liberty, or property without due process of law; nor deny to any person within its jurisdiction the equal protection of the law."

[45] Quoted at Nelson, *The Fourteenth Amendment,* p. 66.

[46] Ibid., p. 65.

[47] Ibid., p. 73.

[48] Ibid.

[49] See, e.g., Thomas Jefferson, *Notes on the State of Virginia,* in William Peden, ed. (New York: W. W. Norton, 1954), pp. 138–43.

but they also thought, as Jefferson had also argued, that blacks were morally equal subjects of the moral sense[50] and that slavery was therefore an abominable deprivation of inalienable human rights. Jefferson—who was, like Madison, a slaveholder—put the point unequivocally:

> Can the liberties of a nation be thought secure when we have removed their only firm basis, a conviction in the minds of the people that these liberties are of the gift of God? That they are not to be violated but with his wrath? Indeed I tremble for my country when I reflect that God is just: that his justice cannot sleep for ever: that considering numbers, nature and natural means, a revolution of the wheel of fortune, an exchange of situation, is among possible events: that it may become probable by supernatural interference! The Almighty has no attribute which can take side with us in such a contest.[51]

Indeed, slavery was not only intrinsically immoral but its immorality was also connected to the consequence of more generalized political attitudes:

> The parent storms, the child looks on, catches the lineaments of wrath, puts on the same airs in the circle of smaller slaves, gives a loose to his worst of passions, and thus nursed, educated, and daily exercised in tyranny, cannot but be stamped by it with odious peculiarities. The man must be a prodigy who can retain his manners and morals undepraved by such circumstances. And with what execration should the statesman be loaded, who permitting one half the citizens thus to trample on the rights of the other, transforms those into despots, and these into enemies, destroys the morals of the one part, and the amor patriae of the other.[52]

Jefferson anticipated in this case what in fact happened in the slaveholding parts of America, the emergence of what abolitionist political morality properly analyzed as the moral corruption that sustained belief in the legitimacy of slavery—full-blown racist theories of race-linked moral incapacities that removed slaves entirely from the scope of Lockean republican morality.[53]

The abstract imperative of the equal protection clause was to require that *all* political power that is exercised by the states be reasonably justifiable to *all* persons who are subject to its power in terms of respect for rights and pursuit

---

[50] See, e.g., ibid., pp. 142–43.

[51] Ibid., p. 163.

[52] Ibid., pp. 162–63.

[53] See, generally, Eric L. McKitrick, ed., *Slavery Defended: The Views of the Old South* (Englewood Cliffs, N.J.: Prentice-Hall, 1963); Michael D. Biddiss, ed., *Gobineau: Selected Political Writings* (New York: Harper & Row, 1971). Locke had argued that slavery was only justified when people attack one's rights by putting themselves in an unjust state of war, and extended only to such cases and not beyond it (for example, to the children of an unjust aggressor). See, e.g., John Locke, *The Second Treatise of Government,* in Locke, *Two Treatises of Government,* Peter Laslett, ed. (Cambridge: Cambridge Univ. Press, 1960), pp. 301–3 (secs. 22–24). See, for commentary, Ruth W. Grant, *John Locke's Liberalism,* (Chicago: Univ. of Chicago Press, 1987), pp. 67–68, 71. Locke's argument could not justify slavery as it existed in America. See *idem,* p. 68, n.22.

of the common interests of all. Consistent with the abolitionist political morality and analysis that motivated this imperative,

> there was one point on which nearly all Republicans [the 1868 "founders"] agreed. No Republican was prepared, as a matter of general principle, to defend as rational a distinction grounded in race. Republicans found "prejudice against race" irrational and "unaccountable," having "its origins in the greed and selfishness of a fallen world" and "belong[ing] to an age of darkness and violence."[54]

The Lockean theory of political legitimacy—assumed by the 1787 founders and 1868 founders—affords the requisite moral discrimination indispensable to understanding the condemnation of such stigmatizing prejudices by equal protection and the connections of such condemnation to the earlier constitutional traditions on which it builds.

Reasonable justification requires, as we have seen, a range of guarantees that validate our central capacities for personal and moral self-government. We identify substantive rights of conscience, free speech, and privacy, for example, by reference to the underlying capacities for moral independence in thought, speech, and action that require protection from the kind of imposition of sectarian orthodoxies that entrenches unreasonable structures of arbitrary hierarchy and privilege. Failure to respect the rights of reasonable self-government is a kind of contempt or of insult to such valued capacities.

The critical analysis of American historical experience by the abolitionists, who had maintained faith with their republican heritage, was that slavery in the American South was now supported by the corrupt moral attitudes Jefferson had anticipated, namely, a grotesque theory of intrinsic racial differences in basic moral competences.[55] Based on a morally irrelevant fact (race), many southerners alleged that an entire class of people lacked elementary moral capacities and were so childlike and even animalistic that they are, as Aristotle called them, "by nature slaves."[56] The "founders" of the equal protection clause, reflecting this analysis, knew that the 1787 Constitution itself bore responsibility for giving rise to the political force that such factionalized attitudes enjoyed in support of slavery, and that these factionalized racist attitudes would continue after the Thirteenth Amendment (1865) abolished slavery and, if allowed unregulated expression in law, would justify imposing a de facto, if not de jure, slavery status.[57] They understood that some states might deprive blacks of basic civil rights on the racist ground that, lacking elementary moral capacities, blacks could not be accorded equal civil rights (the Black Codes). The consensus reached by the "founders" of the Fourteenth Amendment was that their work in rectifying the legitimation of slavery by

[54] Nelson, *The Fourteenth Amendment,* p. 124.

[55] See, e.g., Stanley M. Elkins, *Slavery* (New York: Grosset & Dunlap, 1959), pp. 164–193.

[56] Aristotle, *The Politics of Aristotle,* Ernest Barker, trans. (New York: Oxford Univ. Press, 1962), p. 13.

[57] See, in general, Nelson, *The Fourteenth Amendment.*

the 1787 Constitution could not be complete unless they constitutionally addressed the political consequences of the Constitution's complicity with this republican political immorality, namely, the expression through law of these types of illegitimate political attitudes. They regarded the equal protection clause as forbidding these attitudes from ever enjoying the force of law. Laws using racial classifications that expressed such attitudes were consequently suspect in the way that we now associate with the strict scrutiny of legislative classifications.[58]

The basis for this constitutionally enforceable judgment was that republican principles of equality condemned as immoral the political expression of racist attitudes.[59] The racist attitudes in question used a morally arbitrary and immutable fact (race) as the basis for the unjustified and stereotypical claim that the class of people thus identified lacked elementary moral capacities, but this claim was in fact the viciously circular product of the long-standing institution of slavery, which itself deprived people of the rights and opportunities necessary to the exercise of capacities of moral self-government. In effect, the very consequences of the unjust practice of moral degradation were with vicious circularity adduced as the grounds to justify this practice[60] or its functional equivalent (the Black Codes). The 1868 "founders" identified the political expression of these attitudes as another kind of contempt for human rights—not a contempt for one kind of right but a denial of the existence in a class of persons of all such moral powers across the board. The use of racial classifications to express judgments of race-linked incapacities failed reasonably to justify political power, indeed subverted capacities of moral self-government and entrenched the most unreasonable form of arbitrary hierarchy, what Madison had rightly called "the most oppressive dominion ever exercised by man over man."[61] This type of moral contempt not only deprives persons of the equal rights that are their due, but its denial of their moral status as persons also independently insults their moral dignity.

Each aspect of stricter scrutiny under the equal protection clause (fundamental rights and suspect classification analysis) thus gives expression to the requirement of reasonable justification. Each aspect responds to a different threat to equal protection. Fundamental rights analysis, on the model of the equal liberty principles of the Bill of Rights extended by the Fourteenth Amendment to the states, ensures the required respect for basic rights of reasonable self-government. Suspect classification scrutiny strikes down laws or policies that explicitly or implicitly use stereotypes that deny, in the way abolitionists identified in stigmatizing racial classiciations, the human dignity necessary for a creature to be capable of any rights at all.

Finally, equal protection jurisprudence has a residual requirement. All laws (not abridging fundamental rights or using suspect classifications) must

---

[58] See, e.g., *Palmore* v. *Sidoti*, 466 U.S. 429 (1984).

[59] See, e.g., Elkins, *Slavery*. pp. 169–70.

[60] See, e.g., Biddiss, ed., *Gobineau: Selected Political Writings;* McKitrick, ed., *Slavery Defended*.

[61] Farrand, ed., *Records of Federal Convention*, vol. 1, p. 135.

have a fair rational basis for the classifications they use. This constitutional requirement suggests that even fair interest group politics (fully consistent with fair representation) may nonetheless be inconsistent with the requirement of reasonable public justification of all forms of political power, which all legislation must express.[62] That constitutional mandate, however judicially underenforced, is happily explained by the account of equal protection proposed here, which requires that all political power must be reasonably justifiable in terms of either respect for rights or pursuit of the public good.

Suspect classification analysis is the most arresting and absorbing contribution of the Reconstruction amendments to American constitutional argument. Its interpretive problems are so different from those so far discussed that the remaining interpretive discussion of this chapter is devoted to it. Its innovativeness should not, however, blind us to its continuity with the larger ambitions of the 1787 founders; the 1868 "founders" used the critical history of American constitutionalism since the founding in order to promote a deeper and more principled analysis of the theory of faction. American constitutionalism was, as already stated (Chapter 4), notable for the ways in which it distrusted the kinds of "natural" group identities on which previous political thought often had depended for political community, and used and promoted heterogeneity as a device to achieve the deeper levels of consensus necessary to realize its new conception of a constitutional community of principle. The American experience of slavery from the 1787 Constitution to the Civil War compelled republican Americans critically to come to terms with the narrow vision the founders brought to this project, a vision that led them to make the most vicious form of "natural" identity (race) invisible in this larger project.

This narrow vision was, of course, implicit in the larger pattern of European humanist thought that the American founders both assumed and elaborated. James Baldwin, an American black who lived much of his life in Europe, ably summarized the different place of race in the European and American political experience:

> Europe's black possessions remained—and do remain—in Europe's colonies, at which remove they represented no threat whatever to European identity. If they posed any problem at all for the European conscience, it was a problem which remained comfortingly abstract: in effect, the black man, *as a man,* did not exist for Europe. But in America, even as a slave, he was an inescapable part of the general social fabric and no American could escape having an attitude toward him.[63]

Americans thus had to confront the tensions implicit in their European heritage:

---

[62] See, e.g., Cass R. Sunstein, "Naked Preferences and the Constitution," 84 *Col. L. Rev.* 1689 (1984).

[63] James Baldwin, *Notes of a Native Son* (Boston: Beacon Press, 1984), p. 170.

The idea of white supremacy rests simply on the fact that white men are the creators of civilization . . . and are therefore civilization's guardians and defenders. Thus it was impossible for Americans to accept the black man as one of themselves, for to do so was to jeopardize their status as [European] white men. But not so to accept him was to deny his human reality, his human weight and complexity, and the strain of denying the overwhelmingly undeniable forced Americans into rationalizations so fantastic that they approached the pathological. At the root of the American Negro problem is the necessity of the American white man to find a way of living with the Negro in order to be able to live with himself.[64]

Baldwin's view plausibly explains two remarkable facts about American constitutional history: first, how the 1787 founders could have even tolerated compromise on an issue of republican principle like slavery; and second, the importance of constitutional arguments, successfully made by and on behalf of black Americans, in the deeper understanding and realization of American constitutionalism for all Americans.

On the first point, we should find it astounding that Madison could bring himself to tolerate compromise over slavery with more evident ease than the compromise over equal state representation in the Senate to which he made extensive and repeated objections of republican principle at the constitutional convention.[65] It is at least plausible to suppose, as Baldwin's analysis suggests, that even an intellectual and moral leader among the founders like Madison could not bring the same force of conviction to slavery as to senatorial representation because his very brilliance and depth in elaborating the European humanist tradition limited natural sympathy with those mistakenly assumed to be outside that tradition. Jefferson had, after all, both urged abolition of slavery and the removal of emancipated blacks to separate colonies,[66] which suggests the same confusion of a cultural achievement (open, in principle, to all) and racial supremacy (closed and exclusive to the supreme race).

If the legitimation of slavery was constitutional original sin, the equal protection clause was a principled effort at redemption. As expressed in the equal protection clause of the Fourteenth Amendment, the abolitionist political morality resolved the contradiction between the consequences of tolerance of slavery and republican principle by critical use of the theory of faction to identity both a central defect in the 1787 Constitution itself and the pathological attitudes it had unleashed. Prejudices like racial degradation were not only expressly identified as factions but were forbidden expression through law. The evil here is the moral unreasonableness of the race-linked degradation of moral powers—a degradation that entrenches unnatural hierarchies of power and privilege, which makes them immune from evidence or criticism. The Fourteenth Amendment subjected to constitutional scrutiny and constraint

---

[64] Ibid., p. 172.

[65] See, e.g., Farrand, ed., *Records of Federal Convention*, vol. 1, pp. 446–50, 463–65; vol. 2, pp. 8–10.

[66] See Jefferson, *Notes on the State of Virginia,* pp. 137–38.

this most "natural" of group identities in promotion of the more nearly coherent realization of the community of principle.

The constitutional attack on race as a group identity has been the greatest test of principle of American constitutionalism and, when successful, its glory. As Baldwin suggests, arguments made by and on behalf of black Americans have played a leading role in modern American constitutional history in bringing Americans to a deeper understanding and realization of what a community of principle is. American and black identity have, as in no other multiracial nation, become one question. Another fact of our constitutional history that should astound us is that a group so stigmatized as political, social, and economic outcasts should have played the role of moral and constitutional leader to a nation. That confirms, to my way of thinking, the deepest aspiration of the American founding: that Americans would unite around a new conception of moral community, a community of principle that identifies its integrity by the quality of abstract and impartial justice it brings to the lives of each and every person subject to political power. Black Americans play a central role in the formation of modern American constitutional identity because they raise and continue to raise the most reasonable tests of the quality of our principles and thus of constitutional government itself. Have we been adequate to these tests?

The Unconstitutionality of Racial Segregation

The work of the "founders" of 1868, like those of 1787 and 1791, must itself be interpreted by later generations of Americans—consistent with the requirements of constitutionally legitimate argument, namely, the reasonable justification of political power to all on grounds of principle. The interpretation of equal protection requires us to address the appropriate kind and level of meaning to be ascribed to the clause. That issue may be usefully focused by interpretive investigation of one of the most important interpretive changes in the recent history of constitutional government, namely, the decision of a unanimous Supreme Court in 1954 to reverse the 1896 decision of the Court upholding the constitutionality of state-imposed racial segregation.[67]

Americans now largely agree (Raoul Berger perhaps excepted) that more abstract connotative meanings are to be preferred in the interpretation of the scope of congressional powers and enumerated rights like those of the First and Fourth Amendments. However, there is another level of interpretation about which there is more controversy, namely, over the interpretation of abstract constitutional guarantees like due process or equal protection or the prohibition on cruel and unusual punishments. These guarantees appeal to the most abstract kinds of ethical and political values. Due process is nothing less than the most abstract requirement of justice, giving people their due;

---

[67] See *Brown* v. *Board of Education*, 347 U.S. 483 (1954), reversing *Plessy* v. *Ferguson*, 163 U.S. 537 (1896).

equal protection states the core requirement of justice, treating like cases alike.

Controversy over interpretation of these guarantees is not over denotative versus connotative meaning, but over different levels of interpretation of connotative meaning. The equal protection clause, for example, may be taken to protect a wide range of different connotative meanings: some more concrete, others much more abstract. One such concrete interpretation forbids state-endorsed racial discrimination in a certain narrow range of civil rights (including equal access to the protection of life and property under criminal and civil law, but excluding rights to vote, to serve on juries, to go to integrated public schools, or to intermarry racially).[68] A more abstract interpretation forbids state-endorsed racial discrimination in distributing all rights and benefits but would not extend beyond racial discrimination.[69] A still more abstract interpretation forbids all state-endorsed prejudice through law, which might forbid other prejudices in addition to racism (e.g., sexism) but not protect inequality in the distribution of fundamental rights.[70] Finally, one of the most abstract interpretations forbids state use of all constitutionally unreasonable classifications, including both those that express constitutionally unreasonable prejudices and those that unjustly abridge fundamental rights.[71] The equal protection clause is subject to a wide range of such alternative connotative meanings, each of them amenable to even further interpretive discussion and refinement.

Which interpretation should be preferred? There are a few American advocates of the concrete interpretation view, who either reject all constitutional law that is inconsistent with such interpretations,[72] or urge the radical abandonment of any originalist concern with the founders' intent, calling, in its place, for an open-ended appeal to moral prophecy.[73] These views do not, however, represent either dominant conservative or liberal opinion in the United States. American conservatives defend, for example, the judiciary's prohibition of state-sponsored racial segregation,[74] although this application of the equal protection clause is outside the consensus of Berger's "founders."[75] Rather, dominant interpretive controversy is over different views of the preferred abstract interpretation (e.g., over whether the abstract prohibition on racial discrimination legitimates or forbids racial preferences,[76] or

---

[68] Raoul Berger takes this view. See Raoul Berger, *Government by Judiciary* (Cambridge, Mass.: Harvard Univ. Press, 1977).

[69] See, e.g., Justice Rehnquist's dissent applicable to both *In re Griffiths*, 413 U.S. 717, 729 (1973) and *Sugarman v. Dougall*, 413 U.S. 634, 649–94 (1973).

[70] See, e.g., Ely, *Democracy and Distrust*.

[71] See, e.g., David Richards, *Toleration and the Constitution*, (New York: Oxford Univ. Press, 1986), pp. 296–303.

[72] Berger, See *Government by Judiciary*.

[73] See Michael J. Perry, *The Constitution, the Courts, and Human Rights* (New Haven, Conn.: Yale Univ. Press, 1982).

[74] See Berger, *Government by Judiciary*.

[75] See Berger, *Government by Judiciary*, pp. 117–133.

[76] See, e.g., *Regents of Univ. of California v. Bakke*, 438 U.S. 265 (1978).

should be extended beyond racial to gender discrimination[77]). In order to understand why this is so, we must interpret not parrot history.

As we have seen, the Fourteenth Amendment was centrally motivated by the concern to limit state oppression of the blacks emancipated by the Thirteenth Amendment. The amendment inhibited the southern Black Codes that deprived blacks of civil liberties in order to maintain de facto, if not de jure, slave status. The debates in the Reconstruction Congress and the nationwide ratification debates show that the clauses of the Fourteenth Amendment embody the egalitarian moral values of the abolitionist movement.[78] The language of the Fourteenth Amendment, guaranteeing "privileges and immunities," "due process of law," and "equal protection," is quite general in form. These clauses were initially open to a wide range of interpretive disagreements over how they should be understood. There appeared to be, as Berger points out,[79] broad consensus that the equal protection clause forbids state deprivation of blacks' right to equal access to the criminal and civil law (which the Black Codes had egregiously violated), but there was no comparable consensus that the clause forbids racial classifications affecting other rights or state benefits in general. There was even more interpretive disagreement over how the quite general language of the clause would affect the legitimacy of nonracial classifications. Thus, although the general theme was that the equal protection clause required constitutionally reasonable classifications and that racial classifications depriving people of certain civil rights were per se unreasonable, there was disagreement about almost everything else.[80]

However, the natural question should be: what was the interpretive basis of the limited consensus reached by the founders? As we have seen, that judgment reflected the universal view among them that the expression through law of unjustified racist attitudes was unreasonable and therefore forbidden. If the "framers" of the equal protection clause went this far to condemn racial prejudice, we naturally must ask why they did not interpretively generalize their condemnation to include state-sponsored racial discrimination in political and social rights such as voting, jury duty, schooling, and intermarriage. Although some "framers" did, most others did not.[81] We must understand their interpretation of the most abstract connotation of the equal protection clause contextually: the common sense of the late nineteenth century was shaped by the now-discredited racist and sexist science of Social Darwinism.[82] Although this theory would not justify the deprivation of basic

---

[77] See, e.g., *Craig v. Boren*, 429 U.S. 190 (1976).

[78] See, in general, Nelson, *The Fourteenth Amendment*.

[79] See Berger, *Government by Judiciary*, pp. 1–19, 407.

[80] See Nelson, *The Fourteenth Amendment*.

[81] See ibid.

[82] See, e.g., Richard Hofstadter, *Social Darwinism in American Thought* (Boston: Beacon Press, 1944); John Higham, *Strangers in the Land* (New York: Atheneum, 1967); John S. Haller, Jr., *Outcasts from Evolution* (New York: McGraw-Hill, 1971); Thomas F. Gossett, *Race: The History of an Idea in America* (New York: Schocken Books, 1965); Stephen Jay Gould, *Mismeasure of Man* (New York: W.W. Norton, 1981).

civil liberties, it explained racial differences in a way that other distinctions among races did not appear similarly unreasonable. Thus, the scope of suspect classification scrutiny was truncated. When *Plessy* v. *Ferguson*[83] validated state-imposed racial segregation as a noninvidious and thus nonsuspect racial classification, it relied on this theory.[84] However, that interpretation of the proper scope of the equal protection clause was equally contestable in both 1868, the date of the Fourteenth Amendment, and 1896, the date *Plessy* v. *Ferguson* was decided.[85]

If *Plessy* rested on the then-dominant ideology of Social Darwinian race differences, *Brown* v. *Board of Education*[86] (which overruled *Plessy*) reflected the thorough discrediting of those assumptions. Not only did critical science come to regard those assumptions as factually unwarranted,[87] but we also realized that the widespread belief in those assumptions reflected neither factual nor moral reality. Rather, it reflected the ideological need for rationalizing the justification of societies already committed to practices of racial domination in either the social fabric of segregation at home or imperialist designs over "inferior" peoples abroad.[88] The quintessence of this evil was, of course, the racial genocide of Nazi Germany, in which racist science was wedded to the goal of racial purification.[89] A critical public opinion thus crystallized that the science of racial differences—which underlay cases like *Plessy*—did not reflect any natural or moral reality of racial differences, but ideologically created inequalities where none naturally or justly existed.[90] The racial classifications, which expressed these attitudes, were now interpreted as perfectly irrational. The most abstract moral imperative of the equal protection clause—that reasonable classifications serve constitutionally acceptable purposes—now required that state-imposed segregation (which maintains a

---

[83] 163 U.S. 537 (1896).

[84] See generally Charles A. Lofgren, *The Plessy Case* (New York: Oxford Univ. Press, 1987).

[85] See *Plessy* v. *Ferguson*, 163 U.S. at 533 (J. Harlan, dissenting).

[86] 347 U.S. 483 (1954).

[87] See, e.g., Gunnar Myrdal, *An American Dilemma* (New York: Harper & Row, 1962), pp. 83–153; Gossett, *Race,* pp. 409–30; Gould, *Mismeasure of Man* (1981); N.J. Block and Gerald Dworkin, eds., *The IQ Controversy* (New York: Pantheon, 1976).

[88] See, e.g., Elkins, *Slavery;* Myrdal, *American Dilemma;* Edmund S. Morgan, *American Slavery American Freedom;* David Brion Davis *The Problem of Slavery in Western Culture* (Ithaca, N.Y.: Cornell Univ. Press, 1966); idem, *Slavery and Human Progress* (New York: Oxford Univ. Press, 1984); Orlando Patterson, *Slavery and Social Death* (Cambridge, Mass.: Harvard Univ. Press, 1982). On the imperialist idea of "backward peoples" and the need for appropriate moral theories justifying colonial rule, see Eric Stokes, *The English Utilitarians in India* (Oxford: Clarendon Press, 1959); Philip Mason, *Patterns of Dominance* (London: Oxford Univ. Press, 1970); Frantz Fanon, *The Wretched of the Earth,* Constance Farrington, trans. (New York: Grove Press, 1963).

[89] See, e.g., Hannah Arendt, *The Origins of Totalitarianism* (New York: Harcourt Brace Jovanovich, 1973).

[90] See, e.g., Myrdal, *American Dilemma,* pp. 75–78, 101, 144–49, 207–9. For the transformation of critical public opinion, of the sort reflected in Myrdal's book, into public law, see Richard Kluger, *Simple Justice* (New York: Vintage, 1975).

racism now discredited as irrational and unjustly invidious) be struck down as per se unreasonable. *Brown* v. *Board of Education* so held.

Brown does not abandon the historic principles crystallized in 1868; rather, it interpreted them in a way that contextually interprets the equal protection clause's limited application then and the clause's broader application now. Berger's history, in contrast, tells us how a range of "founders" applied the equal protection clause and then claims that these views must forever freeze interpretive constitutional thought regarding the scope of equal protection.[91] However, this reading constitutionalizes a historically contingent fact without reading the background principles, understandings, and context that explain that fact and, even during the fact's own historical period, sharply qualified its meaning. For example, Berger's argument fails to explore the range of interpretive disagreement that existed even at that time over the consensus (e.g., some would have applied the clause to integrated public services), let alone the disagreement over almost every other important issue of equal protection that would later arise.[92] For this reason, his approach prevents us from reading interpretations of the equal protection clause either then or now as a historically continuous community of principle; that is, his approach prevents responsible interpretive attempts to articulate and implement the most constitutionally reasonable formulations of enduring constitutional principle.

This task requires that we read constitutional principles in ways responsive to changing economic circumstances (the commerce clause) or technological innovations (the Fourth Amendment). It also requires that we bring to the elaboration of arguments of constitutional principle, as we saw earlier in the areas of both enumerated and unenumerated rights (Chapters 5 and 6), those factual and normative arguments that can offer to all persons the most reasonable justifications for the exercise of the state's coercive power in light of the substantive and procedural guarantees of the written constitution. This justifiability creates the interpretive pressure to abstraction, that is, to ascribe to the constitutional text the more abstract connotations that are often alone capable of being justified to all in the required way. The factual and normative premises underlying the consensus of the 1868 "founders" are no longer reasonable interpretations of the abstract value of equal dignity that they respected, and the attempt to limit the interpretive scope of equal protection by adopting these premises insults the intelligence and morality of a community of principle that does find and should find this interpretation no longer reasonable.

The most powerful objection to Berger's approach is that it flouts the very principles that are fundamental to equal protection; that is, its interpretive approach serves the political expression of racist hatred and degradation. In fact, the very factual and normative assumptions that interpretively explain the 1868 consensus almost certainly reflect the false and vicious theory of

---

[91] For a related criticism of Berger's views on the death penalty, see Richards, *Toleration and the Constitution*, pp. 34–45.

[92] See Nelson, *The Fourteenth Amendment*.

racial differences that is the root of the racism that the equal protection clause was intended to inhibit. However, racism is an interpretive paradigm of a suspect classification because, as we saw earlier, facts and values are themselves factitiously manufactured by a history of unjust racist degradation and then used to justify further such degradation.[93] We now know that this corruptive evil digs deeper than the 1868 "founders" of the Reconstruction amendments understood, and that, indeed, their very acceptance of their generation's "commonsense" conception of certain race differences rests on this evil. Therefore, the enforcement of the 1868 consensus today would introduce a fundamental incoherence into the law of equal protection: it would enforce a now constitutionally unreasonable and anachronistic concrete interpretation that in fact perpetuates, indeed advances, the very evil that the clause's more abstract principle condemns. That is not an argument that either conservative or liberal constitutionalists today are inclined to accept, not because it is immoral or bad policy (although it is both) but because it is interpretively unprincipled.

Affirmative Action

The consensus of both conservative and liberal constitutional thought about the unconstitutionality of state-imposed racial segregation breaks down over other issues of the interpretation of equal protection, for example, the constitutionality of racial classifications used in affirmative action programs and of nonracial classifications like gender. A good interpretive theory should clarify the areas of consensus and advance critical interpretive understanding of areas of dissension. The discussion begins with the issue of affirmative action and then turns to nonracial classifications like gender.

Affirmative action programs use racial classifications to define a class of persons, often a racial minority, who may be subject to different standards of evaluation and acceptace. For example, the grade point average required for admission to a law or medical school may be lower for minority candidates than that required for nonminorities.[94] If racial classifications were constitutionally forbidden entirely, then these sorts of programs would be constitutionally equated with de jure segregation, and would therefore be unconstitutional.

State-imposed racial segregation was subjected to the strict scrutiny test of

---

[93] See, e.g., Myrdal, *American Dilemma*, pp. 75–78, 101, 144–49, 207–9.

[94] The leading case on this issue is *Regents of Univ. of California* v. *Bakke*, 438 U.S. 265 (1978), which upheld the principle of affirmative action albeit invalidating the kind of plan (allocating a fixed number of places for admission to to minorities) used for admission to the Medical School of the University of California at Davis. Justice Powell, writing for the Court, objected more to the symbolism than the reality of the Davis plan because his opinion clearly allows state universities to reach the same result by giving appropriate weight to race among other considerations against which all applicants are to be assessed. If my argument about affirmative action is correct, Powell draws a distinction without a constitutional difference and the Davis plan should have been upheld as it stood.

equal protection review. Under that test, a law can pass constitutional muster only if it pursues a compelling and legitimate state purpose and does so neither overinclusively nor underinclusively.[95] A law is underinclusive when it omits some things from its scope of application that advance its purpose; conversely, a law is overinclusive when it includes some items that do not advance its purpose. In the analysis of suspect classifications, strict scrutiny is used in circumstances in which a law is likely to be motivated by the constitutionally forbidden purpose of irrational racial prejudice. In effect, strict scrutiny acts as a filter to check whether or not such a law could have a compelling nonracist justification. The racial classifications used in state-imposed racial segregation failed the test and were unconstitutional because they rested on wholly irrational racial distinctions. On the other hand, when the strict test does not apply, a highly deferential test of whether a law has a rational basis is applied. Under that test, both underinclusiveness and overinclusiveness are acceptable, and most laws pass such constitutional muster easily.

The critical issue of constitutional interpretation in this arena is whether *all* racial classifications should be subjected to the force of the strict test. However, this interpretive question, like all other questions of constitutional interpretation, cannot be addressed in a historical vacuum. Race has historically been the interpretive paradigm of a suspect class because of the facts of American history to which the equal protection clause was addressed, namely, slavery and the intractable racist attitudes to which it had given rise. Furthermore, the modern American interpretive consensus that racial segregation must be condemned arises, as we have seen, from the reasonable conviction that such attitudes improperly motivated segregation, degrading blacks in the way equal protection condemns. However, if a decision like *Brown* v. *Board of Education* is correctly decided, as it clearly is, then the principle of that decision must be accorded its full reasonable force.

Brown stands for the critical principle that the central mission of the Reconstruction amendments had not been achieved because racial segregation enjoyed the force of law and expressed and legitimated the moral degradation of blacks from their proper standing in a community of free and equal persons. *Brown* spoke directly to the special constitutional wrong of moral degradation in educational opportunity, the subjection of morally innocent children to substandard, shabby, and shallow education in support of a publicly legitimated conviction that they are unworthy and subhuman. A constitutional culture, really sensible of its complicity in this wrong to black Americans, could not, as a matter of principle, regard affirmative action programs as unconstitutional on equal protection grounds.

Equal protection requires that state classifications must be reasonable and condemns the expression through law of irrational racial hatred. However, the use of racial classifications in affirmative action programs, when read against the historical background of *Brown,* is not constitutionally unreason-

---

[95] The leading doctrinal exposition of these tests is Joseph Tussman and Jacobus tenBroek, "The Equal Protection of the Laws," 37 *Calif. L. Rev.* 341 (1949).

able in this way. There is no abstract moral or political right, for example, to be tested for admission to professional schools exclusively by one measure.[96] Schools offer complex educational services to both their students and the larger society, and their conception of the proper mix of a student body must serve the aims of good education and the larger social purposes that graduates render to the larger community. In light of American history, schools would be educationally irresponsible not to give some special weight to race in addition to other relevant considerations in determining composition of its student body both to make allowance for the special educational deprivations to which all blacks have been subjected, to establish the stature and standing of blacks as professionals, and to educate all students in the ethical responsibilities of citizens in a community of principle. This responsibility has particular force in law that can neither be properly taught nor practiced without the full participation of a group whose experience and arguments have shaped the best constitutional thought of the generation.

The racial classifications used in affirmative action programs are not analogous to those used in de jure segregation. The latter classifications expressed a long history of intractable prejudice against blacks, and the stringent requirements of the strict test skeptically monitor attempts to justify such laws on nonracist grounds. That skepticism does not properly attach to racial classifications that are not rooted in irrational hositility to racial groups, but that express the reasonable weight racial classifications should be given in programs that attack the continuing effects of our historical legacy of legitimating racial hatred through public law.

Nonracial Classifications (Gender)

The question of race in American history and culture may have opened a new chapter in the American experiment in constitutional controls of faction, but it would trivialize the constitutional struggle and achievement of coming to terms with race on grounds of principle to suppose that this issue can, should, or will end the discussion. The interpretive elaboration of the law of equal protection, like every other area of public law, creates a pressure to abstraction, that is, to work out the implications of arguments of principle in a reasonably justifiable way to all persons. Reasonable elaboration of race as an interpretive exemplar of a suspect classification has advanced our understanding of the depth of the problem in both the racial area (racial segregation, once constitutional, is now unconstitutional) and nonracial areas. That pattern of revision, reconsideration, and elaboration expresses the self-critical reflection of a community of principle on the enduring meaning of its binding historical understanding of the ways in which political power must reasonably be justified consistent with respect for human rights and pursuit of the public

[96] Cf. Ronald Dworkin, *Law's Empire* (Cambridge, Mass.: Harvard Univ. Press, 1986), pp. 387–97.

good. If the constitutional analysis of race is, as Americans believe, a major achievement and advance in the understanding of their community of principle, then its critical methods are a precious legacy of civilizing political argument that we have the responsibility to interpret as a general argument of principle available to all persons on equal terms.

Race has been the American interpretive exemplar of a suspect classification because of our history and experience (in Europe, the comparable issue would be anti-Semitism[97]). In the United States, critical reflection on the sources of the republican evil of slavery led the 1868 "founders" to identify and constitutionalize a new kind of analysis and principle that identified and condemned corruptive forms of faction that unreasonably degraded whole classes of persons from their rightful standing in a community of free and equal persons. The modern judiciary has properly met its distinctive institutional obligations among American constitutional structures when it acted as a forum of principle of reasoned public discourse for giving full effect to this argument of principle in contemporary circumstances, including its application in nonracial areas.

In 1869, John Stuart Mill's *The Subjection of Women*[98] powerfully explored the analogy of race and gender as a common form of unjust degradation of persons from their moral standing as free and equal. If Mill's argument was as reasonable as the comparable arguments about race, then it would require some kind of comparable constitutional scrutiny of gender as a suspect classification. It is not difficult to make a forceful argument for an analogy based on a common constitutional analysis and principle. The analysis begins with the traditional arguments for women's inferior moral capacities, and then turns to constitutional analysis and principle.

Gender has traditionally been regarded as defining women as capable of only one kind of life, namely, childbearing and childrearing within the home. The underlying belief as expressed universally among primitive peoples is that women have an inferior status relative to men, because they are passive, autochtonous creatures who are subject to the rhythms of nature, including uncontrollable and polluting menstrual flows and the burden of bearing and rearing children; indeed, the task of rearing children supposedly makes a woman a kind of child.[99] In contrast, men are thought of as having the capacity for independence of natural processes, developing and cultivating tools and culture and testing themselves in the public world of other mature and independent individuals. Woman's place, in this view, is defined by her limited

---

[97] See, for example, Jean-Paul Sartre, *Anti-Semite and Jew*, George J. Becker, trans. (New York: Grove Press, 1948).

[98] See John Stuart Mill, *The Subjection of Women*, Wendell Robert Carr, ed. (Cambridge, Mass.: MIT Press, 1970).

[99] See Michelle Z. Rosaldo, "Woman, Culture, and Society: A Theoretical Overview," in Michelle Z. Rosaldo and Louise Lamphere, eds., *Woman, Culture, and Society* (Stanford, Calif.: Stanford Univ. Press, 1974), pp. 17–42; Nancy Chodorow, "Family Structure and Feminine Personality," in idem, pp. 43–66; Sherry B. Ortner, "Is Female to Male as Nature Is to Culture?", in idem, pp. 67–87.

nature; to depart from this pattern is literally unnatural, a thought expressed among primitive peoples by the idea that deviational women are witches.[100]

These ideas have been buttressed by philosophical and religious thinkers, as well as by supposed scientific theories. Aristotle, for example, placed women below men but above slaves, so that considerations of equal justice (with men) do not apply to women.[101] Indeed, Aristotle thought of women as biologically defective human male beings, the result of an accident to the male sperm, which contained the full human potential for intellectual knowledge, whereas women's capacities were limited to their procreational and nurturing function.[102] The Aristotelian view, absorbed into Christian philosophical thought by Thomas Aquinas,[103] was confirmed for Christian and Jewish thought by scripture as well. The Old Testament thus is replete with prohibitions enforcing ideas of women's place,[104] ideas carried forward by St. Paul.[105] Finally, later scientific thought, even into the late nineteenth century, mustered data about cranial capacity and evolutionary differentiation that allegedly proved that women, like blacks, were inferior[106] and that feminism, if unchecked, would cause the dissolution of western civilization.[107]

Such an ancient and powerful tradition of thought has understandably led to a traditional conception of women as not persons in the full sense.[108] Literally, moral personality, involving ideas of the capacity for independent and disinterested moral reflection, is supposed to be by definition male. Women, limited by nature exclusively to their sexual processes (as wives and mothers), are conceived of as having moral and legal identity only by their relation to full moral persons, that is, their husbands.[109] Being childlike, women are supposed to be incapable of public life in the world of work and

---

[100] See Rosaldo and Lamphere, *Woman, Culture, and Society*, pp. 34, 38, 86, 290–91; see also Elizabeth Janeway, *Man's World, Woman's Place* (New York: Delta, 1971), pp. 119–33.

[101] On the inferior nature of women and their justifiable inferior status, see Aristotle, *Politics*, 1.12–13.

[102] See Aristotle, *The Generation of Animals*, 737a in Jonathan Barnes, ed., *The Complete Works of Aristotle* vol. 1 (Princeton, N.J.: Princeton University Press, 1984).

[103] See Thomas Aquinas, *Summa Theol.* I, q. 91, 1; I, q. 99, 2; III, q. 32, 4, excerpted in Anton C. Pegis, ed. *Introduction to St. Thomas Aquinas* (New York: Modern Library, 1948). For commentary, see Eleanor C. McLaughlin, "Equality of Souls, Inequality of Sexes: Woman in Medieval Theology," in Rosemary R. Reuther, ed., *Religion and Sexism* (New York: Simon & Schuster, 1974), pp. 213–66, pp. 215–21.

[104] See Phyllis Bird, "Images of Women in the Old Testament," pp. 41–88; also Judith Hauptman, "Images of Woman in the Talmud," pp. 184–212: both in Reuther, ed., *Religion and Sexism*.

[105] See, e.g., I *Corinthians* 11, I *Corinthians* 14. For a sympathetic reading of these and other passages, see Constance F. Parvey, "The Theology and Leadership of Women in the New Testament," in Reuther, ed., *Religion and Sexism*, pp. 117–49.

[106] See John S. Haller and Robin M. Haller, *The Physician and Sexuality in Victorian America* (Urbana: Univ. of Illinois Press, 1974), pp. 48–61.

[107] See ibid., pp. 61–87.

[108] Cf. Simone de Beauvoir's concept of woman as "the Other," in Simone de Beauvoir, *The Second Sex*, H.M. Parshley, trans. (New York: Vintage, 1974), pp. xv–xxxiv.

[109] See Leo Kanowitz, *Women and the Law* (Albuquerque: Univ. of New Mexico Press, 1969), pp. 35–99.

politics. Accordingly, women on paternalistic grounds are by law or convention denied the right to participate in that world, or are given that right only in special areas on terms of protections not accorded to men.[110]

Against this moral and political background, Mill argued that both the assumptions about woman's nature and the weight given them are unreasonable in the same way as the comparable views about race.[111] In particular, the traditional view of women's inferior moral nature—like views of racial differences—is viciously and immorally circular. Traditional societies deprive women of the range of rights, benefits, and opportunities accorded to men, including those to education, culture, employment, politics, and the like, and then take facts about women that result from such stereotypically unequal treatment as dispositive of women's moral powers as persons. In effect, women are deprived of inalienable human rights due persons (analogous to enslavement of blacks), and then the apparent talents, interests, and propensities of such deprivation (enslavement) are taken to be the measure of their intrinsically subpersonal moral capacities. Moreover, the argument of moral inferiority is as factually and normatively unreasonable in the area of gender as it is for race. Treating women as inferior could rest on a scintilla of rationality if it were based on some testing of women under conditions free of coercion, intimidation, and exploitation, but the tradition irrationally and immorally refuses to accord them this opportunity. Such irrationality bespeaks a prejudice that takes pleasure in the unjust degradation of the moral powers of half the human species.[112]

Degrading women—however rooted in long-standing traditions—fails to take seriously women's inalienable right to personal and ethical self-government. Indeed, in contemporary circumstances the enforcement on them of the traditional moral view is a particularly grievous and debilitating imposition of what are, in essence, unquestioned moral orthodoxies of women's inferior moral nature that cannot and should not reasonably enjoy the force and support of law. The imposition of such views ideologically entrenches arbitrary structures of "natural" gender hierarchy and domination, and subverts the intellectual and moral foundations of the integrity of women in coming to know, claim, and pursue their rights and interests in a community of free and equal persons.

The protection of women from "natural" gender hierarchy, though recent, is at the very heart of the larger project of American constitutionalism as we have come to know and understand it in this book. The very legitimacy of American constitutionalism was its constructive aspiration, however flawed and imperfect, reasonably to justify political power to all persons in terms of respect for rights and pursuit of the common interests of all. The equal protection clause advanced that project by its criticism and rectification of cor-

---

[110] See ibid., pp. 7–99.

[111] My argument of principle in the spirit of Mill's *Subjection of Women* is here independently developed. My argument, in contrast to Mill's, is not founded on utilitarianism.

[112] See ibid., pp. 21–29.

ruptive abuses of political power. Traditional treatment of women reflects factionalized prejudices, and the modern judiciary has justifiably recognized women's reasonable claims to protection from prejudice by scrutinizing gender classifications with increasing vigor.[113]

These remarks, comparing race and gender as suspect classifications, have been fairly schematic. Closer examination of the analogy will justify our additional attention, because it clarifies the foundation of the constitutional analysis at issue, and it shows why the model of a defectively majoritarian political process permits at best an imperfect understanding of these issues. Ely's model of equal protection, as we earlier saw, had critical defects because it took this view. Ackerman has recently developed a similar model that is objectionable for similar reasons.[114]

Ackerman argues that constitutionally legitimate judicial protection of minorities secures a politically pluralist majoritarianism in which all groups have the political right to realize their ends unencumbered by unfair bargaining disadvantages. From this perspective, Ackerman argues that the discreteness and insularity of racial minorities in the United States may no longer be bargaining disadvantages. The group solidarity among blacks—which originated from their discreteness and insularity—may at least in contemporary circumstances give them an effective bargaining advantage even over comparably sized groups unencumbered by bargaining disadvantages. In contrast, various nonracial groups, whose historical situation robs them of the bargaining advantages of group solidarity originating in such discreteness and insularity, may, for Ackerman, require special protection—for example, women (discrete and diffuse), homosexuals (both anonymous and somewhat insular), and victims of poverty (both diffuse and anonymous).

The political process model invoked by Ackerman, like that of Ely, fails interpretively to explain even the central cases of the constitutional evils condemned by the equal protection clause. Ackerman thus focuses on comparative bargaining disadvantages, but these disadvantages hardly rise to the level of justifying the kind of absolute condemnation of certain kinds of racist and sexist legislation that is typical of modern equal protection jurisprudence. Ackerman's theory essentially seeks to equalize the bargaining positions of groups of roughly similar numbers, presumably to yield better the utilitarian advantages of a pluralist political process in which all groups have equal access over time to building coalitions, logrolling, and the like. However, this theory does not recommend and thus does not fit the constitutional concern with racism per se. The equalization of bargaining power model would call only for greater political weight of claims, not for an absolute protection against certain kinds of injuries. Where the political bargaining model focuses on a continuum of bargaining advantages and their equalization, the law of equal protection con-

---

[113] See, e.g., *Craig v. Boren*, 429 U.S. 190 (1976); *Frontiero v. Richardson*, 411 U.S. 677 (1973). For discussion, see David Richards, *The Moral Criticism of Law* (Encino, Calif.: Dickenson-Wadsworth, 1977), pp. 162–78.

[114] On Ely, see earlier discussion in this chapter. For Ackerman, see, e.g., Ackerman, "Beyond *Carolene Products*."

demns as qualitatively evil certain kinds of political actions. That evil cuts deeper than the political powerlessness associated with it, and we can understand it only if we interpret the political power issues as themselves consequences of this substantive moral evil. However, to understand this evil, we must examine the analogy between race and gender not in terms of political models of defective majoritarian processes, but from the perspective of the ethical ideal of equality that is fundamental to constitutional legitimacy.

The Analogy between Race and Gender

The clarity of the constitutional perception of race as a suspect classification—which has if anything grown with time (consider the interpretive development from *Plessy* to *Brown*)—is rooted in at least five characteristics that naturally center on race. First, race is naturally thought of as an immutable fact for which persons bear no personal responsibility; second, it is typically salient, something obvious to everyone. Third, race has been a historically familiar ground of immoral prejudice, the basis of both stereotyping and degrading assumptions of moral incapacity. Fourth, race is in fact irrelevant to any legitimate state purpose, and fifth, black people in the United States have been traditionally powerless, either deprived of their constitutionally guaranteed right to vote by blatantly unconstitutional racial prejudice, or—when their right to vote was belatedly guaranteed by the Voting Rights Act of 1965—their voting power was undermined by the pervasive force of racial prejudice (prejudiced people will not recognize common interests with them, and thus not form with them the democratic coalitions typical of normal interest group politics).

These five characteristics relate to the nature of the injury to moral personality that racial prejudice inflicts. The injury is associated with the nature of prejudice itself as an operative force in social life. Prejudice is thus defined in the social psychological literature as a negative attitude toward groups and members of groups not based on—indeed resistant to—facts,[115] which marks prejudice as a kind of irrationality. However, the injurious irrationality of prejudice is not mere cognitive conservatism—the tendency of an overburdened mind to use crude generalizations[116]—but the distinctive nature and force of the inflexible stereotypes[117] that prejudice expresses. In particular, the stereotypical judgments expressed by prejudice, in themselves rationalize conduct to which we are already committed,[118] conduct premised on degrading assumptions of moral incapacity. The moral irrationality of such operative

[115] For a list of some current definitions along these lines, see Howard J. Ehrlich, *The Social Psychology of Prejudice* (New York: John Wiley & Sons, 1973), pp. 3–4.

[116] See Gordon W. Allport, *The Nature of Prejudice* (Garden City, N.Y.: Doubleday Anchor, 1958), pp. 9–10.

[117] Cf. Ehrlich, *Social Psychology of Prejudice,* pp. 20–60.

[118] See Allport, *Nature of Prejudice,* p. 187.

prejudices is not their factual falsity (some may be true[119]), but their misdirected emphasis on some facts and denial of others in support of assumptions of moral incapacity themselves without rational basis. These assumptions in turn create the thing on which they feed, the vicious circularity Myrdal characterizes as follows:

> The Negro is judged to be fundamentally incorrigible and he is, therefore, kept in a slum existence which, in its turn, leaves the imprint upon his body and soul which makes it natural for the white man to believe in his inferiority.[120]

Prejudice, thus understood, is morally irrational in the sense that it injures the capacity for moral personality, the basis of respect for persons as ethical beings. The nature of the injury is defined by the moral interests it frustrates, for example, our interests in self-determination in a community of equal respect. By definition, prejudice condemns the stereotyped group to the terms of the stereotype, a point aptly put by Sartre by reference to French anti-Semitism: "having qualities and a fate *attached* to them—to be Jews as a stone is a stone."[121] By thus reducing the wide range of individual difference and diversity to one granitic fact (e.g., race or religious background), prejudice not only distorts reality, but remakes it in a Manichean image of moral vice[122] that imputes to the target group incapacities of moral personality. That Manichean motivation is the key to the moral irrationality that defines racism and anti-Semitism as distinctive sorts of political and constitutional evils, condemned as such by the equal protection clause.

Earlier in this book, this constitutional evil was compared to the related evil of religious intolerance that was condemned by the religion clauses of the First Amendment, clauses that independently condemn anti-Semitism as a violation of the equal liberties of conscience they protect. The equal protection clause builds on this moral tradition, which is shown by the way in which it concurrently condemns anti-Semitism. However, the special force of the equal protection clause appears when anti-Semitism is not a purely religious intolerance, but is associated—as it was in Nazi Germany—with racist assumptions as well: on this view, Jews are not a religion, but a distinct racial group.[123] The condemnation of anti-Semitism, in this characteristically European form, is one with the condemnation of racism. The condemnation is not built on the Manichean assumption of a willfully disordered conscience, but on a more fundamental Manichean assumption, that a certain group lacks moral capacities across the board (irrespective of their will). In this case, the irrationality is the compulsive ascription of moral incapacities along stereotypical lines in a way that itself injures moral capacities never accorded any fair

---

[119] See ibid., p. 188.
[120] Myrdal, *American Dilemma* p. 101; cf. idem, pp. 75–78, 207–9.
[121] Sartre, *Anti-Semite and Jew,* p. 108.
[122] See ibid., pp. 39–41.
[123] See, e.g. Lucy S. Dawidowicz, *The War Against the Jews 1933–1945* (New York: Holt, Rinehart & Winston, 1975), pp. 3–47.

measure of equal respect. Legislation, reflecting this sort of prejudice, is a paradigm of constitutional unreasonableness, because it affronts constitutional ideals of equal respect in the most directly damaging way: rather than fairly extending equal respect to persons on fair terms, it degrades a class of persons from the equal respect that is their due as persons.

Race is the interpretive exemplar of a suspect classification because it naturally combines five features: immutability, salience, degrading prejudice, irrelevance to legitimate state purposes, and powerlessness. *Degrading prejudice* is, in my view, the essential constitutional evil condemned by the equal protection clause, which suggests that the other four features are elaborations or consequences or frequent concomitants of this evil, but not similarly constitutionally fundamental. Certainly, *irrelevance to legitimate state purposes* elaborates the theme of moral irrationality; that is, it is because race is not, in fact, a proxy for any factual difference relevant to legitimate state purposes that its use is, in part, understandably suspect. However, many other constitutionally acceptable legislative generalizations, used by the state, are at least as crude and inaccurate, which suggests that there is some deeper moral motive for our suspicion of racial classifications. That motive is the way in which such factual inaccuracy serves the constitutional evil of degrading prejudice; that is, the facts under consideration in themselves reflect a long history of prejudice and cannot justly therefore be used (as they are) in support of such prejudice.

Correspondingly, both the *immutability* and *salience* of race make the oppression of the target easier and less avoidable in line with the Manichean ideology that motivates it. However, degrading prejudice per se does not require immutable and salient targets. The constitutional evil may arise in contexts in which the target is not in the same way (as race) immutable or salient, but nonetheless subject to the same history of degrading prejudice (e.g., sexual preference). Neither is it, in principle, unjust for the state to distribute benefits and burdens to characteristics over which the individual has little control if the distribution is otherwise justifiable on grounds of distributive justice or the pursuit of the public good. If there were such a principle, then any reward of the exercise of talent for the public good would be immoral. Racism is evil not because it is based on an immutable characteristic, but because it serves an intrinsically immoral purpose, the degradation of moral personality. This is why the ameliorative use of racial classifications in affirmative action programs should *not* raise constitutional problems. The reason is that these classifications serve no intrinsically immoral purpose; rather, they serve larger aims of justice and the public good.

Finally, *powerlessness* is often a consequence of the substantive moral irrationality of degrading prejudice. It is because degrading prejudices like racism have historically had such political force in the United States that blacks have been denied effective protection of their constitutional right to vote, and—even in those situations in which the right has been guaranteed—have been isolated from the usual logrolling coalitions of interest group politics. However, the constitutional evil of racism cuts deeper than political powerlessness, and thus would not be expunged even if blacks in contemporary circumstances enjoyed, as Ackerman argues that they do, political bargaining advantages in virtue of their discreteness and insularity. Even in these circumstances, laws motivated by degrading prejudice are intrinsically a constitutional evil in the terms condemned by the equal protection clause, and should and would be judicially condemned as such. Furthermore, surely not all forms of political powerlessness or bargaining disadvantages call for special constitutional scrutiny, but only those condemned because they are based on a moral evil like racism or violate fundamental rights (like the right to vote[124]).

The moral model proposed here offers a special interpretive richness in the understanding of the burgeoning constitutional jurisprudence that condemns stigmatizing gender classifications. In *Frontiero* v. *Richardson,*[125] for example, four justices of the Supreme Court were willing to regard gender as a fully suspect class on a par with race and thus subject to strict scrutiny. Because the law in question used gender as a basis for giving spouses of servicemen an advantage not accorded spouses of servicewomen, it used a suspect class, and was therefore unconstitutional (it was both overinclusive and underinclusive as a measure of dependency). Three other justices concurred in the judgment, but on the ground of the "rational basis" irrationality of the statute (they were unwilling to find gender to be a fully suspect class). Writing for the four justices, Brennan argued that, for purposes of suspect classification analysis, gender was exactly analogous to race, because it was an immutable fact, salient, and the object of a long-standing prejudice (the first, second, and third features of our analysis of suspect classifications). Prejudice based on gender is rooted, like racism, in the deprivation of basic rights of the person, because sexism stereotypically reduces the diversity and individuality of women to one crude fact (their gender) and makes on that basis degrading assumptions about their natural moral capacities as persons. In fact, gender, Brennan argues (the fourth feature), "bears no relation to ability to perform or contribute to society." Finally, whereas women now vote and are a statistical majority of the American populace, Brennan argues (the fifth feature) that their effective social powerlessness is shown by the minuscule numbers of women occupying positions of political power in the United States.

There are two natural objections to regarding gender as a suspect class on a par with race: political powerlessness, and the relevance of gender to some legitimate state aims. The former objection seems hardly decisive, but the latter is more weighty. However, both are clarified by the moral model of degrading prejudices.

The political powerlessness of blacks arises from both their prolonged disfranchisement by American racists and—even when blacks achieved the vote—the effective isolation of their minority voting power from larger political coalitions. However, although women acquired the legal right to vote later than blacks, they have exercised an effective right to vote for much

---

[124] See, e.g., *Reynolds* v. *Sims,* 377 U.S. 533 (1964).
[125] 411 U.S. 677 (1973).

longer. Their actual voting power is that of a statistical majority: they could potentially constitute a majority coalition dominating democratic politics (they are not required, unlike blacks, to engage in coalition politics to achieve working majorities). However, on the view of the evil of racism taken earlier, political powerlessness is, at best, a typical consequence of the underlying constitutional evil. Even if, as Ackerman suggests, blacks may now not be subject to bargaining disadvantages in the democratic political process, the evil of racist legislation remains as an independently cognizable constitutional wrong. Correspondingly, if sexism is a degrading prejudice, on a par with racism (as Brennan argues it is), then it is that degradation, in and of itself, that is a constitutional wrong, and that shapes the way in which powerlessness should be understood as a natural (though not inevitable) consequence or concomitant of this moral wrong. From this perspective, Brennan is surely correct that powerlessness—as an aspect of the evil of sexism—cannot be understood independent of the debilitating effects of a long history of degrading prejudice, which has so eroded the bases of self-respect that capacities for autonomous self-government and effective political action have been unjustly stunted. That has certainly been the effect of racism, and the statistics offered by Brennan suggest that it is true of sexism as well. If sexism is as much an insult and indignity to a just estimate of moral worth as racism, then it is a corresponding evil, and requires a corresponding remedy.

Because the theory of racial differences has been exploded, race appears simply irrelevant to any legitimate state purpose. However, it is natural to object that gender is not fully analogous, because there *are* gender differences. If so, it should be a central issue in the judicial interpretation of gender as a suspect classification question whether or to what extent reasonable arguments might be made for differences between genders that do not correlate with facts attributable to the vicious circularity that equal protection analysis clearly condemns. For example, in addition to biological differences like lactation and pregnancy, psychologists of sex differences point out various statistically significant differences between genders along parameters of various skills (verbal versus mathematical, nonspatial versus spatial), propensities (nurturant versus aggressive), and physique (physical strength).[126] Some of these characteristics are so obviously due to long-standing differences in treatment that they could not, without circularity, be appealed to as neutral facts on which gender distinctions might be reasonably justified. Others, touching on pregnancy and physical strength, might reasonably be thought less prone to such abusive circularity, and thus be the basis of gender distinctions that are constitutionally reasonable.

The Supreme Court has struggled with these issues in recent cases. In *Craig v. Boren*,[127] for example, the Court addressed a gender distinction that

---

[126] See, in general, Eleanor E. Maccoby and Carol N. Jacklin, *The Psychology of Sex Differences* (Stanford, Calif.: Stanford Univ. Press, 1974).

[127] 429 U.S. 190 (1976).

allowed women to drink beer at an earlier age (eighteen) than men (twenty-one) on the ground that there was a pertinent gender difference justifying the distinction, namely, that young men were much more statistically likely than women to drink to excess and to be arrested for drunk driving (the statistically significant difference is 2 percent versus 0.18 percent). A majority of the Supreme Court finally agreed that although gender was not a fully suspect class, it was sufficiently suspect (or semisuspect) that a mere rational basis for the gender distinction would not suffice. In fact, Brennan, writing for the Court, looked closely into the use of evidence of statistical differences between men and women and found them in this case inadequate to support the gender distinction. The Court's difficulty is not just the very low statistical incidence (2 percent) supporting the use of the male gender as a proxy for drinking and driving, but that there is no reliable gender difference (like pregnancy) that might reasonably justify the differential treatment. Attitudes to drinking may themselves be so much the product of sexist stereotype (the alcoholic male, the temperate female) that to rely on such statistics would effectively use the power of law to endorse and legitimate an unjustly degrading cultural stereotype in the same way that the state's use of ethnic stereotypes (based on the alcoholism rates of various ethnic groups) would rest on facts tainted by degrading cultural stereotypes. Although women are technically advantaged by the distinction (they can drink at eighteen while men cannot), such stereotypes are objectionable because of their reinforcement of the sexist image of women on the pedestal that is, in fact, a cage. If the effect of sexist prejudice, like racial prejudice (as we saw earlier), is to degrade stereotypically and diminish the diverse powers and competences of people, then it would be viciously circular to use the social reality created by those prejudices as the ground for perpetuating the injustice. It is that moral wisdom that explains the Court's searching analysis in *Craig* of alleged gender differences.

Whereas the Court has not extended comparably demanding analysis of alleged gender differences in other cases,[128] its approach in *Craig* is to be preferred, and is best explained interpretively by the moral model of degrading prejudice defended here. On this view, the stereotypical assumptions that prejudice often expresses may sometimes be factually supported, but they may still be morally irrational in that their factual support itself reflects a long history of unjust degradation of the moral powers of persons. Accordingly, in cases involving gender discrimination, there should be a comparably heavy burden of justification for the use of any allegedly neutral gender difference as the basis of unequal treatment. In particular, any gender difference, the force of which depends or may depend on a cultural history of degrading prejudice, should be denied the support of law, because it lends the support of law to degrading prejudice.[129]

---

[128] See, e.g., *Michael M.* v. *Superior Court,* 450 U.S. 464 (1981) (statutory rape); *Rostker* v. *Goldberg,* 453 U.S. 57 (1981) (registration for conscription).

[129] Cf. Sylvia A. Law, "Rethinking Sex and the Constitution," 132 *U. Pa. L. Rev.* 955 (1984).

In order to be faithful to its legacy, the reasonable elaboration of this analysis and principle in the future must be contextually sensitive to facts and values that reasonably bear on the issue in dispute. Homosexuals, for example, may have been subjected to a history of sectarian oppression about "natural" sexuality quite as corruptive of their just moral autonomy as the comparable insult inflicted on women (see Chapter 6). If so, the judiciary's refusal to accept sexual preference as a suspect classification must be reexamined.[130] Other reasonable developments may, from our current vantage, be much more remote but no less worth making or attempting to make.

Poverty is assuredly not a suspect classification under current American constitutional law,[131] reflecting perhaps a long-standing myopia in republican theory and practice that tended to blame the victims of poverty as natural slaves unworthy of full republican citizenship.[132] However, suppose reasonable argument could be made and elaborated about unjust structures of permanent poverty unworthy of a community that regards people as equal and free because such conditions crush basic self-respect with the experience of grinding and hopeless poverty, malnutrition, and neglect. If so, we might reasonably come to condemn on grounds of principle widespread social contempt for those in poverty that stigmatizes them as subhuman outsiders to the scope of reasonable political community. We might, just as in the area of race and gender, come to see the traditional republican view of the slavish poor as reflecting an unquestioned natural hierarchy that insults the capacity for reasonable freedom due all persons under republican constitutionalism. It would not have seemed likely that the self-blinding conventionality and popularity of attitudes contemptuous of the poor would make it any more pointless or idle to develop and press reasonable arguments protecting such groups than the comparable such arguments made early in the long constitutional struggle against similarly insuperable odds (pervasively conventional American racism) that eventually culminated in *Brown* v. *Board of Education*. Indeed, constitutional argument might be the natural forum of principle through which the constitutional conscience of the nation might be awakened to its republican responsibilities.

We should have learned one thing at least from our long interpretive journey from the founders of 1787, namely, that their community of principle is a moral community of free and equal persons capable of respecting one another because they have been *guaranteed the resources to respect themselves*. That vision requires struggle to include outcasts into a more critically humane community or principle, and we have both the interpretive right and duty to make the most reasonable sense we can of that vision by our lights and

---

[130] See *Dronenburg* v. *Zech*, 741 F.2d 1388 (D.C.Cir. 1984). See, for further discussion, Richards, *Moral Criticism of Law*, pp. 173–76.

[131] See *James* v. *Valtierra*, 402 U.S. 137 (1971). But see Frank I. Michelman, "Foreword: On Protecting the Poor Through the Fourteenth Amendment," 83 *Harv. L. Rev.* 7 (1969).

[132] See, for example, Morgan, *American Slavery American Freedom*, pp. 322, 324–25, 381–87. Cf. Ian Shapiro, *The Evolution of Rights in Liberal Theory* (Cambridge: Cambridge Univ. Press, 1986).

in our circumstances. The Constitution and its founders are our national symbols of that aspiration and responsibility. The test of our fidelity to that heritage must be the quality of thought and action we bring to the understanding of its interpretive demands. Is our generation adequate to this heritage and its interpretive demands?

8

Constitutional Decadence and Educational Responsibility

The dominant approaches to constitutional interpretation—the appeals to historical exemplars, to moral reality, and to positivistic conventionalism—possess an impoverished explanatory and critical power of constitutional interpretation (Chapter 1). Two of these interpretive approaches (moral reality and positivistic conventionalism) do not take the founders seriously at all, and the third (historical exemplars) does not take them seriously in the right way (Chapters 1 and 4). Each offers a separate, narrowly viewed insistence on one aspect of the interpretive process (history or conventions or political theory) that fails to do justice to the important place each one of them has in the densely structured interpretive complexity of American constitutional argument. My argument, in contrast, has tried to suggest a holistic interpretive approach incorporating each of these elements. Its strategy has been to construct such an approach by taking the founders seriously at the interpretive and critical level of thought, argument, and deliberation that they brought to their task and self-consciously innovated for both their own and future generations. That account (Chapters 2–4) showed that taking the founders seriously requires that we take seriously each of the critical methods they used and advanced: interpretive history (including the comparative political science of Machiavelli, Harrington, Montesquieu, and Hume), the Lockean political theory of legitimate government, and a common-law model for interpretive practice over time that reasonably justified the Constitution to each generation on terms of respect for rights and pursuit of the common interests of all. If the founders thus transcended the now-conventional boundaries separating history, political theory, and conventionalism, then taking their project seriously today requires that we do no less.

My constructive alternative proposal is now complete. It gives a perspicuous account of the basic institutional structures of American constitutionalism (Chapter 4), reveals common principles that clarify much of the modern law of the First Amendment (Chapter 5), gives a sensible and defensible interpretation of the founders' clear textual and historical commitment to the protection of unenumerated rights of the person (Chapter 6), and advances understanding

287

of how the equal protection clause interprets, criticizes, and advances the founders' project of a community of principle (Chapter 7). It is a better interpretive theory in both breadth and depth. It explains a wide range of structures and doctrines in a convincing way. Furthermore, it not only articulates the deeper structures of argument common to these structures and doctrines, but also convincingly explains them as the kind of argument for the legitimacy of political power that is the most reasonable justification of the ongoing historical project of the amended U.S. Constitution. The account thus gives interpretive weight to all aspects of the familiar commonsense canon of constitutional argument (i.e., history, text, interpretive practice, and political theory), because it takes them all seriously as features of the new kind of republican community of principle that the founders innovated. This view is superior to the alternatives because it gives weight to the whole canon, reveals interpretive structures that other accounts ignore, makes clear their roots in history and tradition, and yet gives a sense of why the enduring value of the enterprise requires that it be interpreted as an ongoing project of reasonable justification of political power for each generation of Americans.

This chapter will explore the interpretive responsibilities defined by this approach in the course of a critical perspective on the ways in which American culture has failed to meet these responsibilities. The three areas that are of special concern to me as a lawyer and educator are the constitutionally decadent standards of interpretive argument recently advocated at the highest levels of government as grounds for judicial appointments, the educational responsibilities of American universities, and the special educational responsibilities of American law schools.

On Constitutional Decadence

As we have seen (Chapter 4), the founders of the Constitution self-consciously assumed, as an important aspect of their own project, the later emergence in American public life of a decline in republican morality. Madison's argument in *The Federalist* no. 49 against Jefferson assumed that later generations of Americans would tend to read the Constitution through factionalized lenses, and that it must be protected from easy amendment precisely for that reason. His argument was based on agreement with Jefferson (though to different effect) about the importance of taking seriously how later Americans would recede from the republican morality that actuated the vision of their founders. Jefferson had contrasted the integrity of the current generation with what a constitutional founder should reasonably anticipate:

> Mankind soon learned to make interested uses of every right and power which they possess, or may assume. . . . With money we will get men, said Caesar, and with men we will get money. Nor should our assembly be deluded by the integrity of their own purposes. . . . They should look forward to a time, and that not a distant one, when corruption in this, as in the country

from which we derive our origin, will have seized the heads of government, and be spread by them through the body of the people, and make them pay the price. Human nature is the same on every side of the Atlantic, and will be alike influenced by the same causes. The time to guard against corruption and tyranny, is before they shall have gotten hold on us. It is better to keep the wolf out of the fold, than to trust to drawing his teeth and talons after he shall have entered.[1]

Such sober Machiavellian constitutional calculations were at the heart of the founders' sense of the role that the Constitution and their founding of it might usefully play in later American constitutional experience (Chapter 4). Machiavelli's constitutional thought had used and elaborated the Roman idea of ruthless founders and the importance of restorations of their original principles to maintain republican institutions. Harrington's constitutionalism appealed to a man of genius (Cromwell) to put in place the dream of a written constitution that would use political science to serve the ends of republican morality by designing an immortal commonwealth protected from corruption because designed to use the political psychology of human nature to serve republican ends. In contrast to Machiavelli and Harrington, the founders innovated methods of argument, deliberation, and justification that eschewed, in principle, the legitimacy of the imposition of republican government by ruthless men of genius. Rather, the only authority they claimed for themselves and their work was its reasonable justifiability on terms of respect for rights and pursuit of the common interest of all; furthermore, the broadly democratic and deliberative ratification given the Constitution was itself the appropriate political decision-making procedure to legitimate the Constitution because it made this deeper point of reasonable justifiability. In effect, the founders gave a Lockean interpretation to the conception of founding of Machiavelli and Harrington, and thus transformed their related idea of restoration of the founders' constitution from a comparable act of ruthless genius to a continuing project of reasonable justifiability to all centered in historical memory of the kind of legitimacy brilliantly innovated and displayed by the 1787 Constitution and 1791 Bill of Rights.

For this reason, American constitutional thought naturally gravitated to an idea quite foreign to Machiavelli and Harrington and not suggested by the constitutional thought of Montesquieu and Hume that otherwise so absorbed them, namely, judicial supremacy over interpretation of the Constitution. The judiciary could play for American constitutionalists this quite unprecedented role among basic constitutional structures because, of all available and ongoing institutions at hand, it could best express the Lockean supremacy of the impartially reasonable justification of political power embodied in the written constitution. Lockean impartiality in judging and enforcing rights and the public good—fundamental to the very legitimacy of the Constitution—naturally culminated in the interpretive supremacy of judicial processes. In

[1] Thomas Jefferson, *Notes on the State of Virginia,* in William Peden, ed. (New York: W. W. Norton, 1954), p. 121.

effect, the Machiavellian conception of restoration of the original republican principles of the founding men of genius was interpreted in terms of a judiciary that was guaranteed sufficient independence and power to be authoritative custodians of the memory of the legitimacy of America's founding; the judiciary could thus hold accountable to original republican principles later generations of Americans otherwise inclined to the natural corruptions of impartial republican morality that time and circumstances would work.

The founders identified these corruptions with people's view of interpretive questions not from the required perspective of impartial Lockean reasonableness, but through the prism of factionalized perceptions of how such interpretive judgments affected them. Madison observed that any interpretive debate

> could hardly be expected to turn on the true merits of the question. It would inevitably be connected with the spirit of pre-existing parties, or of parties springing out of the question itself. It would be connected with persons of distinguished character and extensive influence in the community. It would be pronounced by the very men who had been agents in, or opponents of the measures, to which the decision would relate. The *passions* therefore not *the reason,* of the public, would sit in judgment. But it is the reason of the public alone that ought to controul [sic] and regulate the government. The passions ought to be controuled [sic] and regulated by the government.[2]

The judiciary would not always be the final word on correct constitutional interpretation; it could, for example, make interpretive mistakes that free critical debate by other officials (state and federal) and by the larger society (protected by guarantees of liberty of conscience and speech) could analyze and identify. However, in order to preserve adequate institutional space for a forum of principle free from factionalized perceptions of these interpretive questions, the judiciary would be the final word on authoritative interpretation at least until such time as it acknowledged and corrected its interpretive mistakes.

However, the judiciary can be adequate to its institutional responsibilities only if it brings to its interpretive task the qualities of thought and deliberation that are required for it to produce the kind of reasonable arguments about the text, history, political theory, and interpretive practices that hold both the mind and heart of the nation accountable to the principles of a republican community. There are, of course, a wide range of approaches to understanding and giving effect to this project, and we must assess their relative adequacy, for example (as we have at length in this book), in terms of how they serve or do not serve the project—constitutional interpretation—to which all pay homage. However, some approaches to constitutional interpretation are, for reasons we have already canvased (Chapters 1, 4, 6, 7), subject to criticism in a way that distinguishes them from other views.

As we have seen (Chapter 6), in 1987—a year that marked the bicenten-

---

[2] *The Federalist,* pp. 342–43.

nial celebration of the constitutional convention of 1787—Robert Bork's name was placed in nomination for a seat on the Supreme Court of the United States because his views of constitutional interpretation reflected what the Reagan administration, represented by Attorney General Meese, regarded as the proper interpretive attitude to the founders' intent that Americans were then celebrating. Bork had himself prominently applied his interpretive views to a number of areas, but he had been particularly forceful in applying his views to the criticism of the constitutional right to privacy. That right was, Bork argued, not in the text of the Constitution, was not supported by history or any sound view of interpretive practice, and violated the political theory of the constitution because it trammeled majority rule on wholly unsupported interpretive grounds.

The founders had, as we have seen, anticipated later corruptions in republican morality, and regarded constitutional institutions as a new kind of protection against such corruptions. When Julius Caesar subverted the Roman republic to Cicero's dismay, he may have been corrupt in this way—whatever he may have said. For the founders, the Constitution was directed against the Caesarist corruptions of power that they called faction. Bork's interpretive views pay homage to the project of American constitutionalism; indeed his views are distinguished from other views (like the appeal to political theory and to positivistic conventionalism) by an insistence on making his interpretive claims serve the founders' intent (restoring original republican principles). There is no reason to believe that Bork's arguments were attempts to subvert American constitutionalism to a Caesarist worship of power that is antagonistic to republican political morality. Bork's arguments were consistent with the founders' republican project against such corruptions, and must be assessed in light of that ambition.

However, the very terms in which Bork justified his position undercut it in a way that suggests not just reasonable interpretive mistake, but constitutionally decadent standards of the kind of argument that could count as interpretations of the founders' project. As we have seen (Chapter 6), Bork's criticism of the principle of constitutional privacy was unreasonable in a remarkable way; his argument was wrong on the very grounds that he adduced in its support, namely, the text, history, political theory, and judicial method and role. His argument, ostensibly made in the name of excavating the founders' intent, was blatantly oblivious to both the text and history that put the protection of unenumerated rights at the very center of the 1787 Constitution and 1791 Bill of Rights. His interpretive views assumed a morally vacuous universe, but the founders of the U.S. Constitution were not moral skeptics. Indeed, their conviction that persons had inalienable human rights was the normative premise that gave force and sense to their continuing revolutionary and constitutional project to create forms of government the legitimacy of which would be tested by respect for both enumerated and unenumerated rights. Their use of the theory of faction, for example, addressed the pervasive political psychology—expressed in republics through majority rule—that subverted the respect for rights that are fundamental to the legitimacy of political power. For this reason, constitutional arguments of principle were the test of legitimate political power because they subjected power to this continuing scrutiny and accountability. However, Bork's theory of judicial method and role truncated arguments of principle precisely when the reasonable elaboration of such arguments was most justified and legitimate. The judiciary plays its great historical role as the forum of principle not when it protects the rights of majorities not at serious threat, but when it articulates and elaborates with integrity the constitutional arguments of public reason against the self-blinding views of factionalized majorities not otherwise reasonably to understand and give weight and respect to the equal claims to human rights that are, in constitutional principle, immune from legitimate political power. From this perspective, Bork's commitment to majoritarianism as the standard of proper judicial review comes close to making the mere fact—namely, that an interpretive view (however uninformed or unreasonable) is shared by a majority of other persons—the measure of constitutionally legitimate judicial interpretation. That would, as we have shown at some length (Chapters 2–4), entrench what the founders regarded as the demonic, antirepublican force of faction as the measure of the constitutional arguments justified by them as a necessary republican throttle on faction. In effect, a shallow and stifling majoritarianism, based on a parochial pride in the mere congruence of opinion and sentiment, would subvert the constitutional morality of public reason and the emancipation of personal and moral self-government it makes possible. The issue was, for the founders, not peripheral or marginal, because the tyranny of the majority was their central concern long before De Tocqueville analyzed it as an American democratic pathology.[3] Indeed, protections against it were at the very heart of what they valued in their innovative constitutionalism, which they consciously directed against an anachronistic interpretive style, like Bork's, that would read rights out of the Constitution because they were not expressly enumerated or not protected in 1787 to the extent later generations might and should regard as reasonable (Chapters 4 and 6). We need better interpretive understanding of the founders' project because it contains the cultural resources for understanding and containing our worst demons. Bork's argument is, as an interpretive view of their project, perverse, because he offers an account of constitutional interpretation they clearly and for good reason rejected, and he takes seriously neither their acute introspective psychology of the corruptions of power nor their political ethics of inalienable human rights. He offers the American people not the precious memory of the founders' republican morality of the self-discipline of public reason of a free and democratic people but the kind of comfortable and conscience-saving oblivion from the memory of those demands and responsibilities that legitimates the republican immorality of faction.

The critical point is not the substance of Bork's views, which could be justified in other ways not open to the kind of objection made here. One

[3] See, e.g., Alexis de Tocqueville, *Democracy in America* vol. 1, Phillips Bradley, ed. (New York: Vintage, 1945), pp. 201–2.

could, for example, straightforwardly adopt and defend a critical political theory of democracy that takes Bentham's view that rights are "nonsense on stilts,"[4] and urge the critical editing of American constitutional text, history, and tradition, as Learned Hand and John Hart Ely[5] did, in service of such a political theory. Such arguments would, in my view, be wrong and unreasonable,[6] but they would reflect a coherent political philosophy (utilitarianism) the terms of which are understood and open to reasonable public discussion and debate. One can identify and discuss the reasons offered for the position and assess them in light of larger considerations of coherence and adequacy. These arguments are not decadent in the sense that is explored here.

My objection is to the kind of argument Bork chose to make for his substantive positions and that his argument could have been supposed (by himself and others) to observe the highest intellectual standards of interpretive responsibility. Bork chose, in contrast to other interpretive alternatives, to define himself as someone who took a reasoned interpretive stance on what they ignored, namely, text and history. However, Bork's views, whatever they are, are not serious interpretations of either text or history, and whatever authority he drew from the founders' intent was unearned and, on the founders' views of political legitimacy, quite illegitimate (Chapter 4).

It critically indicts the state of American constitutional culture that Bork's arguments should have been made, advertised, and credited as they were. That criticism may be usefully understood and analyzed as pointing to a decadent state of interpretive argument in which the kinds of critical standards necessary to maintain reasonable discourse about the Constitution have been so little identified, cultivated, and discussed that people, including Bork himself, lose their hold on reality. Decadence, as a general term for artistic and cultural degeneration, may well be an incoherent critical concept.[7] The term is used here stipulatively in a specific sense that is appropriate to constitutional law and discourse. Arguments like Bork's are constitutionally decadent because they do not engage the wider public standards of reasonable discussion and debate that are appropriate to an interpretive issue like the founders' intent. Both the substantive claims made (e.g., unenumerated rights are foreign to the text, history, and traditions of American public law) and the grounds offered for such claims (e.g., that unenumerated rights illegitimately abridge the scope of majority rule) lack any coherent connection with wider

[4] See Jeremy Bentham, "Anarchical Fallacies," in *The Works of Jeremy Bentham,* Book II (published under superintendence of Bentham's executor John Bowring: Edinburgh, 1843), p. 501.

[5] See Learned Hand, *The Bill of Rights* (New York: Atheneum, 1968); John Hart Ely, *Democracy and Distrust* (Cambridge, Mass.: Harvard Univ. Press, 1980).

[6] See, for example, my discussion of Ely's views in Chapter 7.

[7] In this arena, the term may be no more than invective and epithet. See, e.g., Richard Gilman, *Decadence* (New York: Farrar, Straus & Giroux, 1980). The term does have a more local usage to identify a European artistic movement of the late nineteenth century. See, e.g., Jean Pierrot, *The Decadent Imagination, 1880–1900,* Derek Coltman, trans. (Chicago: Univ. of Chicago Press, 1981); Geoffrey Grigson and Charles H. Gibbs—Smith, *Ideas* (New York: Hawthorn, n.d.), pp. 102–4.

standards of reasonable argument. They state clear conclusions but offer no reasons. Ostensible arguments are not arguments at all: labels become a substitute for reason, and will does the work of the intellect.

Constitutional conservatives take a just pride in defending the Constitution and the history of the founders' intent. When arguments as interpretively rigid and willfully nescient as Bork's could be supposed by national leaders to be those of a constitutional conservative, then the public understanding of constitutional argument has become decadent as well. Both Bork and these leaders have lost touch with the standards of reasonable justification of a community of principle when Bork's appeal to founders' intent could be supposed authoritatively to define what his arguments do not remotely justify or explain—the text and history of the founders' intent or the tradition in which constitutional conservatives take pride. Bork and these politicians have allowed self-deceiving moral insularities of faction to enjoy uncritical sway instead of subjecting their "interpretive" arguments to the discipline of democratic reason that was the founders' test for legitimate political power, that is, respect for equal rights and the public good.

Because Bork was a former law professor from an elite American law school (Yale), the diagnosis of constitutional decadence naturally raises correlative questions of educational responsibility. The discussion of this responsibility begins with university education and then turns to law schools.

Educational Responsibility: Universities

Educated Americans are currently engaged in a complex public debate about the status and role of higher education in American society. In particular, arguments have been forcefully advanced that American universities have abdicated their essential responsibilities, in a free and democratic society, both to maintain and to advance the critical standards of morally and intellectually independent critical thought and action that are traditionally associated with humanistic learning.[8] However, it is a symptom of the constitutional decadence referred to previously that these arguments are oblivious to the most apparent and striking failure of educational responsibility in this arena, namely, the failure of universities to maintain and advance the kind of humanistic learning that is central to our most important institution of national unity as a people, American constitutionalism. The argument of this book enables us at least to state the problem in a way that permits a more general discussion of these matters.

The strategy of this book has been to articulate better standards of constitutional interpretation by taking seriously the powerful, pivotal, and uniquely American role accorded the founders of the republic in our interpretive practices. To do so, we must take seriously those methods of analysis, deliberation,

---

[8] See, for example, Allan Bloom, *The Closing of the American Mind* (New York: Simon & Schuster, 1987); E.D. Hirsch, Jr., *Cultural Literacy* (New York: Vintage, 1988).

and justification that the founders politically pioneered. The focus of my argument has thus been on the kinds of critical and interpretive procedures that the founders brought to their own work, for example, interpretive history (including the comparative political science of Machiavelli, Harrington, Montesquieu, and Hume), the Lockean political theory of legitimate government, and a common-law model for interpretive practice over time that reasonably justified the Constitution to each generation on terms of respect for rights and pursuit of the common interests of all. The founders' arguments brilliantly combine history, political philosophy, and law in a way consistent with the European humanist tradition, that they used and transformed, and they defined their methods, task, and ambitions against the background of that tradition.

That tradition originated with the intrinsically critical and comparative project of European humanists of the Renaissance and Reformation. They found the Augustinian synthesis of pagan philosophy and Christian revelation no longer acceptable in part because it had united political and religious power in ways that humanists came to regard as corruptive of the democratic emancipation of our rational and moral powers in ethics, religion, and politics. Accordingly, they applied humanist learning to biblical interpretation and criticism as well as to the reading of the great pagan works in philosophy, history, and science. They undertook the rethinking of both the structures and effects of political power in religion and politics that had unreasonably blocked such inquiry and its availability to all. Modern political science and philosophy was born out of that latter study.

The founders were thoroughly absorbed by the political philosophy of Locke and the political science of Machiavelli, Harrington, Montesquieu, and Hume because they regarded the critical procedures of philosophy and political science as the most reasonable way to think about their own extraordinary opportunity to establish the legitimacy of republican government among a commercial people in a large territory. Locke's political theory of inalienable human rights stated, for them, the ends of legitimate political power that took seriously the reasonable powers of self-government of free and equal people. The political science of Machiavelli, Harrington, Montesquieu, and Hume thoroughly absorbed them because the comparative study of republican and constitutional government reasonably advanced their understanding of how political power might be shaped and channeled permanently to serve their ends of realizing now and for their posterity a political community committed to Lockean democratic emancipation.

Their new conception of political community (a community of principle) was a work of humanist public reason—argued over and justified to the people at large in terms of views of political psychology (the theories of faction and of fame), of comparative political science (including America's own political experience), and of the ends of politically legitimate government (respect for rights and pursuit of the public good). The ambitions of their project for a community of principle have, if anything, been more reasonably elaborated over time than they could achieve in 1787. The scope of the community of principle has, for example, been expanded as its republican principles require

(Chapter 7). Correlatively, our cumulative experience—in America with racism and in Europe with the modernist barbarities of anti-Semitism—has deepened our reasonable understanding of the depth of the political evil of faction and our need for constitutional government to elaborate its structures and principles accordingly. Locke's theory of political legitimacy has been supplanted by better philosophical theories of his basic insights,[9] but these theories clarify—consistent with these constitutional developments—both the scope and depth of the basic project of reasonable justification of political power.[10]

The interpretation of the work of the founders absorbs Americans. Their work is honored not only as a remarkable cultural achievement of democratic reason for 1787–1788, but also because their interpretive and critical procedures reasonably define, at the deepest level of the sense of ourselves as a historically continuous political community of principle, our interpretive responsibilities today (Chapter 4). However, those interpretive responsibilities require that we, as a people, remain capable of the kind and quality of humanist learning required both to understand and to continue their project. However, we can neither appreciate our legacy nor carry it on if we cannot bring to our interpretive role the competence to study history, to do political philosophy, and to engage in principled legal argument as *one* interpretive process.

To illustrate, American constitutional thought was importantly shaped by its critical interpretation of classical republican political theory and practice and the perfectionist political philosophy that justified it (Chapter 2). Neither the originality nor point of American constitutionalism can be fully understood without engaging in the kinds of empirical and philosophical arguments that led the founders to develop a new conception of republican government as an alternative to the classical model. A people incapable of understanding and giving weight to these arguments has only a shallow appreciation of both their own institutions and the political theory that is required by those institutions. The failure of basic higher education to cultivate in students an understanding of the critical philosophical confrontation of the founders with the classical philosophical tradition of the ancient world leads to both overestimation and underestimation of the continuing importance of that tradition to contemporary democratic thought. Plato and Aristotle were not liberals or democrats in our sense, and an exploration of how the founders critically appreciated this fact might debunk the kind of fashionable appeal these thinkers enjoy today both in general[11] and in constitutional theory.[12] However, the

---

[9] See, e.g., John Rawls, *A Theory of Justice* (Cambridge, Mass.: Harvard Univ. Press, 1971); Thomas Nagel, "Moral Conflict and Political Legitimacy," 16 *Phil. & Pub. Aff.* 215 (1987).

[10] See, e.g., Ronald Dworkin, *Law's Empire* (Cambridge, Mass.: Harvard Univ. Press, 1986); David Richards, *Toleration and the Constitution* (New York: Oxford Univ. Press, 1986).

[11] See, e.g., Alasdair MacIntyre, *After Virtue* (Notre Dame, Ind.: Univ. of Notre Dame Press, 1981); idem, *Whose Justice? Which Rationality?* (Notre Dame, Ind.: Univ. of Notre Dame Press, 1988).

[12] See, e.g., Paul Eidelberg, *The Philosophy of the American Constitution* (New York: The Free Press, 1968).

founders' critical confrontation with classical thought acted as the crucial matrix for defining and realizing their own distinctive humanist enterprise. American higher education greatly underestimates the continuing importance of humanist education and thought in enabling Americans today to engage in the same kind of critical and comparative inquiry.

The sterile dichotomies of current interpretive approaches (Chapter 1) define both the problem of public culture and the issue of educational responsibility. The universities, which have produced these inadequate interpretive theories, reproduce in theory the consequences of their inadequate educational and intellectual practice. History is studied, when at all, as a discipline autonomous from political philosophy and law. Philosophy is isolated from both history and law, and identifies its problems in increasingly technical and politically esoteric terms. Furthermore, law is isolated in professional schools that are hardly on speaking terms with the discourse of the larger universities in which they are paradoxically located.

As the devotion of Jefferson and Madison to founding the University of Virginia so clearly attests,[13] universities bear a heavy burden of responsibility under the founders' Constitution to educate a free and democratic people in their essential intellectual and ethical obligations as participants in one of history's greatest achievements of democratic reason. In fact, they are complicitous with the conditions of constitutional decadence. It is not credible that they are not able to act more responsibly.

Educational Responsibility: Law Schools

Could American lawyers be more nearly adequate to their interpretive responsibilities? The issue crucially relates to the conception of the mission of the American law school.

American lawyers' attitudes toward constitutional interpretation are formed in American law schools in which isolation from the larger dialogue of the university is self-justified on the basis of the lawyer's need to master the autonomous legal traditions of bench and bar. Both academic and practicing lawyers thus gravitate to positivistic conventionalism, which in fact distorts the complexity of our interpretive practices and impoverishes the contribution of the American law school and legal profession to what they should maintain and advance: the best interpretive and critical thought about constitutional interpretation.

The consequences of this failure are dramatically underscored by the superficial approaches that academic lawyers like Bork bring to the critical analysis of judicial interpretive conventions with which they substantively disagree. Such conventions are, as already argued (Chapter 1), sometimes interpretively wrong, and it is a defect in positivistic conventionalism that it fails to

---

[13] See e.g., Adrienne Koch, *Jefferson and Madison: The Great Collaboration* (London: Oxford Univ. Press, 1980), pp. 260–90.

capture the kinds of important and often true interpretive arguments that make this point and sometimes change the law. However, critical interpretive arguments of this sort require the kind of critical education in both history and political philosophy that often best enable lawyers to make such true, reasonable, and convincing arguments. Even the most intelligent legal scholars, like Bork, lack this training, and thus sometimes make their criticisms in quite intellectually shallow ways that do them and their arguments no credit. Such scholars, often moved by apparent failures in the Supreme Court to have adequately discharged its interpretive responsibilities, become ideologues of fixed positions on substantive issues, and advance neither their own nor the nation's capacity to conduct reasonable debate over the central questions of interpretive mistake that should absorb the reason, not the passions, of a free people.

The American lawyers at the center of the legal thought of the revolution and the subsequent constitutional experiments (including, to name only a few, John Adams, Thomas Jefferson, James Wilson, Alexander Hamilton, and John Dickinson) took a different view of both legal argument and education. They regarded law as a subject at the heart of the larger tradition of humanist critical thought, and they studied and used history, political philosophy, and the procedures of the common law as one interpretive and critical enterprise (Chapters 2–4). Their model for a broad humanist legal education was that of the Scottish universities where Wilson studied and from which Madison profited under Witherspoon at Princeton.[14] Law was, for the Scottish Enlightenment of Hume, Smith, Ferguson, Millar, and the like, the central humane subject at which history, philosophy, and political science intersected, and the founders thought of law as a discipline in that kind of learning and argument.

American law schools do not define their educational and intellectual mission to cultivate and advance this kind of disciplined critical learning. A student who today comes to an elite law school with the good fortune of an adequate college or graduate school background in humanism encounters not the critical deepening of this training, but its stultification, not the education of Adams or Jefferson, but that of Bork. Furthermore, law students whose educational misfortune is the lack of such training, experience law not as a study that could absorb the intellectual and moral powers of a life well spent, but as a shallow technique. Critical theory taught in elite law schools usefully suggests some of the dimensions of the problem,[15] but it does not do adequate justice to the interpretive and critical issues of educational responsibility at the core of the problem, namely, the insularity of legal scholarship from the wider discourse of the university. Indeed, this theory is itself sometimes a symptom of the underlying problem it fails to identify or address.

Law school training precludes the kind of contribution that American

---

[14] For later Scottish developments of this model of education, see George Davie, *The Democratic Intellect: The Crisis of the Democratic Intellect* (Edinburgh: Polygon, 1986).

[15] See, e.g., Roberto M. Unger, *The Critical Legal Studies Movement* (Cambridge, Mass.: Harvard Univ. Press, 1986); Mark Kelman, *A Guide to Critical Legal Studies* (Cambridge, Mass.: Harvard Univ. Press, 1987).

lawyers could make in bridging the rifts of theory and practice that blemish the landscape of American public life: the constitutional decadence of public argument about constitutional values, the hermetic conversations of university elites. Legal practice in the United States is in all respects illuminated by a humanistic education that seeks constructively to understand and critically to evaluate law by the use of the best available methods of critical historiography, political philosophy and science, normative and positive economics, and the like. The sophistication of intellectual work of the most authentic integrity and depth might well be sharpened and illuminated if such work could see its problems, as the founders saw theirs, embedded in the very fabric of law as the central study of civilized political order. The American law school, which is clearly deficient in training in the critical skills of legal practice, is thus deficient for the same reason in its conception of legal theory. Its failure to sharpen the intellectual understanding of the interpretive practices of law is consistent with its unreal conception of what practice is and could be.

Educated Americans today gravitate to two kinds of attractive but apparently inconsistent claims: that Americans need a deeper sense of community and that they need higher standards of critical argument and learning. On the view of the foundations of American constitutionalism that has been described in this book, the two claims express, in fact, a common hunger the object of which is our uniquely American aspiration to be a community of principle.

The deepest level of American consensus is about the Constitution. All Americans have a place in that enterprise, because it supplies the grounds of principle that dignify the lives of outcasts (e.g., blacks or women or homosexuals) from majority factions in terms of respect for the rights and common interests of all persons. However, the appeal to public reason embodied in the Constitution requires the cultivation of humane learning both to understand what the project is and to carry it forward on the reasonable terms it requires. Humane learning is, in short, the requisite tool and self-discipline of democratic reason to achieve and maintain the community of principle that is, if anything is, America's moral community.

These are interpretive responsibilities no democrat can shirk, a heritage no conservative would squander, a vision of emancipation of our moral powers to which no liberal could be insensible. However, Americans are, at once, democratic and conservative and liberal. Our common ground is the community of principle that our founders bequeathed to us as a moral heritage to posterity. Most of us are not their lineal heirs in fact; however, for that very reason, we are all the more their moral posterity. Our bonds of community are neither ethnic nor racial nor sexual nor familial nor religious nor any other of the "natural" groups around which most polities organized their identities, but a new vision of republican political community the morality of which is democratic reason.

Index

Abolitionist political morality, 261, 262, 263, 264, 269

Abortion: constitutionality of restrictions on, 203, 204, 205, 206, 207, 208, 209, 214, 236, 240, 245, 252, 253; morality of, 218, 219

Abortion Control Act, Pennsylvania, 203, 204

Abrams v. *United States,* 191

Absolutism, 122, 123

Abstractness, tendency to, 167, 168, 170, 241, 271

Ackerman, Bruce, 278, 279, 282, 283

Adair, Douglass, 111

Adams, John, 3, 19, 22, 23, 24, 28, 30, 32, 44, 48, 50, 51, 52, 98, 298; on American constitutionalism, 22, 53, 93, 94; on bicameralism, 93, 123, 124; on British constitution, 65, 67, 69, 70, 79, 92, 123, 124, 298; *Defence of the Constitutions of Government of the United States of America,* 22, 93, 124; *Dissertation on the Canon and Feudal Law,* 25, 32, 51; on emancipation of political intelligence, 24–25, 51; on independent executive, 93, 123; on Locke's constitutionalism, 90; on Massachusetts state constitution, 54, 93, 123, 124; on natural aristocracy, 44, 53, 100, 114; on political legitimacy, 48; on political psychology. *See* Fame, theory of; on public service, 50, 53; on separation of powers, 124; on uses of political science, 94, 124; on theory of fame, 52, 53, 54, 55; on veto power, 124

Advertising. *See* Commercial advertising

Affirmative action, constitutionality of, 154, 251, 268, 272, 273, 274; Ely on, 253

Agrarian: American rejection of, 100; Harrington on, 60, 99; Hume on, 112; Madison on, 59, 60, 62

Albany Plan of 1754, 68

Alien and Sedition Act, 174, 181

Amendment procedures, Madison on, 103, 132, 134

Amendments to Constitution, 132, 151, 165, 166. *See also* Reconstruction amendments

American Revolution, 3, 13, 18, 19, 32, 65
—grounds for, 65, 66, 68, 74, 75, 78, 79, 80, 91, 95, 96; Madison on, 95, 96; Wilson on, 138
—philosophy of, 32, 65, 93, 143, 181, 232, 233, 291

Anal intercourse, 209; constitutionality of laws forbidding, 244, 245

Animals as non-bearers of rights, 230

"Answer to the Nineteen Propositions" (Charles I), 72

Antiestablishment clause, 173, 178, 179, 186, 217. *See also* Religious liberty

Anti-Federalists: appeal to contractualist legitimacy, 82; appeal to posterity, 105, 133; dependence on Montesquieu, 111; on homogeneity in political order, 110, 111, 116, 117; on need for bill of rights, 82, 220, 221, 222, 223; on need for commerce power, 64, 111; on need for religious qualifications, 111; on restricting or disqualifying immigrants, 111; on small territories for republics, 111, 116

Anti-Semitism, 275, 280, 296

Arendt, Hannah, 122

Aristocracy, hereditary, 36, 72; Montesquieu on, 72, 123, 129

Aristocracy, natural. *See* Natural aristocracy

Aristotle, 21, 40, 41, 263, 276, 296; on moral inferiority of women, 41, 276; on morality of slavery, 41, 263; on perfectionist ethics, 41, 42, 43, 44, 45, 49, 53, 145

Article I, section 8, U.S. Constitution, 159

Article IV, U.S. Constitution, 214, 230, 255

Article V, U.S. Constitution, 165

Articles of Confederation, viii, 20, 21, 33, 35, 36, 52, 64, 75, 78, 91, 95, 105, 107, 110, 114, 123, 160, 163; Madison's criticism of, 36, 39–40, 95, 96, 113, 117, 160, 161, 163

Association, democratic right of, 224, 225, 226

Atheism: toleration of, 178, 183, 184, 186, 198

Athens, 30, 40, 41, 46, 109, 145